CONFUCIANISM
for the Contemporary World

SUNY series in Chinese Philosophy and Culture
───────────
Roger T. Ames, editor

CONFUCIANISM
for the Contemporary World

Global Order, Political Plurality,
and Social Action

Edited by
Tze-ki Hon and Kristin Stapleton

Cover Image: "Shanghai Skyline" © cuiphoto / iStockphoto.com

Published by State University of New York Press, Albany

© 2017 State University of New York

All rights reserved

Printed in the United States of America

No part of this book may be used or reproduced in any manner whatsoever without written permission. No part of this book may be stored in a retrieval system or transmitted in any form or by any means including electronic, electrostatic, magnetic tape, mechanical, photocopying, recording, or otherwise without the prior permission in writing of the publisher.

For information, contact State University of New York Press, Albany, NY
www.sunypress.edu

Production, Dana Foote
Marketing, Fran Keneston

Library of Congress Cataloging-in-Publication Data

Names: Hon, Tze-ki, 1958– editor. | Beyond the New Confucianism: Confucian Thought for Twenty-first Century China (Conference) (2012 : Buffalo, New York)
Title: Confucianism for the contemporary world : global order, political plurality, and social action / edited by Tze-ki Hon and Kristin Stapleton.
Description: Albany, NY : State University of New York Press, 2017. | Series: SUNY series in Chinese philosophy and culture | "This volume originated in an April 2012 international conference sponsored by the UBCI: "Beyond the New Confucianism: Confucian Thought for Twenty-first Century China." Tze-ki Hon and I organized the event. With the exception of one chapter, all of the essays in this volume were originally presented and discussed at the 2012 conference in Buffalo"—Preface. | Includes bibliographical references and index.
Identifiers: LCCN 2016047191 (print) | LCCN 2016047800 (ebook) | ISBN 9781438466514 (hardcover : alk. paper) | ISBN 9781438466521 (ebook) | ISBN 9781438466507 (pbk. : alk. paper)
Subjects: LCSH: Philosophy, Confucian—China. | Confucianism—China. | Confucianism—Economic aspects—China. | Confucianism—Political aspects—China. | Confucianism—Social aspects—China.
Classification: LCC B127.C65 C643 2017 (print) | LCC B127.C65 (ebook) | DDC 181/.112—dc23
LC record available at https://lccn.loc.gov/2016047191

10 9 8 7 6 5 4 3 2 1

Contents

List of Illustrations   vii

Preface   ix
    Kristin Stapleton

Introduction: Confucianism for the Contemporary World   xi
    Tze-ki Hon

Part One: Capitalism and the Global Order

1. Global Capitalism with Chinese Characteristics   3
   Fang Keli's New Confucian Research Project (1986–1995)
       Tze-ki Hon

2. Confucianism, Community, Capitalism
   Chen Lai and the Spirit of Max Weber   19
       Els van Dongen

3. Realizing *Tianxia*   45
   Traditional Values and China's Foreign Policy
       Daniel A. Bell

4. Confucianism to Save the World   65
       Tongdong Bai

Part Two: Political Plurality and Civil Society

5. Building Democracy   81
   The Theory and Practice of Contemporary New Confucianism
       Ming-huei Lee

6. Self-Restriction and Progressive Confucianism 91
    Stephen C. Angle

7. Confucianism and Civil Society
    The New Meanings of "Inner Sage" and "Outer King" 107
    An-wu Lin

8. A Mission Impossible?
    Mou Zongsan's Attempt to Rebuild Morality in the Modern Age 117
    Ke Sheng

9. The Challenge of Totalitarianism
    Lessons from Tang Junyi's Political Philosophy 131
    Thomas Fröhlich

10. A Critique of Colonialism and Capitalism
    Tang Junyi's Views on Plurality and Openness 167
    Hok Yin Chan

PART THREE: SOCIAL RESPONSIBILITY AND SOCIAL ACTION

11. Worshipping Ancestors in Modern China
    Confucius and the Yellow Emperor as Icons of Chinese Identity 183
    Marc Andre Matten

12. The Chinese Media's Campaign for Confucianism
    Motivations, Implications, and Problems 209
    Junhao Hong, Miao Liu, and Wen Huang

Epilogue
    Beyond New Confucianism
    Expanding the Contemporary *Rudao* 225
    John H. Berthrong

Bibliography 243

Notes on Contributors 267

Index 271

Illustrations

Figure 11.1	Worship of Confucius at his tomb in March 2012.	195
Figure 11.2	Statues of Confucius in Qufu at Confucius Research Institute, Qufu Normal University, and Lunyu Garden.	196
Figure 11.3	Confucius sculpture in the Park of the Four Books (Sishuyuan 四書苑).	198
Figure 12.1	Growth of Confucius Institutes (2004–2013).	213
Figure 12.2	Geographic distribution of Confucius Institutes.	217
Figure 12.3	Are you interested in learning about Chinese culture?	220
Figure 12.4	How do you feel about Chinese culture?	221
Figure 12.5	Why are you not interested in learning about Chinese culture?	221
Figure 12.6	Where do you obtain your knowledge of Chinese culture?	222
Figure 12.7	What is the most important element of China's soft power?	223

Preface

Kristin Stapleton

Confucian teachings have been reinterpreted, expanded, and reassessed continuously since the Sage himself walked the earth. The last twelve decades, however, have been a particularly fertile time for debate about their value and meaning. As a historian of Chinese cities and social life, I am by no means an expert on the intellectual aspects of the struggle over Confucianism set in motion by the crises at the end of the Qing. Like many who have read and enjoyed modern Chinese literature, however, I have long been familiar with the dramatic story of how basic Chinese understandings of humanity and the world came under attack in the twentieth century. In excavating the historical background of Ba Jin's popular anti-Confucian novel *Family*, I have even contributed to the large body of scholarship on the May Fourth Movement and its condemnation of Confucian thought as "feudal."

This book helps us piece together a different, but no less striking, story. In his introduction, "Confucianism for the Contemporary World," Tze-ki Hon calls this story a "cultural miracle"—the preservation and adaptation of Confucian thought for the contemporary world, despite the attempts of its critics to consign it to the dustbin of history. As the scholars whose work is represented here make clear, even as Confucianism was being condemned during the first decades of the People's Republic of China (PRC), a core group of scholars outside of the PRC worked tirelessly to carry on the scholarly tradition of careful mastery and exegesis of a huge body of sophisticated texts. They also sought to find the terms through which Chinese philosophy could engage with other schools of thought, and particularly with European philosophy, which dominated—and still dominates—philosophical studies in Western and Western-style academies.

Since the 1980s, Confucian thought once again has become a subject of interest in mainland China. PRC scholars are now at the forefront of Confucian studies, and enthusiasm for Confucian culture extends far beyond the scholarly world, as the chapters in this volume demonstrate. The decision of the PRC government to choose "Confucius Institute" as the name for a global network of centers for the study of Chinese language and culture is just one of many indications of the renewed respect for the Sage in his geographical homeland.

The Confucius Institute at the University at Buffalo (UBCI) was established in 2009 as one node of this network, as a partnership between UB and Capital Normal University in Beijing. Its primary goal is to encourage study of Mandarin, particularly among schoolchildren across Western New York. In addition to working with regional school systems to establish Chinese-language programs, though, it also organizes cultural events and scholarly conferences. This volume originated during an April 2012 international conference UBCI sponsored, "Beyond the New Confucianism: Confucian Thought for Twenty-First Century China." Tze-ki Hon and I organized the event and, with the exception of one chapter, all of the chapters herein were originally presented and discussed at the 2012 Buffalo conference. The organizers would like to thank the staff of the UB Asian Studies Program, the UB History Department, and the UBCI for their assistance with the conference. In particular, Dr. Eric Wenzhong Yang, then serving as UBCI executive director, handled myriad logistical details with his usual extraordinary energy, efficiency, and cheerfulness.

Several scholars whose work is not included in this volume participated in the conference, presenting their research, chairing sessions, or serving as discussants. These include James Beebe, Thomas Burkman, Zuyan Chen, Roger Des Forges, Daniel Elstein, Todd Goehle, On-cho Ng, Paul Poenicke, and Hagop Sarkissian. We thank them for their contributions. We are also grateful to Thomas Fröhlich, who was not a conference participant, for writing a chapter on Tang Junyi and thereby helping to round out the volume's analysis of the scholars who kept Confucian studies alive in the mid-twentieth century. John Berthrong's commentary enlivened our conference discussions, and the epilogue he wrote is as graceful as it is thoughtful.

Working with the chapter authors as they refined their work for publication was a pleasure. The editors wish to thank Gregory Epp and Therese Myers for their excellent work in copyediting the chapters. In the course of our work on the book, Nancy Ellegate, our SUNY Press editor, unexpectedly passed away. We join her SUNY Press colleagues—as well as many Asian studies scholars whose work she brought into print—in paying tribute to her service and mourning her passing.

Introduction

Confucianism for the Contemporary World

Tze-ki Hon

We all know that China's economy has grown rapidly since the early 1980s. Over three decades, China has become "the factory of the world," producing manufactured goods ranging from cellular phones and solar panels to T-shirts and sneakers. Today, this spectacular growth is creating millions of nouveaux riches in the country—men and women who are eager to show off their wealth by purchasing high-end luxury goods from international brands such as Gucci and Louis Vuitton.

Nevertheless, we often forget that, concomitant with this "economic miracle," a "cultural miracle" has unfolded. Condemned as a relic of feudalism for more than half a century, Confucianism suddenly enjoyed a robust revival during the 1980s and 1990s, as post-Mao China was gradually integrated into the global economy.[1] Not so long ago, when cultural iconoclasm was at its height during the May Fourth Movement (1915–1923) and the Cultural Revolution (1966–1976), Confucianism was blamed for everything that had gone wrong in the country—elitism, foreign defeats, imperial autocracy, local separatism, patriarchy, xenophobia, and so on.[2] In the ten years from the mid-1980s to the mid-1990s, however, the image of Confucianism changed completely. It became a theory of modernization that supported economic development, individual growth, and social progress.

During this revival, a particular form of Confucian thought—combining the moral cultivation of Lu Xiangshan (1139–1192) and Wang Yangming (1472–1529) with a creative interpretation of Kantian and Hegelian philosophies—gained widespread attention. Known as "contemporary New Confucianism" (*xiandai xinrujia* or *xiandai xinruxue*), this Confucian school of thought was said to have contributed to economic success in Japan and the Four Mini Dragons (Hong Kong, Singapore, South Korea, and Taiwan) in the postwar period. It was also considered to be a strategy for modernizing China that would preserve the country's cultural heritage on the one hand and enable the country to catch up with advanced nations on the other.

This Confucian school of thought—first started in overseas Chinese communities in Hong Kong and Taiwan during the 1950s and 1960s—quickly took root in China, creating what some scholars call "mainland Confucianism."[3] Responding to economic disparity and social injustice in post-Mao China, mainland Confucians challenged the party-state system and introduced the notions of "the division of power," "civil society," and "public realm" to the expanding Chinese middle class.[4] Recently, we see indications that grassroots organizations have begun to adopt Confucian terminology to demand social justice and better services in local communities.[5] Whether the "Confucian torch" has been successfully passed to the masses is unclear, but it is fair to say that Confucianism (or more precisely, Confucian ethics) is no longer monopolized by cultural elites. It has become a school of thought that speaks to the educated and the uneducated, the rich and the poor, and the powerful and the powerless when facing the challenges of a rapidly growing economy.

The Openness of the 1980s and 1990s

Over the years, experts have offered numerous reasons for this Confucian revival. In the mid-1990s, Arif Dirlik and Jing Wang were the first Western scholars bringing attention to this Confucian revival and linking it to global capitalism.[6] In the early 2000s, Gloria Davis examined the Confucian revival through the lens of the social changes in post-Mao China.[7] In recent years, insightful studies have been published about key figures, such as Xiong Shili (1885–1968) and Mou Zongsan (1909–1995), who built the philosophical foundations for New Confucianism—a school of thought that inspired the Confucian revival in China during the 1980s and 1990s. To highlight the contributions of these thinkers, John Makeham, Umberto Bresciani, and Ming-huei Lee trace their roots to earlier attempts at reviving Confucianism in the late nineteenth and early twentieth centuries.[8] By demonstrating a link to previous Confucian revivals, these scholars show that New Confucianism (and by extension, the recent Confucian revival on the mainland) is part of a long-standing "conservative movement" in modern China that opposes "total westernization," unbridled consumption, and excessive industrialization. For Serina Chan and Sébastien Billioud, however, New Confucianism is not only aimed at the Chinese, but also at anyone in the world who is interested in the balanced development of humanity.[9] To prove their point, they pay special attention to "A Manifesto for a Re-appraisal of Sinology and Reconstruction of Chinese Culture," issued in 1958 by four New Confucian thinkers: Mou Zongsan, Tang Junyi (1909–1978), Xu Fuguan (1903–1982), and Zhang Junmai (1886–1969).[10] In the manifesto, they argue, the four authors spelled out their goal of transforming Confucianism into a critique of the Western mode of thinking, particularly the notions of empiricism, linear progression, materialism, and scientism.[11]

However stimulating intellectually, this philosophical explanation does not clarify why New Confucianism—once a peripheral intellectual current among a small group of overseas Chinese thinkers—quickly gained popularity in mainland China during the 1980s and 1990s. The New Confucian thinkers were, after all, exile scholars who left the mainland for Hong Kong and Taiwan in the context of the 1949 Communist Revolution. In their adopted lands, they did not receive strong support for reinterpreting Confucianism. This was particularly true in Hong Kong, which, as a British colony, was an entrepôt privileging English-speaking businessmen rather than scholars of Chinese classical learning.[12] More important, as exile scholars, the New Confucian thinkers did not have strong ties to the mainland to start a cultural revival. Faced with the "capitalism versus communism" bipolarity of the Cold War, they were preoccupied with opposing communism. As a result, their writings, however insightful and inspiring, had to be reformulated within a new framework in order to reach mainland readers of the post–Cold War period.[13]

For these reasons, scholars (such as John Makeham and Song Xianlin) correctly focus attention on what was happening on the mainland during the 1980s and 1990s when discussing contemporary Confucian revival.[14] They point to, for example, the atmosphere of skepticism—particularly about communism and Maoism—that led Chinese intellectuals to be open to new ideas, new thinking, and new learning.[15] This openness, they argue, gave rise to the "culture craze" (*wenhua re*) in the mid-1980s and the "national learning craze" (*guoxue re*) in the early 1990s, both of which were essential to the appeal of New Confucianism.[16] Today, in their writings, well-known "mainland Confucians" (such as Jing Haifeng) still fondly recall the openness of the 1980s and 1990s as the impetus for their turn to New Confucianism.[17] Clearly the interest in New Confucianism during the 1980s and 1990s was due more to the perception that it provided answers to many of China's problems of modernization than to the claim that it captured the essence of Confucius's thought.

Global and Local Factors

The sociocultural explanation for the rise of New Confucianism is broader in scope, but does not account for the concrete steps by which New Confucianism was transformed into a theory of modernization that supported the economic reforms in mainland China. If indeed the rise of New Confucianism occurred during China's transition from making socialist revolution to joining neoliberal global capitalism, which actors and factors made this transformation possible? What were the crucial events that turned an erstwhile esoteric philosophy into a theory of East Asian capitalism?

On this question, Arif Dirlik offers the most convincing argument. In the lengthy article "Confucius in the Borderlands: Global Capitalism and the Reinvention of Confucianism," Dirlik highlights two interlocking events. The first event was a change in the structure of global capitalism: after the 1973 oil crisis, East Asia (especially Japan) rose rapidly at the expense of Europe and the United States.[18] Mixing a market economy with aggressive state intervention, the "East Asian development model" (a term sociologist Peter Berger coined) appeared to provide an alternative to capitalism and socialism. Sometimes referred to as "the third way," the East Asian development model was unique in achieving capitalistic modernity based on a reinvention of Confucian culture, such as transforming the traditional concept of filial piety into a family-based work ethic for modern capitalistic enterprise.[19] In the 1980s and 1990s, when China was transitioning from socialist revolution to global capitalism, the East Asian development model was attractive to Chinese intellectuals because it promised both capitalistic productivity and a reinvention of Chinese heritage.

The second event was Tu Wei-ming's 1985 visit to China and the subsequent academic exchanges between Chinese and U.S. scholars studying East Asian capitalism. Known to some as "the American Confucius," Tu Wei-ming (in pinyin, Du Weiming) repackaged New Confucianism by incorporating elements of Weberian sociology and process theology.[20] Expanding a point Mou Zongsan made, he argued that over centuries Confucianism had gone through three major transformations: (1) the codification of Confucian cosmology, epistemology, and ethics during the classical period; (2) the reformulation of Confucianism to respond to Indian Buddhism during the late imperial period; and (3) the restructuring of Confucianism to meet the challenge of the West during the modern period.[21] These "three epochs," Tu explained, not only demonstrated the breadth and depth of Confucianism, but also highlighted the creativity of Confucian thinkers in encountering the pressing issues of their times.

For Tu, the challenge of contemporary Confucian thinkers in the "third epoch" (*di san qi*) was to solve the problems of the modern metropolis such as alienation, atomization, bureaucratization, commodification, and excessive rationalization. He claimed that in the third epoch Confucianism must first show its relevance to the modern world by making an impact on cities such as London, New York, Paris, and Tokyo before returning to its homeland, China.[22] In many ways, Tu's argument was based on his experience as an advisor to the Singapore government in the early 1980s. Partly to explain Singapore's economic success and partly to justify teaching "Confucian values" in the school system of the city-state, Tu highlighted "the triad chord" that linked Confucian ethics to the success of East Asian economy from the perspective of Max Weber's sociology.[23]

Although Dirlik acknowledges Tu's contribution to the transformation of New Confucianism into a theory of modernization, he blames him for being uncritical of capitalism. For all that Tu's writings offer new approaches to social policy, Dirlik argues, "what has been untouched by, and in fact benefited from, the Confucian 'challenge,' is capitalism itself."[24] And yet, in retrospect, Tu's role is far more important than Dirlik admits. First and foremost, Tu's contribution lies in linking two separate discourses: the discourse of "the East Asian development model" among economists and sociologists in the United States and the discourse of "New Confucianism" among a small group of scholars in overseas Chinese communities. And the bridge between these two discourses was Max Weber's *The Protestant Ethic and the Spirit of Capitalism*. Drawing from the former discourse, Tu used Weber's text to highlight the uniqueness of "East Asian capitalism," which, he claimed, successfully developed the spirit of capitalism based on Confucian ethics.[25] Drawing from the latter discourse, Tu used Weber's text to show how certain Confucian concepts (e.g., *ren*, humanity, and *li*, rituals) could help people develop "inner sagehood" amid the hustle and bustle of the modern city.[26] Even though it was not exactly Herbert Marcuse's critique of industrial society from the perspective of "one dimensional man," Tu's interpretation of Confucian ethics registered problems of urban life while attempting to bring fluidity, creativity, and hope to modern existence.

Thus, by "Weberizing Confucianism," Tu presented a compelling argument that the Chinese could develop an East Asian form of capitalism that would allow them to build an advanced economy on the one hand and remain culturally Chinese on the other. Although lacking a clear explanation of how Confucianism would develop capitalism, Tu's argument fit the general atmosphere of the 1980s and 1990s, when the Chinese government was promoting "socialism with Chinese characteristics." Certainly Tu had no interest in building socialism in China, but his argument resonated with Chinese readers who wanted to break down the "capitalism versus socialism" dichotomy of the Cold War and were eager to revive some forms of Chinese tradition to boost their national identity.[27]

In addition to Tu's 1985 lecture tour, we should note that state-sponsored studies also helped spread New Confucianism around China. For ten years from 1986 to 1995, through generous grants from the Department of Education of the Chinese government, many conferences were held to discuss New Confucianism, and many collected works of New Confucian thinkers (particularly Mou Zongsan, Tang Junyi, and Xu Fuguan) were printed and distributed. While some scholars questioned the motives behind these concerted efforts to introduce New Confucianism,[28] these government-sponsored activities were clearly instrumental in spreading Confucianism across China. By the early 1990s, there were self-proclaimed "mainland Confucians" (such as Luo Yijun) whom the state had formerly employed to study New Confucianism and found themselves sympathetic to it. Later, as the number of "mainland Confucians" grew, the leaders of the "New Confucian research project"—such as Fang Keli—faced fierce criticism for spreading subversive learning within China.[29]

As China becomes more affluent and diverse after the turn of the millennium, the Confucian revival adopts a variety of forms. Although one can still trace its roots to New Confucianism of the 1980s and 1990s, the recent Confucian revival reaches many sectors of Chinese society and touches the lives of millions of people across the country. The Confucian revival becomes, as mentioned earlier, a platform for critiquing the party-state and pressing the government to provide more local services.[30] It has been transformed into self-help advice to manage fears and anxiety in a fast-growing economy, as seen in Yu Dan's popular television programs from 2006 to 2007.[31] It has also become part of the propaganda campaign of the Chinese government to promote "harmonious society" and Chinese nationalist identity.[32] More recently, various groups that identify themselves as Confucian have appeared across China to address issues ranging from political rights and social justice to environmental protection and early child education.[33] Theorists of world politics also apply Confucian concepts to international issues, envisioning a new global order in which the major players are no longer nation-states.[34] In sum, contemporary Confucian revival has become a broad cultural phenomenon responding to the economic, existential, political, and social issues of the twenty-first century.[35]

Nevertheless, despite its strong impact on Chinese politics and society, the contemporary Confucian revival is still understood in the West primarily as a philosophical movement with a strong emphasis on moral metaphysics.

Major publications continue to portray contemporary Confucian revival as an intellectual enterprise confined to scholars in the academy. While this ivory-tower image of contemporary Confucian revival is built on decades of Western publications promoting East Asian civilization, clearly a glaring discrepancy exists between contemporary Confucianism in China and its representation in the West.

New Confucianism as a Modernization Theory

Based on the papers presented at the "Beyond the New Confucianism" April 2012 conference held at the University at Buffalo, this volume examines the contemporary Confucian revival as a potent force in shaping politics and society in mainland China, Hong Kong, Taiwan, and overseas Chinese communities. Consisting of twelve chapters, an introduction, and an epilogue, it links the contemporary Confucian revival to debates—both within and outside China—on global capitalism, East Asian modernity, political reforms, civil society, and human alienation. Thematically divided into three sections, it offers a fresh view of the contemporary Confucian revival as a broad cultural phenomenon consisting of an interpretation of Confucian moral teaching, a theory of political action, a vision of social justice, and a perspective for a new global order.

Part 1 focuses on New Confucianism (*xin rujia*) as a theory of modernization. The section begins with Tze-ki Hon's chapter "Global Capitalism with Chinese Characteristics: Fang Keli's New Confucian Research Project (1986–1995)," which provides an account of the transformation of New Confucianism from a moral metaphysics into a social theory. In the chapter, Hon argues that the 10-year New Confucian research project played a crucial role in "Weberizing" New Confucianism, and therefore provides a framework linking the philosophical discourse of overseas Chinese to the broader question of East Asian capitalism. Certainly, as critics point out, the research project was strong in popularizing the writings of New Confucians and weak in analyzing their thoughts. Nevertheless, Hon contends that the research project was significant in bringing Confucianism back to mainland China after a thirty-year absence under Mao. More importantly, the research project paved the way for applying Confucianism (particularly Confucian ethics) in resolving political, social, and existential problems caused by China's fast-growing economy.

If "Weberization" was indeed the key to transforming New Confucianism from a philosophy into a social theory, different interpretations of Weber's work invigorated Chinese intellectuals as they pondered the relationship between Confucianism and capitalism. In her chapter "Confucianism, Community, Capitalism: Chen Lai and the Spirit of Max Weber," Els van Dongen draws attention to two opposing views of Weberian sociology. In an approach known as the "Weberian thesis," some scholars focus on Weber's argument in *The Protestant Ethic and the Spirit of Capitalism* that the Protestant ethic contributed to the rise of capitalism. The other approach, known as the "Weberian critique," focuses on Weber's *Economy and Society*, in which he stressed the negative consequences of modernization-as-rationalization, described as the "iron cage of modernity." To Chinese scholars (particularly Chen Lai), the tension between the two views did not seem problematic. In fact, Chinese scholars understood New Confucianism as both a *sociopolitical* argument for economic development in the post–Cold War world and a *moral* project to create a fiduciary community in response to the alienation and fragmentation of modern society. Like many intellectuals in developing countries, Chinese scholars were eager to find a way to develop the economy and to avoid excessive rationalization and bureaucratization.

After being transformed into a theory of modernization, New Confucianism has been applied to concrete political problems. The next two chapters in part 1 are examples of using Confucian concepts to envision a new political order nationally and internationally. In both chapters, the authors go beyond what is conventionally considered as New Confucianism, namely, the moral teachings of Lu Xiangshan and Wang Yangming and the intellectual genealogy that stretches from Xiong Shili to Mou Zongsan. For instance, in "Realizing *Tianxia*: Traditional Values and China's Foreign Policy," Daniel A. Bell explains how some Chinese thinkers envision a new global order based on the Confucian concept *tianxia* (all-under-heaven). For these Chinese thinkers, Bell argues, *tianxia* encapsulates a vision of global order that does not involve a world government that has ethical and political priority over national states. Rather, a transnational global order will be established by being cognizant of the "obligations that we owe to people living outside the territorial boundaries of our states, even though they are not as intense as the obligations we owe to fellow citizens." Bell further argues that, although the ideal of *tianxia* would have to be modified somewhat to fit the political reality of the twenty-first century, he sees a "Confucian-inspired foreign policy" as being both realistic and humane, especially in three areas: a hierarchical world order, political meritocracy, and social harmony.

Similarly, in "Confucianism to Save the World," Tongdong Bai employs Confucian concepts to envision a pluralistic political order. Adopting an argument shared by many mainland Confucians, Bai considers Confucianism more a political philosophy than a moral metaphysics. In Bai's words, "not only is Confucianism chiefly a political philosophy, but it is a modern political philosophy." This political interpretation of Confucianism allows Bai to achieve two goals. First, he emphasizes the similarity between the so-called Spring and Autumn and Warring States Periods (when Classical Confucianism emerged) and the multipolar international environment that we see today. This similarity, he contends, makes Confucianism an inspiring political philosophy because it balances multiplicity with unity, agency with structure. Second, he can imagine a Confucian government that would, like many Western democratic governments, support freedom of speech, the rule of law, and civil liberties. While Bai's argument in this part may seem controversial to some readers, we need to remember that he is proposing an alternative form of governance substantially different from the party-state system of the People's Republic of China. Like other mainland Confucians (such as Jiang Qing),[36] he is suggesting a new political structure that may one day be accepted in China as well as in the rest of the world.

The Moral Foundation of Contemporary Democratic Institutions

While part 1 focuses on the contemporary Confucian revival as a cultural force of modernization, part 2 examines the moral dimension of the revival by focusing on two thinkers: Mou Zongsan and Tang Junyi.[37] This turn to morality, however, is not just to affirm the moral roots of the Confucian revival, particularly the moral metaphysics of New Confucianism. It is also to clarify the role of Confucian ethics in the pluralistic society of the twenty-first century. Collectively the six chapters in part 2 demonstrate that the contemporary Confucian revival is a result of and a response to rapid sociopolitical changes in Chinese communities across the Taiwan Strait. The chapters show that through creative interpretation of its core ideas, Confucianism can be a vital force for a diverse and pluralistic society of the twenty-first century.

This creative use of Confucianism for contemporary life is particularly clear in Ming-huei Lee's chapter, "Building Democracy: The Theory and Practice of Contemporary New Confucianism." A philosopher trained in Germany, Lee begins his chapter with an explanation of the subtlety of Mou Zongsan's moral metaphysics, particularly his seemingly opaque concept "the self-negation of moral consciousness" (*liangzhi zhi ziwo kanxian*). Then he shows why Mou emphasizes the development of "the inner sage" as the precondition for "the outer king." By giving preference to the moral mind over political institutions, Lee points out, Mou highlights the importance of recovering moral sensitivity to counter the individualism, materialism, and pragmatism of contemporary society. His observation of recent Taiwan politics leads Lee to conclude that Mou's moral metaphysics is even more relevant today because it stresses the need for training clear-headed citizens to make political decisions based on moral intuition rather than utilitarian goals.

Similarly, in his chapter "Self-Restriction and Progressive Confucianism," Stephen C. Angle expands on Mou Zongsan's moral metaphysics. Like Ming-huei Lee, Angle focuses on Mou's concept of "the self-negation of moral consciousness," but, unlike Lee, he is interested in Mou's thought on the *indirect* relationship between morality and politics. By keeping morality and politics separate but connected, Angle argues, Mou provides a new model for political participation that can be described as "Progressive Confucianism." In this new model, Angle envisions the possibility of political engagement where "politics emerges out of the ethical activity of individuals as they merge together in political life, and a certain kind of political structure is ultimately needed as the indirect means to more complete ethical practice." In this manner, Angle asserts, "Progressive Confucianism" not only will provide a basis for pluralistic governance in China, but it will also make important contributions to political theory in democratic societies around the world.

An-wu Lin's chapter, "Confucianism and Civil Society: The New Meanings of 'Inner Sage' and 'Outer King,'" reinforces some of the themes covered in Angle's article. For two decades since the 1995 death of Mou Zongsan, Lin has fought a battle in Taiwan to replace "New Confucianism" with "Post–New Confucianism" (*hou xinrujia*). As part of Post–New Confucianism, as Lin conceived, New Confucian thinkers will turn their attention from developing personal morality to developing "civil society" through the cultivation of what Jürgen Habermas calls "communicative acts" in the public sphere. Calling his version of New Confucianism a "Civil Confucianism" (*gongmin ruxue*), Lin, like Angle, hopes to establish a dynamic relationship between morality and politics while keeping the two spheres separate. As such, Lin is determined to create a new image of Confucianism by focusing on "the modern proclivity for privacy and individual rights."

In "A Mission Impossible? Mou Zongsan's Attempt to Rebuild Morality in the Modern Age," Ke Sheng reflects on the role of New Confucianism in the twenty-first century. Unlike the previous three authors, Sheng does not believe that the New Confucian thinkers are capable of resolving "the modern predicament." Citing Scottish philosopher Alasdair MacIntyre, Sheng defines the modern predicament as the universal problem of establishing moral values in a thoroughly secular and materialistic world. Employing this definition, Sheng finds New Confucianism ill-equipped to solve the modern predicament because it is basically an invention of modern times. In addition, Sheng also finds that New Confucianism lacks the flexibility to adapt to different circumstances even though it makes universal claims of relevance to all people in the world. In the end, Sheng concludes, even Mou Zongsan (the most original thinker among the New Confucians) could not find a solution; hence the title of the article: a mission impossible.

For readers who want to see Confucianism play an active role in the twenty-first century, Sheng's article may come as a surprise. It is particularly intriguing, coming after three articles that demonstrate the possibilities of building a pluralistic society based on a creative interpretation of the New Confucian moral metaphysics. At the same time, Sheng's pessimism is a healthy reminder that the reinvention of Confucianism in the twenty-first century is by no means an easy task.[38] As Sheng points out, the main obstacle to a Confucian revival is not the Confucian moral values, but the changed world. In a world driven by competition, consumption, and material gains, convincing people—particularly the poor and the disenfranchised—to patiently develop their "inner sagehood" so that they may one day become "outer kings" is difficult.

New Understanding of Tang Junyi

As shown in the first four chapters in part 2, Mou Zongsan is the key thinker behind the development of New Confucian moral metaphysics. Consequently, current literature on New Confucianism often focuses on him, as if he is the New Confucian thinker par excellence. By contrast, Tang Junyi is less familiar to Western readers, even though he was a contemporary of Mou and one of the authors of the 1958 Manifesto. This imbalance is unfortunate because in his lifetime Tang was better known than Mou due to his esteemed position as a top administrator at New Asia College in Hong Kong. In addition, his charismatic personality and moral passion won him numerous followers, many of whom are still promoting his version of Confucianism to high school and college students in Hong Kong and Taiwan.

To redress this imbalance, part 2 includes two chapters on Tang Junyi. In "The Challenge of Totalitarianism: Lessons from Tang Junyi's Political Philosophy," Thomas Fröhlich discusses Tang's struggle with totalitarianism.[39] Based on a close reading of Tang's writings, Fröhlich identifies an inner tension in Tang's political view: his unbounded optimism for political modernization on the one hand, and his acute sensitivity to the danger of totalitarianism on the other. Fröhlich finds out that throughout his active life as a scholar, Tang was unable to resolve this inner tension, although the crimes against humanity unleashed by totalitarian regimes were increasingly clear to Tang, particularly from reports on the Holocaust and the political campaigns in mainland China. This inability to conceptualize (let alone resolve) the inner tension, Fröhlich argues, shows a bigger problem of New Confucian thinkers, namely, their reluctance to come to grips with barbarism and dehumanization in modern society.[40] Fröhlich's observation also reminds us of the misreading of Weber's works that Els van Dongen discusses in her chapter in part 1. From Tang Junyi to Chen Lai, Chinese thinkers have been consistently missing Weber's grim diagnosis of modern society. They embrace the Weberian thesis because it supports their optimism about modernization, but they are not interested in the Weberian critique because they do not see the danger of "the iron cage of rationality" destroying humankind and human civilization.

In "A Critique of Colonialism and Capitalism: Tang Junyi's Views on Plurality and Openness," Hok Yin Chan offers a different view of Tang, focusing on the political environment of colonial Hong Kong that provoked Tang to develop his Confucian humanism. Chan argues that, although it was often criticized for being broad and uncritical, Tang's Confucian humanism was actually a critique of colonialism and capitalism. More importantly, his promotion of the Confucian Five Relationships (especially the relationship between friend and friend) was aimed at ameliorating the alienation and fragmentation of modern society. From Tang's critique of colonialism and capitalism, Chan draws a stern lesson. He finds that the problems that Tang confronted in the 1950s and 1960s (such as social injustice and alienation) are the same ones that we are facing today in neoliberal global capitalism. Certainly it is comforting to know that Tang's writings are still relevant to this day; at the same time, it is disturbing to learn that the world has not made much progress in improving the human condition in the last five decades.

Taking seriously the complicated history of Confucian revivals of the twentieth century, the six chapters in part 2 seek to offer a broad and inclusive understanding of a multifaceted cultural movement that has recently become an important cultural, political, and social force in mainland China, Hong Kong, and Taiwan. By presenting different images of Mou Zongsan and Tang Junyi as political actors and thinkers, the six chapters demonstrate that Confucianism of the twenty-first century is capable of addressing a wide range of issues, such as alienation in a big city, commodification in a market economy, the concentration of power by the state, and social injustice in monopolistic capitalism.

Introduction / xxiii

Confucius as a Commodity and a Cultural Icon

As mentioned earlier, although started with an interest in New Confucianism in the 1980s and 1990s, recently contemporary Confucianism has been driven by its broad appeal to different sectors of Chinese society. In part 3, two chapters examine the wide variety of ways that Confucianism is presented in contemporary China. To begin the discussion, Marc Andre Matten compares two forms of ancestral worship in "Worshipping Ancestors in Modern China: Confucius and the Yellow Emperor as Icons of Chinese Identity." Through a comparison of the rituals that have grown up around the Yellow Emperor and Confucius since the late nineteenth century, Matten argues that the two have been closely linked to the construction of Chinese national identity, even though the concept behind the two forms of worship is quintessentially Confucian (i.e., filial piety). Despite the vicissitude in the rituals due to politics, Matten points out, cultural iconoclasm does not appear to have had a lasting negative effect on them. Even at the height of cultural iconoclasm—notably the May Fourth Movement and the Cultural Revolution—worship of Yellow Emperor and Confucius continued as long as political leaders saw the value in mobilizing the Chinese citizens. In this sense, Matten argues, modern China has experienced no rise or fall in Confucianism. The Confucian concept of filial piety, directed at these important cultural forefathers, has continuously served the cause of nation-building.

In "The Chinese Media's Campaign for Confucianism: Motivations, Implications, and Problems," Junhao Hong, Miao Liu, and Wen Huang give us a detailed study of how Confucianism is portrayed in mass media in contemporary China. Focusing on the culture industry (particularly movies, television, newspapers, magazines, and the Internet), the three authors compare the ways that Confucianism is disseminated as a cultural product, both to consume as a commodity and to exchange as a currency.[41] Revealingly, this study shows that the dissemination of Confucianism as a cultural product is facilitated by both the market and the state. For the former, the goal of the dissemination is for profit; for the latter, the goal is for domestic security and international recognition. Despite their different goals, the entrepreneurs and the government have plenty of reasons to continue to promote Confucianism as a cultural icon.

Together these two chapters highlight obstacles and shortcomings when one looks at Confucianism today. According to the two authors, contemporary Confucianism has been highly susceptible to political use. Whether it is for building a national identity or for improving the country's image abroad, Confucianism (and Confucius particularly) is often deployed as a tool to achieve a political goal. This susceptibility for political use is significant, especially if we take into account the long history of Confucianism serving as a ruling ideology during the imperial period. How can we distinguish radical Confucianism (or Angle's "Progressive Confucianism") from state Confucianism? Where do we draw the line between the government's promotion of Confucianism as a culture and the government's cooptation of Confucianism as a measure of thought control? These are indeed difficult questions to answer.

Confucianism of the Twenty-First Century

In the epilogue, "Beyond New Confucianism: Expanding the Contemporary *Rudao*," John H. Berthrong concludes this volume by reflecting on the history of Confucian revivals since the beginning of the twentieth century. As a "Boston Confucian" who participated in intense debates with Tu Wei-ming and Robert Neville during the 1980s and 1990s, Berthrong brings an insider's perspective to Confucian revivals as cultural phenomena in China and the United States. In his account, he explains the complex process by which contemporary Confucianism becomes a transnational cultural movement that stretches across the Pacific Ocean. In this unfolding of Confucianism that began in mainland China in the early twentieth century, spread overseas in the midcentury, and then returned to China at the end of the century, Berthrong sees an expansion of the contemporary *Rudao* (the Confucian Way) in which communities, big and small, are joined for the same purpose of building a better world based on an understanding of Confucian teachings. What makes this contemporary *Rudao* fascinating is its diversity. Different groups of people may look at Confucian teachings differently: some stress the political vision; some emphasize the social agenda; some focus on the moral philosophy. And yet, Berthrong sees a common thread among these groups that, in one way or another, are looking for ways to improve the human condition and turning to the Confucian canon for guidance.

In short, Berthrong demonstrates that contemporary Confucianism is able to address issues and questions of the twenty-first century because of its creativity, openness, and, above all, its acute sensitivity to human suffering and all forms of injustice. Contrary to the idea that Confucianism becomes a "lost soul"—an irreparable disconnection between Confucianism as a system of thought and a contemporary Chinese society no longer founded on an agrarian, kinship-based, and gentry-led structure,[42] Berthrong argues that the many forms of contemporary Confucianism are not only relevant to the pluralistic society of the twenty-first century, but also capable of transforming the world into a better place. As such, Berthrong reiterates the main theme of this volume: both within and outside China, New Confucianism is, and continues to be, a major force of change in the twenty-first century.

Notes

1. For a stimulating account of this "cultural miracle," see Kenneth J. Hammond and Jeffrey L. Richey, "The Death and Resurrection of Confucianism, in *The Sage Returns: Confucian Revival in Contemporary China*, edited by Kenneth J. Hammond and Jeffrey L. Richey (Albany, NY: State University of New York Press, 2015), 1–9.

2. Much has been written about the May Fourth Movement and the Cultural Revolution. For the May Fourth Movement, see esp. Chow Tse-tsung, *The May Fourth Movement: Intellectual Revolution in Modern China* (Cambridge, MA: Harvard University Press, 1960); Lin Yü-sheng, *The Crisis of Chinese Consciousness: Radical Anti-Traditionalism in the May Fourth Era* (Madison: University of Wisconsin Press, 1979); and Vera Schwarcz, *The Chinese Enlightenment: Intellectuals and the Legacy of the May Fourth Movement of 1919* (Berkeley: University of California Press, 1986). For the Cultural Revolution, see William Joseph, Christine P. W. Wong, and David Zweig, eds., *New Perspectives on the Cultural Revolution* (Cambridge, MA: Council on East Asian Studies, 1991); Elizabeth J. Perry and Liu Xin, *Proletarian Power: Shanghai in the Cultural Revolution* (Boulder, CO: Westview, 1997); and Joseph W. Esherick, Paul G. Pickowicz, and Andrew G. Walder, eds., *The Chinese Cultural Revolution as History* (Stanford, CA: Stanford University Press, 2006).

3. I thank Ming-huei Lee for pointing out the difference between New Confucianism of overseas Chinese community and "mainland Confucianism" that has emerged since the 1990s.

4. For the political and social background of the spread of New Confucianism in mainland China, see Song Xianlin, "Reconstructing the Confucian Ideal in 1980s China: The "Culture Craze" and New Confucianism," in John Makeham, ed., *New Confucianism: A Critical Examination* (New York: Palgrave Macmillan, 2003), 81–104. For the political ramifications of this Confucian revival, see Daniel A. Bell, *China's New Confucianism: Politics and Everyday Life in a Changing Society* (Princeton, NJ: Princeton University Press, 2008), 3–18.

5. See Sébastien Billioud, "Carrying the Confucian Torch to the Masses: The Challenge of Structuring the Confucian Revival in the People's Republic of China," *Oriens Extremus* 49 (2010): 201–224.

6. See Arif Dirlik, "Confucianism in the Borderlands: Global Capitalism and the Reinvention of Confucianism," *Boundary 2*, 22, no. 3 (Fall 1995): 229–273; Jing Wang, *High Culture Fever: Politics, Aesthetics, and Ideology in Deng's China* (Berkeley: University of California Press, 1996), 64–71.

7. See, e.g., Gloria Davis, ed., *Voicing Concerns: Contemporary Chinese Critical Inquiry* (Lanham, MD: Rowman & Littlefield, 2001), esp. 123–134.

8. See John Makeham, ed., *New Confucianism: A Critical Examination* (New York: Palgrave Macmillan, 2003); John Makeham, *Lost Soul: "Confucianism" in Contemporary Chinese Academic Discourse* (Cambridge, MA: Harvard University Asia Center, 2008); Umberto Bresciani, *Reinventing Confucianism: The New Confucian Movement* (Taipei: Taipei Ricci Institute for Chinese Studies, 2001); Ming-huei Lee, *Der Konfuzianismus im modernen China* (Leipzig: Leipziger Universitätsverlag, 2001).

9. See N. Serina Chan, *The Thought of Mou Zongsan* (Leiden: Brill, 2011), and Sébastien Billioud, *Thinking through Confucian Modernity: A Study of Mou Zongsan's Moral Metaphysics* (Leiden: Brill, 2012).

10. The 1958 Manifesto is also known as the 1958 Declaration. For a translation of the Manifesto see Carsun Chang, *The Development of Neo-Confucian Thought* (New York: Bookman Associates, 1957–1962), vol. 2, 455–483. In the epilogue of this volume, John Berthrong discusses the background and interpersonal relationships of the authors of the Manifesto.

11. For the significance of the 1958 Manifesto, see N. Serina Chan, *The Thought of Mou Zongsan*, 260–279.

12. For a discussion of the cultural milieu of colonial Hong Kong, see chap. 10 by Hok Yin Chan herein.

13. To his death, Mou Zongsan was adamantly anti-Communist. For an account of one of Mou's stormy encounters with mainland scholars, see Fang Keli, "Xiandai xinruxue de yishi xingtai tezheng" 现代新儒学的意识形态特征 [The characteristics of the New Confucian ideology], in *Xiandai xinruxue yu Zhongguo xiandaihua* 现代新儒学与中国现代化 [Contemporary New Confucianism and Chinese modernization], edited by Fang Keli (Tianjin: Tianjin renmin chubanshe, 1997), 210–222.

14. See John Makeham's introduction to *Lost Soul* and Song Xianlin's article "Reconstructing the Confucian Ideal in 1980s China" in *Lost Soul*.

15. One way to appreciate the openness and creativity that prevailed during the 1980s and 1990s is to read Li Zehou's 李泽厚 writings. In the late 1970s, his essays exposed the misuse of history under the Gang of Four, thereby setting the tone for an intellectual liberation; see *Zhongguo jindai sixiang shi* 中国近代思想史 (Beijing: Renmin chubanshe, 1979). In the mid-1980s, he reexamined the intellectual history of modern China, thereby encouraging readers to look for new ideas and new perspectives; see *Zou wo ziji de lu* 走我自己的路 (Beijing: Sanlian, 1986) and *Zhongguo xiandai sixiang shilun* 中国现代思想史论 (Beijing: Dongfang chubanshe, 1987). In the early 1990s, after relocating to the United States, Li continued to influence Chinese readers by asking them to "bid farewell to revolution"; see *Gaobie geming* 告别革命 (Hong Kong: Tiandi, 1995).

16. For the openness of the 1980s and 1900s, see Gan Yang 甘阳, ed., *Bashi niandai wenhua yishi* 八十年代文化意识 [The Cultural Consciousness of the 1980s] (Shanghai: Shijie chuban jituan, 2006). See also Xu Jilin 许纪霖 and Luo Gang 罗

岗, *Qimeng de ziwo wajie: 1990 niandai yilai Zhongguo sixiang wenhua jie zhongda lunzheng yanjiu* 启蒙的自我瓦解：1990 年代以来中国思想文化界重大论争研究 [The self-dissolution of Enlightenment: Studies of the major intellectual and cultural debates since the 1990s] (Jilin: Jilin chuban jituan, 1997), esp. 1–36. For specific examples of how the openness helped to inspire a Confucian revival, see the memoirs of those who participated in the "culture craze" and the "national learning craze" in Liang Tao 梁涛 and Gu Jianing 顾家宁, eds., *Guoxue wenti zhengming ji (1990–2010)* 国学问题争鸣集 (1990–2010) [A collection of polemical writings on national learning, 1990–2010] (Guilin: Guangxi shifan daxue chubanshe, 1990), esp. 3–9, 24–27, 35–44.

17. Jing Haifeng 景海峰 is explicit about the impact of the cultural milieu of the 1980s and 1990s on his study of New Confucianism. See his *Xinruxue yu ershishiji Zhongguo sixiang* 新儒学与二十世纪中国思想 [Contemporary New Confucianism and Twentieth-Century Chinese thought] (Zhengzhou: Zhongzhou guji chubanshe, 2005), 315–317.

18. Dirlik, "Confucianism in the Borderlands," 236–247.

19. For the original argument of Peter Berger, see Peter L. Berger and Hsin-Huang Michael Hsiao, eds., *In Search of an East Asian Development Model* (New Brunswick, NJ: Transaction Books, 1988), 3–11.

20. Dirlik, "Confucianism in the Borderlands," 254–268.

21. For Tu Wei-ming's full argument about the three epochs and the significance of the third epoch, see Tu Wei-ming 杜维明, "Rujia disanqi fazhan de qianjing wenti" 儒家第三期发展的前景问题 [The question of the development prospect of the Third Epoch of Confucianism], in *Rujia chuantong de xiandai zhuanhua: Du Weiming xinruxue lunzhu jiyao* 儒家传统的现代转化：杜维明新儒学论著辑要 [The modern transformation of Confucian tradition: A collection of writings on New Confucianism by Tu Wei-ming], edited by Yue Hua 岳华 and Guan Dong 关东 (Beijing: Zhongguo guangbo dianshi chubanshe, 1992), 234–277.

22. Tu does not talk explicitly about this "global tour" of New Confucianism. But Yue Hua and Guan Dong emphasize the "global tour" in their editorial preface, or "bianxu" 编序. See "bianxu" in *Rujia chuantong de xiandai zhuanhua*, esp. 14.

23. See Tu Wei-ming, ed., *The Triadic Cord: Confucian Ethics, Industrial East Asia and Max Weber* (Singapore: Institute of East Asian Philosophies, 1991), esp. 3–56.

24. Dirlik, "Confucius in the Borderlands," 267.

25. See Tu Wei-ming 杜维明, "Cong shijie sichao de jige cemian kan ruxue yanjiu de xin dongxiang" 从世界思潮的几个侧面看儒学研究的新动向 [Looking at new development in New Confucianism from the perspective of several currents of world thought], in *Rujia chuantong de xiandai zhuanhua*, 303–329.

26. Tu Wei-ming 杜维明, "Rujia lunli yu dongya qiye jingshen" 儒家伦理与东亚企业精神 [The Confucian ethic and the East Asian entrepreneurial spirit], in *Rujia chuantong de xiandai zhuanhua*, 329–360.

27. For the influence of Tu Wei-ming on Chinese philosophers, see chap. 2 by Els van Dongen herein.

28. Some Taiwan scholars have suggested that the massive New Confucianism research project was part of the Chinese Communist Party's efforts to "unify" Taiwan. See Fang Keli, "Xiandai xinrujia de yishi xingtai tezheng."

29. For an analysis of the contributions and limitations of the "New Confucian research project," see my chapter herein.

30. See Kenneth J. Hammond, "The Return of the Repressed: The New Left and 'Left' Confucianism in Contemporary China," in *The Sages Return*, 93–111.

31. See Anthony DeBlasi, "Selling Confucius: The Negotiated Return of Tradition in Post-Socialist China, in *The Sages Return*, 67–92. For a glimpse of how Yu Dan interprets Confucianism, see her English-language publication *Confucius from the Heart: Ancient Wisdom for Today's World* (New York: Atria Book, 2006).

32. See Daniel A. Bell, *China's New Confucianism*, 3–56. See also chap. 12 by Junhao Hong, Miao Liu, and Wen Huang herein.

33. See reports of these grassroots organizations in Sébastien Billioud, "Carrying the Confucian Torch to the Masses." See also the discussion of Confucian religious activities in Sébastien Billioud and Joël Thoraval, *Le Sage et le people: Le renouveau confucéen en China* (Paris: CNRS Éditions, 2014) and the broad range of social issues discussed online in Jeffrey L. Richey, "Chat Room Confucianism: Online Discourse and Popular Morality in China," in *The Sage Returns*, 113–125.

34. For Chinese debates about the new global order, see chap. 3 by Daniel A. Bell herein.

35. For studies of the wide range of circumstances in which Confucianism (broadly defined) is invoked in contemporary China, see Sébastien Billioud and Joël Thoroval, "Confucianism, 'Cultural Tradition,' and Official Discourse in China at the Start of the Century," *Chinese Perspectives* 3 (2007): 50–65; Sébastien Billioud and Joël Thoroval, "Jianhua: The Confucian Revival as an Educative Project," *Chinese Perspectives* 7 (2007): 4–20; Anna Sun, *Confucianism as a World Religion*, esp. chaps. 7–9.

36. In the last few years, thanks to Daniel A. Bell's summaries and translations, Jiang Qing's political views are available in English. See Daniel A. Bell, *China's New Confucianism*, 175–191; Jiang Qing, *A Confucian Constitutional Order: How China's Ancient Past Can Shape Its Political Future*, translated by Edwund Ryden, edited by Daniel A. Bell and Ruiping Fan (Princeton, NJ: Princeton University Press, 2013).

37. Part 2 would be more complete if I could include articles about Xu Fuguan and Zhang Junmai, the other two authors of the 1958 Manifesto. Unfortunately, over the three years when this volume was prepared, I was unable to find scholars interested in contributing chapters on Xu and Zhang. For those interested in Xu as a political thinker, Aihe Wang's *Cosmology and Political Culture in Early China* (Cambridge, UK: Cambridge University Press, 2000), esp. 1–22, offers a glimpse of his critique of authoritarianism. For those interested in Zhang as a transnational scholar, please read Joseph Ciaudo, "Questioning Sinodicy: An Inquiry into Zhang Junmai's Cultural Discourse (1919–1937)" (PhD diss., 2016, College de France).

38. A similar view is found in the chapters by Thomas Fröhlich, Hok Yin Chan, Marc Andre Matten, and Junhao Hong herein.

39. For another study of Tang Junyi's philosophy, see Thomas A. Metzger, *A Cloud across the Pacific: Essays on the Clash between Chinese and Western Political Theories Today* (Hong Kong: Chinese University Press, 2005), 185–290.

40. Thomas A. Metzger and Zhang Hao 張灝 have also pointed out the absence of critical reflection on modernity among Chinese thinkers. For Metzger, the absence is due to the Chinese propensity toward "epistemological optimism." See Thomas A. Metzger, *A Cloud across the Pacific*, 1–184. For Zhang Hao, the absence is due to the lack of an awareness of human evil. See Zhang Hao, *Youan yishi yu minzhu chuantong* 幽暗意识与民主传统 [Consciousness of darkness and the democratic tradition] (Beijing: Xinxing chubanshe, 2006), esp. 23–43.

41. Recently, detailed studies have been written about Confucianism as a cultural icon and a commodity. See, for instance, articles by Robert L. Morre and Julia K. Murray in *The Sage Returns*, 129–194; Lionel M. Jensen, "Culture Industry, Power, and the Spectacle of China's "Confucius Institutes," in *China in and beyond the Headlines*, edited by Timothy B. Weston and Lionel M. Jensen (Lanham, MD: Rowman & Littlefield, 2012), 271–299.

42. Yu Ying-shih coined the term "lost soul" (*you hun* 游魂). For Yu, any attempt to revive Confucianism is doomed to failure because of the immense gulf between thought and social reality. See Yu, *Xiandai ruxue de huigu yu zhanwang* 现代儒学的回顾与展望 [Contemporary Confucianism: Retrospect and prospect] (Beijing: Sanlian shudian, 2004), esp. 53–58, 263–270. John Makeham reiterates Yu's view in his introduction to *Lost Soul*. Some mainland Chinese scholars also support Yu's and Makeham's views. See Fang Chaohui 方朝晖, *Xuetong de mishi yu zaizao: Rujia yu dangdai Zhongguo xuetong yanjiu* 学统的迷失于再造: 儒家与当代中国学统研究 [The loss and reconstruction of intellectual paradigms: Studies of Confucianism and contemporary intellectual paradigms] (Xi'an: Shaanxi shifan daxue, 2010), esp. 9–29.

Part One

Capitalism and the Global Order

1

Global Capitalism with Chinese Characteristics

Fang Keli's New Confucian Research Project (1986–1995)

TZE-KI HON

> Placed in the museum of history by Joseph Levenson three decades ago, Confucianism has reemerged from the museum "to advance toward the twenty-first century with a smile on his lips," to quote a recent article in the *Renmin ribao*.
>
> —Arif Dirlik

Having been a prime target of attack and denunciation for more than half a century, Confucianism enjoyed a robust revival in China during the 1980s and 1990s. By all accounts, this resurgence of Confucianism was spectacular. Rather than a relic of feudalism and a stumbling block to Chinese modernity, as the May Fourth cultural iconoclasts once insisted, Confucianism was seen as an indispensable cultural force that would bring China into global capitalism. Rather than a sociopolitical system that exploited women, peasants, and the poor, as the Red Guards of the Cultural Revolution once disdainfully claimed, Confucianism was considered a source of cultural authenticity that would anchor China's rise in the late twentieth century.[1] A result of this spectacular revival is that Confucianism has become, once again, an important social and cultural force in China after thirty years of absence, giving rise to speculations that a transformation "from Communism to Confucianism" is under way.[2]

Commonly known as "New Confucianism" (*xin rujia* 新儒家 or *xin ruxue* 新儒學),[3] this late-twentieth-century revival of Confucianism was fundamentally different from earlier attempts the "National Essence group" (*guocui pai* 國粹派, 1905–1911) and the Critical Review scholars (Xueheng pai 學衡派, 1922–1933) made.[4] First and foremost, the Confucian revival was triggered by a state-sponsored research project to analyze and classify the writings of a group of scholars known as New Confucian thinkers. The list of these thinkers was long and had been revised several times. In general, the list included luminaries such as Liang Shuming 梁漱溟, Zhang Junmai 張君勱, Feng Youlan 馮友蘭, Xiong Shili 熊十力, Ma Yifu 馬一浮, He Lin 賀麟, Qian Mu 錢穆, Mou Zongsan 牟宗三, Tang Junyi 唐君毅, Xu Fuguan 徐復觀, Fang Dongmei 方東美, Tu Wei-ming 杜維明, Liu Shu-hsien 劉述先, Yü Ying-shih 余英時, and Cheng Chung-ying 成中英.[5] With these New Confucian thinkers, a genealogy was created to denote a lively intellectual movement that began in the 1920s and continued into the 1990s.

Furthermore, concomitant with Deng Xiaoping's economic reforms, the research project of New Confucianism projected an image of a China that was open to ideas from overseas Chinese, particularly those in Hong Kong, Singapore, Taiwan, and the United States. And by including scholars who left the mainland in 1949 (e.g., Qian Mu, Tang Junyi, Mou Zongsan, and Xu Fuguan) as New Confucian thinkers, the researchers showed a willingness to go beyond the Cold War binary of communism versus democracy, offering opportunities for cooperation and partnership among various Chinese communities around the world. Above all, at a time when Marxism-Leninism and Mao Zedong Thought had lost their appeal to many Chinese on the mainland, the study of New Confucianism provided a cultural framework for building "socialism with Chinese characteristics." Particularly, it promoted Confucian capitalism by focusing attention on economic successes in Japan and the Four Mini Dragons (Hong Kong, Singapore, South Korea, and Taiwan).

This chapter examines the New Confucian research project Fang Keli 方克立 (b. 1938) led. Funded by the Chinese government as part of the seventh (1986–1990) and eighth (1991–1995) five-year plans for philosophy and the social sciences, Fang's research project defined the scale and scope of New Confucianism. It also linked New Confucianism to Confucian capitalism, thereby explicitly putting the research at the center of the debate on building "socialism with Chinese characteristics." Certainly, as Arif Dirlik has pointed out, Fang's research project was strong in popularizing the writings of New Confucians but weak in analyzing them.[6] Despite the generous government funding and the warm support from scholars inside and outside China, Fang and his cohort were reluctant to engage in a theoretical discussion of Confucian capitalism, leaving many questions unanswered as to how Confucianism—widely known for its emphasis on filial piety, hierarchy, elitism, and patriarchy—could be a driving force of economic productivity and global connectivity. Nevertheless, from a historical perspective, Fang Keli's ten-year research project is significant in China's tumultuous transition from Mao's socialist revolution to state-capitalism of the post-Mao era. Despite being plagued by missteps and miscalculations, Fang's research project helped to bring Confucianism back to mainland China after a thirty-year absence.[7] More importantly, it was part of a discourse of state-capitalism that focused on modernity rather than revolution. Whether bidding "farewell to revolution" (*gaobie geming* 告別革命)[8] is truly in China's best interest, modernity (*xiandai xing* 現代性) has now replaced revolution (*geming* 革命) as a key word in Chinese intellectual debate.

To highlight the significance of Fang's research project, this chapter is divided into three sections. The first section discusses Fang's purpose for creating a genealogy of New Confucian thinkers. Through what John Makeham calls "a retrospective creation of New Confucianism,"[9] this section argues that Fang not only promoted New Confucianism based on the traditional notion of *daotong* 道統 (the Genealogy of the Way), but also challenged the "revolutionary historiography" that marked the last century of Chinese history as a series of revolutions.[10] The second section traces Fang's various efforts to create an acceptable genealogy of New Confucian thinkers. Although controversial in its selection, Kang's genealogy of New Confucian thinkers introduced a new perspective that viewed the last one hundred years of Chinese history as a continuous saga of building state-capitalism. This section examines the way Fang presented Confucian capitalism. Even though Fang attempted to avoid discussing Confucian capitalism, it was undoubtedly a core idea that drove the retrospective creation of New Confucianism. Its absence—or, more precisely, its absent presence—revealed a dilemma that Fang faced when, in the intellectual milieu of the 1980s and 1990s, he could not directly discuss state-capitalism and yet his task was to introduce the concept of state-capitalism into the debate of modernity. The chapter ends by analyzing Fang's brief entry on "Confucian capitalism" in the *Dictionary on Confucius* (Kongzi da cidian 孔子大辭典), which clearly shows his ambivalence about Confucian capitalism. In analyzing this entry, I highlight the limits of Fang's research project in justifying China's entry into global capitalism of late twentieth century.

Three Intellectual Currents

For many Chinese who grew up after 1949, the history of their country in the last century is filled with revolutions: the 1911 Revolution, the May

Fourth Movement (1915–1923), the 1949 Communist Revolution, and the Great Proletarian Cultural Revolution (1966–1976). Although not considered a revolution, the opening Deng Xiaoping initiated in 1979 has once again transformed life for Chinese. Although distinct in their own right, these events are linked as a historical teleology of continuous revolution. According to this narrative, twentieth-century China began with a political revolution to transform the imperial state into a nation-state; then it underwent an intellectual revolution to replace Confucianism with modern science and democracy; finally it developed a socialist revolution to drastically change the socioeconomic structure of the nation. The underlying theme of this narrative is that China's modernization could be achieved only by severing its ties with the past, particularly through a complete restructuring of the country's political, cultural, and social systems.[11]

What drives this teleology of revolution is the dichotomy between tradition and modernity. Understood as the totality of the Chinese imperial system, tradition must make way for modernity because it is not only a remnant of the past but also a stumbling block to modernizing China's political, social, and economic structures. From this dichotomy comes a long chain of binary oppositions, those of autocracy versus democracy, classical language versus vernacular language, elitism versus populism, morality versus science, patriarchy versus gender equality, and so on. At its root, the teleology of revolution is a form of modernization theory that upholds the West (particularly Western Europe and the United States) as the model of global progress and measures the developments of countries around the world according to how closely they resemble the Western experience. Embedded in this teleology is the concept of linear progression, which assumes that the present must supersede the past and the best is yet to come.

During the 1980s, Deng Xiaoping's "reform and opening up" (*gaige kaifang* 改革開放) quietly called into question this historical teleology. By replacing "revolution" (*geming* 革命) with "reform" (*gaige* 改革) as a key term in political discourse, Deng put emphasis on cultural continuity and gradual change. Encapsulated in his enigmatic phrase "building socialism with Chinese characteristics," he stressed China's uniqueness in modernization. In the academic field, Deng's "reform and opening up" had had important consequences. One of them was the call to "bid farewell to revolution" in which scholars such as Li Zehou 李澤厚 and Liu Zaifu 劉再復 asked their colleagues to stop interpreting modern Chinese history from the perspectives of revolutions.[12] The other development was the rise of the "new national learning" (*xin guoxue* 新國學) in which cultural conservatism was presented as a vital force of modernizing China, along with Liberalism and radicalism.[13] Accomplished scholars in the Republican period who were foreign trained but had a strong interest in Chinese culture (such as Chen Yinke 陳寅恪 and Tang Yongtong 湯用彤) were touted as models for a postrevolutionary scholarship that would recover the "suppressed Chinese modernity" when China was building a nation-state. Fang Keli's ten-year research project on New Confucianism emerged in this context of "bidding farewell to revolution" and "recovering the suppressed Chinese modernity." As Song Xianlin reminds us, the study of New Confucianism appeared between the "culture craze" (*wenhua re* 文化熱) of the 1980s, when the revolutionary historiography was under attack, and the "national studies craze" (*guoxue re* 國學熱) of the 1990s, when cultural conservatism was in vogue as an alternative to the "total westernization" of the liberals.[14]

From Fang's writings, he was clearly fully aware of the significance of the intellectual debates in the 1980s and 1990s when he discussed the goal of studying New Confucianism. He repeatedly stressed that the premise of his study was the coexistence of three "intellectual currents" (*sichao* 思潮) since the 1920s: Marxism-Leninism, Liberalism, and Conservatism. In spite of their differing assumptions and approaches, Fang reiterated, these three intellectual currents offered valuable insights and inspirations to China's quest for modernity. For instance, in a key statement about New Confucianism, he wrote:

> New Confucianism has been undoubtedly one of the influential and vital intellectual movements in modern China since the May Fourth Movement. It forms a triad with Marxism and the liberals' Westernization. It is an intellectual current that develops in opposition to the "total westernization" [of the liberals] on the one hand and the triumph of Marxism in China on the other. Despite differences in their approaches, the three intellectual currents share the same goal of modernizing China.[15]

Two points are important in this quote. First, Fang dates the beginning of New Confucianism to the 1920s, despite the fact that some forms of Confucian revival had already appeared in the late Qing period (e.g., Kang Youwei 康有為 and Deng Shi) and during the 1911 Revolution (e.g., Zhang Taiyan 章太炎 and Liu Shipei 劉師培). By dating the beginning of New Confucianism to the 1920s, Fang makes it contemporaneous with the May Fourth Movement and the arrival of Marxism-Leninism. The date conveniently supports Fang's claim that the three intellectual currents were codependent and constantly in dialogue. Second, Fang stresses the common goal of the three intellectual currents. According to Fang, they are in essence theories of modernization aimed at bringing wealth and power to China. This common goal not only drew the three intellectual currents together but also gave each of them its own uniqueness: the Marxists' vision of socialist modernity based on the leadership of the party-state, the liberals' vision of capitalistic modernity based on the invisible hand of the market economy, and the New Confucians' vision of using some of the East Asian cultural values to boost industrial production and to smooth the corporate-labor relationship.[16]

This composite view is significant because it offers a new perspective on China's modernization. Certainly, as self-professed Marxists, Fang and his cohort affirmed the supremacy of the party-state system over the market economy and East Asian values.[17] At the same time, they also emphasized the importance of dialogue and partnership among supporters of the three intellectual currents. By championing an open and fluid relationship among the three intellectual currents, Fang and his cohort tacitly acknowledged that Marxism-Leninism had lost its august status as the only option in modernizing China. Instead, China's development had to draw resources from all three forms of modernity: the one party-state for political structure, a dynamic and robust market for the economy, and a strong cultural identity among Chinese citizens.

In addition, this composite view provides a different interpretation of modern Chinese history. Rather than a time divided into waves of revolution, the last one hundred years of Chinese history is understood as a single but highly dynamic process of sociopolitical change undergirded by three streams of thought sharing a common goal of modernizing China. Of course, at each given movement, only one stream of thought was dominant; for instance, Liberalism was in vogue during the May Fourth Movement and Marxism-Leninism was the ruling ideology in Mao's China. Nevertheless, the dominance was never total because there was space for conversation, contestation, and dissent because of the existence of alternative views.

Three Generations of New Confucians

Despite making an important breakthrough in historiography, Fang and his cohort were not sure how to reconcile the fundamental differences among the three streams of thought, especially with regard to the conflict between the party-state, the neoliberal market economy, and the Confucian emphasis on kinship and bloodlines. But at the time, Fang and his cohort clearly needed to explore and explicate what was known as Confucian capitalism—a particular form of state-market relationship in East Asia during the 1970s and 1980s. Variously referred to as "the East Asian development model," "the capitalistic development state," "the planned rational economy," or "the second case of capitalist modernity," Confucian capitalism was based on a Weberian argument for the cultural aspect of capitalism. Instead of the Protestant ethic that Max Weber suggested was the driving force of the capitalistic spirit, the supporters of Confucian capitalism regarded Confucian ethics as the cultural foundation of East Asian capitalist success.[18] The argument was complex, and it included an export-oriented economy, state planning, family-based entrepreneurship, social harmony, team-player spirit, and a long-hours work ethic. And it was proven, supporters claimed, by the rapid economic growth in Japan and the Four Mini Dragons.[19] But, as Arif Dirlik has pointed out, the significance of Confucian capitalism is not limited to economic performance or the improvement in the standard of living of East Asian people. More importantly, Confucian capitalism challenges the Euro-American model of neoliberal global capitalism and underscores the importance of incorporating traditional practices into modernization to boost consumption, innovation, and production.[20]

For Fang Keli and his cohort, the goal of their study was to gain a handle on the theory and practice of Confucian capitalism through the study of New Confucianism. To that end, they needed to determine what New Confucianism meant and who the New Confucians were. In 1987, a year after the New Confucian research project was formally launched, Fang attempted to define New Confucianism, and that definition later became the basis for deciding which scholars to include in, or exclude from, the genealogy of New Confucian thinkers. Fang's definition states:

> New Confucianism began in the 1920s and is still a vital school of thought to the present day. Its goal is to continue the genealogy of the Confucian Way and to revive the Confucian learning. It builds on Neo-Confucianism of the Song-Ming period, particularly the Confucian practices of moral cultivation. In its bid to achieve Chinese modernity, New Confucianism stresses the centrality of Confucian learning in absorbing, adapting, and transforming Western learning. Although it is essentially a school of thought, we can also call it an intellectual current.[21]

Besides reiterating the time frame and the link to Chinese modernity, Fang's definition added one new dimension to understanding New Confucianism. It highlighted three characteristics of New Confucian learning: (1) its goal of reviving Confucianism in the modern age, (2) its emphasis on moral self-cultivation drawn from Song-Ming Neo-Confucianism, and (3) its strategy of balancing the competing claims of preserving Chinese uniqueness and opening China to foreign theories and practices.

In hindsight, these three characteristics of New Confucian teaching were by no means random. Rather, they were intended to set a baseline for building a genealogy of New Confucianism. In particular, the three characteristics clearly privileged Xiong Shili and his students (Tang Junyi, Mou Zongsan, and Xu Fuguan), who claimed to continue the Lu-Wang school of Song-Ming Neo-Confucianism. In other words, from the beginning, Fang and his cohort decided that Xiong and his students formed the core group of New Confucians.

Fang focused on Xiong and his students for several reasons, one of which was that, after leaving the mainland in 1949, Xiong's students had produced numerous writings critiquing the modern life from a Confucian perspective. Among Xiong's students, Mou Zongsan was particularly important in using the Lu-Wang school of Song-Ming Neo-Confucianism to challenge the Kantian philosophy, thereby also challenging the authority of Europe as the model of modernity.[22] Mou's bold attempt signified the possibility of a dialogue between the Eastern and Western philosophies and the importance of transforming Confucianism into a philosophical system to address questions and issues of modern life. Another reason for privileging Xiong's students was that they had managed to attract a small but solid group of supporters in overseas Chinese communities, most prominently the Fazhu 法住 group in Hong Kong and the Ehu 鵝湖 writers in Taiwan.[23] The success of Xiong's students proved that their learning had had direct impact on overseas Chinese communities in facing the challenges of modern life, such as cutthroat competition in a market economy, alienation of urban life, and social polarization caused by appropriation and dispossession of wealth.[24] Furthermore, Xiong's students had successfully trained several young scholars who became spokesmen for New Confucianism in international academic circles. Among these scholars, Tu Wei-ming played a special role in globalizing New Confucianism. He promoted the concept of "the third epoch of Confucianism," namely, a Confucianism for the modern age that is different from Confucianism in early China and imperial China.[25]

Even though Fang focused on Xiong and his students, he also made efforts to include other scholars, particularly those who remained on the mainland after 1949. To include as many mainland scholars as possible, he adopted a broad definition of Song-Ming Neo-Confucianism. In addition to the Lu-Wang school—which Xiong and his students supported—Fang also included the Cheng-Zhu school. By taking a broad definition of Song-Ming Neo-Confucianism, he opened the possibility for including other scholars (such as Qian Mu and Feng Youlan) who supported the Cheng-Zhu school of Neo-Confucianism.[26]

Feng Youlan, in particular, was important to Fang's attempt at including more mainland scholars into the pantheon of New Confucians. Unlike Liang Shuming, who established his credentials for being a Confucian philosopher in the 1920s, Feng's status as a Confucian was questionable because he was primarily a historian of Chinese philosophy with no particular preference for Confucianism or a particular Confucian school. Active in the mainland Chinese academy until his death, his reputation as an independent scholar was somewhat tarnished after he worked for the Gang of Four during the "anti-Lin Bao and anti-Confucius" campaign. Yet Fang and his cohort made strenuous efforts to include him in the pantheon of New Confucians. In so doing, they made clear that mainland scholars, although working under difficult conditions, had played an important role in developing New Confucianism.

On this score, John Makeham is right that the genealogy of New Confucianism has to be understood as a "retrospective creation." The purpose of the retrospective creation is particularly clear in how the New Confucian thinkers are divided into three successive generations. The first generation of New Confucians, stretching from the 1920s to the 1940s, includes Liang Shuming, Ma Yifu, Zhang Junmai, Feng Youlan, He Lun, and Xiong Shili. With this list of scholars, Fang Keli conveniently juxtaposes New Confucianism with major cultural events in Republican China: the May Fourth Movement (1915–1923), the debate on science and the philosophy of life (1923), the debate on "total westernization" (1935), and the wartime rethinking of philosophy (1937–1945). More importantly, the list is deliberately inclusive, such that Xiong Shili is at best one of the early New Confucians. This inclusiveness in the first generation of New Confucians sends a clear signal to Xiong's students that, despite what they claim, they are not the only New Confucians in contemporary China.

The second generation of New Confucians, extending from the 1950s to the 1980s, includes Tang Junyi, Mou Zongsan, Xu Fuguan, and Fang Dongmei. By including only scholars who left the mainland in 1949, Fang highlights that New Confucianism played no role on the mainland under Mao's rule. The third generation of New Confucians, spanning from the 1980s to the present, includes Tu Wei-ming, Liu Shu-hsien, Yü Ying-shih, and Cheng Chung-ying. All of them received their graduate training in the United States and are prominent scholars in the English-speaking world. With this list of scholars, Fang makes clear that the future of New Confucianism lies in its transformation into a modern philosophy for both Chinese and the global community.

Of the third generation of New Confucians, Fang Keli gave special attention to Tu Wei-ming and Liu Shu-hsien. He identified these two scholars as the leaders of the third generation and provided detailed summaries of their writings.[27] Even after other scholars such as Yü Ying-shih and Cheng Chung-ying were added to the list of the third generation, Fang still regarded Tu and Liu as the most influential and significant New Confucians of their generation. On one level, it seems obvious that Fang would regard Tu and Liu as the representatives of the third generation. First, they are U.S.-trained scholars who have had successful academic careers teaching Confucian philosophy in well-regarded universities (Harvard University for Tu, and the Chinese University of Hong Kong for Liu). Together, they represent the success of the third generation New Confucians in globalizing Confucianism. Second, the two scholars are more open to dialogue with colleagues on the mainland than earlier New Confucians such as Mou Zongsan.[28] Their openness fit perfectly the relaxed and fluid atmosphere that Fang wanted to cultivate in promoting "the co-existence of the three intellectual currents of modern China."

On another level, however, Fang saw Tu and Liu not only as New Confucian thinkers but also as key players in the discourse of modernity on the mainland. In summarizing the writings of Tu and Liu, Fang stressed their contributions in highlighting the importance of humanistic learning in modern society[28] and in reforming the Confucian social system to serve the needs of modern life.[30] In short, in Tu and Liu, Fang found concrete evidence of New Confucianism being a modern philosophy that provides inspirations to deal with the anxiety and alienation of late-twentieth-century capitalism.[31]

Confucian Capitalism

Interestingly, despite Fang's emphasis on the modernity of New Confucianism, he said little about Confucian capitalism. In Fang's writings, the term "Confucian capitalism" often appeared when he discussed New Confucianism, but he did not give "Confucian capitalism" a clear definition, treating the term as an empty signifier with neither substance nor concrete reference. A clear example of Confucian capitalism being an empty signifier is Fang's entry on the subject in *The Dictionary of Confucius*. There, he defines Confucian capitalism as:

> a path or a model of development adopted by New Confucians to achieve capitalistic modernity based on Confucian culture and Confucian thought. It is different from the developmental models of industrialization and modernization that appear in

Western Europe and North America on the one hand and in the Soviet Union and Eastern Europe on the other. According to New Confucians, the recent twenty years of rapid economic growth in Japan, South Korea, Taiwan, Hong Kong, and Singapore disprove [Max] Weber's theory of secularization. They believe that alongside the Protestant ethic, Confucian ethics is also a potent force of the capitalistic spirit because of its unique form of religiosity and its secularizing function. [As a result,] Confucian ethics has been a main reason for the East Asian economic miracle.[32]

By cleverly linking New Confucianism to Confucian capitalism, Fang reiterates the prominent role that New Confucian thinkers play in the discourse of modernity. Nonetheless, besides using the East Asian economic miracle as evidence of the success of Confucian capitalism, Fang says little about what exactly Confucian capitalism entails. Nor does he specify the type of Confucian ethics that is supposed to lead to the success of "industrial East Asia." Although by the early 1990s a large body of work examining the East Asian "development state" and "bureaucratic capitalism"[33] had already been developed in the West, Fang seems to have had no knowledge of that literature. Instead, he relied on Tu Wei-ming when he mentioned, in passing, the Confucian impact in education, social cohesion, work ethic, and entrepreneurship.[34]

Even more striking, however, is how Fang ended the entry. In concluding the entry, he changed his position sharply and abruptly. Rather than continue to discuss the link between Confucian ethics and Confucian capitalism, he adopted the voice of a critic. Without giving any specific example, he argued that the East Asian economic miracle could not be understood solely from the perspective of culture and ideas. He wrote: "In looking for the reasons that have led to the rapid economic growth in some of the East Asian countries and places, other scholars find that it is incorrect to put the emphasis on cultural and intellectual factors, linking the success mechanically to the positive impact of Confucian cultural values. These scholars reject the view of New Confucian thinkers who interpret the economic success in East Asia as a manifestation of extending the Confucian learning of the 'inner sage' into the management of world affairs of the 'outer king.'"[35] Completely contradicting what he said earlier, Fang cautioned his readers neither to accept the New Confucians' argument for Confucian capitalism nor to adopt the New Confucian perspective in contemplating an East Asian modernity.

Practically split into two halves with two opposite arguments, the short entry shows Fang's predicament in using New Confucianism to promote Confucian capitalism. Caught in the volatile political environment of the 1980s and 1990s, when the Marxists, liberals, and conservatives were competing for power and influence to shape the policies of the Chinese Communist Party (CCP), Fang realized that in supporting Confucian capitalism the situation was fraught with difficulties. To protect himself and his project, Fang had to be less than forthcoming in his work. His evasiveness became even more frequent in the mid-1990s when he was attacked from three sides: (1) the "mainland Confucians" (such as Luo Yijun 劉義俊 and Jiang Qing 蔣慶) who wanted to use New Confucianism to challenge the CCP's authority; (2) the CCP ideologues who were unhappy with Fang's being uncritical of Confucian capitalism; and (3) the scholars in Taiwan and Hong Kong who increasingly saw Fang's research project as a political ploy to reach out to overseas Chinese communities. Consequently, his writings became polemical and defensive. He became less forthcoming in promoting dialogue and cooperation with scholars outside China.[36]

Conclusion

His evasiveness notwithstanding, the significance of Fang's research project does not lie in promoting New Confucianism or introducing Confucian capitalism into the Chinese debate over modernity. Its true contribution is bringing two important issues into the Chinese discourse of modernity. The first issue is how to preserve Chinese cultural authenticity in modernization. Whether as a result of cultural nationalism or of cultural conservatism, since the beginning of the 1990s Chinese intellectuals had been adding increasingly more items to the list of "Chinese characteristics" when following the CCP's call for "building socialism." Certainly, several factors (including the advertising strategies of the culture market) led to this emphasis on Chinese characteristics. Nevertheless, the rationale for Fang's research project was to examine the New Confucians' efforts at reinventing the Confucian tradition to serve in modern times. On this score, Fang's research is a resounding success.

The second issue is the relationship among Marxism, Liberalism, and New Confucianism as three interdependent intellectual forces in modern China. While vague on what Confucian capitalism meant and unclear on how New Confucianism could help to achieve capitalistic growth, Fang's emphasis on "the coexistence of Marxism, Liberalism, and Conservatism" forms the groundwork for building what Rebecca Karl calls "the state-market-intellectuals complex" in China during the 1990s.[37] In hindsight, while Fang's research project might have begun with the modest goal of exploring and explicating New Confucianism, it quickly turned into an academic rehearsal for the legitimization of state-capitalism in China. By linking the party-state (Marxism-Leninism), the market economy (Liberalism), and the educated elite (New Confucianism), Fang's research project set the tone for the sociopolitical order that has dominated China since the 1990s.

Notes

Author's note: An early version of this chapter appears as "From Culture to Cultural Nationalism: A Study of New Confucianism of the 1980s and 1990s," in *Contemporary Confucian Thought and Action*, edited by Guy Alitto (Berlin, Heidelberg: Springer, 2015), 27–39.

1. For a study of this contemporary revival of Confucianism, see John Makeham, *Lost Soul: "Confucianism" in Contemporary Chinese Academic Discourse* (Cambridge, MA: Harvard University Asia Center, 2008), esp. 42–73.

2. For an optimistic interpretation of contemporary Confucian revival, see Daniel A. Bell, *China's New Confucianism: Politics and Every Life in a Changing Society* (Princeton, NJ: Princeton University Press, 2008). The phrase "from Communism to Confucianism" comes from the title of chap. 1.

3. Although *xin rujia* (New Confucianism) and *xin ruxue* (New Confucian learning) have slightly different meanings, many researchers use the two terms interchangeably. For instance, Fang Keli (the head of the New Confucian research project) considers the two terms synonyms.

4. For a study of the Confucian revivals of the Guocui and Xueheng scholars, see my book *Revolution as Restoration: Guocui xuebao and China's Path to Modernity, 1905–1911* (Leiden: Brill, 2013), and my article "National Essence, National Learning, and Culture: Historical Writings *Guocui xuebao, Xueheng*, and *Guoxue jikan*," *Historiography East and West* 1, no. 2 (2003): 242–295.

5. For a complete list of New Confucians, see Fang Keli 方克立 and Zheng Jiadong 鄭家棟, eds., *Xiandai xinrujia renwu yu zhuzuo* 現代新儒家人物與著作 [The modern New Confucians and their writings] (Tianjin: Nankai daxue chubanshe, 1995); Fang Keli, Li Jinquan 李錦全, eds., *Xiandai xinrujia xuean* 現代新儒家學案 [Intellectual biographies of modern New Confucians] (Beijing: Zhongguo shehui kexue chubanshe, 1995).

6. Arif Dirlik, "Confucius in the Borderlands: Global Capitalism and the Reinvention of Confucianism," *Boundary 2*, 22, no. 3 (1995): 261–271.

7. John Makeham, for one, emphasizes Fang's contribution in this respect. See John Makeham, *Lost Soul*, 331–350.

8. In critiquing the "farewell to revolution," Wang Hui coins the term "depoliticized politics." See Wang Hui, *The End of the Revolution: China and the Limits of Modernity* (London: Verso, 2009), 3–19. For a succinct summary of the significance of critiquing "the end of the revolution," see Rebecca Karl's foreword to *The End of the Revolution*, vii–x.

9. John Makeham coins the phrase "a retrospective creation of New Confucianism." For the details of Makeham's argument see the chapter "The Retrospective

Creation of New Confucianism" in *New Confucianism: A Critical Examination*, edited by John Makeham (New York: Palgrave Macmillan, 2003), 25–53.

10. On the significance of *daotong* in the construction of the genealogy of New Confucians, see John Makeham, "The New *Daotong*," in *New Confucianism: A Critical Examination*, 55–78. Although I agree with Makeham that the traditional notion of *daotong* played a role in the creation of a genealogy of New Confucian thinkers, the main purpose of the genealogy was to reshape the Chinese collective memory of the history of their country since the 1920s. For details of my argument, see the section on three intellectual currents.

11. To this day, this saga of continuous revolution is still frequently portrayed in films, novels, operas, songs, and television documentaries in China. In historical writings, a key text that explains this historical view is Fan Wenlan 范文澜, *Zhongguo jindai shi* 中国近代史 [History of modern China] (Beijing: Renmin chubanshe, 1955).

12. Li Zehou and Liu Zaifu, *Guobie geming: Huiwang ershi shiji Zhongguo* 告别革命：回望二十世紀中國 [Farewell to revolution: Looking back on twentieth-century China] (Hong Kong: Tiandi tushu youxian gongsi, 1995), esp. 267–305.

13. Jing Wang, *High Culture Fever: Politics, Aesthetics, and Ideology in Deng's China* (Berkeley: University of California Press, 1996), 37–117.

14. Song Xianlin, "Reconstructing the Confucian Ideal in 1980s China: The 'Culture Craze' and New Confucianism," in *New Confucianism: A Critical Examination*, edited by John Makeham, 81–104.

15. Fang Keli, "Lüelun xiandai xinrujia zhi deshi" 略论现代新儒家之得失 [A brief assessment of the strengths and weaknesses of modern New Confucianism], *Xiandai xinrujia yu Zhongguo xiandai hua* 现代新儒家与中国现代化 [Modern New Confucianism and China's modernization], edited by in Fang Keli (Tianjin: Tianjin renmin chubanshe, 1997), 46. The original is: 在"五四"以來的中国现代思想史上，现代新儒家无疑是最具有影响力和生命力的思想派别之一．它和马克思主义以及自由主义的西化派可谓鼎足而三，是在反对"全盘西化，"抵制马克思主义在中国的胜利行进中产生和发展的一个思想派别．这三个派别都主张中国要现代化，但各自选择的道路不同．

16. In his writings, Fang did not explicitly spell out what exactly drew the "three intellectual currents" into a dialogue and collaboration, but on several occasions he linked the "three intellectual currents" to the debate among the Marxists, the liberals, and the conservatives in the 1980s and 1990s. The debate, as Wang Hui has pointed out, was how to reconfigure the political and socioeconomic structure of the Maoist party-state in the name of "building socialism with Chinese characteristics." See Wang Hui, "The Year 1989 and the Historical Roots of Neoliberalism in China," in Wang Hui, *The End of the Revolution*, 19–66.

17. See, for instance, Fang Keli, "Guanyu xiandai xinrujia yanjiu de jige wenti" 关于现代新儒家研究的几个问题 (A few questions regarding the study of modern New Confucianism), in *Xiandai xinrujia yu Zhongguo xiandai hua*, 17–34.

18. The discussion of Asian capitalism began in 1973 after the oil crisis caused an economic downturn in the United States. Among the first who started this discussion was historian Edwin O. Reischauer, who coined the term "the Sinic world"

to draw attention to the economic development in East Asia. See Reischauer, "The Sinic World in Perspective," *Foreign Affairs* (Jan. 1974): 341–348. Extrapolating from the economic achievements in Japan during the 1960s and 1970s, Herman Kahn predicted the rise of East Asia as a new economic powerhouse in the late twentieth century. See Kahn, *World Economic Development* (Boulder, CO: Westview, 1979). Soon after, the sociologist Peter Berger brought the Weberian perspective into the "Sinic world" discussion by focusing on Confucian cultural values as an important force of East Asian capitalism. See Berger, "An East Asian Development Model?," in *In Search of an East Asian Development Model*, edited by Peter L. Berger and Hsin-huang Michael Hsiao (New Brunswick, NJ: Transaction Books, 1988), 3–11. For a summary of the discussion of East Asian capitalism, see Tu Wei-ming, "The Rise of Industrial East Asia: The Role of Confucian Values," *Copenhagen Journal of Asian Studies*, 4 (1989): 81–97. Regarding the role of Weberian sociology in conceptualizing Asian capitalism, see Tu Wei-ming, ed., *The Triadic Chord: Confucian Ethics, Industrial East Asia and Max Weber* (Singapore: Institute of East Asian Philosophies, 1991), particularly the essays by Wolfgang Schluchter and Hwang Kwang-kuo.

19. For a cogent argument for Confucian capitalism, see Gilbert Rozman, *The East Asian Region: Confucian Heritage and Its Modern Adaptations* (Princeton, NJ: Princeton University Press, 1991). See also Hung-chao Tai, ed., *Confucianism and Economic Development: An Oriental Alternative?* (Washington, DC: Washington Institute Press, 1989).

20. Arif Dirlik, "Reversals, Ironies, Hegemonies: Notes on the Contemporary Historiography of Modern China," in *History after the Three Worlds*, 135.

21. Fang Keli, "Lüelun xiandai xinrujia zhi deshi" 略论现代新儒家之得失 [A brief assessment of the strengths and weaknesses of modern New Confucianism], in *Xiandai xinrujia yu Zhongguo xiandai hua*, 19. The original is: 现代新儒家是产生于本世纪20年代, 至今仍有一定生命力的, 以接续儒家"道统", 复兴儒学为己任, 以复膺宋明理学 (特别是儒家心性之学) 为主要特征, 力图以儒家学术为主体为本位, 来吸引, 融合, 汇通西学, 以寻求中国现代道路的一个思想流派, 也可以说是一种文化思潮.

22. See Mou Zongsan, *Xinti yu xingti* 心體與性體 [The essence of human mind and the essence of human nature] (Taipei: Zhengzhong shuju, 1968), 1–196.

23. Fang Keli, "Xiandai xinrujia de fazhan lichen" 现代新儒家的发展历程 [The development process of modern New Confucianism], in *Xiandai xinrujia yu Zhongguo xiandai hua*, 139–141.

24. For a thoughtful summary of how New Confucian thinkers in Hong Kong and Taiwan addressed the challenges of modern life, see Wang Bangxiong 王邦雄, "Cong Zhongguo xiandaihua guocheng zhong kan dangdai xin rujia de jingshen" 丛中国现代化过程中看当代新儒家的精神 [The spirit of New Confucianism from the perspective of China's modernization], in *Ping xinrujia* 评新儒家 [Assessing New Confucianism], edited by Luo Yijun 罗义俊 (Shanghai: Shanghai renmin chubanshe, 1989), 74–97. Wang's article was first published in 1984 in the Taiwan journal *Erhu*.

25. Tu Wei-ming, "Ruxue disanqi fazhan de qianjing wenti" 儒學第三期發展的前景問題 [The prospect for the development of the third epoch of

Confucianism], in *Bainian Zhongguo zhexue jingdian: Bashi naindai yilai juan* 百年中國哲學經典: 八十年代以來卷 [The classics of Chinese philosophy in the last hundred years: Section on the post-1980s] (Shenzhen: Haitian chubanshe, 1998), 502–530. Tu's article first appeared in 1986 in *Mingbao yuekan*.

26. For the differences between the Cheng-Zhu and Lu-Wang schools of Neo-Confucianism, see Shu-hsien Liu, *Understanding Confucian Philosophy: Classical and Sung-Ming* (Westport, CT: Praeger, 1998), 131–230.

27. Fang Keli, "Xiandai xinrujia de fazhan licheng" 现代新儒家的发展历程 [The development process of modern New Confucianism], in *Xiandai xinrujia yu Zhongguo xiandai hua*, 143–150; "Du Weiming xinrujia sixiang shuping 杜維明新儒家思想述評 (A study of Tu Wei-ming's New Confucian thought), in *Xiandai xinrujia yu Zhongguo xiandai hua*, 362–381.

28. Fang Keli complained bitterly about Mou Zongsan's anticommunist stand. See Fang Keli, "Disandai xinrujia lüeying" 第三代新儒家掠影 [Glimpses of the third generation New Confucians], in *Xiandai xinrujia yu Zhongguo xiandai hua*, 54–63.

29. Fang Keli, "Xiandai xinrujia de fazhan licheng" 现代新儒家的发展历程 [The development process of modern New Confucianism], in *Xiandai xinrujia yu Zhongguo xiandai hua*, 143–146.

30. Ibid., 146–150.

31. Fang Keli, "Guanyu xiandai xinrujia yanjiu de jige wenti" 关于现代新儒家研究的几个问题 [A few questions regarding the study of modern New Confucianism], in Fang Keli, *Xiandai xinrujia yu Zhongguo xiandai hua*, 31.

32. Fang Keli, "Rujia ziben zhuyi" 儒家资本主义 [Confucian capitalism], in *Xiandai xinrujia yu Zhongguo xiandai hua*, 458. The original is: 现代新儒家设想的以儒家文化为背景或以儒家思想为指导来实现资本主义现代化的发展道路或模式. 它不同于西欧北美和苏联东欧实现工业化, 现代化的道路或模式. 现代新儒家认为, 近20年日本, 南朝鲜, 台湾, 香港, 新加坡等东亚国家和地区经济的迅速发展, 否定了韦伯的"世俗化理论", 即认为并非只有新教伦理才能促进资本主义的发展, 儒家伦理也有其特定的宗教性和世俗功能, 它是造成"工业东亚"经济奇迹的一个重要原因.

33. See, for instance, Gilbert Rozman, *The East Asian Region*.

34. Fang Keli, "Rujia ziben zhuyi" 儒家资本主义 [Confucian capitalism], in *Xiandai xinrujia yu Zhongguo xiandai hua*, 458.

35. Ibid., 459. The original is: 另外一些学者则认为, 探讨东亚部分国家和地区经济迅速发展的原因, 主要不能从思想文化去解释, 把它归结为儒家伦理价值观积极作用的结果; 不能像新儒家那样, 把东亚经济发展说成是儒家"内圣"之学合乎逻辑的开出"外王"事功.

36. After 1992 Fang Keli was criticized from many sides. For instance, he identified 1992 as the year when "mainland New Confucians" made their voices known in public. For a clear example of Fang's change, see his article "Xiandai xinrujia yanjiu de ziwo huixing—jingda zhuwei pipingzhe" 现代新儒家研究的自我回省—敬答諸位批評者 (Self-critical reflections on my study of modern New Confucianism—A respectful reply to my critics), in *Xiandai xinrujia yu Zhongguo xiandai hua*, 192–209.

37. Rebecca Karl's foreword to *The End of the Revolution*, ix.

2

Confucianism, Community, Capitalism

Chen Lai and the Spirit of Max Weber

Els van Dongen

Ever since Confucianism rose to the forefront of discussion among sociologists, scholars of religion, philosophers, and area specialists during the 1980s, debates on the topic have been characterized by a central tension between Confucianism as a *moral* project to create a fiduciary community through self-cultivation and Confucianism as a *sociopolitical* argument about the role of values in economic development.[1] The tension between these two forms of Confucianism is not inherent to Confucianism. Rather, it originates in Max Weber's critique of modernity, a critique that was influential in shaping the debate on the role of Confucianism in the modern world. Weber's critique was at the same time concerned with the negative consequences of modernization-as-rationalization—the "iron cage of modernity"—and with the role of religious values in capitalist modernization. Whereas the former leads to the question of how to lead a meaningful life in a rational world devoid of meaning and what values could play a role in this, the latter leads to the question of the instrumental role of values in the process of rationalization. As for the latter, Weber is most famous for exploring this question in his *The Protestant Ethic and the Spirit of Capitalism*, in which he argued that the Protestant ethic—duty, discipline, and rational behavior—had benefited the rise of capitalism.[2]

The same double-edged role of values in relation to modernity can be found in Weber's understanding of rational action, which could also be based both on intrinsic values and on instrumental motivations. In his *Economy and Society* (1922), Weber outlined the distinction between two types of social action, namely "value rationality" (*Wertrationalität*) and "instrumental rationality" (*Zweckrationalität*). According to Weber, "instrumental rationality" is a type of rational action in which the actor calculates how to reach a certain end. This type of action is present in modern capitalism and in the modern bureaucracy.[3] "Value rationality," on the contrary, refers to an action that is not a means to an end, but that is inspired by "unconditional demands," as Weber calls it. As Weber himself explains the difference between the two types of action, *instrumentally rational behavior* is "determined by expectations as to the behavior of objects in the environment and of other human beings; these expectations are used as 'conditions' or 'means for the attainment of the actor's own rationally pursued and calculated ends.'" *Value-rational action*, on the other hand, is "determined by a conscious belief in the value for its own sake of some ethical, aesthetic, religious, or other form of behavior, independently of its prospects of success."[4]

Weber adds that these ideal types are heuristic devices; in practice, however, finding action that can be reduced to only one type of rational action is difficult.[5] For Weber, rationalization and rationalism occur in all world religions, but distinctions are made based on the *sphere* in which they occur and the *direction* rationalization and rationalism take. Instrumental rationalization takes place in the sphere of the world and has a practical orientation; value rationalization not only takes place in the sphere of the "afterworld" (*Hinterwelt*), but it *also* has a practical orientation. We find a theoretical orientation in both the "scientific rationalism" in the world and the "metaphysical rationalism" in the afterworld. Weber argues that in the modern West, scientific and technical rationalism gradually *reject* metaphysical and ethical rationalism; at the same time, an *inclusive* notion of both theoretical rationalism and practical rationalization that includes both scientific and metaphysical rationalism and both instrumental and value rationalization becomes more unlikely. In other words, rationalism becomes scientific only and rationalization turns into instrumental rationalization only.[6]

Debates on Confucianism since the 1980s have manifested these two sides of the Weberian coin—the treatment of values as antidotes against the consequences of the process of rationalization that rejects value rationality and the discussion of values as instruments to rationalization. On the one hand, advocates of Confucianism argued that Confucianism as "value rationality" could be a moral cure against the erosion of meaning and community in a modernized world built on "instrumental rationality." Thus, some Chinese scholars (such as Chen Lai and Tu Wei-ming) framed their Confucian project as a critique of modernity, defending the free-spirited value rationality against the instrumental rationality of modern industrial society. On the other hand, however, Chen Lai and Tu Wei-ming also made references to the second aspect of Weber's thought, the question of the relation between Confucianism and capitalism, which was a question regarding the instrumental role of values that was in tension with their defense of Confucian values based on their inherent worth. Here, scholars and advocates of Confucianism engaged with Weber's argument that Confucianism had not served the rise of capitalism because of its focus on moral perfection, its lack of asceticism, and its emphasis on education instead of business. This chapter is concerned with the tension between these two positions, one of which involves a defense of the value rationality of Confucianism and the other of which implies the recognition of the instrumental rationality of Confucian values.

To understand why the discussion on Confucianism became prominent among advocates of Confucianism and beyond during the 1980s and the 1990s, we need to consider three contextual factors in particular. First, in mainland China, Deng Xiaoping's program of reform and opening up—which was launched during the late 1970s and which intensified in 1992 with Deng's famous Southern Tour—not only created the conditions for the revaluation of Confucianism but also triggered debates on the relation between tradition and modernity. Second, as a consequence of these changes, the intellectual world was exposed to theories from scholars outside of China on a scale unprecedented in decades. An intellectual frenzy occurred that consisted of an engagement with comparisons of "Eastern" and "Western" cultures and that also engaged in debates on the relation between tradition and modernity and the question of historical continuity. Following this trend during the mid- to late 1980s, both the Tiananmen Square Incident in 1989 and the seventieth anniversary of the May Fourth Incident led to a continued engagement with these themes, both in mainland China and beyond. Finally, the rise of the so-called Four Mini Dragons (Hong Kong, Taiwan, South Korea, and Singapore) led scholars to reconsider Weber's verdict that Confucianism had not benefited the rise of capitalism, thereby engaging with the possibility of a "Confucian capitalism."

This chapter investigates the tension between the moral and the sociopolitical positions in Confucian discourse primarily through the writings of the mainland Confucian scholar Chen Lai 陈来 (b. 1952), a philosopher based at Tsinghua University. However, it also connects Chen Lai's writings with the work of Tu Wei-ming 杜维明 (b. 1940), the "Boston Confucian" who is perhaps the most famous exponent of "New Confucianism" (*xiandai xin rujia* 现代新儒家, *dangdai xin rujia* 当代新儒家, or *dangdai xin ruxue* 当代新儒学).[7] The reason behind this choice is that Tu Wei-ming played a prominent role in the debates in the United States, as well as in introducing the debates in a mainland Chinese context. Tu had linked the criticism of the May Fourth Movement as having been too radical in its rejection of the Chinese past, which spread on mainland China during the early 1990s, to the question of the role of Confucian values in the modern world in a broad sense. He influenced Chen Lai's thinking on the matter. In addition, the two scholars were intellectually related: Chen Lai studied with Tu Wei-ming twice. He first studied with Tu when Tu was a visiting scholar at Peking University in 1985, and then when Chen was a visiting scholar at the Harvard-Yenching Institute between 1986 and 1988.[8] However important the connection between both scholars is, looking at Chen Lai's writings per se offers us a valuable insight into debates on Confucianism in the light of changes in mainland China specifically. This chapter focuses on Chen Lai's writings from the 1990s because significant discussions on New Confucianism took place in mainland China during this period following the seventieth anniversary of the May Fourth Incident and the demonstrations on Tiananmen Square in 1989 (for the importance of this period, see Tze-ki Hon's introduction and chapter 1 herein).

Additionally, this chapter incorporates analyses and critiques from before and after the 1990s, as well as writings by other scholars, in an attempt to extend the discussion and to ponder the fate of Confucianism in the twenty-first century. This chapter raises the question whether Confucianism can function in two opposite roles. Can it be an antidote against the ills of capitalism and the dehumanization inherent in modernization on the one hand, and a driving force of East Asian capitalism on the other? To some Chinese scholars (including Chen Lai and Tu Wei-ming), the contradiction between the two opposite roles of Confucianism does not seem to be problematic. More interestingly, they tend to speak of the two roles of Confucianism as if they are mutually supportive. Although they claim their view is derived from Max Weber, they do not seem to grasp the subtlety of Weber's two types of rationality and the inherent contradiction between these types of rationality. In a final section, some possible explanations why both Tu Wei-ming and Chen Lai do not perceive any contradiction between the two types of rationality will be explored further.

Confucianism as a Moral Project: The Critique of Instrumental Rationality

In order to understand the tension between the moral and the sociopolitical debate in the work of Chen Lai, we first need to understand what is entailed in his engagement in the moral project and how this relates to the moral project of the so-called New Confucians. As Tze-ki Hon's chapter and others in this volume explain, New Confucianism is a reinterpretation of the

Neo-Confucianism that flourished during the Song (907–1279) and Ming (1368–1644) dynasties. Although some advocates trace the movement back to the early twentieth century, Makeham has argued that that the movement became a distinct school of thought only in the late 1970s.[9] Whereas Chen Lai does not belong to this lineage, we will see that many of Chen's arguments in fact reflect the concerns of the New Confucians.[10]

The two main schools in Song and Ming Neo-Confucianism were (1) the "heart-mind centered learning" (*xinxue* 心学) of Lu Xiangshan (1139–1192) and Wang Yangming (1472–1529), and (2) the "principled-centered learning" (*lixue* 理学) of Cheng Yi (1033–1107) and Zhu Xi (1130–1200). According to the Lu-Wang school, the universe was identical with the mind, and the unity between man and heaven was to be realized through the development of the innate knowledge of the good and the native ability to do good. For the Cheng-Zhu school, the principles of the universe had to be grasped through the "investigation of things," which would in turn enable the realization of one's good nature. In spite of the differences between the schools, both focus on ethical cultivation.

A core concept from Neo-Confucianism that twentieth-century New Confucians elaborated is the so-called doctrine of learning of the mind and nature (*xinxing zhi xue* 心性之学). As Chang Hao explains, for New Confucians, nature (*xing* 性) has to be understood in a metaphysical sense; it implies the belief in inner transcendence. This inner transcendence is connected with the outer transcendence of heaven (*tian* 天); together, they constitute the "unity between man and heaven" (*tianren heyi* 天人合一). Another critical concept is *ren* 仁 (benevolence, humaneness), which is actualized through self-cultivation. Having become an "inner sage" (*neisheng* 内圣), one has to rise above this moral cultivation by taking part in the outer world and by becoming an "outer king" (*waiwang* 外王).[11]

In the 1958 document that has generally been treated as the "manifesto" of New Confucianism, the "Declaration on Behalf of Chinese Culture Respectfully Announced to the People of the World," the authors Mou Zongsan (1909–1995), Tang Junyi (1909–1978), Xu Fuguan (1903–1982), and Zhang Junmai (1886–1969) argued that the core of Chinese culture was the doctrine of *xinxing* 心性 or the "conformity of heaven and man in virtue."[12] They disapproved of the use of external standards to evaluate Chinese culture and criticized the "feverish pursuit of progress" of the West.[13] The authors envisioned a modernization that included both science and democracy and Confucian ethics. The Declaration was hence a plea for the continued importance of Chinese culture in the modern world.[14]

In the works of Tu Wei-ming, we clearly see the concern with self-cultivation, the realization of a moral community, and the continued existence of morality under modernity.[15] Tu is most known for his theory of "the third epoch of Confucianism," which involves the contemporary revival of Confucianism on a global scale after the first epoch of Confucius, Mencius, and Xunzi, and the second epoch of Song and Ming Neo-Confucianism.[16] This is also in line with his theory of a "Cultural China," according to which a Confucian revival from the "periphery" can impact developments in the "center," the People's Republic of China.[17] Tu Wei-ming has conducted much research on Wang Yangming, which links him to the heart-mind centered learning of the Lu-Wang school.

Chen Lai is not a New Confucian in the sense that Tu Wei-ming is. He belongs to a different generation of scholars and his teachers are not all considered New Confucians. In addition, he is much less publicly involved in the New Confucian project than Tu Wei-ming is. However, as a Confucian scholar, he has been a central figure in the revaluation of Confucianism in mainland China. He not only has studied the writings of Zhu Xi rigorously, but he has also written about the thought of Wang Yangming.[18] Like New Confucians, Chen Lai is convinced that core Confucian values can foster community in an environment of increased social rationalization. Chen's emphasis on Confucian values can be read as an engagement with Weber's argument that modern rationality becomes exclusive of value rationality and dominated by instrumental rationality.

In 2006, Chen Lai's *Chuantong yu xiandai: Renwen zhuyi de shijie* [Tradition and modernity: The Scope of Humanism] was published.[19] Central themes in this collection include the autonomy of culture versus the politicization of culture, the historical continuity of Chinese tradition, instrumental rationality versus value rationality, and the particularity versus the universality of Confucian values. The collection includes writings on both aspects of the debate over the nature of Confucianism, which is why it is interesting for our purposes. The word "humanism" in the book's title needs to be understood in relation to Chen Lai's interpretation of Confucianism as "a human way rather than a way of the spirits."[20] According to Chen, since ancient times, *rujia* culture has gone through a process of "humanization" and "rationalization" through which magic and religious elements were replaced by the cultivation of spirituality in education and rites.[21] The word "humanism" also refers to the New Confucian understanding of Confucianism as an ethical system in which the main concern is, in the words of Tu Wei-ming, "how we learn to be human."[22]

The main title *Tradition and Modernity* reveals that, especially in mainland China, the Confucian discourse was embedded in a larger debate on the relation between tradition and modernity, a theme that gained importance in the context of the so-called culture fever (*wenhua re* 文化热) of the 1980s, the seventieth anniversary of the May Fourth Incident in 1989, and the revaluation of Confucianism since the 1990s.[23] Before the 1990s, China had witnessed decades of "antitraditionalism" under both the May Fourth Movement (with the exception of a brief return to tradition during the 1930s) and the Marxist notion of progress since 1949. Although the criticism of the May Fourth legacy became widespread among intellectuals during the early 1990s, some had already begun to question this legacy during the 1980s.[24] In the context of the seventieth anniversary of the May Fourth Incident, the May Fourth legacy was scrutinized in a multitude of volumes and conference volumes.[25] Academic journals such as *Dongfang* 东方 (Orient), *Wenxue pinglun* 文学评论 (Literary review), *Xueren* 学人 (Scholar), and *Yuandao* 原道 (Tracing the way) published debates on the topic.

Chen Lai's revaluation of the May Fourth legacy corresponds with his overall argument that morality, and Confucianism in particular, is very much needed in modern society. Since the late 1980s, Chen Lai has addressed the issue of the crisis of Confucianism—which he conceives of as both a cultural crisis and a crisis of the belief in values—in a number of articles.[26] Before May Fourth, although Confucianism had been erased from politics and education, it still stood firm in the ethical and spiritual realms. With May Fourth, it also disappeared from these realms; after 1949, its position was damaged fiercely, this time not by liberals but by dogmatism and "extreme leftist false Marxism."[27] In the article "A Propitious New Start," written for *Twenty-first Century* during the winter of 1992, however, Chen Lai describes how, after decades of denial, a shift had taken place: "Confucianism has already passed the hardest time; it has already left the low ebb."[28]

In one of the key articles of *Tradition and Modernity*, Chen Lai addresses the "antitraditionalism" of the May Fourth era, the Cultural Revolution, and the so-called New Enlightenment of the 1980s in an article on "cultural radicalism" (*wenhua jijin zhuyi* 文化激进主义).[29] In a reference to Max Weber, Chen Lai introduces the concept of "value rationality" (*jiazhi lixing* 价值理性), which he associates with the "cultural conservatives" during the May Fourth era. Those who advocated traditional values during the May Fourth era did so because of their belief in the inherent value of these values. "Cultural radicals," on the other hand, rejected these values based on "instrumental rationality" (*gongju lixing* 工具理性), or the reliance on external standards of economic or political usefulness.[30] For this division, Chen Lai draws on Max Weber's distinction between "value rationality" (*Wertrationalität*) and "instrumental rationality" (*Zweckrationalität*), the two types of social action that Weber had outlined in his *Economy and Society*. In an article in which Chen Lai seeks ways to dissolve the tension between tradition and modernity, he explains the distinction between these two types of rationality: "The standard of instrumental rationality refers to taking the efficiency of politics or economics of a certain society as a starting point. The standard of value rationality is taking ethical and cultural values in itself as a yardstick."[31] Chen Lai also makes use of Weber's two types of rationality to read the 1923 debate on "Science and Metaphysics," in which the main participants had been Zhang Junmai (1886–1969), Ding Wenjiang (1887–1936), Liang Qichao (1873–1929), Hu Shi (1891–1962), and Wu Zhihui (1865–1953).[32] For Chen Lai, those participants in the debate who argued against scientism, such as Zhang Junmai, were "conservatives" who stood on the side of "value rationality." Advocates of scientism, such as Ding Wenjiang, on the other hand, were "radicals" who had reduced modern civilization to "instrumental rationality." For Chen Lai, "value rationality" does not lend itself to an opposition between "old" and "new": it is continuous. Chen's defense of "value rationality" through his reading of the 1923 debate and his insistence on it being "continuous" clearly reveals the side of the Weber debate in which Confucianism is understood as a moral antidote against the social rationalization inherent in capitalism that is especially important in today's world.

Chen Lai's notion of "value rationality" and his defense of the autonomy of values need to be understood in relation to his conception of Confucianism as a moral system detached from social referents or institutions. This view is opposed to the view of scholars such as Lin Yü-sheng (b. 1934), who argued in favor of the "creative transformation" of Chinese tradition, and Yü Ying-shih (b. 1930), who claimed that modern Chinese thought had witnessed a "radicalization process." For Lin and Yü, Confucianism was tied to concrete social referents, and it was very much intertwined with social institutions.[33] For Yü particularly, the preservation of intermediate organizations was driven by the fact that these institutions were embodiments of Confucian culture as a living culture. For Chen Lai, conversely, Confucianism cannot be equated with its social amalgamations, as the latter harms its transcendental values.[34] Like Tu Wei-ming, Chen makes a clear distinction between Confucianism as a system of thought and orthodox state Confucianism.

In this context, Chen Lai criticizes the leading May Fourth intellectual and cofounder of the Chinese Communist Party Chen Duxiu (1879–1942), who had reduced Confucian ethics to the "three bonds" (*sangang* 三纲)—the bonds between ruler and official, father and son, and husband and wife—and who had claimed that "advocating respect for Confucius must necessarily lead to an emperor ascending the throne."[35] Chen Duxiu's fierce attack on Confucianism had been directly related to the attempts at revival of the Chinese monarchy by Yuan Shikai (1859–1916) and Zhang

Xun (1854–1923), both of whom invoked Confucianism in their political maneuvers. "Radicals" such as Chen Duxiu committed the fallacy of overgeneralization (*yipian gaiquan* 以偏概全): in their assault on Confucianism, they focused on political ethics, family ethics, and sexual ethics, and on the basis of this, they discarded Confucianism as a whole.[36] The argument that Confucianism had been distorted in the process of its practical usage in political and social life is not unique to Chen Lai; Tu Wei-ming also makes a distinction between a distorted politicized Confucianism and everyday-life Confucianism.[37] For both Tu Wei-ming and Chen Lai, then, Confucianism stands for certain values—*ren* in particular—that are detached from social referents.

Tu Wei-ming has engaged on numerous occasions in a critique of the "instrumental rationality" and the quest for world mastery that underlay the "Enlightenment mentality."[38] For Tu Wei-ming, Confucianism has a religious dimension—it is a "religio-philosophy"—and its core element is *ren* (humaneness), which Tu also translates as "human-relatedness."[39] As indicated in the title of Chen Lai's collection of essays, humanism (*renwen zhuyi* 人文主义) is also a focal concern for Chen. For Chen Lai, the virtues that make man human are benevolence (*ren* 仁) and harmony (*he* 和), values that Tu Wei-ming also identifies as the kernel of Confucianism. Chen Lai claims that *harmony* can form an antidote to the exploitation of nature, the distance between people, the anxiety of the individual, and the lack of tolerance and peaceful coexistence between cultures. As Chen Lai phrases it, "One could say that '*ren*' is the representation of Confucian value rationality and the concentrated manifestation of substantive tradition."[40]

In line with the New Confucian agenda, then, for Chen Lai, the renunciation of Confucian values is a result of the rationalization process of modernization that renders all human activities into cost-benefit calculations. To highlight the importance of "value rationality," Chen refers to the American neoconservative Daniel Bell's criticism of late industrial societies. In his *The Cultural Contradictions of Capitalism* (1976), and relying on Max Weber, Bell argues that in the postindustrial era, capitalism erodes the very virtues that are so important to the "spirit" of capitalism, such as self-discipline, restraint, and frugality. Chen Lai asserts that this criticism can also be applied to China because it addresses the question of "how to establish a humanist environment suited to the modernization project [of late-twentieth-century China]."[41]

In his promotion of "value rationality," Chen Lai also invokes Liang Shuming's (1893–1988) concept of *lixing* 理性. According to Alitto, between 1930 and 1949, Liang Shuming focused on the concept of *lixing* instead of *ren* 仁 (benevolence) and *zhijue* 知觉. Alitto has argued that *lixing* was for

Liang "the normative sense that directs moral action . . . the sense of right and wrong which makes man human."[42] For Chen Lai, Liang Shuming's concept of *lixing* in some aspects resembles Habermas's concept of "communicative rationality" because it was a "manner of interaction," a "mutual understanding," or a "mentality of mutual connection."[43] This, Chen Lai notes, is like benevolence.[44] Whereas Habermas's theory of "communicative rationality" accords a central role to communication in the establishment of rationality, Chen Lai interprets this communication as a moral concept that connects people and that offers normative guidance, that is, communication is essential to the formation of a community.

Like Chen Lai, Tu Wei-ming also indicates the importance of communicative rationality instead of instrumental rationality in the Confucian education system in particular. Tu finds this especially in the *Analects*.[45] He is concerned with the Mencian tradition of humaneness, with personal cultivation, and with the universality of Confucian values. Tu Wei-ming argues that Confucian morality enables the creation of a "fiduciary community," a community that is not just an aggregate of individuals, but that is based on a relation of mutual trust.[46] Similarly, he emphasizes the importance of communication in Confucianism because of its nature as a "philosophy of mutuality."[47] The relation between the individual and the community under the conditions of modernity, then, are central concerns for Tu Wei-ming, as they are for Chen Lai. What we can see from this is that Weber's critique of modernity has inspired this side of the New Confucianism discourse, not only in mainland China, but also through Tu Wei-ming's advocacies in the United States. As will be explored further, however, some differences exist between their advocacies as well, and the specific context of mainland China during the 1980s and the early 1990s played an important role in this.

Instrumental Rationality and East Asian Development

Apart from the debate on tradition and modernity in the context of the revaluation of Confucianism, the 1980s also witnessed an upsurge of debates on the role of Confucianism in the modern world in the context of the rise of the Four Mini Dragons. Already in the late 1970s, some Japan scholars had made reference to Confucianism in their analyses of Japan's economic success. In 1978 economist Michio Morishima employed the term "Confucian capitalism"; one year later, both Japan scholar Ezra Vogel in his *Japan as Number One* and sociologist Herman Kahn in his *World Economic Development* also tied Confucianism to Japan's economic rise.[48] Shortly after, scholars also applied the concept of Confucian capitalism to a broader context.

For example, in 1980, China scholar Roderick MacFarquhar wrote about a "post-Confucian challenge." Since then, the East Asian Development thesis has become popular in the United States, and sociologist Peter Berger is one of its supporters.[49]

Ironically, the very same "ideational factors" that had been designated as a hindrance to development in the 1950s and 1960s were now considered to contribute to economic success.[50] For instance, John King Fairbank, operating in the context of post–World War II modernization theories, famously argued that China had failed to respond to the impact of the West precisely because of a Confucian worldview "of China as central, superior, and self-sufficient."[51] In the field of intellectual history, Joseph Levenson similarly exposed the rupture between Confucianism and modern life in the well-known trilogy *Confucian China and Its Modern Fate*.[52]

Despite the irony, scholars and advocates of Confucianism eagerly joined economists, area studies specialists, and sociologists to discuss the role of Confucianism in capitalism. In 1987 Yü Ying-shih expanded the application of the Weber thesis to China by arguing that the connection between Confucianism and capitalism could be traced back to the Ming dynasty (1368–1644).[53] Contemporaneously, Tu Wei-ming entered the debate by editing several conference volumes on Confucian capitalism.[54] Later, Yü and Tu were also involved in the development of a Confucian ethics course in Singapore.[55]

Of the many publications at the time, the 1991 conference volume *The Confucian World Observed: A Contemporary Discussion of Confucian Humanism in East Asia* clearly shows the relationship between Confucianism and capitalism.[56] Conference participants pointed out that in order to solve the tension between Confucianism and capitalism, in the past, scholars had attempted to legitimate profit-making in Confucianism as a way to serve the community and to improve the conditions of the people. In the West, the tension between ethics and profit-making had similarly been resolved by referring to Adam Smith's "invisible hand": profit-making was justified as being part of a larger goal.[57] Here, we already see a clear tension between the moral debate and the sociopolitical debate, a tension being resolved through the argument that profit-making had to be understood in a broader sense as a *moral* project.

At the time, participants in the conference who were advocates of Confucianism, including Tu Wei-ming, resolved this tension through ambivalence: neither did they embrace the relation between Confucianism and the so-called East Asian Development Model wholeheartedly, nor did they criticize or reject it. This uneasy compromise allowed them to be involved with both groups. With regard to the "Weber question" of the relation between Confucianism and capitalism, Tu Wei-ming states that we need to rethink the notion of modernity, as well as the relation between tradition and modernity.[58] Hence, the "Weber question" is central to the discussion of capitalism, but the point is not to focus on finding the counterpart of the Protestant ethic in Confucian ethics, which would be too simplistic. Rather, the question of "Confucian ethics" leads to the question of "alternative modernities," pointing to the fact that the East Asian model has some distinct characteristics, such as the lack of distinction between the public and the private, and the importance of the family and duty.[59]

Furthermore, Tu Wei-ming also stressed that Confucian ethics were compatible with the capitalist spirit in many respects. Although he attempted to frame the relationship between Confucianism and modernization in broader terms—such as the recreation of community through the notion of the self as a "center of relationships"—one cannot deny that Tu endorsed this relation between Confucianism and capitalism in the narrow Weberian sense as well. At a 1982 seminar at the National University of Singapore, for example, Tu discussed the link between East Asian capitalism and the "Confucian ethics."[60] From this, we can see that in the understanding of advocates of New Confucianism, such as Tu Wei-ming, the tension between Confucian values as an antidote to capitalism and the question of whether Confucian values benefited capitalism was not problematic at all. Instead, they considered the question of the role of Confucian values in the modern world to be an extension of the question of the relation between Confucian values and capitalism: both concerned the relation between tradition and modernity.

Why was demonstrating that Weber's argument regarding the relation between Protestant values and the rise of capitalism could be applied to China so important? In order to answer this, we need to understand the historical background of the debate. In *The Protestant Ethic and the Spirit of Capitalism*, Weber held that the Calvinist doctrine of predestination affected the formation of capitalism because mystical contemplation was exchanged for ascetic and this-worldly action. Ascetic Protestantism in particular provided a "systematic rational ordering of moral life as a whole."[61] It was this "spirit" of rational conduct, duty, and discipline on the basis of the idea of the calling that gave rise to modern rational capitalism. In his *The Religion of China: Confucianism and Daoism*, Weber further asserted that "Protestant rationalism" was marked by its "disenchantment" with the world; there was a tension between the rational ethical imperatives of Protestantism and this-worldly irrationalities.[62]

For Weber, Confucianism did not bring capitalism to China because it differed from Protestantism in three critical respects. First, the tension between the ethical demands of Confucianism and this-worldly realities was minimal. For Confucians, "the world was the best of all possible worlds; human nature was disposed to the ethically good."[63] Confucian ethics aimed at an affirmation of and adjustment to the world, and although both Confucianism and Protestantism demanded self-control, the former aimed at the moral perfection of the "man of the world," whereas the latter's goal was to enable man to focus on God's will.[64] Furthermore, in contrast to Protestants, Confucians were not ascetics; they exalted material wealth instead.[65] Like Protestants, they were sober and thrifty, but they invested their savings in education, not in business.[66] Finally, relations between people were personalized instead of rationalized; they were based on tradition, custom, and personal favors.[67] Although the Chinese social structure consisted of elements both suitable and not suitable to capitalism, Weber claimed that the "spirit" of capitalism was lacking in China because of the above-mentioned factors.[68] Nevertheless, Weber considered both Protestantism and Confucianism examples of practical rather than theoretical rationalism."[69]

Already during the 1970s and 1980s, U.S. scholars of China criticized Weber's China thesis. They attacked his argument that there was no tension between Confucianism and reality and that Confucianism was "this-worldly" because it was characterized by adjustment to the world.[70] Although Weber's *The Protestant Ethic and the Spirit of Capitalism* was translated into Chinese only in 1986, mainland scholars had eagerly studied Weber before that time, and Weber had also appeared in the translation series *Culture: China and the World*.[71] The topic of the relation between Confucianism and modernization was taken up during the mid-1980s, when many mainland intellectuals went to the United States, where both the writings of Max Weber and Talcott Parsons were in vogue. Already in 1985, Chen Lai recalls, a doctoral dissertation on Weber was completed in China.[72] After the interest in Weber peaked in 1986, the New Confucian discourse changed from a revaluation of Confucianism in China to a debate on the existence of an East Asian development model.[73]

In this context of reform and opening up and increasing scholarly exchange, in combination with the economic rise of East Asia and the "culture fever" of the mid- to late 1980s, the question of the relation between Confucianism and capitalism arose in mainland China. By applying Weber's "Protestantism thesis" to Confucianism, Chinese scholars refuted Weber's verdict on Confucianism in *The Religion of China*. Like Tu Wei-ming, Chen Lai held that the economic miracle of East Asia formed a serious challenge to Weber's theories on Confucianism: the success of the Four Mini Dragons demonstrated that the notion of a Confucian capitalism was not oxymoronic.

Chen Lai further argued that the debate on Confucian ethics and East Asian modernization did not focus on the "coming into being" (*chansheng* 产生) of capitalism but rather on the "assimilation" (*tonghua* 同化) of it.[74] Following Tu Wei-ming, Chen Lai argued that Weber himself made the distinction between "creation" and "assimilation." Weber states in his last chapter of *The Religion of China* that "the Chinese in all probability would be quite capable, probably more capable than the Japanese, of assimilating capitalism."[75] Although Weber did not specify whether Confucian ethics could play a role in this "assimilation," for Chen Lai, they clearly could, at least in the initial stage.

Here, Chen Lai referred to Boston sociologist Peter Berger's term "vulgar Confucian ethics" (*shisuhua de rujia lunli* 世俗化的儒家伦理).[76] Whereas Weber had focused on the ethics of Chinese imperial ideology, Berger had analyzed the daily ethics of the commoners. He had concluded from this that daily ethics had indeed played a role in economic development and that the existence of an "East Asian development model" in the Four Mini Dragons confirmed it.[77] Berger's argument, Chen Lai posited elsewhere, in fact addressed an inconsistency in Weber, who had looked at ethical beliefs and attitudes in daily life in the case of Protestantism, but who had analyzed religion instead of beliefs and attitudes in daily life in the case of Confucianism.[78] This is again reminiscent of Tu Wei-ming's distinction between orthodox Confucianism and Classical Confucianism: both Chen Lai and Tu Wei-ming advocate a focus on Confucian ethics as distinct from imperial ideology.

Occasionally, Chen Lai admitted that a cultural explanation of East Asian development was too simplistic. Modernization could not be reduced to economic function, and even if Confucian values had nothing to do with the coming into being and assimilation of capitalism, this did not mean that they lost value in a modern society. Precisely because Confucianism, as a system of thought, focused not merely on economy, Confucian values could exist in a creative tension with the "instrumental rationality" of modern industrial society. Therefore, Chen Lai distinguished between Confucian values as a critique of modern society and the sociopolitical debate on "Asian values," in which these values were turned into "instrumental rationality" to boost industrial production. In a further attempt to justify his participation in both debates, Chen added that political scientists first raised the issue of the role of Confucian values in East Asian capitalism, not New Confucians.[79] This reveals once more the ambivalence of the position of the advocates of New Confucianism: if it is really more about values in the modern world than about the role of these values in economic development, then why is proving that the values did play a role in the latter, thereby confirming their instrumental role rather than their intrinsic worth, important?

My questioning of the participation of Chen Lai and New Confucians in the Weber debate does not mean that Confucianism must be an abstract moral system unrelated to society. Many critics have accused Tu Wei-ming and Chen Lai of focusing only on moral metaphysics at the expense of sociopolitical institutions. Several chapters in this volume—particularly those by Stephen Angle (chapter 6), Ming-huei Lee (chapter 5), and An-wu Lin (chapter 7)—discuss the tension between ethical (*neisheng*) and political (*waiwang*) Confucianism. A crucial concern regarding Confucianism in the modern world is the question of its compatibility with existing political systems, as exemplified by the discussion on the compatibility between Confucianism and liberal democracy and the foundation of new political institutions as demonstrated in the proposals of Jiang Qing (b. 1953). The crux of the matter is that Confucianism is a system of thought that includes both a moral dimension and a sociopolitical dimension. For instance, the Confucian concept of self-development (*xiushen* 修身) is directly connected to ordering the family, governing the state, and harmonizing with the world.

Chen Lai and Tu Wei-ming would answer that we need to separate the two debates and that we ought to understand both the relation between Confucianism and capitalism in a broad sense, namely as a continuity between past and present, and the relation between tradition and modernity. We can ask ourselves, however, whether this answer is sufficient: When entering the realm of the "Weber question," can we really avoid "Weberizing Confucianism"?[80] If the answer is negative, what does this mean for the future development of New Confucianism as a moral project? On a broader level, this question is part of the argument that Ke Sheng makes in chapter 8 herein regarding the fate of any moral project since the nineteenth century: Given the dominance of rationality and utilitarianism since this time, is not any moral project bound to fail?[81]

Chen Lai, Max Weber, and the Chinese Discourse on Modernity

Because the desire to modernize leads to a lack of structural criticism of modernity, leftist critics have attacked both Confucianism and Chinese thought as an unreflective confirmation of a capitalist system. One of the fiercest critics of the Confucian revival has been Arif Dirlik, who describes it as a "manifestation in East Asia of a global postcolonial discourse" that led to the "self-Orientalization of the 'Orientals' themselves."[82] For Dirlik, Tu Wei-ming and other Confucian scholars confirmed the utility of Confucianism for capitalism; their goal was "modernizing tradition." The final result was that "Confucius has been moved from the museum to the theme park."[83] In the same vein, Timothy Brook emphasizes the irony of Confucianism being used both as an antidote against the ills of capitalism and as a driving force of capitalism.[84] Similarly, Zhang Xudong has maintained that the New Confucians' resort to culture was simply a way to revive national politics in the face of the universalism of global capital.[85] Liu Kang has added "regional anticommunism" to "global capitalism" as the ideological and political implications of New Confucianism.[86]

If we look beyond the "global capitalism" criticism, a more fundamental contradiction is clearly at work here, namely the tension between value rationality and instrumental rationality that goes back to Max Weber. Gan Yang had already noted this by arguing that the attempt to prove how Confucian values suited modernization went against the essence of value rationality that Confucians upheld. Does it not, he asked, harm the basic Confucian principle of "learning for oneself" (*weiji zhixue* 为己之学)?[87] Jing Wang has similarly argued that the alliance between Confucianism and capitalism delegitimated its claim of value rationality because "Confucianism is no less susceptible to instrumental reason and materialistic motivation on which capitalism is based than capitalism itself."[88] As exposed in the above, instrumentalist appropriations of Confucian values in the service of modernization, be it in the form of an East Asian development model or in the form of the socialist modernization project in mainland China, have challenged the moral project of Confucianism as a search for "authentic existence."

Chen Lai's dilemma was a continuation of the same ambiguity we find in Max Weber. On the one hand, Weber was critical of the "iron cage" of modern rationality. On the other hand, Weber investigated the relation between the role of ideas, mostly those of ascetic Calvinism, and this very rationalization in the form of capitalism. He sought to demonstrate the force of ideas in the rationalization process, a process that was at the same time detrimental to them, which sociologist Daniel Bell later exposed. Weber's "rationalization," then, as Anthony Giddens has noted, has multiple meanings: it refers to the "disenchantment" (*Entzauberung*) of the world, as well as to rationality to attain both practical and ethical goals.[89] The difference between Weber and the New Confucians, however, was that Weber was not an advocate of Calvinism as a moral value system or the ideas that had played a role in the formation of capitalism. Like New Confucians, he was concerned with the negative aspects of modernization and rationalization. Unlike New Confucians who see Confucianism as a remedy to modern industrial society, Weber did not regard Calvinism as an ideal state of community that would make modern life better.

The reference to both the positive and negative aspects of modernity as expressed in the debate on New Confucianism that originated with Weber was not unique. In German scholarship specifically, the double bind of modernity has received much attention. In *The Dialectics of Enlightenment*, for example, Theodor Adorno and Max Horkheimer have also criticized rationalism and capitalism; in late capitalist modernity, instrumental reason, they argue, has become irrational. However, the Marxist critique in German scholarship would not support the instrumental rationality of Confucian capitalism that advocates of Confucianism neglect to deny. In German critique, rationality itself is being denied, which excludes the possibility of supporting contradicting forms of rationality.

Why, then, did advocates of New Confucianism not consider upholding of both sides of the Weber debate as contradictory? Why did they perceive the debate on Confucian values for community-building against capitalist individualism and the debate on the role of Confucian values in the rise of capitalism as part of a single debate on the role of tradition in the modern world? Apart from the importance of the contextual factors outlined above (economic reform, changes in the intellectual world, and the emergence of the Four Mini Dragons), we can also find some answers in the nature of both Confucianism and Chinese intellectual discourse on modernity on a broader level.

As for Confucianism, as Jing Wang notes, Chinese intellectuals do not draw on these Marxist criticisms because they are a "radical critique of reason" that "inevitably leads to the critique of the sovereign rational subject, and, by extension, to a frontal attack on the whole tradition of humanism itself."[90] Chinese New Confucians, conversely, are strong defenders of humanism: their criticism is not directed at the rational subject. In addition, critiques of modernity in China have been ambiguous, a fact attributable to the obsession with "catching up with the West" ever since the nineteenth century. To refer to Chang Hao, this preoccupation with China's wealth and power (*fuqiang* 富强) and the "crisis consciousness" (*youhuan yishi* 忧患意识) of Chinese intellectuals leads to both a critique of modernity in its Western manifestation and an embrace of modernity on another level.[91]

This paradox has been present in Chinese thought since the late Qing, as Wang Hui convincingly argues in his monumental article on contemporary Chinese thought,[92] succinctly summarizing: "Indeed, in China's historical context, the struggle for modernization and the rejection of rationalization have proceeded together, something that has produced profound historical contradictions."[93] One can therefore argue that modernity was never truly challenged because it was rejected only in its Western manifestation, accompanied by the desire to modernize. For this reason, Wang Hui described Chinese thought since the late Qing as an "anti-modern theory of modernization" (*fan xiandai de xiandai zhuyi* 反现代的现代主义).[94] Because the discourse was framed within the binaries China/West and tradition/modernity, problems were situated in Western modernity or in Chinese tradition, instead of being regarded as produced by the modernization process itself.[95]

Furthermore, building on the notion that Chinese intellectuals never fully challenged modernity, Thomas Metzger, in his *A Cloud across the Pacific*, a vast study of moral-political discourse in China and the West, argues that the criticism of Western modernity in Chinese discourse—be it in the form of Marxism, Liberalism, or Confucian humanism—has been a criticism of its *societal* aspects, but not of its *epistemological* tenets. The consequence of this, according to Metzger, is that modernity is upheld, without reflecting on its negative aspects, such as "individualism" or "Liberalism." For Metzger, this "epistemological optimism" accounts for the difference between Chinese and Western critiques of modernity. The latter is characterized by the attack on reason itself. In the Chinese case, however, "rationality" is never questioned.[96]

Even though we need to be skeptical of Metzger's claim because Chinese intellectuals have engaged with the negative aspects of modernity, we can say that a contradiction is indeed present in this engagement. This contradiction is not restricted to China, but manifests itself in different shapes in those countries affected by Western expansionism and imperialism. One example is the discourse on nationalism in India. Dipesh Chakrabarty has argued that Indian nationalism has been characterized by a desire to distinguish India from the West, but at the same time, Indian modernity must be "combined with an aspiration towards a modernity that can be defined only in terms of the post-Enlightenment rationalism of European culture."[97] The criticism of the fundamental tenets of Western modernity, then, is combined with a desire to overcome this very modernity through an embrace of its structural features.

From this, we can understand why Chen Lai and Tu Wei-ming do not perceive of their advocacies as contradictory. First, as Confucians, they uphold humanism and are not engaging in a radical critique of reason and, by extension, of rationalization and rationality. Second, as participants in the Chinese discourse on modernity, which has been characterized by an ambiguous stance toward modernization from the beginning, there is only one debate for both of them, namely that on the relation between tradition and modernity. The debate is really a question of historical continuity, be it instrumental or not. In addition, the individualism in particular that Chen Lai seeks to counter with a quest for community based on Confucian values is the result of a modernity initiated by the West; it is not an attack on rationality *an sich*. The problem for them does not lie in modernity itself, as Wang Hui notes, which is why the broader question really is how to make Chinese tradition, which has universal significance, matter in a world that has witnessed the consequences of what is in essence a process of modernization the West has initiated. Naturally, the agendas of Tu Wei-ming and Chen Lai also differ here because Tu is a "Boston Confucian" removed from the context of mainland China. This, however, also makes us wonder why the difference in their positions regarding the Weber debate is not greater than it is: perhaps we can blame the conditions of late modernity for this lack of difference.

Notes

Author's note: I thank Tze-ki Hon and Kristin Stapleton for their insightful comments on an early draft of this chapter. I also extend my thanks to Chen Lai for making time to share his ideas and to guide me through the Chinese intellectual landscape. Any remaining errors are mine.

1. In this chapter, I use the term "Confucianism" because it is the term most commonly used in the sociopolitical debates of the late 1970s and 1980s. However, those identified as "New Confucians" make a clear distinction between the terms *ru, rujia, rujiao,* and *ruxue*. For a detailed overview of the difference between these terms, see John Makeham, *Lost Soul: "Confucianism" in Contemporary Chinese Academic Discourse* (Cambridge, MA: Harvard University Asia Center, 2008), and John Makeham, ed., *New Confucianism: A Critical Examination* (New York: Palgrave MacMillan, 2003). On the creation of "Confucianism" and the role of the Jesuits in this process, see Lionel M. Jensen, *Manufacturing Confucianism: Chinese Traditions and Universal Civilization* (Durham, NC: Duke University Press, 1997).

2. Although first published in English in 1930, Weber's essays on the topic first appeared in the *Archiv für Sozialwissenschaft* in 1904–1905. The question of the impact of Calvinism and Quakerism on the development of capitalism had already been raised by Werner Sombart in his *Der Moderne Kapitalismus*, vol. 1, *Die Genesis der Kapitalismus*, and vol. 2, *Die Theorie der Kapitalistischen Entwicklung* (Leipzig: Duncker and Humblot, 1902), but Max Weber was the first to explore the relation in detail. See Günther Roth, "Introduction," in Max Weber, *Economy and Society: An Outline of Interpretive Sociology*, edited by Günther Roth and Claus Wittich (Berkeley: University of California Press, 1978), 72, 77.

3. For details, see Weber, *Economy and Society*, chap. 2, "Sociological Categories of Economic Action," and chap. 9, "Bureaucracy."

4. Weber, *Economy and Society*, 24–25. Weber discerned two other types of action, namely "affectual" and "traditional" action. Both of these were situated on

a lower level because they were actions based on habit instead of on worldview or choice. See Weber, *Economy and Society*, 4–5.

5. Weber, *Economy and Society*, 26.

6. Wolfgang Schluchter, "Einleitung: Max Webers Konfuzianismusstudie: Versuch einer Einordnung," in *Max Webers Studie über Konfuzianismus und Taoismus: Interpretation und Kritik*, edited by Wolfgang Schluchter (Frankfurt am Main: Suhrkamp Verlag, 1983), 28–30. I thank Tze-ki Hon for bringing this study to my attention.

7. On "Boston Confucianism," see Robert Cummings Neville, *Boston Confucianism: Portable Tradition in the Late-Modern World* (Albany, NY: SUNY Press, 2000).

8. Chen Lai was also at Harvard in 1997 and 2006–2007, during Tu Wei-ming's directorship of the Yenching Institute (1996–2008).

9. See Makeham, *Lost Soul*, 25–53. On the New Confucian lineage and the notion of *daotong* 道统 (interconnecting thread of the Way), see his "The New Daotong," in *Lost Soul*, 55–78.

10. Makeham, *Lost Soul*, 68.

11. Hao Chang, "New Confucianism and the Intellectual Crisis of Contemporary China," in *The Limits of Change: Essays on Conservative Alternatives in Republican China*, edited by Charlotte Furth (Cambridge, MA: Harvard University Press, 1976), 289–296. See also chap. 6 by Stephen Angle and chap. 5 by Ming-huei Lee herein.

12. For an English version of the manifesto, see Junmai Zhang, "A Manifesto for a Re-appraisal of Sinology and Reconstruction of Chinese Culture," in Junmai Zhang, *The Development of Neo-Confucian Thought*, vol. 2 (New York: Bookman Associates, 1962), 455–483; ref. from 460, 464. The Declaration was published in the journals *Zaisheng* [Renaissance] and *Minzhu pinglun* [Democratic Tribune] in the New Year's issues of 1958.

13. Zhang, *The Development of Neo-Confucian Thought*, vol. 2, 476.

14. On the 1957 Declaration, see chap. 10 by Hok Yin Chan and chap. 5 by Ming-huei Lee herein.

15. See for example his *The Quest for Self-Realization: A Study of Wang Yang-ming's Formative Years* (Ph.D. diss., Harvard University, 1968); *Humanity and Self-Cultivation: Essays in Confucian Thought* (Berkeley, CA: Asian Humanities Press, 1979); and *Confucian Thought: Selfhood as Creative Transformation* (Albany, NY: SUNY Press, 1985).

16. See his *Ruxue disanqi fazhan de qianjing wenti: dalu jiangxue, wennan he taolun* 儒学第三期发展的前景问题: 大陆讲学, 问难和讨论 [Prospective issues of the third epoch of Confucianism: Mainland lectures, questions, and discussions] (Taipei: Lianjing chubanshe gongsi, 1989).

17. See Tu Wei-ming, "Cultural China: The Periphery as the Center," in *The Living Tree: The Changing Meaning of Being Chinese Today*, edited by Tu Wei-ming (Stanford, CA: Stanford University Press, 1994), 1–34.

18. See, e.g., Chen Lai, *Zhu Xi zhexue yanjiu* 朱熹哲学研究 [A study of Zhu Xi's philosophy] (Beijing: Zhongguo shehui kexue chubanshe, 1987); Chen Lai 陈

来, *You wu zhi jing: Wang Yangming zhexue de jingshen* 有无之境: 王阳明哲学的精神 [The realm of "you" and "wu": The spirit of Wang Yangming's philosophy] (Shanghai: Renmin chubanshe, 1991).

19. Chen Lai, *Chuantong yu xiandai: Renwen zhuyi de shijie* 传统与现代: 人文主义的视界 [Tradition and modernity: The scope of humanism] (Beijing: Beijing daxue chubanshe, 2006). This volume is a revised and expanded edition of a volume published in 1997 under the title *Renwen zhuyi de shijie* 人文主义的视界 [The scope of humanism] (Nanning: Guangxi jiaoyu chubanshe, 1997), that included Chen's writings on Confucianism over a period of nearly twenty years (1987–2006).

20. Makeham, *Lost Soul*, 335.

21. Ibid., 286–287.

22. Tu Wei-ming, *Confucian Ethics Today: The Singapore Challenge* (Singapore: Curriculum Development Institute of Singapore, 1984), 4.

23. On the "culture fever," see Jing Wang, *High Culture Fever: Politics, Aesthetics, and Ideology in Deng's China* (Berkeley: University of California Press, 1996).

24. See, e.g., Li Zehou's famous 1986 article on the May Fourth Movement in which he argues, among other things, that tradition was a "cultural-psychological structure" (*wenhua xinli jiegou* 文化心理结构), which is why a denial or confirmation of tradition is impossible. Li Zehou 李泽厚, "Qimeng yu jiuwang de shuangzhong bianzou" 启蒙与救亡的双重奏 [The double variation of Enlightenment and salvation], in Li Zehou, *Zhongguo xiandai sixiangshi lun* 启蒙与救亡的双重变奏 [On modern Chinese intellectual history] (Beijing: Dongfang chubanshe, 1987), 7–49.

25. The revaluation of May Fourth is such a broad topic that it requires a separate study. Some of the main volumes include: Zhou Yangshan 周阳山 et al., eds., *Cong wusi dao xin wusi* 从五四到新五四 [From May Fourth to the New May Fourth] (Taipei: Shibao wenhua chuban qiye youxian gongsi, 1989); Tang Yijie 汤一介, ed., *Lun chuantong yu fan chuantong: Wusi qishi zhounian jinian wenxuan* 论传统与反传统: 五四七十周年纪念文选 [On tradition and antitradition: Commemorative literary selections for the seventieth anniversary of May Fourth] (Taipei: Lianjing chuban shiye gongsi, 1989); Li Zehou 李泽厚 et al., *Wusi: Duoyuan de fansi* 五四: 多元的反思 [May Fourth: Multiple reflections] (Taipei: Dahong faxing, 1989). For a detailed overview of the May Fourth Movement, see Tse-tsung Chow, *The May Fourth Movement: Intellectual Revolution in Modern China* (Cambridge, MA: Harvard University Press, 1960).

26. Chen Lai, "Ershi shiji Zhongguo wenhua zhong de ruxue kunjing" 二十世纪中国文化中的儒学困境 [The predicament of Confucianism in twentieth-century Chinese culture] *Zhejiang shehui kexue* 浙江社会科学 3 (May 1988): 26–32; ref. from 30. See also his "Duoyuan wenhua jiegouzhong de ruxue ji qi dingwei" 多元文化结构中的儒学及其定位 [Ruxue and its place in multicultural structures] *Zhongguo luntan* 中国论坛 27, no. 1 (1988): 21–23.

27. Chen Lai, "Ershi shiji Zhongguo wenhua zhong de ruxue kunjing," 31.

28. Chen Lai, "Zhenxia qiyuan" 贞下起元 [A propitious new beginning] *Ershiyi shiji* 二十一世纪 10 (April 1992): 10–11.

29. Chen Lai, "Ershi shiji wenhua yundong zhong de jijin zhuyi" 二十世纪文化运动中的激进主义 [Radicalism in twentieth-century cultural movements] *Dongfang* 东方1 n.1 (1993), 38–44.

30. Chen Lai also used the term "functional rationality" (*gongyong lixing* 功用理性) instead of "instrumental rationality" (*gongju lixing* 工具理性). See, e.g., "Huajie 'chuantong' yu 'xiandai' de jinzhang: 'Wusi' wenhua sichao de fansi" 化解 '传统' 与 '现代' 的紧张: "五四" 文化思潮的反思 [Dissolving the tension between tradition and modernity: Reflections on the cultural trend of "May Fourth"] in *Chen Lai zixuanji* 陈来自选集 [Self-selected works of Chen Lai] (Guangdong: Guangdong shifan daxue chubanshe, 1997), 377. In other articles, Chen Lai also employed the terms *shizhi lixing* 实质理性 and *xingshi lixing* 形式理性, which appear to be closest to the original Weberian terms. See, e.g., "Xin lixue yu xiandaixing siwei de fansi" 新理学与现代性思维的反思 [New rational philosophy and reflections on modernity thought] in Chen Lai, *Chuantong yu xiandai* (q.v.), 174.

31. Chen Lai, "Huajie chuantong yu xiandai de jinzhang: Wusi wenhua sichao de fansi," *Chen Lai zixuanji,* 373–398, quote from 377.

32. On the debate, see Daniel Kwok Wynn-Ye, *Scientism in Chinese Thought, 1900–1950* (New Haven, CT: Yale University Press, 1965).

33. See Lin Yüsheng, *The Crisis of Chinese Consciousness: Radical Antitraditionalism in the May Fourth Era* (Madison: University of Wisconsin Press, 1979); and Lin Yüsheng, "The Radicalization of China in the Twentieth Century," *Daedalus* 122, no. 2 (Spring 1993): 125–150.

34. Chen Lai, "'Wusi' sichao yu xiandaixing" "五四"思潮与现代性 [The "May Fourth" trend and modernity], in *Chuantong yu xiandai: Renwen zhuyi de shijie*, 60–67; ref. from 62–63.

35. Chen Lai, "Ershi shiji Zhongguo wenhua zhong de ruxue kunjing," 27. Chen Lai referred to Chen Duxiu's text "Fubi yu zunkong" 复辟与尊孔 [Restoration and revering Confucius], *Xin qingnian* [New Youth] 3, 6 (N.d.): n.p.

36. Chen Lai, "Huajie jinzhang," 388.

37. Tu calls the distortions "open attacks" or *mingqiang* 明槍 (the end of the imperial system) and "hidden attacks" or *anjian* 暗箭 (the May Fourth critique).

38. Tu Wei-ming, "Huajie qimeng xintai" 化解启蒙心态 [Beyond the Enlightenment syndrome], *Ershiyi shiji* 二十一世纪 2 (Dec. 1990): 12–13.

39. Neville, *Boston Confucianism*, 56–57; Makeham, *Lost Soul*, 280.

40. Chen Lai, "Rujia sixiang yu xiandai dongya shijie" 儒家思想与现代东亚世界 [Confucian thought and the modern East Asian world], in *Chuantong yu xiandai: Renwen zhuyi de shijie,* 179–187; ref. from 186.

41. Chen Lai, "Renwen zhuyi de shijie" [The scope of humanism]. Dongfang wenhua [Eastern culture] 18, no. 1 (1997): 14–20, ref. from 16.

42. Guy Alitto, *The Last Confucian: Liang Shu-ming and the Chinese Dilemma of Modernity* (Berkeley: University of California Press, 1979), 184.

43. For a similar view on *ren* as "public domain" and "communicative rationality," see chap. 7 Lin An-Wu herein.

44. Chen Lai, "Rujia sixiang yu xiandai dongya shijie," 186.

45. Wei-ming Tu et al., eds., *The Confucian World Observed: A Contemporary Discussion of Confucian Humanism in East Asia* (Honolulu, HI: East-West Center, 1992), 65.

46. Neville, *Boston Confucianism*, 91.

47. Wei-ming Tu, *Confucian Ethics Today: The Singapore Challenge* (Singapore: Curriculum Development Institute of Singapore, 1984), 9.

48. Michio Morishima, "The Power of Confucian Capitalism," *The Observer* (London), June 1978; and Ezra Vogel, *Japan as Number One: Lessons for America* (Cambridge, MA: Harvard University Press, 1979). See also Vogel's later work, *The Four Little Dragons: The Spread of Industrialization in East Asia* (Cambridge, MA: Harvard University Press, 1991). The Japan scholar Robert Bellah, a student of Talcott Parsons, had already applied the Weber thesis to Japan in the 1950s. See Robert N. Bellah, *Tokugawa Religion: The Values of Pre-Industrial Japan* (Glencoe, IL: Free Press, 1957). Another early Weberian approach to Japanese thought is Maruyama Masao's *Nihon seiji shisōshi kenkyū* [Studies on the history of Japanese political thought] (Tokyo: Tokyo Daigaku Shuppankai, 1952); Herman Kahn, *World Economic Development: 1979 and Beyond* (Boulder, CO: Westview, 1979).

49. Roderick MacFarquhar, "The Post-Confucian Challenge," *The Economist*, Feb. 9, 1980, 67–72; and Peter L. Berger, "An East Asian Development Model," in *In Search of an East Asian Development Model*, edited by Peter L. Berger and Hsin-Huang Michael Hsiao (New Brunswick, NJ: Transaction Books, 1988), 3–11.

50. Harriet T. Zurndorfer, "Confusing Confucianism with Capitalism: Culture as Impediment and/or Stimulus to Chinese Economic Development" (paper presented at the Third Global Economic History Network Meeting, Konstanz, Germany, June 2004), 5. Tu Wei-ming has also referred to the fact that the very same values were used by the same people to make the opposite argument as "the most fascinating aspect" of the entire debate. See his *Confucian Ethics Today*, 79.

51. Zurndorfer, "Confusing Confucianism with Capitalism," 7.

52. Joseph R. Levenson, *Confucian China and Its Modern Fate*, 3 vols. (Berkeley: University of California Press, 1958–1965).

53. See his "Zhongguo jinshi zongjiao lunli yu shangren jingshen" 中国近世宗教伦理与商人精神 [The early modern Chinese religious ethic and the mercantile spirit], *Zhishi fenzi* 知识分子 [New York] 2, no. 2 (1985).

54. See, e.g., Wei-ming Tu et al., eds., *The Confucian World Observed*; Wei-ming Tu, ed., *The Triadic Chord: Confucian Ethics, Industrial East Asia, and Max Weber, Proceedings of the 1987 Singapore Conference on Confucian Ethics and the Modernization of Industrial East Asia* (Singapore: Institute of East Asian Philosophies, 1991); and Wei-ming Tu, ed., *Confucian Traditions in East Asian Modernity: Exploring Moral Education and Economic Culture in Japan and the Four Mini-Dragons* (Cambridge, MA: Harvard University Press, 1996).

55. For a detailed overview, see John Makeham, "The Singapore Experiment and Rujia Capitalism," in Makeham, *Lost Soul*, 21–41. See also Tu Wei-ming, *Confucian Ethics Today*.

56. Wei-ming Tu et al., eds. *The Confucian World Observed*, 75.

57. Ibid.

58. Wei-ming Tu, "Introduction," *Confucian Traditions in East Asian Modernity*, 2.

59. Ibid., 6–9.

60. See Makeham, *Lost Soul*, 30, 34–37.

61. Max Weber, *The Protestant Ethic and the Spirit of Capitalism*, translated by Talcott Parsons (New York: Scribner's Sons, 1958), 126.

62. Max Weber, *The Religion of China: Confucianism and Taoism*, translated by Hans Gerth (New York: Free Press and Collier-Macmillan, 1968), 226–227.

63. Ibid., 227. Elsewhere, Weber has formulated it as follows: "Completely absent in Confucian ethic was any tension between nature and deity, between ethical demand and human shortcoming, consciousness of sin and need for salvation, conduct on earth and compensation in the beyond, religious duty and sociopolitical reality." Ibid., 235–236.

64. Ibid., 240.

65. Ibid., 242.

66. Ibid., 247.

67. Ibid., 229, 236–237, 241.

68. Negative structural factors were the lack of an effective monetary system, the lack of politically and militarily autonomous cities, the lack of legal foundations for guilds, and a patrimonial bureaucracy. Other obstacles were the kinship system and the existence of substantive ethical law instead of a rational legal system. Positive elements were the lack of status restriction by birth; free migration and freedom of choice with regard to occupation; the lack of compulsory military service and schooling; and the lack of restraints on trade. Ch'ing-k'un Yang, introduction to Weber, *The Religion of China*, xx–xxviii.

69. See Wolfgang Schluchter, "Einleitung: Max Webers Konfuzianismusstudie: Versuch einer Einordnung," 26. The difference between them was that Confucianism did not have an ethics of ultimate ends and did not recognize the existence of evil.

70. See Thomas A. Metzger, *Escape from Predicament: Neo-Confucianism and China's Evolving Political Culture* (New York: Columbia University Press, 1977). See also the debate that followed in the *Journal of Asian Studies*, Feb. 1980; and Shmuel Eisenstadt, "This-Worldly Transcendentalism and the Structuring of the World: Weber's 'Religion of China' and the Format of Chinese History and Civilization," *Journal of Developing Societies* 1 (1985): 168–186.

71. Wang, *High Culture Fever*, 66.

72. Interview with Chen Lai, Beijing, Aug. 10, 2005.

73. Wang, *High Culture Fever*, 68.

74. Chen Lai, "Shisu rujia lunli yu houfa xiandaihua" 世俗儒家伦理与后发现代化 [Vulgar Confucianism and late modernization] *Ershiyi shiji* 二十一世纪 22 (Apr. 1994): 112–120, ref. from 113. See also "Rujia lilun yu Zhongguo xiandaihua" 儒家理论与中国现代化 [Confucian ethics and Chinese modernization], in *Chuantong yu xiandai: Renwen zhuyi de shijie*, 188–206.

75. Weber, *The Religion of China*, 248. Wei-ming Tu also refers to this statement by Weber in his introduction to *Confucian Traditions in East Asian Modernity*, 4.

76. Chen Lai, "Shisu rujia lunli yu houfa xiandaihua," 112–120.

77. Berger, "An East Asian Development Model," 3–11.

78. Chen Lai, "Rujia lilun yu Zhongguo xiandaihua," 195.

79. Chen Lai, "Rujia sixiang yu xiandai dongya shijie," in *Chuantong yu xiandai: Renwen zhuyi de shijie*, 179–187; and interview with Chen Lai, Beijing, Aug. 10, 2005.

80. The term "Weberizing Confucianism" is taken from Arif Dirlik, "Confucius in the Borderlands: Global Capitalism and the Reinvention of Confucianism," *Boundary 2* 22, no. 3 (Fall 1995): 267.

81. For more details on this argument, see chap. 8 by Ke Sheng herein.

82. Dirlik, "Confucius in the Borderlands," 230, 273.

83. Ibid., 267, 273.

84. Timothy Brook, "Profit and Righteousness in Chinese Economic Culture," in *Culture and Economy: The Shaping of Capitalism in Eastern Asia*, edited by Timothy Brook and Hy V. Luong (Ann Arbor: University of Michigan Press, 1997), 44.

85. Xudong Zhang, "The Making of the Post-Tiananmen Intellectual Field: A Critical Overview," in *Whither China? Intellectual Politics in Contemporary China*, edited by Xudong Zhang (Durham, NC: Duke University Press, 2001), 44.

86. Liu Kang, "Is There an Alternative to (Capitalist) Globalization? The Debate about Modernity in China," *Boundary 2* 23, no. 3 (Fall 1996): 206.

87. Makeham, *Lost Soul*, 38.

88. Wang, *High Culture Fever*, 66, 67.

89. Trevor O. Ling, "The Weberian Thesis and Interpretive Positions on Modernisation," in *The Triadic Chord*, edited by Wei-ming Tu (q.v.), 66, from Anthony Giddens, *Politics and Sociology in the Thought of Max Weber* (London: Macmillan, 1972), 44.

90. Wang, *High Culture Fever*, 76–77.

91. Hao Chang, "New Confucianism and the Intellectual Crisis of Contemporary China."

92. See Wang Hui, "Dangdai Zhongguo de sixiang zhuangkuang yu xiandaixing" 当代中国的思想状况与现代性, originally published in *Tianya* 天涯 (Frontiers) 5 (1997): 133–150; a translation by Rebecca Karl appeared in *China's New Order: Society, Politics, and Economy in Transition*, edited by Theodore Huters (Cambridge, MA: Harvard University Press, 2003), 139–187.

93. Wang Hui, "Contemporary Chinese Thought," 150.

94. Ibid., 150.

95. Ibid., 145.

96. Thomas A. Metzger, *A Cloud across the Pacific: Essays on the Clash between Chinese and Western Political Theories Today* (Hong Kong: Chinese University of Hong Kong Press, 2005), 50–51, 53, 142–143.

97. Dipesh Chakrabarty, "Towards a Discourse on Nationalism," *Economic and Political Weekly* 22, no. 28 (July 11, 1987): 1137.

3

Realizing *Tianxia*

Traditional Values and China's Foreign Policy

Daniel A. Bell

Tianxia, usually translated as "all-under-heaven" or "the world," has been central to Chinese political thinking and it has shaped the way that China has dealt with the rest of the world for more than two millennia. According to Li Yangfan, *tianxia* is the key idea that differentiates Chinese from European political culture.[1] Whereas the idea of the state with fixed territorial boundaries has been central to Western political culture,[2] Chinese political culture was shaped with a more global political vision. Instead of viewing itself as one state in a competitive international environment of other states, China has viewed itself as the center of a world that should be unified and peaceful.

Ironically, China has more recently come to be known as a country that seems distinctly obsessed with sovereignty. The concept of sovereignty had European origins (the term came to China via a process of transplantation that included a Japanese interlude) and it ran counter to core aspects of indigenous Chinese approaches to territory,[3] but it became the mainstream way of thinking about territory among political and intellectual Chinese elites in the twentieth century. The roots of China's political "Westernization" date from China's military defeats at the hands of Western powers in the mid- to late nineteenth century. Chinese elites could no longer see themselves as occupying a symbolic world in which the capital possessed a superior normative value; instead, they became preoccupied with the painful reality that their polity was peripheral within the expanding Westphalian international order. If China was to survive, it had to adjust to this new system.[4]

In the early twentieth century, influential Chinese intellectual Liang Qichao criticized the Chinese people for excessive idealism: "The Chinese people have never taken the state as the highest entity; they believed there must be an entity higher than the state and exercising control over all states. That was *tianxia*." So traditional politics in China "did not take the tranquility and happiness of a single state as its ultimate purpose, but had the tranquility and happiness of all mankind as its final aim." In a dangerous and Darwinian world system of competing states, Liang thought that giving too little weight to the state was a shortcoming that must be corrected immediately, and he repeatedly called on his countrymen to give importance to "the state."[5]

After China established a relatively strong and unified Chinese state in 1949, its survival as a political community was more secure. However, the Korean War, instability in minority regions, and the break with the Soviet Union (as well as a degree of paranoia among ruling elites) led China to adopt a rigid posture regarding territorial boundaries.[6] In the early 1990s, global condemnation of the Tiananmen Square crackdown and the collapse of the Soviet empire made the regime even more sensitive about "outside interference," and the "Western" idea of respect for state sovereignty and territorial boundaries became an entrenched mode of political discourse in China. The key was to ensure survival of the political community, and the Chinese Communist Party (CCP) rulers claimed that opening up China to interference by foreigners would open a Pandora's box, plunging China into civil war, poverty, and chaos.

But such sentiments are receding with time. Clearly China is stronger than before, and it does not have to worry as much about foreign incursions. The realities and responsibilities of being a great power are gradually rendering preoccupation with state sovereignty less central. "To each his own" in international affairs no longer makes any sense. With China's economic integration in the global market, it has the power to influence economic actors around the globe (and vice versa). The environmental consequences of China's economic growth (it has become the largest emitter of greenhouse gases) threaten the rest of the world. It has been blamed for supporting repressive regimes in Ethiopia and Zimbabwe. If China affects the rest of the world, how can it ask the rest of the world not to interfere with its own internal affairs?

Faced with such concerns, China has begun to play a more responsible and cooperative role in international affairs. It has shown willingness to settle long-standing territorial disputes with its neighbors.[7] It has sent 4,000 soldiers and police to participate in fourteen United Nations peacekeeping missions: more than any of the other five members of the U.N. Security

Council.⁸ China has participated in antipiracy operations off the coast of Somalia as well as helping with an increasing number of humanitarian missions abroad: Soon after Japan's devastating earthquake and tsunami in March 2011, Chinese rescue teams were mobilized and sent to help with the recovery process, and Chinese Defense Minister Liang Guangjie publicly offered possible military rescue help. China's response to the Libya crisis in spring 2011 is an even more striking example: China's U.N. representative quickly voted for the U.N. sanctions against the Qaddafi government and for the first time China dispatched a warship and four military aircraft that evacuated 35,860 Chinese nationals and 2,100 foreigners from Libya.⁹

Of course, such efforts often fall short of what the Chinese government ought to do. But what exactly is the government supposed to do? What moral principles should inform China's foreign policy, the way China deals with the rest of the world? Not surprisingly, perhaps, traditional values help Chinese leaders not only make sense of the new emphasis on international responsibility but also help provide moral resources for social critics to expose the inevitable gap between the ideal and the reality. In the context of the broader revival of Confucianism that Tze-ki Hon and others in this volume discuss, the ideal of *tianxia* has been revived for the purpose of rethinking China's role in Asia and beyond.¹⁰ But what exactly is *tianxia*? And how can it help us to think about China's role in the world? The remainder of this chapter focuses on these questions.

The Concept of *Tianxia*

The first point to make about *tianxia* is that it is a vague concept that has been used differently in different times (and differently in the same times).¹¹ To further complicate matters, the term has sometimes been used in a descriptive sense meaning the whole world and other times in a normative sense of an ideal that contrasts with the reality. The use of the term *tianxia* predates Confucianism, but Confucian thinkers—along with other thinkers in the late Warring States Period—emphasized the political, normative dimension the term.¹² In the Mencius, for example, the term is used eighty-six times¹³ and often refers to an ideal of a unified world without any territorial boundaries governed by one benevolent ruler, an ideal that is meant to contrast with the ugly reality of small states competing ruthlessly for territorial advantage in the Warring States Period. Once Qin Shi Huang identified the warring states and the new centralized state he created (and later emperors recreated) viewed itself as the empire at the center of the world, the term often took on more descriptive meanings. In the

Tang dynasty, for example, *tianxia* referred either to the area actually Tang dynasty rulers governed or to the whole world with Zhongguo (China) at its core surrounded by other countries.[14] In the seventeenth century—toward the end of the Ming dynasty and the early stages of the Manchu-governed Qing empire—Confucian thinkers explicitly drew on the normative implications of *tianxia* for critical purposes. Huang Zongxi criticized the rulers of his day for treating *"tianxia"* as something that is meant to serve their own interests rather than the people's interests.[15] His contemporary Gu Yanwu explicitly distinguished between the fall of the state (国家) and the fall of *tianxia*, arguing that the common people's obligation is to the latter but that securing the state or dynastic polity is the concern of rulers or officials.[16] His political point is that political dynasties will collapse when they fail to provide for the people's needs and to gain the trust of the people.[17]

In contemporary times, *tianxia* was famously revived by the philosopher Zhao Tingyang who gave it a normative definition. According to Zhao's influential formulation, *tianxia* has three meanings: (1) a geographical meaning referring to the whole world; (2) a psychological meaning in the sense that the hearts of all the world's peoples are unified, like a big family; and (3) an institutional meaning in the sense of a world government with the power to ensure universal order.[18] Zhao's ideal echoes the early twentieth-century Confucian-inspired thinker Kang Youwei's "Confucian-inspired" political ideal of Taiping Shi (Global Peace) composed of people freed from particular attachments and where all goals are shared in common,[19] but it is worth asking if these ideals are really consistent with Confucian values.

Zhao claims that his ideal derives inspiration from the values and practices put forward by the "founding fathers" of the Zhou dynasty approximately 3,000 years ago—the same sage kings who inspired Confucius—but his ideal is radically inconsistent with the key Confucian value of graded love. Zhao's global government is supposed to be supported by the world's people psychologically bound like an intimate family (the second feature of his ideal),[20] but this ideal owes more to imported traditions like Christianity, Buddhism, and Marxism that aim to break down particularistic attachments. Consider the reference to *tianxia* in the Great Learning. This Han dynasty work—subsequently canonized by the Song dynasty scholar Zhu Xi (1130–1200) as one of the four Confucian classics—opens with the famous passage:

> The extension of knowledge consists in the investigation of things. When things are investigated, knowledge is extended; when knowledge is extended, the will is sincere; when the will is sincere, the mind is rectified; when the mind is rectified, the

personal life is cultivated; when the personal life is cultivated, the family will be regulated; when the family is regulated, the state will be in order; and when the state is in order, there is peace throughout the world (*tianxia*).

Starting from the moral ordering of the individual person and the family, an important goal of Confucianism is to bring order to the state and thereby spread peace throughout the world. The ideal is a harmonious political order of global peace. But nowhere does the Great Learning state that ties to the people outside the state should be as strong as ties to people within the state. The reason is simple: ties should be extended from intimates to others, but with diminishing intensity as we move beyond the circle of intimates. We owe more to intimates (starting with the family) than to strangers, both because they are the main sources of happiness and because we need to reciprocate for what they have done for us. Hence, the web of obligations that binds citizens is more intense than those binding foreigners. As Joseph Chan puts it: "The Confucian view that it is natural and right for a person to show more concern for people close to him or her than to strangers would lead one to accept at least some kind of territorial boundary that distributes more resources to citizens of a community than to outsiders."[21]

But the Great Learning reminds us that it should not end there. Just as we should extend ties beyond the family, so we should extend ties beyond the nation. Extending this concern to outsiders, although with less concern as they extend further and further from the political community, is also natural and right. Hence, Confucianism should not view special concern for fellow citizens as a politically necessary compromise, a second-best deviation from an ideal world. Nor is it just a necessary mechanism on the way to the politics of global love and government. At least some sort of special commitment to a particular political community is required by the logic of graded love,[22] a commitment that should be extended (in diminishing degrees) to outsiders.

In short, a Confucian-inspired defense of the ideal of *tianxia* would not involve a world government that has ethical and political priority over national states (not to mention an anarchist or communist ideal of abolishing the state). It does involve thinking about the sorts of obligations that we owe to people living outside the territorial boundaries of our states, even though they are not as intense as the obligations we owe to fellow citizens. Of course, the ideal of *tianxia* would have to be modified from its understanding in imperial times. Nobody believes that China is the center of the world (or the universe), so the question is not what Chinese rulers owe to "barbarians" living outside the country but rather what they owe to people living in other countries. Given that the Chinese state finds itself at a time of transition from an age of survival to an age of expansion and global influence, it seems like a particularly topical question to think about. But the value of *tianxia* by itself cannot do all the work. We need to look to other values for a fuller picture of a morally-informed approach to Chinese foreign policy. For this purpose, I draw on the works of contemporary Chinese thinkers who work within a Confucian political framework[23] Along the way, I make comparisons with liberal and Marxist approaches, and I then turn to key Confucian political values—hierarchy, harmony, and meritocracy[24]—and say a bit about how they might inform China's foreign policy in both humane and realistic ways.

A Hierarchical World Order

Contemporary Chinese thinkers have explicitly called into question the liberal ideal of equality between sovereign states, arguing instead for more hierarchical arrangements between states in the international arena. As one might expect, critics in the West have raised doubts about this "Chinese" project. William Callahan, for example, has charged that Zhao's ideal of *tianxia* masks an effort to replace Western hegemony with Chinese hegemony.[25] But Zhao's latest work responds to such concerns. He explicitly argues for a world organization that would have more territory and resources than any one state (including the Chinese state): "The world government directly rules a land called King-land, about twice the size of a large sub-state, and four times that of a medium sized sub-state and so on. The military force controlled by the world government is greater than those of large, medium and small substate with a ratio of 6 to 3, 6 to 2 and 6 to 1 divisions. This proportional design limits the King-land of the world government in its advantages over the sub-states either in resources or military power."[26] Zhao's proposal may help alleviate concerns of Chinese hegemony, but how it could be realized in the actual political world is unclear: as Zhang Feng puts it, "the critical flaw of Zhao's thesis is his failure to outline any clear pathway that might lead to the creation of the world institution of the *tianxia* system. . . . He insists on the priority of the world institution, yet surprisingly fails to provide any description of how it might come about . . . and [be] maintained."[27]

Yan Xuetong's defense of a hierarchical world system, with China as a major power, is more realistic. Yan draws on the thoughts of the pre-Qin thinker Xunzi to question the ideal of equality between states:[28] "After the 1648 Treaty of Westphalia, equality of state sovereignty developed to become a universal moral international norm. Xunzi's thought is the exact opposite of equality of sovereignty. . . . According to Xunzi's interpretation of Five Services, distinctions in international norms should be decided according to a state's status in international society."[29] Given China's decisive influence on the global economy and its increasing ability to project military power, Yan argues that China should play a more major role on the world stage and it should be honest in doing so: "China should not adopt the United States' current way of acting, saying that all states are equal while in practice always seeking to have a dominant international status." Moreover, such hierarchical arrangements can actually benefit weaker states because this sense of dominance means that states have extra responsibilities, including assistance to poor countries. Rather than insisting on reciprocity with weaker states, China should try to gain their support by allowing for differential international norms to work in their favor. In the cooperation of the 10+1 (Association of Southeast Asian Nations [ASEAN] and China), for example, "China is required to implement the norm of zero tariffs in agricultural trade before the ASEAN states do. This unequal norm enabled the economic cooperation of the 10+1 to develop more rapidly than that between Japan and ASEAN. Japan's demand for equal tariffs with ASEAN slowed the progress of its economic cooperation with the ASEAN states, which lags far behind that of China and ASEAN."[30] Yan adds that hierarchical norms also contribute to international peace: "If we examine recent international history, we can see that in those areas that implemented international norms, international peace was better maintained than it was in areas that had norms for equality. During the Cold War, the equal status of the United States and the Soviet Union was such that they undertook many proxy wars in order to compete for hegemony, while their special status in the North Atlantic Treaty Organization (NATO) and the Warsaw Pact, respectively, enabled them to prevent the members of those alliances from engaging in military conflict with one another." Here, too, the extra responsibilities for the major powers in hierarchical systems may actually benefit the weaker ones: "China should propose that large states and small states have different responsibilities, and that different states should respect different security norms. . . . If nuclear weapons do not proliferate, then nuclear states must strictly adhere to nonproliferation while providing security guarantees to nonnuclear states."[31]

Allen Carlson suggests that a hierarchical system may also contribute to solving territorial disputes with China's neighbors because China's leaders might place less emphasis on the sanctity of territorial boundaries than is currently the case: "In a reconstituted *tianxia* system, the territorial and jurisdictional concerns which have so preoccupied China's leaders over the course of the last century could be re-imagined as issues involving peripheral regions, not zero-sum disputes over sovereign recognition. In this sense, a *tianxia* order might pave the way for the novel solution of such controversies, and as such lead to greater stability within the region." The problem, as Carlson goes on to note, is that the large states along China's periphery are likely to construe an attempt to impose (or even articulate) a new normative hierarchical order in the East Asian region as a threat: "Within such a system it is clear that it is China that is to occupy the paramount position, while those along its margins are expected to accept such dominance and show fealty to the center. Obviously, within such an order there is no rhetorical space for any external arbitrator of normative principles, such as the United States."32

To be fair, Yan himself explicitly argues that the tribute system is outdated for the modern world: "In fact, any effort to restore the tribute system will weaken China's capability for international political mobilization."33 Yan recognizes that neighboring states in East Asia are not likely to welcome a system that enshrines second-class status. One could also argue that the tribute system itself is a largely an invention of Western sinologists and cannot usefully explain China's interaction with its neighbors over long periods of time.34 In historical practice, Chinese imperial courts did not usually use the idea of "tributary relations" to interfere in the internal affairs of neighboring states, and the states in China's periphery often had complete independence to do as they wished.35 So the charge that neighboring states will be expected to "show fealty" or pay tribute to China may not stick. But there is the issue of U.S. military dominance in the region, and imagining any reconstituted hierarchical order with a greater role for China based on its growing economic and military power would not involve any substantial change in that respect is difficult. So how could China gain the trust of its neighbors such as South Korea and Japan who seem distinctly worried by China's growing military might? China's bellicose approach to regional territorial disputes in 2010 have only reinforced these concerns and any talk of ending U.S. military alliances seems more removed than ever.

Yan does not explicitly address this issue, but his theory of political leadership inspired by pre-Qin political thinkers may be helpful for alleviating concerns. For the sake of making itself a rising power that is welcomed by the rest of the world, Yan says that China should act as a humane authority (王) that does good in the rest of the world. Yan's theory of political leadership is directly inspired by pre-Qin thinkers. In contrast to Marxists who believe that economic might is the key to national power and to neoconservatives who believe that countries should rely on military might to get their way, Yan argues that political leadership is the key to national power and that morality is an essential part of political leadership. Economic and military power might matter as components of national power, but they are secondary to political leaders who act in accordance with moral norms.

Of course, China must show more evidence that it is acting according to humane norms before persuading its neighbors that it should take on more responsibilities in the East Asian region (and that the United States should close its military bases). And it must begin at home. As Yan puts it, "For China to become a superpower modeled on humane authority, it must first become a model from which other states are willing to learn."[36] Yan argues that the modern equivalent of humane authority is democracy—"I think that in their respect for norms, the modern concept of democracy and the ancient Chinese concept of humane authority are alike"—but he does not spell out in detail the implications for domestic political reform.[37] What is clear, perhaps, is that other countries are not likely to be inspired by a thin-skinned regime that imprisons leading artists, peaceful political reformers, and public-interest lawyers.

Political Meritocracy

Whatever their rhetorical support for the idea of democracy, one of the key ideals Confucian-inspired reformers put forward is the value of political meritocracy. Whereas Marxists aim for an ideal world without any government—in "higher communism," the state would have withered away because a classless society has no need for instruments of violence[38]—and liberal cosmopolitans tend be inspired by Immanuel Kant's ideal of a federation of republican (or democratic) governments that can converge on the value of global peace[39]—Confucians are explicit that any government concerned with the world would have to be composed of above-average moral and political talent. There should be equality of opportunity in education (有教无类, as Confucius put it in the *Analects*, 15.39) and government, but not everybody will emerge from the educational process with equal capacity to make competent and morally justifiable political judgments. Hence, an important task of the political system is to identify and select those with above-average capacity.[40]

Perhaps the most influential statement of Confucius's own highest political ideal is the account of "the Great Way" (大道) in the Record of Rites (礼记), a work compiled during the Han dynasty based on older materials. This ideal is described as an age when the world worked for the interests of all people (*tianxia wei gong* 天下为公) and these characters are immediately followed by an ideal of political meritocracy: "The worthy and the able were promoted to office" 选贤与能. In a recent article on *tianxia*, Liu Junping, a philosopher at Wuhan University, draws on this passage to defend a political ideal where the most talented members of the political community occupy political posts.[41] Zhao Tingyang is even more explicit: "The unspoken theory [within the concept of *tianxia*] is that people do not really know what is best for them, but that the elite do, so the elite ought genuinely to decide for the people."[42] Of course, Zhao has a powerful world government in mind—an ideal that is not realistic today—so it is worth asking what the ideal of political meritocracy would mean for a Chinese government that is inspired by the ideals of *tianxia* and political meritocracy.

Yan Xuetong proposes that China should learn from Xunzi's recommendation of strategy for a rising power, which "stresses human talent, that is, focuses on competition for talent." Again, there is a critique of the status quo: "At present, China's strategy of seeking talent is still mainly used for developing enterprises and has not yet been applied to raising the nation as a whole. Talent is still understood as having to do with technicians rather than politicians or high-ranking officials." Talented people are available but they are not always chosen: "Xunzi thinks that there are many talented people with both morality and ability, and the key is whether the ruler would choose them."

Drawing on historical examples, Yan puts forward some strategies for finding talent. First:

> The degree of openness is high: choosing officials from the whole world who meet the requisite standards of morality and ability, so as to improve the capability of the government to formulate correct policies. For example, in ancient times, the Tang Dynasty in China and the Empire in North Africa, Spain, and the Middle East, in the course of their rise, employed a great number of foreigners as officials. It is said that at its peak more than 70 percent of officials in the Umayyad Empire were foreigners. The United States has attained its present hegemonic status also by its policy of attracting talented and outstanding foreigners.[43]

In other words, the main competition with the United States should be competition for human talent rather than for economic or military superiority.

Second, Yan argues that officials should be held responsible for their mistakes. He opposes lifetime job security that increases the risk of officials becoming corrupt, lazy, and prone to repeating mistakes. In the more meritocratic societies, "unsuitable government officials could be speedily removed, reducing the probability of erroneous decisions. This applied to all politicians and officials, if they lost their ability to make correct decisions for any reason, such as being corrupted by power, being out-of-date in knowledge, decaying in thought, suffering a decline in their ability to reflect, or experiencing deterioration in health. Establishing a system by which officials can be removed in a timely fashion provides opportunities for talented people and can reduce errors of policy and ultimately increase political power."

Yan also argues for the establishment of independent think tanks that would provide professional advice on policy. At the moment, "the research institutions attached to our government agencies are not think tanks in the strict sense. Their main task is to carry out policies, not to furnish ideas. To undertake the work of a think tank is to exercise social responsibility." Institutions similar to think tanks existed in the past (e.g., Confucian academies in the Song dynasty), but "since the founding of the new China in 1949, the state has not allowed high officials to have their own personal advisors or to rely on nongovernmental advisory organizations."[44]

In short, China can increase its political power by adopting a more meritocratic system of selection of political officials and advisors. But this leads to the question of what exactly these talented and public-spirited politicians and advisors should aim for. I leave aside the question of domestic policy; here the question is how to aim for the good of people living outside China's boundaries who are affected by China's policies. To repeat, China does not have the same obligations to foreigners as to its own citizens, but the value of *tianxia* means that it does have some obligations to foreigners. So how to increase the likelihood that China would aim for the good of non-citizens? In addition to Yan's suggestions—more employment of foreigners, more job accountability, and more independent think tanks—there are other possibilities.

Most important, perhaps, is the need to recognize that China's own policies such as release of greenhouse gases may have negative consequences for other countries. Hence, a separate political institution of deputies who have the explicit task of deliberating about and serving the interests of noncitizens may be needed. The deputies could be selected at least partly by modernized competitive examinations that test for knowledge of international affairs, basic economics, as well as the Confucian political classics, and their power can be checked by means such as term-limits and stiff penalties for corruption.[45] Of course, such proposals are far removed from the current reality: not just in China, but also in democratic states, where rulers selected by the people owe their obligations to the community of voters and nobody represents the community of nonvoters (including foreigners) who are affected by government policies. But they are less utopian than Zhao's proposal for a world institution that has ethical and political priority over existing states. And if China is really moving toward a form of government inspired by *tianxia* and related Confucian political values, imagining an institution explicitly designed to serve the interests of non-citizens is not difficult.

More realistic (in the short term), China can assist other countries seeking to build meritocratic rule. Just as the United States promotes democracy abroad via government-funded foundations such as the National Endowment for Democracy, so the Chinese government can fund an institution—for example, the National Endowment for Meritocracy—that would fund experiments for political meritocracy designed to improve governance in other countries. Western powers may not be interested, but those in Africa and elsewhere will be.[46]

Social Harmony

The value of harmony is central to Confucian political ethics and the famous line from the *Analects* that exemplary persons should pursue harmony (和) but not sameness/uniformity/conformity (同) is well known to most Chinese intellectuals. The contrast between harmony and sameness owes its origins to the *Zuo Zhuan*—a text of narrative history of the Spring and Autumn Period compiled no later than 389 BCE that was canonized as one of the thirteen Confucian classics—where it clearly referred to the idea that the ruler should be open to the different political views among his advisors. As Li Chenyang explains, the value of harmony also affirms the value of mutual accommodation between cultures: "In the harmony model, when cultures conflict, the best way to handle conflict is not to protect one's own ground and try to eliminate the opponent; it is to find a way to work out an arrangement that allows oneself as well as one's opponent to adjust. . . . Through mutual adjustment and mutual accommodation we reshape the situation into a harmonious one."[47] Hence, contemporary defenders of the ideal of *tianxia* repeatedly draw on the ideal of harmony to argue for respect of different cultures and value systems.[48]

But respect for different cultures does not mean equal respect for all cultures. Just as Christians think that Christian values are superior to other religions values and liberals believe that liberal values are superior to other political values, so Confucians believe that Confucian values are superior to non-Confucian values. Societies that value meritocracy, harmony, and other Confucian values such as ritual are superior to those that do not. The early Confucians recognized that the Spring and Autumn and Warring

States Periods had different kinds of states, but they differentiated between peoples on the basis of level of cultural development, meaning commitment to Confucian culture, rather than ethnicity or territory. The term "China" referred to a cultural entity bound by Confucian culture, and in principle it was open to anybody who partook of those norms, regardless of race or ethnicity. Those who did not partake of Confucian culture were considered to be "barbarians," but everyone in principle could be "civilized."[49]

What are the implications for China? On the one hand, Confucianism can serve as the moral basis for a critique of ethnic-based notions of nationalism and citizenship. Certainly, the reality has often deviated from the ideal. Han Chinese racism was far from uncommon in imperial Chinese history.[50] In the early twentieth century, the Confucian reformer Kang Youwei (1858–1927) selectively appropriated Western racial categories and created a taxonomy of hierarchical races according to "white," "yellow," "red," and "black" skin colors, with the former two as superior to the latter two.[51] Today, however, Confucian intellectuals in China no longer use such racial or ethnic categories. John Makeham argues that "cultural nationalism"—the conviction that the unique culture associated with the nation constitutes the basis of national identity—is shared by a wide spectrum of participants in the contemporary Chinese discourse on Confucianism.[52] But (re-)Confucianizing China—meaning the building of a national identity centered on commitment to Confucian values—does not rule out the possibility that non-Chinese (people who are not ethnically Han, or do not have Chinese citizenship, or both) cannot be Confucians. Tu Wei-ming, the most prominent Confucian in the English-speaking world, even argues that Confucianism must take root outside of China before it can be promoted successfully within China: "Whether Confucianism [will have] vitality in the [remaining period of the] twentieth century will principally be determined by whether it is able to make its way fully back to China via New York, Paris, Tokyo. . . . It must confront the challenges of American culture, European culture, and East Asian culture (i.e., industrial East Asia), and furthermore sow seeds and take root in these cultures."[53] Jiang Qing, the most prominent political Confucian in mainland China, argues that Confucian values cannot accommodate central Western values, but he also rejects racialist and ethnic forms of nationalism. The only relevant criterion for admittance to the "Confucian nation" is commitment to Confucian values.[54]

Still, there may be a worry that Confucianism's confidence in its values could translate in "civilizing missions" outside the "Confucian" nation, similar to John Stuart Mill's justification for British imperialism in India on the grounds that the "barbarians" were insufficiently rational to govern themselves.[55] But Confucians argue for the use of "soft power"—moral example, ritual, and persuasion—to bring the "non-Confucians" into the fold. It is true that the practice has often deviated from the ideal. The Ming dynasty's strategy against the Mongols, for example, "placed a high degree of value on the use of pure violence to solve conflicts."[56] But Jiang Shidong, who teaches law at Beijing University, argues that Confucian political values have also underpinned relatively humane ways of dealing with cultural conflict. He argues that the "one country, two systems" formula for Hong Kong is rooted in Confucian values such as *tianxia* that justify a "hands-off" approach for the rule of outlying territories.[57] The model was implemented in Tibet during the Qing dynasty and in the early days of Mao's rule, and Jiang suggests that the same model can be used to govern Tibet in the future.[58]

The ideal of *tianxia*, however, suggests that China should concern itself not just with cultural groups within the country and neighboring jurisdictions, but also with the question of how to promote its political values to the rest of the world. If Confucians rule out force (except in cases of just war; see note 24), then other mechanisms are available. U.S.-based nongovernment offices (NGOs) such as Freedom House rank countries according to their adherence to political freedoms, the implication being that other countries should conform to the ideals espoused in the U.S. Constitution. China, in contrast, can promote the ideal of harmony. It is perhaps best promoted via NGOs because official support is likely to arouse political suspicion. Hence, one might imagine an NGO—for example, Harmony House—that relies on rigorous empirical methods to determine the extent of harmony in the world. Countries could be ranked according to a "social harmony index" that measures rates of crime and incarceration, gaps between rich and poor, and success in dealing with cultural conflict peacefully. Countries that do well on the index could be a model for other countries.[59]

Conclusion

In sum, I have drawn on the works of contemporary Chinese political thinkers to review some of the practical and institutional implications of a Chinese foreign policy that would be inspired by *tianxia* and related Confucian political values. This is not to imply, however, that we need to stick to a Confucian framework when thinking about a morally justified approach to Chinese foreign policy. Nor do I mean to deny that freedom, democracy, and human rights have a place in China's future. But a Confucian moral framework might be most psychologically compelling in a Chinese context and hence might have more causal power than other frameworks. From a normative standpoint, my own view is that a Confucian-inspired foreign policy is both realistic and humane and can improve on some of the drawbacks of liberal and Marxist approaches to the topic. But the reader will no doubt disagree, and I look forward to the criticisms.

Notes

Author's note: I am grateful for written comments by Kristin Stapleton, Tze-ki Hon, and Ban Wang, as well as for comments from participants at the University at Buffalo's conference on New Confucianism, April 27–28, 2012, and the *Tianxia* workshop at Stanford University, May 6–11, 2011. I am also grateful for helpful emails and articles from Yuri Pines and Justin Tiwald.

    1. Li Yangfan 李扬帆, "《天下》观念" *("Tianxia" guannian)* [On the concept of *"Tianxia"*], 《国际政治研究》 *(Guoji zhengzhi yanjiu)* [Research in international politics] 1 (2002), 113–114.

    2. To be more precise, the idea of the state with fixed territorial boundaries was central to "Western" political culture in ancient Greece and since the 1648 Treaty of Westphalia. One could argue that the Roman sense of territory was no stricter than in Han or Tang's China. I thank Qian Jiang for this point.

    3. This may oversimplify imperial Chinese history. As early as the Song dynasty, there were values and practices that anticipated modern-day concerns with sovereignty. The Chinese empire was subject to repeated invasions from outside and boundaries became more rigid and fortified, outsiders were portrayed more negatively, wars were justified in terms of the protection of territory, and Confucian intellectuals penned novels and historical works and defended rituals that justified "patriotic" attachment to China (as opposed to *tianxia*). See Ge Zhaozhao 葛兆兆, "*Songdai (Zhongguo)—Yishi de tuxian—Guanyu jin shi minzuzhuyi sixiang de yi ge yuanyuan*" 宋代《中国》意识的凸显—关于近世民族主义思想的一个远源 [The prominence of "China" consciousness in the Song dynasty: A distant source of nationalist thought in modern times], *Wen shi zhe* 文史哲 (Journal of history, literature, and philosophy), no. 1 (2004): 5–12.

    4. Allen Carlson, "Reimagining the Frontier: Patterns of Sinicization and the Emergence of New Thinking about China's Territorial Periphery" (paper presented at the Civilizations and Sinicization Workshop, Beijing University, Mar. 25–26, 2011), 3–4.

    5. Quoted in Luo Zhitian, "From '*Tianxia*' (all-under-heaven) to 'the world': Changes in the Late Qing Intellectuals' Conceptions of Human Society," *Social Sciences in China* 29, no. 2 (May 2008): 96. Liang gradually came round to take a more positive view of the world thinking implied in *tianxia*. After World War I, he argued that political rulers should not only be concerned with making their own nation strong and prosperous, but they should also be concerned with the fate of the world. Liang explicitly criticized Western nationalism for being too narrow, and he argued that the West should learn from the traditional Chinese idea of *tianxia* to expand concern beyond then nation (Chen Zehuan, "Individuals, Nation States, and

the World: A Study of Liang Qichao's Views on Human Rights" (paper presented at the Chinese Academy of Social Sciences [CASS], Beijing, 2010).

6. China's participation in the Bandung conference in 1955 and Zhou Enlai's efforts to establish friendly ties with newly independent states in Asia and Africa that were strongly interested in a strict view of sovereignty is another factor. (I thank Kristin Stapleton for this point.)

7. Taylor Travel, "Regime Insecurity and International Cooperation: Explaining China's Compromises in Territorial Disputes," *International Security* 2, no. 30 (Fall 2005): 46.

8. Bates Gill and Yanzhong Huang, "Sources and Limits of China's Soft Power," *Survival* (Summer 2006): 22.

9. Yan Xuetong, "How Assertive Should a Power Be?," *New York Times*, Mar. 31, 2011.

10. Allen Carlson, "Moving beyond Sovereignty? A Brief Consideration of Recent Changes in China's Approach to International Order and the Emergence of the *Tianxia* Concept," *Journal of Contemporary China* 20, no. 68 (2011), 96.

11. Li Yangfan 李扬帆, "'*Tianxia*' guannian" 天下观念 [On the concept of "*Tianxia*"], 《国际政治研究》 *Research in International Politics*, no. 1 (2002): 107, 111.

12. Yuri Pines, "Changing Views of *Tianxia* in Pre-Imperial Discourse," *Oriens Extremus* 43 (2002): 1/2, 105–106 (http://www.oriens-extremus.de/inhalt/pdf/43/OE43–09.pdf).

13. Ibid, 108.

14. Li Fang 李方, "Shilun Tangchao de 'Zhongguo' yu '*Tianxia*'" 试论唐朝的"中国与"天下 [An analysis of "China" and "*tianxia*" in the Tang dynasty]," *Zhongguo bianjiang shi di yanjiu* 中国边疆史地研究 (Research on the history and geography of China's borderlands) 17, no. 2 (June 2007).

15. Liu Junping 刘军平, "*Tianxia*" yuzhouguan de yanbian yu qi zhexue yiyun "天下"宇宙观的演变及其哲学意蕴 (The development and philosophical meaning of the cosmological concept of "*tianxia*"), *Wen shi zhe* 文史哲 (Journal of literature, history, and philosophy), no. 6 (2004): 101–107, serial no. 285.

16. The phrase "天下兴亡，匹夫有责" (adapted from Gu Yanwu's original formulation: 保天下者，匹夫之贱与有责焉耳) is known to most high school students in China but it is used almost interchangeably with "heaven" or "state" at the front. The critical import of Yan's phrase is lost because either way the phrase is taken to mean that ordinary citizens should serve and care about the well-being of the state.

17. Gan Chunsong 干春松, *Rujia gailun* 儒学概论 [An introduction to Confucian studies] (*Beijing: Zhongguo renmin daxue chubanshe*, 2009), 250.

18. For Zhao's latest formulation, see Zhao Tingyang, "All-under-Heaven and Methodological Relationism: An Old Story and New World Peace," in *Contemporary Chinese Political Thought: Debates and Perspectives (Chinese Political Thought Today: Debates and Perspectives)*, edited by Fred Dallmayr and Zhao Tingyang (Lexington: University of Kentucky Press, 2012), 46–66.

19. This ideal also influenced Sun Yat-sen and a youthful Mao Zedong; see my book *China's New Confucianism: Politics and Everyday Life in a Changing Society*, new ed. (Princeton, NJ: Princeton University Press, 2010), 23–24.

20. Zhao, "All-under-Heaven and Methodological Relationism," 79.

21. Joseph Chan, "Territorial Boundaries and Confucianism," in *Boundaries, Ownership, and Autonomy*, edited by David Miller and Sohail H. Hashmi (Princeton, NJ: Princeton University Press, 2001), 81

22. In principle, that community need not be the nation. The nation has emerged as the main source of political identity in the modern world, but things can always change in the future, e.g., cities can become a more important source of political identity. See Daniel A. Bell and Avner de-Shalit, *The Spirit of Cities: Why the Identity of a City Matters in a Global Age*, new ed. (Princeton, NJ: Princeton University Press, 2013).

23. I use this term loosely. For example, Yan Xuetong draws on a wide-range of pre-Qin thinkers including non-Confucians (Yan, *Ancient Chinese Thought, Modern Chinese Power*, edited by Daniel A. Bell and Sun Zhe, translated by Edmund Ryden [Princeton, NJ: Princeton University Press, 2011]), but in this chapter I draw on his interpretation of Xunzi, who can (controversially) be labeled a Confucian.

24. Another key Confucian political value is the idea that tyrants should be punished, but I have drawn implications for debates about just and unjust war in my books *Beyond Liberal Democracy* (chap. 2) and *China's New Confucianism* (chap. 2) and will not repeat myself here. See also Luke Glanville, "Retaining the Mandate of Heaven: Sovereign Accountability in Ancient China," *Millennium* 39, no. 2 (2010): 323–343.

25. William A. Callahan, "Chinese Visions of World Order: Post-Hegemonic or a New Hegemony?," *International Studies Review* 10 (2008): 749–761.

26. See, Zhao Tingyang, "All-under-Heaven and Methodological Relationism: An Old Story and New World Peace," in *Contemporary Chinese Political Thought: Debates and Perspectives*, 73–74.

27. Zhang Feng, "The *Tianxia* System: World Order in a Chinese Utopia," *Chinese Heritage Quarterly* 21 (Mar. 2010).

28. Xunzi was not typically viewed as a Confucian thinker in imperial Chinese history because he began with the assumption that human nature is bad, in contrast to the official Mencian view (from the Song onward) that human nature is good. In my view, however, the starting point does not make much difference because Xunzi allowed for the possibility of moral transformation via the use of ritual and his core moral concerns fit in the Confucian tradition (see my *China's New Confucianism*, chap. 3).

29. Yan, *Ancient Chinese Thought, Modern Chinese Power*, 104–105.

30. Ibid., 16–17.

31. Ibid., 106–107.

32. Carlson, "Moving Beyond Sovereignty?," 101–102.

33. Yan, *Ancient Chinese Thought, Modern Chinese Power*, 104.

34. Zhang Feng, "Rethinking the 'Tribute System': Broadening the Conception Horizon of Historical East Asian Politics," *Chinese Journal of International Politics*, 2 (2009): 545–574.

35. Zhuang Guotu 庄国土, "Luelun chaogong zhidu de xuhuan: Yi gudai zhongguo yu dongya de chaogong guanxi yi li" 略论朝贡制度的虚幻: 以古代中国与东南亚的朝贡关系为例 [An account of the unreality of the tributary system: An example of the relationships in tributary system in ancient China and East Asia]," 南洋问题研究 *Nanyang wenti yanjiu* [Research on problems in Nanyang], 3 (2005): 1–8.

36. Yan, *Ancient Chinese Thought, Modern Chinese Power*, 99.

37. Ibid., 17. For a detailed account of what "humane authority" (王道) means for domestic constitutional reform, see Jiang Qing, *A Confucian Constitutional Order: How China's Past Can Shape Its Political Future*, translated by Edmund Ryden, edited by Daniel A. Bell and Fan Ruiping (Princeton, NJ: Princeton University Press, 2012). Jiang argues that democracy is only one of three sources of political legitimacy (the others being heaven 天 and earth 地) and on that basis he defend a tricameral legislature, with each legislature expressing a different source of legitimacy.

38. Karl Marx did not spell out what he meant by higher communism in any detail, but his last major work, *Critique of the Gotha Program*, provides a brief outline of his vision.

39. See, e.g., Michael Doyle, "Kant, Liberal Legacies and Foreign Affairs," *Philosophy and Public Affairs*, I and II, 12 (1983): 205–235, 323–353.

40. While Confucians do agree that those in public office should have superior qualities, there is much less agreement about whether and how to enshrine this ideal in standards for office. For contrasting views, see Kim Sungmoon's *Confucian Democracy in East Asia: Theory and Practice* (Cambridge, UK: Cambridge University Press, 2014) and my *The China Model: Political Meritocracy and the Limits of Democracy* (Princeton, NJ: Princeton University Press, 2015).

41. Liu Junping 刘军平, "*Tianxia*" *yuzhouguan de yanbian yu qi zhexue yiyun*, 102.

42. Zhao Tingyang, "Rethinking Empire from a Chinese Concept 'All-under-Heaven' (*tianxia*)," *Social Identities*, 12, no. 1 (2006): 32.

43. In a similar vein, Zhao Tingyang advocates the freedom of migration on (at least partly) meritocratic grounds, noting that "most of the famous ministers, generals and think tankers in states, for instance in the later period of the Zhou dynasty, were foreigners from other states, never accused as traitors. Traveling far and wide, Confucius was one of those who tried their fortune in other states" ("All-under-Heaven and Methodological Relationism," 74).

44. I've drawn here on my introduction to Yan's book *Ancient Chinese Thought, Modern Chinese Power*, 13–15.

45. For similar ideas, see Jiang Qing, *Shenming xinyang yu wangdao zhengzhi: Rujia wenhua de xiandai jiazhi* 生命信仰与王道政治:儒家文化的现代价值 [A faith in life and the kingly way of politics: The modern value of Confucian culture] (Taipei: Yang Zheng Tang, 2004); Tongdong Bai, "A Mencian Version of

Limited Democracy," *Res Publica* 14, no. 1 (2008), 19–34; Joseph Chan, "Democracy and Meritocracy: Toward a Confucian Perspective," *Journal of Chinese Philosophy* 34 no. 2 (June 2007): 179–193; Li Chenyang, "Where Does Virtuous Leadership Stand?," *Philosophy East and West*, 59 no. 4 (2009): 531–536; and my *Beyond Liberal Democracy* (chap. 6) and *China's New Confucianism* (chap.1).

46. Such efforts are already taking place on an ad hoc basis: for example, several government officials from Africa, Latin America, and South Asia are training at the China National School of Administration (国家行政学院) in Beijing. South Africa's President Jacob Zuma has praised China's relatively meritocratic system of selecting and training cadres. As the African National Congress transforms itself from a revolutionary movement to a modern party that is responsible for running a state, it can learn from the experience of the CCP, which has gone from rewarding "red" (commitment to the revolution) to rewarding expertise and talent (again, I do not mean to imply that the Chinese political system is as meritocratic as it should be; the reality is that factors such as *guanxi* and loyalty to leaders influence political promotion more than they should). In Ukraine, the Meritocratic Party stands for "meritocracy as a basic principle for effective functioning of society, politics, and government" (http://www.linkedin.com/company/meritocratic-party-of-ukraine) and here too the Chinese experience of economic development under the guidance of meritocratically selected cadres may be helpful.

47. Li Chenyang, "The Confucian Ideal of Harmony," *Philosophy East and West* 56, no. 4 (Oct. 2006): 583–603.

48. See, e.g., Wang Dasan 王达三, "Rujia *tianxia* guannian yu shijie chengxu zhongjian 儒家天下观念与世界秩序重建 [The Confucian concept of *Tianxia* and the construction of the global order]," http://vpapers.cn/rujia/137; 5, 8–10, 12–13; Liu Junping 刘军平, "*Tianxia*" yuzhouguan de yanbian yu qi zhexue yiyun," 102; Mou Zhongjian 牟钟鉴, *She tianxia yi jia haishi ruorouqiangshi*" 是天下一家还是弱肉强食—儒学天下观的当代意义? ([Is it *tianxia* or the strong prey on the weak?], 本刊特稿 *Benkan tegao* [Special issue of Benkan] 1 (2007): 2.

49. Gan Chunsong 干春松, "Wangzhi wuwai yu yixia zhi fang: Gongyang san shi shuo yu yixia guannian de chongtu yu xietiao" 王者无外 与 夷夏之防: 公羊三世说与夷夏观念的冲突与协调 [The kingly way without outsiders and protection against barbarians: The conflict and compromise between the Gongyang shishuo and the concept of barbarians], paper presented at People's University, Beijing, Oct. 24, 2010, 9.

50. Frank Dikotter, *The Discourse of Race in Modern China* (Hong Kong: Hurst, 1992).

51. http://science.jrank.org/pages/10955/Race-Racism-in-Asia-Race-Racism-in-China.html.

52. John Makeham, *Lost Soul: "Confucianism" in Contemporary Chinese Academic Discourse* (Cambridge, MA: Harvard University Asia Center, 2008), 9.

53. Quoted in ibid., 36.

54. Let me support this point with an anecdote. A couple of years ago, I visited the Confucian temple in Beijing with Jiang Qing and about fifteen young

Confucian scholars. We made our way to the main hall to bow to the statue of Confucius and Jiang was asked to lead the ritual. One of the young scholars questioned whether I was supposed to join the ceremony. Jiang forcefully objected to the ethnic nationalism underpinning the question. Confucianism, he said, is for *"tianxia."* I joined the ritual.

55. See, e.g., John Stuart Mill, "Considerations on Representative Government," chap. 4.

56. Alasdair Ian Johnston, *Cultural Realism: Strategic Culture and Grand Strategy in Chinese History* (Princeton, NJ: Princeton University Press, 1995), xi. Zhangd Feng, however, argues that the Chinese state during the same period relied more on moral power vis-à-vis the Japanese and (especially) the Koreans (Zhang Feng, "Regionalization in the *Tianxia*: Continuity and Change in China's Foreign Policy," paper presented at the China-West Intellectual Summit, Paris, Feb. 23–24, 2009).

57. The gap between the ideal of a "hands-off" system and the political reality in Hong Kong seems to have widened of late (see, e.g., Lian Yi-Zheng, "Hong Kong's Missing Booksellers," *New York Times*, Jan. 20, 2016).

58. Jiang Shigong, *Zhongguo Xianggang: Wenhua yu zhengzhi de shiye* [China's Hong Kong: The establishment of culture and institutions] (Hong Kong: Oxford University Press, 2008), 112–121, 149–158. But for a critique of Jiang's view, see Chen Guanzhong 陳冠中, "Zhongguo tianchaozhuyi yu xianggang" 中國天朝主義與香港 [China's tributary system and Hong Kong], *Xianggang: Dushi xiangxiang yu wenhua jiyi guoji xueshu yantaohui* 香港: 都市想像與文化記憶國際學術研討會, paper from the Imagining the City and Cultural Memory International Academic Symposium, Hong Kong, Dec. 17, 2011.

59. For a preliminary effort to construct such an index, see Daniel A. Bell and Yingchuan Mo, "Harmony in the World 2013: The Ideal and the Reality," *Social Indicators Research* 118, no. 2 (Sept. 2014): 797–818.

4

Confucianism to Save the World

Tongdong Bai

Which Confucianism?

In contrast to the exuberance in the 1990s when Francis Fukuyama's declaration that "history ends with liberal democracy" was in the air, recent crises both financial and political make some wonder whether the model of liberal democracy plus market economy has failed, and a new model needs to be developed to save the world. This chapter outlines why and how Confucianism can do this job. First, however, I want to be clear about my use of the Confucian model and Confucianism.

As an armchair philosopher, by offering a Confucian model to the world, I do not mean to describe how historically Confucianism has saved the world, and what I argue in this chapter should be clearly distinguished from the various proposals of the China models—that is, China offers different political and economic models to development that are superior to those Western countries offer or prescribe. Indeed, financial and political failures in the United States and in Europe, and China's relative immunity to these crises have given much credibility to those who argue for the China models as an alternative to liberal democracy and free markets. Not being an expert on economic matters, I cannot pass reasonable judgments one way or the other on whether there are indeed China models of economic development (I doubt that many who advocate such models have this expertise). Even if there were such models, I doubt that features in these models (such as strong state control of the economy) would find approval among Confucians. Claiming that China now is still a Confucian state, after so many years of radical "modernization," is also dubious. Besides, tying the merit of a philosophical model to the fate of a particular economy is dangerous. If the merit of a Confucian model is connected hand-in-hand with a rising China, the former will be spoiled if China experiences an economic downfall. Thus, I focus on what ought to be a Confucian ideal political model and why this model will be a better alternative to the regimes available today.[1]

Before introducing this model, I need to explain my understanding of Confucianism. Among those who are devoted to reviving traditional Chinese thoughts, one group, including thinkers such as Jiang Qing (蒋庆),[2] maintains that Western liberal democracy is rooted in Western culture—Christianity in particular—while the dominant Chinese culture is rooted in Confucianism (understood as a state religion), meaning that China cannot adopt Western political regimes in general and liberal democracy in particular. But this argument has a few problems. First, whether Confucianism was *the* state ideology in traditional China is debatable, in spite of the famous claim of "respecting Confucianism only" (独尊儒术), *allegedly* a proposal the Han Confucian Dong Zhongshu (董仲舒) made and Emperor Wu (汉武帝) (around 134 BCE) accepted and dictated. Even if it were, what form of Confucianism—Confucianism is a broad concept with many different and even opposing schools—was taken as the state ideology is another controversial question. Whether Confucianism as Jiang Qing understands it, as a state religion interpreted through a particular *gongyang* (公羊) reading of the Classics, has ever been a mainstream ideology is questionable. And, after more than one hundred years of vicious attacks on it, how much of the Confucian tradition remains relevant is yet another controversial issue.

Second, even if (some form of) Confucianism still were or could be reinstituted to be the dominant culture of China, the above argument of the incompatibility between Confucianism and Western political regimes has additional problems. The aforementioned incompatibility argument claims that the Chinese people and the Western peoples have different cultures, and different regimes are good for peoples of different cultures. This argument is based on a culture-specific, culture-relativistic, and even postmodernist view of Confucianism and Western regimes. Also based on this view is the idea that Chinese thoughts are so peculiar that any attempt to understand and interpret them with (Western) philosophical terminology is doomed to be misleading, and they can only be understood by the Chinese, or by using traditional Chinese vocabularies. Ironically, though, this culture-specific understanding is shared by many who are highly critical of Confucianism. For example, the May Fourth radicals also held the incompatibility view, and in order to embrace Western democracy and science they advocated uprooting Confucianism and adopting Western culture. Those who think that Confucianism is too deep-rooted to be uprooted then advocate a view of the clash of civilizations. Of course, the latter two groups may hold only a culture-specific view vis-à-vis Confucianism, while believing Western regimes and culture are universal. The fact that the aforementioned pro-Confucianism conservatives and the anti-Confucianism radicals share the same culture-specific view of Confucianism actually reveals a problem with the former.[3] This view is a betrayal of the view of early Confucians that Confucianism is universal, applicable to all those who are *hua xia* (华夏)—a term now often associated with those who are ethnically Chinese, but that originally referred to the civilized people[4]—and even to the uncivilized barbarians.[5] Only when China was under siege by Western powers in the early twentieth century did Chinese intellectuals start adopting the culture-specific view of Confucianism. That some cultural conservatives or "Confucian fundamentalists" should adopt this view of Confucianism is ironic. Based on this view, the defense of a Confucian regime this group of thinkers often offers is that it is good because it is Confucian, which obviously lacks any power of persuasion to those who are not believers in (their brand of) Confucianism. Their objection to Western regimes—since they are Western, they cannot be applicable to us—is equally problematic. Just because liberal democracy was first developed in the West does not mean that it is not applicable to China. China has adopted many things that are not originally indigenous.

Another group of Confucian promoters, New Confucians (新儒家) such as Mou Zongsan and his followers, seems to believe in the universality of Confucianism. But for them, Confucianism is a moral metaphysics. They often ignore or even find distasteful the political aspect of Confucianism.[6] In this regard, they are quite close to the May Fourth radicals, differing only from the radicals on whether Confucianism can be made compatible with liberal democracy. Mou Zongsan (牟宗三) shows this compatibility by reading Kantianism into Confucianism. In other words, Confucianism can only become universal by turning itself into a Western philosophy. This is an implicit acknowledgement of the universality of Western values and an implicit denial of the universality of an "unmassaged" version of Confucianism. What New Confucians "massage out" is the political dimension of Confucianism.[7] Interestingly, Yu Dan (于丹), a television personality who has made the *Analects* popular among average Chinese viewers, also champions this depoliticized version of Confucianism, offering what many dub "chicken soup for the soul." She does it probably out of the desire to appeal both to the viewers and to the government, which may worry about the political aspect of Confucianism. The New Confucians, as well as many anti-Confucian liberal intellectuals (both in China and elsewhere), however, look away from and look down on the political aspect of Confucianism because they view it as representing "feudalistic authoritarianism" (封建专制), a common label for traditional Chinese politics.

But this characterization of traditional Chinese politics—and the role of Confucianism in it—is seriously mistaken. The term "feudalistic authoritarianism" itself is self-contradictory. A key feature of feudalism in the Chinese context (if not also in the European context), as practiced during the Western Zhou regime, is that the central authority appointed local rulers as its delegates, allowing political autonomy to a very great degree.[8] This poses a sharp contrast to authoritarianism, a key feature of which is a comprehensive and all-powerful central authority.

As we know, Confucianism emerged when the Western Zhou regime collapsed. A pressing issue of that time was to find a new regime able to address a newly emerging political reality. Confucianism should be then understood first and foremost as a political philosophy. Moreover, as I have argued elsewhere, the political transition from the Western Zhou to the Qin dynasty resembles the European early modernity (before the industrial revolutions) in many respects. In this sense, not only is Confucianism chiefly a political philosophy, but it is a modern political philosophy.[9] That is, Confucianism as a political philosophy is not outdated, as New Confucians and many others believe, but is still relevant to us moderns.

What eventually emerged from the ruins of feudal regimes in China was the *junxian* (郡县) system, in which the central government had authority all the way down to the county level in that, from the county magistrate up, the central government had to appoint all officials. This regime dominated traditional China since the Qin dynasty, and the power concentrated in the position of the emperor makes characterize the system as authoritarianism appropriate. Early Confucians were no supporters of a hereditary emperorship, but of the rule of the wise and virtuous. Some of them tried to abolish hereditary emperorship in the early Han, but their proposals were marginalized and even disappeared after Wang Mang's (王莽) disastrous rule, the beginning of which was inspired, sincerely or as an excuse, by the Confucian idea that a ruler should be based on Confucian merits and not on pedigree. Then, some Confucians tried to check the power of the emperor by taking control of the education of the crown prince by advocating for an administration consisting of Confucian scholar-officials and by assigning responsibility for running affairs below the county level to Confucian scholars and Confucian gentry. Whether these institutions were effective in checking the power of the emperor is debatable, but we can clearly see labeling traditional Chinese regimes simply as authoritarian and considering Confucians minions and enablers of authoritarianism is plainly wrong.

Moreover, to understand Confucianism as a comprehensive doctrine of moral metaphysics not only fails to capture the mainstream of Confucianism (this understanding catches a dominant branch or aspect of Neo-Confucianism at best), but also fails to deal effectively with pluralism in the modern world. We only need to be reminded of how fiercely Neo-Confucians fought against each other across the centuries from Song to Qing times in order to realize the impossibility for all-under-heaven to adopt one moral metaphysical doctrine.

The above challenge to the understanding of Confucianism as primarily a moral metaphysics does not mean that in order to be universal Confucianism should not have anything to do with moral and ethical issues, but it means that we need to see how "thick" its moral dimension is.[10] For example, claiming that by nature we are good is controversial, but claiming that it is possible not only for us to be compassionate but also necessary that we be compassionate for a good society is far less controversial. Additionally, Confucians value family. But instead of insisting on a particular metaphysical foundation for this value, a Confucian can persuade many people by making the following arguments. The stability and harmony of a state is an important good, and a state consists of families.[11] Therefore, to maintain and promote certain family relationships (such as what can offer children materially and emotionally stable environments) is an important good. Moreover, if we agree that a good society needs people who care about others, and the family is a natural ground for cultivating this care ("you should leave this cookie for your baby sister"; "you should let grandma sleep in the warm room on such a cold winter night"), we can see the significance of Confucians' emphasis on family and filial piety.

In short, a Confucianism that is built on a "thin" moral conception and centers on the political is both faithful to the root of Confucianism and has the potential to be universal. This is the Confucianism that I am advocating.

How Can Political Confucianism Save the World?

What can this brand of Confucianism offer to the world other than a thin family ethics? As mentioned earlier, many still believe that the history of humanity's struggle for a just society ends with liberal democracy. Even if history did end with liberal democracy, what is the meaning of the latter? Many identify it as one person, one vote. But that simple formulation obscures the fact that liberal democracy also includes constitutionalism, rule of law, protection of basic liberties and rights, and so forth. In fact, these features are some of the most desirable aspects of liberal democracy. Confucians can endorse them, although they may have different readings of them. For example, Confucians would not consider freedom of speech a sacred right that is not subject to any higher good. But Confucians do consider good governance a good, and if freedom of speech is necessary for good governance, Confucians can endorse it as a good secondary to the higher good of good governance. Confucians also emphasize the rule of virtue, but they can endorse the rule of law as a fallback mechanism when the rule of virtue fails. Indeed, to emphasize the practical benefits of the rule of law and civil liberties can be more persuasive to many than a sanctimonious assertion of the sacredness of laws and liberties. To an ordinary citizen, which argument is more persuasive: "the rule of law is sacred, and we human beings have inborn rights," or "to have the rule of law means that you won't be punished simply because you complain to a governmental agency, a journalist, or on the internet, or take a peaceful action against the political or commercial infringement on the interests of your community?" Even powerful officials who know they will not stay in power forever and who do not possess a gambler's mentality would consider yielding part of their power to the law a reasonable compromise because although they would lose some of the arbitrary power they enjoy, the rule of law will protect them from the abuse of powerful people in the future when they step down or lose influence. Constitutionalism, rule of law, and (certain) civil liberties, rather than a particular mechanism for political representation, may be the true universal values of liberal democracy.[12]

What is often considered the core of liberal democracy, the institution of one person, one vote, however, is perhaps the most problematic part. I have discussed this issue and its solution elsewhere,[13] so the following is merely a summary of my views on this issue. The public's lack of sound political judgment is clearly shown in far too many incidents. The most recent striking example is the world financial crisis of 2008 in which the irrational actions of ordinary people played an important role. Such incidents and the search for their underlying causes lead many to doubt a basic premise behind one person, one vote: voters are rational (and moral in a minimum sense). Many thinkers acknowledge this problem and have tried to correct the wrongs from within. They believe the factors that lead to the apathy of average voters are, for example, the lack of economic equality, the failure of the educational system, the influence of money in politics, and so on. But if they are mistaken (and I think they are), then their "internal" solutions will not be sufficient. Does this mean that we should abolish one person, one vote completely? Certainly letting a small circle of the allegedly wise and virtuous make all the political decisions is politically dangerous and harmful. The solution seems to lie, then, in some form of hybrid regime that combines the democratic element with a meritocratic element. This regime is precisely the ideal regime for Confucians such as Mencius. For him, a government should be of the people and for the people, and he argued that a key to good governance is receptivity to the popular will. But he also saw the limitations of the popular will and the discrepancy between the popular will and the true will of the populace (i.e., what people would truly want if they could see the situation clearly). Therefore, he believed that an ideal government cannot be "by the people" if we wish to realize people's true will (Rousseau's general will?). Rather, the wise and the virtuous have to play a significant role in political decision making. Putting Mencius's two considerations together, then, we can imagine that he would support the kind of hybrid regime mentioned earlier. This regime becomes ever more relevant to addressing problems in today's states in which political affairs are too complicated due to the size of each state and the interconnectedness of the world, to be grasped by the masses, who under the present economic reality have to work to make a living and are thus too busy to devote themselves fully to politics the way the ancient Greeks and Romans did during the republican eras. If we understand the emergence of democracy in the West as a reaction to the nobles' abuse of power, we should see that now we are moving toward the other extreme, in which an uninformed populace that lacks a minimum sense of morality—the kind of morality even liberal thinkers such as John Rawls consider essential to a real democracy—has too much power in politics. This means that we now need to establish more checks and balances against the power of the people. Confucians are advocating precisely a hybrid regime that establishes checks and balances between the meritocrats and the common people, and their experiences of checking the power of the emperor can be a good guide for our attempts to tame the populace. Therefore, both Confucian political philosophy and Confucian political practices in traditional China are still relevant to today's world.

In short, the Confucian domestic political model embraces liberties and the rule of law (with a different interpretation and understanding of them than is found in liberal political theory) and checks the popular participation in politics. On the basis of constitutionalism and the rule of law, the Confucian ideal regime adopts a hybrid legislature, for example, through a bicameral legislature in which members of the lower house are democratically elected to represent the popular will and members of the upper house are meritocrats selected through various mechanisms.[14] At the same time, in this regime, a thin version of Confucian ethics is promoted, which is both the foundation of and supplement to the rule of law. This regime is not only what a developing country should pursue, but also a cure to the disease of populism in Western democracies.

Another cause of the turmoil and potential dangers in the world is the nation-state model that was developed from the sovereign-state model, which had its beginning in Europe in the Westphalian treaties.[15] This model has had its positive role in enabling citizens within a state by, for example, promoting solidarity among all its nationals (citizens of the same nation) and the care between each other, especially between the ruling class and the ruled, through the belief in their shared nationality. Increasingly, however we see the problematic consequences of this model: domestically, absolute state sovereignty leads to the suppression and even eradication of powerless people by the powerful with no possibility of outside intervention and, internationally, it leads to *realpolitik* in interstate relations, according to which might makes right.

With regard to China, in the past one hundred years or more, the mainstream view within China is that modernization means adopting the nation-state model. As a result, domestically the Chinese communist government has *created* fifty-six ethnicities[16] and reinforced them by various policies, such as allowing those who are not ethnically Han Chinese to enjoy preferential policies for college admission and family size; internationally, due to the lack of an alternative model of international relations, many worry about the rise of China, convinced that China will be assertive with regard to its national interests and thus violently disrupt the present balance of powers. Some people, such as Henry Kissinger, who are better informed about the history of traditional China, have argued that China will adopt an alternative model based on the traditional tributary system in which China is the middle kingdom, the center of the world, and can only tolerate other states if they accept a tributary relationship.

Clearly, the peace and the prosperity of the world are in danger if China is striving for the tributary system. But these people forget that, at the origin, Confucians were facing a world of competing independent and de facto sovereign states, which is comparable to today's world of nations. Each state in this era desperately needed to discover a new social glue that could hold it together and find a new model of international relations because the old system under the Western Zhou regime had stopped working. The glue Confucians offered is not that of the European nation-state, which uses imagined national identity to attach the people to it, but is based on humanity (*ren* 仁) and compassion, as well as the distinction between the civilized and uncivilized worlds. This is a key to the phenomenon of continuity in traditional China. Although nomadic tribes invaded and conquered China many times, China remained China because these invaders, if they stayed long enough, eventually adopted the Chinese culture (even as they contributed to it and transformed it to some extent) and became Chinese themselves. Internationally, the Confucian model is "if people from a different state are un-submissive and even pose a potential threat, we should improve our civilization and moral character to attract them" (see 16.1 of the *Analects*). That is, Confucians would support an open (but regulated) border that allows people to vote with their feet, which is more humane than the immigration policies of most developed countries today.[17] Likewise, they support a peaceful expansion as Chinese culture is adopted in neighboring territories, a dynamic that is also far more humane than the expansion by force, which is a common strategy among nation-states.

But Confucians are not pacifists. Cautioning against a casual appeal to war as a solution to political problems, early Confucians nevertheless supported wars of humanitarian intervention. Humanity (*ren*), in particular, the concern with whether or not those who are affected by wars will be better off, is the supreme principle of both wars of humanitarian intervention and defense. Its motto might be expressed as "humanity overrides sovereignty." It may sound similar to the cosmopolitan idea of "human rights override sovereignty," but the Confucian concept of humanity is more sophisticated than human rights as understood in liberal theory and can thus lead to a more nuanced theory of just war. I cannot elaborate on this point in this short chapter.[18]

In general, the Confucian model of international relations that is based on its concept of humanity is clearly more humane than the *realpolitik* model, which is the model of international relations for nation-states. Moreover, the Confucian concepts of humanity and compassion require that each person take loving everything in the world as his or her goal, but also emphasize the gradation or hierarchy of love. For example, even when a Confucian sage achieves the ideal stage of being compassionate about everything, he or she will still love his or her mother (or whomever he or she feels closest to) more than a stranger. Following this Confucian idea of humanity that advocates universal but unequal care, we can justify a moderately preferential treatment of one's own national interests, although this preferential treatment does not allow for disregard of or intentional harm to the interests of other states and peoples.[19] This model is more realistic and more in line with humans' natural sentiment than the (extreme?) cosmopolitan model, which is built on notions of universal and equal love. As mentioned earlier, the Confucian model, because of the subtlety of the Confucian concept of humanity, is also more realistic than the idea of "human rights override sovereignty." Therefore, the Confucian model of national identity, international relations, and just war, developed in the turmoil of warring states after the collapse of the Western Zhou regime, is more idealistic than the nation-state model and more realistic than the cosmopolitan model.

Indeed, we can conceive of the world since European modernity as a rerun, albeit on a larger scale, of the Spring and Autumn and Warring States Periods (roughly 770 BCE to 222 BCE) in the history of China. Then, following the history of China, we can predict that in the future, a world government will emerge that has real power (in comparison to the U.N.), policing the world. Most likely it will be a national alliance rather than one strong state, in contrast to what happened in Chinese history (when China was the center of its known world). But whether it is Confucian and desirable depends on whether or not this alliance bases its rule and its policing on the principle of humanity. There is no guarantee, but the Confucians should fight for it. In this regard, they may find allies even among today's liberals, such as John Rawls, who envisions the well-ordered peoples enforcing the law of peoples,[20] although differences between Confucians and liberals still remain.

China as a Role Model?

How can the Confucian ideal regime become reality? Again, space constraints compel me merely to offer an outline of an answer to this question. To achieve the Confucian ideal, we need a role model, and naturally, people may think that China will be such a model. However, as mentioned, we Chinese have not cherished our own tradition and have even been actively antitradition for many years, denouncing and demolishing much of our heritage. Then, how much tradition is left in China? Without proper human relationships and without cultural heritage, even if China becomes rich and powerful, in what way can we Chinese call ourselves Chinese? No wonder many are fearful of the rise of China.

Witnessing the destruction of tradition and claiming that the Chinese are losing their soul, those who want to see China revive itself as China and not another faceless machine of a capitalistic nation-state, have been trying to promote the revival of traditional learning. But many take a "literal" or "fundamentalist" attitude in their revival effort, following rituals and codes of conduct "as they were." Whether what they are doing is really "as they were" is questionable, a problem haunting fundamentalist efforts. More importantly, although many doubt that Confucianism can adjust itself to a liberal democratic world, I do not think that this is a problem. Indeed, Confucianism can even contribute to the improvement of present regimes. The real problem, in my view, is how Confucianism can adjust itself to an industrialized and highly mobile society. There were commercial, "industrial" (in a less developed form), and political activities in traditional China that made it a mobile society. But the mobility in traditional China is dwarfed by that in today's world. The commercial and political elites in traditional China were highly mobile, but the masses were not. To adapt themselves to mobility, the elites were well-educated, and the masses were not in spite of the Confucian ideal of offering educational opportunity to everyone. Traditional institutions were designed for such a society, but things have changed. Therefore, an urgent question for a traditionalist is how to develop institutions with Confucian characteristics that are well-adjusted to the new world. But precisely in this endeavor lies the spirit of Confucianism: "Zhou is an old state, but its mission/mandate is ever renewing" (周虽旧邦其命维新).[21] That is, Confucianism has had such a long life precisely because it can reinvent itself in different historical contexts while preserving its core.

Now, how can this reinvention be done? Let me offer one example. An important Confucian ritual is the mourning ritual for one's deceased parents and ancestors. One way to mourn is to visit their tombs on certain days during the year. But this is often quite a challenge now that many people have moved far from their ancestral residence. Moreover, the population boom in recent decades means that the living and the dead are fighting for a shrinking land supply. In Chinese history, there was actually a debate about whether the sacrificial ceremony for the ancestors should be done at the tombs or at the family shrine. Perhaps we can draw lessons from these debates. Indeed, people could reserve a place in their homes, setting up a table for the memorial tablets of the ancestors and a genealogy next to them? These areas would be a constant reminder of where they have come from and where they are going; and one day, they will become an entry in the family tree and a tablet on the table. This is precisely an intended function of the Confucian emphasis on family: to guide people to have a longer view of the self and thus to discourage people from making short-sighted decisions. Clearly, with its intention so understood, this practice is not only good for the Chinese, but also for all human beings.

In addition to cultural reinventions in China, many individuals are promoting traditional learning on all levels, and some universities have established schools of traditional learning (国学院). While these are all admirable efforts, a more effective way to promote tradition is to institutionalize its studies on all levels of education. If traditional learning can become a part of state-sponsored education on all levels, students not only will be exposed to traditional learning, but it will also offer a career path for those who study it at higher education. This will create a healthy cycle of reviving tradition. Of course, it is a pluralistic world now, and students will be given choices about which traditional subject they wish to study, and this will be only a part of a comprehensive curriculum. As I have argued, Confucianism can contribute to China, the Chinese, and the world, and thus such institutionalized traditional learning will help the Chinese to understand where they come from and where they are going—not only for the Chinese but also for the world.

Notes

Author's note: The research for this chapter was supported by the Program for Professor of Special Appointment (Eastern Scholar) at Shanghai Institutions of Higher Learning, Shanghai Educational Development Foundation (Shuguang Project), and the Shanghai Philosophy and Social Sciences Projects.

1. One can challenge this by arguing that if this model has never been realized, why does the discussion of it matter? This is perhaps a sin of all political philosophers because their proposals are always a bit utopic. Nevertheless, for their proposals to be good ones, they should be realistic to some extent. Although no real-world regimes embody the Confucian model presented in the rest of this chapter, we can find elements of it in various regimes. Moreover, although this is just an imagined regime on paper, it will gain traction if the present dominant model(s) keep failing and people are driven to search for alternatives.

2. Jiang Qing (蒋庆), *Political Confucianism* 政治儒学 (Beijing: Sanlian, 2003), and *Political Confucianism Revisited* 再论政治儒学 (Shanghai: East China Normal University Press, 2011).

3. Jiang Qing is quite explicit about the culturally specific nature of liberal democracy, and rejects it on the ground that China is a Confucian country. How he would address the issue of whether his Confucianism can one day become a universal teaching for everyone is not clear.

4. See 3A4 of the *Mencius*. For an English translation, see D. C. Lau, *Mencius*, rev. and bilingual ed. (Hong Kong: Chinese University Press, 2003), 117.

5. For example, Confucius maintained that if an exemplary person settles among barbarians, there will no longer be any crudeness or lack of culture among them (9.14 of the *Analects*). For an English translation, see D. C. Lau, *Confucius: The Analects* (paperback bilingual ed.) (Hong Kong: Chinese University Press, 2002), 81.

6. See Shuxian Liu 刘述先, *Rujia sixiang kaituo de changshi* 儒家思想开拓的尝试 [Attempts to explore Confucian thoughts], edited by Jiadong Zheng 郑家栋 (Beijing: Zhongguo shehui kexue chubanshe, 2001), 16; and *Lun rujia zhexue de sange dashidai* 论儒家哲学的三个大时代 [On the three epochs of Confucian philosophy] (Guiyang: Guizhou renmin chubanshe, 2009), 3, 5.

7. For a more sympathetic account of Mou's philosophy, see chap. 6 by Stephen Angle herein. See also Stephen Angle, *Contemporary Confucian Political Philosophy* (Cambridge, UK: Polity Press, 2012) for a detailed account of a Confucian political philosophy based on some of Mou's insights. For a response to this account, see my review of Angle's book published in *Notre Dame Philosophical Review* (http://

ndpr.nd.edu/news/36870–contemporary-confucian-political-philosophy/ accessed on Jan. 23, 2014).

8. Whether "feudalism" can be applied to medieval Europe or Western Zhou China is a controversial issue. On the former, see Elizabeth A. R. Brown, "The Tyranny of a Construct: Feudalism and Historians of Medieval Europe," *American Historical Review* 79, no. 4 (1974): 1063–1088; and Susan Reynolds, *Fiefs and Vassals* (Oxford, UK: Clarendon Press Reynolds, 1994). On the latter, see Feng Li, *Landscape and Power in Early China* (Cambridge, UK: Cambridge University Press, 2005), and *Bureaucracy and the State in Early China* (Cambridge, UK: Cambridge University Press, 2008). But I use "feudalism" to refer to a political structure in which rulers on lower levels enjoy much political autonomy, which may hold true in both medieval Europe and China in the pre-Qin era.

9. From the perspective of the contemporary mainstream scholarship on China, the claims that the Zhou-Qin transition is a form of modernization and that Confucianism is primarily a political philosophy are quite unorthodox. For more detailed discussions and support for this argument, see my articles: "How to Rule without Taking Unnatural Actions (无为而治): A Comparative Study of the Political Philosophy of the *Laozi*," *Philosophy East and West* 59, no. 4 (Oct. 2009): 481–502; "Preliminary Remarks: Han Fei Zi—First Modern Political Philosopher?" *Journal of Chinese Philosophy* 38, no. 1 (Mar. 2011): 4–13. I also express similar view in my book *China: The Political Philosophy of the Middle Kingdom* (London: Zed Books, 2012), and my manuscript "Nietzsche, Mencius, and the Nature of Compassion as a Modern Virtue."

10. By a "thick" reading, I mean a metaphysical and literal reading of the texts, with a comprehensive metaphysical system and with a "fundamentalist" attitude that does not allow adaptations to different contexts. A "thin" reading, in contrast, is an ametaphysical reading that, under the condition of following a minimum set of general principles, allows different interpretations and even revisions of ideas in the relevant texts.

11. What counts as a family is a controversial question today, against, among other things, the debate over gay marriages. The Confucian stance on this issue is equally controversial, depending on which Confucian texts one takes as essential and how one interprets them. I think that Confucians can take a more "liberal" view of families in that the couple in a family does not have to be one man and one woman.

12. For a detailed discussion, see my article "The Price of Serving Meat—On Confucius's and Mencius's Views of Human and Animal Rights," *Asian Philosophy* 19, no. 1 (Mar. 2009): 85–99.

13. See, e.g., Tongdong Bai, "A Mencian Version of Limited Democracy," *Res Publica* 14, no. 1 (Mar. 2008): 19–34; and "A Confucian Version of Hybrid Regime: How Does It Work, and Why Is It Superior?," in *The East Asian Challenge to Democracy—Meritocracy in Comparative Perspective*, edited by Daniel A. Bell and Chenyang Li (Cambridge, UK: Cambridge University Press, 2013), 55–87.

14. Of the possible mechanisms to select meritocrats in a fair and reliable manner, see my book chapter "A Confucian Version of Hybrid Regime: How Does

It Work, and Why Is It Superior?" in *The East Asian Challenge to Democracy—Meritocracy in Comparative Perspective*, edited by Bell and Li, 55–87.

15. For more detailed discussion of the problems with this model and Confucian solutions of them, see my two articles: "Renquan gaoyu zhuquan—Mengzi de zhengyi zhanzhengguan" 仁权高于主权—孟子的正义战争观 [Humanity (Ren) overrides sovereignty—On Mencius's view of a just war], *Shehui kexue* 社会科学 [Journal of social sciences] 1 (2013): 131–139; and "Xiandai guojia renting yu guoji guanxi—Rujia de lilun yuqi dui minzu guojia yu ziyou zhuyi fanshi zhi youyue xing 现代国家认同与国际关系—儒家的理论及其对民族国家与自由主义范式之优越性 [National identity of modern states and modern international relations—A Confucian theory and its superiority to the nation-state and liberal models], *Zhishi fenzi luncong* 知识分子论丛 (Intellectual forum) 11 (2013): 103–119.

16. Some of the ethnic identities were recognized and the basis for different political treatments under the Qing dynasty. But most of the ethnicities were newly identified and were introduced into and reinforced by the political system in the communist China—in this sense they are created.

17. Although early Confucians supported the idea that people vote with their feet, they also recognized or could recognize as justified other political factors with regard to migration policies, such as the well-being of those who are already in the state in question. This is why the regulations over migration can be considered justified and even necessary by Confucians.

18. For a more detailed discussion of this issue, please see my two articles: "Humanity (*Ren*) Overrides Sovereignty" and "National Identity of Modern States and Modern International Relations."

19. Daniel Bell also presents a similar account in his chapter herein. For my own detailed discussion of these ideas as well as of Bell's account, see my two articles: "Humanity (*Ren*) Overrides Sovereignty" and "National Identity of Modern States and Modern International Relations." Tongdong Bai, "Humanity (*Ren*) Overrides Sovereignty—On Mencius's View of a Just War 仁权高于主权—孟子的正义战争观," *Journal of Social Sciences* 社会科学 1 (2013): 131–139; and "National Identity of Modern States and Modern International Relations—A Confucian Theory and Its Superiority to the Nation-State and Liberal Models" 现代国家认同与国际关系—儒家的理论及其对民族国家与 自由主义范式之优越性, *Intellectual Forum* 知识分子论丛 11 (2013): 103–119.

20. John Rawls, *The Law of Peoples with "The Idea of Public Reason Revisited"* (Cambridge, MA: Harvard University Press, 1999).

21. The line is from *The Book of Odes* (《诗经·大雅·文王》).

Part Two

Political Plurality and Civil Society

5

Building Democracy

The Theory and Practice of Contemporary New Confucianism

MING-HUEI LEE

TRANSLATED FROM THE CHINESE BY TZE-KI HON

During the 1950s, at the height of the Cold War, the New Confucians in Hong Kong and Taiwan raised a theory of "developing democracy from Confucianism." They were so confident about their theory that they even debated with Taiwan's liberals. They argued that, despite its long history supporting imperial authority, Confucianism was capable of producing democracy in modern China. They further argued that Confucianism, particularly its moral metaphysic, was essential to cultivating an ethos of responsibility among citizens in a democratic society. To this day, few people fully understand the New Confucians' argument, even though it is directly relevant to building democracy in today's China and Taiwan.[1] This chapter summarizes the New Confucians' argument and compares it with that of the liberals.[2]

In their debates in the 1950s, the New Confucians and the liberals focused on two issues. First was the role of Chinese tradition (particularly Confucianism) in developing science and democracy in modern China. The two sides differed on whether the Chinese tradition was a hindrance to China's modernization. They had different views on whether a successful modernization in China would require a totalistic critique of Chinese tradition. The second issue was the role of ethics in democratization. The two sides agreed on the importance of promoting political freedom (e.g., freedom of speech, assembly, and dissent) as a precondition for democracy, yet they had different opinions on whether political freedom must be linked to a moral foundation. More importantly, they disagreed on whether political freedom must be based on citizens' moral freedom.[3]

Confucianism and Democracy

Regarding the role of Chinese tradition in modernization, the New Confucians emphasized the continuity between past and present. They did not oppose adopting new ideas or institutions from abroad. Yet they stressed that new ideas or institutions must not be mechanically transplanted into China, as if adding a new technology to an industrial production process. Rather, new ideas and institutions must be organically integrated and creatively absorbed into Chinese tradition in a manner similar to the way a farmer nurtures a new crop. Modernization, they concluded, was a multifaceted process that allowed each country to develop its own model in accordance with its cultural and ethnic uniqueness.

By contrast, the liberals saw a rupture between past and present. They argued that, because Chinese tradition had failed to produce science and democracy in premodern times, it must be in conflict with modern needs. To successfully bring Western ideas and institutions into China, they contended, Chinese tradition (Confucianism, in particular) must first be discarded. From this perspective, the liberals found the New Confucians' perspective completely indefensible, holding onto the past as a psychological self-defense against the challenges from the West. Worse still, they accused them of prolonging imperial autocracy even though the imperial system had been discredited and destroyed after the 1911 Revolution.

Regarding the role of ethics in democratization, the New Confucians believed that political freedom must be based on moral ideals. Although they accepted a conceptual distinction between politics and morality, they stressed that in practice the two were codependent and intertwined. More specifically, they saw democratization as a complex process that included both the founding of a political system and the cultivation of a moral view that supported the democratic institution. In other words, like Isaiah Berlin, the New Confucians saw liberty (the core value of democracy) as meaning both "negative liberty" and "positive liberty." In their view, citizens in a democratic society must not only be "freed from" outside interference but also be "freed to" pursue self-realization. From this perspective, the New Confucians viewed Liberalism as one-sided. It was concerned only with political democratization and failed to cultivate the moral values that would sustain democracy. As such, New Confucians considered the liberals to be failing to counter communism—the biggest enemy of democracy at that time—on moral grounds.

The 1958 Declaration

In 1958, in "A Declaration to the World for Chinese Culture," the declaration's four authors (Tang Junyi, Mou Zongsan, Xu Fuguan, and Zhang Junmai [Carsun Chang]) clearly articulated the New Confucian view on democracy.[4] Of the twelve sections in the declaration, sections 8 and 9 are particularly germane to our discussion. In those two sections, the four authors frankly admit the shortcomings of Chinese tradition, especially its failure to develop democracy and science in China. They also accept that in modernization the Chinese must learn from advanced countries in Europe and other parts of the world. Yet they point out that, despite its failure to develop science and democracy in premodern times, Chinese tradition contains "seeds" (*zhongzi*) and "tendencies" (*qingxiang*) that can help to build science and democracy in modern China.[5] For this reason, the four authors urge their readers to view China's modernization as a multifaceted process that includes at least four interlocking aspects: (1) the cultivation of a moral subject based on the Neo-Confucian learning of heart/mind (*xin*) and nature (*xing*); (2) the creation of a political subject based on a democratic political structure; (3) the development of a cognitive subject based on a deep knowledge of the natural world; and (4) the training of a technological subject based on a rigorous schooling in modern science and technology.[6] To develop these four types of modern subjectivity, the four authors argue, China's modernization must not begin with acquiring scientific and technological knowledge. Rather, it must begin with the cultivation of a moral subject who, in turn, will have the determination to transform the political, cultural, and technological environments.

Seemingly idealistic, the logic of the four authors' argument is stunningly profound. For them, the sequence of modernization is aimed at addressing the long history of autocracy in China, where rulers frequently govern as if the country were their personal property. One result of this long history of autocracy is that the Chinese people are used to taking a passive role in moral cultivation and in political participation. Morally, they wait for a sage ruler to teach them how to behave properly. Politically, they wait for a benevolent ruler to provide them with what they need. Hence, throughout the 2,000 years of imperial rule, several accomplished rulers brought peace and prosperity to China, but few were morally sensitive souls willing to risk their lives to challenge the imperial autocracy. To the four authors, the success of China's modernization depends on a clean break from this unhealthy reliance on sage kings. And the best way to change the Chinese system is to turn millions of Chinese people into active and reflective citizens who will take charge of their lives.[7]

For this reason, the four authors argue that the starting point of China's modernization must be a moral justification of it. The four authors frequently use the technical terms of Song-Ming Neo-Confucianism to describe the moral and political processes of China's modernization. They refer to the moral process as the learning of "inner sagehood" (*nei sheng*) and to the political process as the learning of "outer kingship" (*wai wang*). For them, the problem with traditional Confucianism is its heavy emphasis on the learning of inner sagehood at the expense of the learning of outer kingship. In modern times, to redress the imbalance, both the learning of inner sagehood and the learning of outer kingship must be emphasized, the former providing the basis for the latter.

Mou Zongsan's Contribution

After the publication of the 1958 Declaration, Mou Zongsan further elaborated the New Confucian view of modernization. For instance, in *Lishi zhexue* (The philosophy of history), Mou separates the "synthetically rational spirit" from the "analytically rational spirit." In *Zhengdao yu zhidao* (The principle of legitimation and the principle of governance), he distinguishes two additional dichotomies: functional presentation versus constructive presentation of reason, and intensional presentation versus extensional presentation of reason. With these three dichotomies, Mou explains the difference between two modes of thinking: the synthetic mode of thinking originates from the moral mind, and the analytical mode of thinking activates when the human mind is applied to solving practical problems of everyday life. In the former, the moral mind gives human beings the ability to comprehend the outside world from a particular perspective and to become part of the outside world by assuming the perspective of the whole. Through this dual process of internalization and externalization, human beings form a union between Subject and Object, Part and Whole, Self and Other.[8] To emphasize his point, Mou describes this synthetic mode of thinking as "subordination," in which differences and distinctions are homogenized and similarity and unity are highlighted. In contrast, the analytical mode of thinking emphasizes the distinction between Subject and Object, Part and Whole, Self and Other. Mou describes this mode of thinking as "coordination," in which the horizontal relationships among actors and factors are stressed.[9]

In separating the synthetic mind from the analytical mind, Mou clearly drew his inspiration from the Kantian distinction between Noumenon and Phenomenon. He equated the synthetic mind to the realm of Noumenon and the analytical mind to the realm of Phenomenon. But Mou adopted the Kantian distinction not only for philosophical reasons but also to answer two crucial questions regarding how to develop democracy from Confucianism. First, the Kantian distinction helped to explain the failure of the Confucian tradition in producing science and democracy in premodern times. According to Mou, the failure was due to a one-sided emphasis on developing the synthetic mind. Overly tilted to homogenizing differences and distinctions, the Confucian tradition inadvertently provided justification for imperial autocracy, literati elitism, and restrictive social hierarchy. Focusing excessively on subordinating Part to Whole and Self to Other, the Confucian tradition did not provide enough intellectual stimulation for scientific breakthrough. Second, the Kantian distinction shed light on the potentials in Confucianism for developing democracy in modern times. While in imperial China the synthetic mind of Confucianism had led to autocracy and elitism, in modern China it would be a much-needed antidote to the excess of analytical thinking in an industrial economy. According to Mou, in the modern context, the synthetic mind not only gave human beings the means to escape from what Max Weber calls "the iron cage" of instrumental rationality but also authenticated them as "moral subjects" who are able to make decisions based on their moral intuition.[10]

In short, Mou saw the development of democracy from Confucianism as a dialectical process. By itself, the synthetic mind of Confucianism cannot produce pluralistic politics and independent-minded citizens. But after the analytical mind is fully activated to develop modern science and democracy, the synthetic mind is needed to inject moral idealism into a society that is excessively pragmatic and calculative. In his writings, Mou describes this dialectical process as "the self-negation of moral consciousness" (*liangzhi zhi ziwo kanxian*) (see Angle's chapter 6 herein). To him, this self-negation is absolutely necessary to counter the extremes of "scientism" and "excessive politicization." In both cases, the lofty goal of developing science and democracy in modern China is turned into a means to bring wealth and power to China. What is lacking is the true spirit of science and democracy, namely, the creativity and self-confidence of human beings who are motivated not by achieving a utilitarian goal but by a moral intuition.

The Perfect Balance

In today's political debates, the New Confucians' view on democracy is even more important because it is fundamentally different from that of the conservatives who question or reject Western democracy and that of the radicals who see Confucianism playing no role in China's modernization. For the conservatives (e.g., the "mainland New Confucian," Jiang Qing), the New Confucians are quasi-Westernizers because they do not support building "a democracy with Chinese characteristics" that would emphasize China's cultural uniqueness.[11] For the radicals (including both the Chinese Christians and the liberal thinkers Yin Haiguang, Lin Yü-sheng, and Li Hongxi), the New Confucians are defending a dying tradition that is no longer relevant to contemporary life.[12]

In this climate of political debate, the contribution of New Confucians lies precisely in their attempt to strike a perfect balance between adopting a democratic system from abroad and preserving China's subjectivity in political modernization. One can see their significance by comparing their view with that of Southeast Asian leaders who promote "Asian values." As we recall, in the 1990s some Southeast Asian leaders (e.g., Singapore's Lee Kuan Yew and Malaysia's Mahathir ben Mohamad) questioned the universality of Western democracy. They argued that Western concepts such as liberty, equality, and human rights are specific to Euro-American culture and that therefore they are not necessarily applicable to East and Southeast Asian countries where kinship and collectivity are treasured over individuality and privacy. They suggested that because of this cultural uniqueness in East and Southeast Asia, the political system in the region should be paternalistic rather than individualistic, hierarchic rather than pluralistic.

The New Confucians do not agree with this view. First, they support the universality of Western democracy. They admit that, due to historical accident, Confucianism was part of imperial autocracy and that its association with the imperial system created distortions in its basic teaching. To dissociate Confucianism from imperial autocracy, the New Confucians gladly welcome Western democratic concepts and institutions. Second, they support the particularity of Chinese culture, especially its emphasis on communitarian values. Yet unlike the promoters of "Asian values," they do not see the particularity of Chinese culture as interfering with political democratization. Rather, they see political democratization as an application of universal Western democratic values in the cultural milieu of China. The result of connecting the universal with the particular, they argue, would be a "Confucian application of democracy": a democratic system that follows basic Western democratic values but differs from Western democracies because of its Confucian elements, such as its emphasis on kinship and community.

Taiwan Democracy

When considering the role of New Confucianism in Taiwan's democratization, one must keep in mind that, despite the debates in the 1950s, the academic discussion about democracy has had, at best, an indirect impact on political development on the island. This relationship is similar to the limited influence of John Rawls's *A Theory of Justice* on U.S. politics and elections. In the pluralistic democracies of modern times, a single factor most likely will not determine political life.

In the last fifty years, Taiwanese have made remarkable progress in democratization, from the one-party state in 1949 to the triumph of a multiparty political system at the turn of the millennium. The contrast is even stronger if the "prohibition policies" that the Chinese Nationalist Party (Kuomintang or KMT) used in the 1950s and 1960s to suppress opposition parties are compared to the more recent orderly and peaceful transition of power from the KMT to the Democratic Progressive Party (DPP) in 2000 and from the DPP back to the KMT in 2008. Paradoxically, during this process of democratization, the liberals have been increasingly marginalized and their influence has become limited. In today's Taiwanese politics, Liberalism is basically displaced by "populism" (pitching to the populace): the major political philosophy is defined only by what will win elections.

To some observers, New Confucianism fares no better. Because of their emphasis on resuscitating Confucianism in modern democracy, New Confucians seem to support the KMT's efforts to strengthen its one-party rule on the basis of a selective revival of Chinese tradition. Even those writers who are sympathetic with Confucianism complain about the "absence" of New Confucianism in the momentous changes in the politics of Taiwan during the last few decades.[13]

These criticisms of New Confucianism are not fair. As mentioned earlier, New Confucians wholeheartedly affirm the universality of democracy. In particular, they support parliamentary democracy rather than authoritarian democracy (i.e., the form practiced in Singapore). In action, New Confucians are fearless defenders of liberty and freedom. For instance, Zhang Junmai was one of the authors of the 1946 Constitution of the Republic of China that is still in use in Taiwan today. Although the constitution was not completely put into practice when the KMT ruled Taiwan under the "prohibition policies," it was a democratic constitution that defined the rights and duties of citizens. To champion his model of democracy, Zhang spent decades living overseas to protest the KMT's authoritarian rule. Similarly, Xu Fuguan made his name by publicly criticizing the KMT and supporting the opposition parties. His views were so sharp that they led to the suppression of the journal *Minzhu pinglun* (Democratic review) in 1966. Afterward, Xu was forced to move to Hong Kong.

In addition, New Confucians founded New Asia College in Hong Kong. In the 1950s, under the leadership of Qian Mu and Tang Junyi, New Asia College became a base for defending Confucianism and democracy in colonial Hong Kong, which was shaped politically by several political forces that included the British, the communists, and the Americans.[14] Through the New Confucians' efforts, New Asia College became part of the Chinese University of Hong Kong in the 1960s, and since then it has been a center for the study of Chinese culture.

If we turn our attention to developments in China and Taiwan since the 1980s, we can see the New Confucians more concretely.[15] In China, after the implementation of the reform policies, the 1990s saw a "culture craze" and a "national learning craze" demonstrating a strong interest in traditional culture among many mainland Chinese. In Taiwan, despite the DPP's policies of "decentering China" in the early 2000s, the Taiwanese still fervently follow Chinese cultural practices. In today's Taiwan, imagining that we can avoid discussing the relationship between democratic politics and Chinese traditional culture is difficult.

In this regard, the New Confucians' plan to connect Confucianism with democracy is not a far-fetched one. Using Heiner Roetz's terms, the combination of Confucianism and democracy would be a product of a "reconstructive hermeneutics of accommodation," in which both sides will yield to each other to produce something totally new.[16] Or, following the view of sociologist Ambrose King, the combination of Confucianism and democracy would produce a "democratically Confucian" system rather than a "Confucian democracy." In the former, the democratic system would be based on Western democracy adjusted to fit the Confucian tradition. In the latter, the democratic system would be derived from Confucianism and adapted to fit democratic criteria.[17]

Finally, in the last half century of democratization in Taiwan, New Confucians have been a hidden but potent force in politics. In particular, their participation in theorizing democracy has helped to create a political environment in which democratic ideals are accepted as universal. One should not underestimate this contribution from the New Confucians. Without their relentless insistence on the universality of democracy, there would have been supporters of "Asian values" in Taiwan who argued for an

Asian way of building democracy or, worse still, the equivalent of Islamic fundamentalists who argued for a total rejection of democracy. Even at the height of the KMT's one-party rule in the 1950s and 1960s, the presence of the New Confucians helped to maintain hope for a democratized Taiwan, where the power of the authoritarian party-state would be checked and curtailed.

In retrospect, one may say that the influence of New Confucians has been stronger among the KMT's leaders and supporters than among the Taiwanese liberals and the Taiwanese local elites. Ironically, New Confucians' fervent interest in connecting Confucianism to democracy makes their view appealing to the KMT's leaders and supporters, who also wish to selectively revive Chinese tradition to support their one-party rule. Sharing the same discourse of "reviving Chinese tradition" but for different purposes, the New Confucians are able to convince leaders and supporters of the KMT that the best way to democratize Taiwan is to adopt a multiparty system. By the same token, one must also recognize the contribution of New Confucianism in creating an environment in Taiwan in which "Confucian fundamentalism"—in the form advocated by the mainland scholar Jiang Qing, who wants to replace Marxism with Confucianism but without accepting Western democracy—does not appear. As New Confucians have repeatedly pointed out, building democracy is a delicate and complicated process that can easily be derailed by taking extreme measures.

Notes

1. See, for instance, the report of the 1982 roundtable discussion held in Taipei on New Confucianism and China's modernization, *Zhongguo luntan* 中國論壇 165 (Oct. 10, 1982). The participants in the roundtable discussion included well-known historians, philosophers, psychologists, anthropologists, sociologists, jurists, and political scientists. But the views expressed in the discussion reveal misunderstanding of the New Confucians' perspective.

2. I explain the New Confucians' perspective in Ming-huei Lee, *Ruxue yu xiandai yishi* 儒學與現代意識 [Confucianism and modern consciousness] (Taipei: Wenjin chubanshe, 1991). See also Ming-huei Lee, "Culture et démocratie: Réflexions à partir de la polémique entre libéraux taiwanais et néo-confucéens contemporains," *Extrême-Orient, Extrême-Occident* 31 (2009): 33–62.

3. For the details of the debates of the 1950s, see Ming-huei Lee, *Dangdai ruxue zhi ziwo zhuanhua* 當代儒學之自我轉化 [The self-transformation of contemporary Confucianism] (Taipei: Zhongyang yanjiuyuan Zhongguo wenzhe yanjiusuo, 1994), esp. 89–127.

4. The 1958 Declaration was then titled "Zhongguo wenhua yu shijie" 中國文化與世界 [Chinese culture and the world]; it may be found in Tang Junyi's work

"Zhonghua renwen yu dangjin shijie" 中國人文與當今世界 [Chinese humanistic culture and the contemporary world] (Taipei: Taiwan xuesheng shuju, 1975).

5. Ibid., 897.
6. Ibid., 896.
7. Ibid., 903–904.
8. For the details of these two modes of thinking, see Ming-huei Lee, *Ruxue yu xiandai yishi*, 106–115.
9. Mou Zongsan, *Zhengdao yu zhidao* 政道與治道 [The principle of legitimation and the principle of governance] (Taipei: Taiwan xuesheng shuju, 1987), 52–53; see also *Mou Zongsan Xiansheng quanji* 牟宗三先生全集 [Collected works of Mr. Mou Zongsan] (Taipei: Lianjing chuban gongsi, 2003), vol. 10, 58.
10. Mou Zongsan, *Zhengdao yu zhidao*, 140; see also his *Collected Works*, vol. 10, 155.
11. Jiang Qing 蔣慶, *Zhengzhi ruxue: Dangdai ruxue de zhuanxiang tezhi yu fazhan* 政治儒學：當代儒學的轉向, 特質與發展 [Political Confucianism: The reorientation, characteristics, and development of contemporary Confucianism] (Taipei: Yangzhengtang wenhua shiye gongsi, 2003), 82–83, 174–175.
12. For the liberals' critique of New Confucianism, see Yin Haiguang 殷海光, "Genzhe wusi de jiaobu qianjin" 跟著五四的腳步前進 [Going forward by following the footsteps of the May Fourth movement], in *Yin Haiguang quanji* 殷海光全集 [Collected works of Yin Haiguang], edited by Lin Zhenghong 林正弘 (Taipei: Guiguan tushu gongsi, 1990), vol. 11, 577.
13. See Chen Zhaoying 陳昭瑛, "Xu Fuguan yu ziyou zhuyi de duihua" 徐復觀與自由主義的對話 [The dialogue between Xu Fuguan and the liberals], *Sixiang* [Thought] 20 (Nov. 2012): 175.
14. See Zhou Ailing 周愛靈, *Huaguo piaoling: Lengzhan shiqi zhimindi de xinya shuyuan* 花果飄零：冷戰時期殖民地的新亞書院 [The dispersion of flowers and fruits: The New Asia College under colonial rule during the Cold War], translated by Luo Meixian 羅美嫻 (Hong Kong: Shangwu yinshuguan, 2010).
15. See Ming-huei Lee, ed., *Rujia sixiang zai xiandai Dongya: Zonglun pian* 儒家思想在現代東亞：總論篇 [Confucianism in modern East Asia: A general perspective] (Taipei: Zhongyang yanjiuyuan Zhongguo wenzhe yanjiusuo, 1998), 81–98. See also Ming-huei Lee, *Konfuzianischer Humanismus: Transkulturelle Kontexte* (Bielefeld: Transcript, 2013), 129–143.
16. Heiner Roetz, "The 'Dignity within Oneself': Chinese Tradition and Human Rights," in *Chinese Thought in a Global Context*, edited by Karl-Heinz Pohl (Leiden: Brill, 1999), 257.
17. Ambrose Y. C. King, "Confucianism, Modernity, and Asian Democracy," in *Justice and Democracy: Cross-Cultural Perspectives*, edited by Ron Bontekoe and Marietta Stepaniants (Honolulu: University of Hawaii Press, 1997), 174–177.

6

Self-Restriction and Progressive Confucianism

STEPHEN C. ANGLE

Traditional Confucianism conceived of the ethical and political realms as continuous and unified. Either the most virtuous should rule or, in a concession to hereditary monarchy, rulers should strive to be as virtuous as possible and be guided by their still-more-virtuous ministers. In theory, the possession of virtue enabled the ruler to care for all in the realm; the exemplary nature of the ruler's character, especially as manifest in his concern for members of his family, was supposed to lead all in the realm toward virtue as well. To be sure, a variety of intermediary institutions evolved to enhance and spread the effects of the ruler's virtue, including bureaucrats and the system of examinations that produced them, a broad system of rituals, and a penal code designed to preserve order when all else failed. "Order" was a central goal, but it was conceived in ethical terms and virtuous rule was understood to be both necessary and sufficient for its attainment.

Two of the main competing approaches to contemporary Confucian political philosophy are "political" or "institutional" Confucianism, on the one hand, and "ethical" (*xinxing* 心性) Confucianism, on the other. According to advocates of the former such as Jiang Qing or Kang Xiaoguang, "Confucian constitutionalism" should be based on revised versions of traditional Confucian political values and institutions. Advocates of the latter follow the lead of Mou Zongsan (1909–1995) in arguing that Confucian politics must emerge out of, although still be independent from, Confucian ethics. The independence of the political was crucial because Mou was worried about political systems that rely on leadership by individuals who claim to have highly developed moral insight. He had in mind the periodic, terrible excesses of both the traditional Confucian state and the modern Communist one: in both cases, leaders who believed in their own virtue sometimes sought to impose their vision of morality on the realm, with bloody consequences. Mou characterized this as politics being "swallowed" by morality.[1] To be sure, Mou was deeply committed to the importance of striving for sagehood. Among other things, he saw laws and rights themselves as rooted in and emerging from moral struggles as we will see. Without morality there would be no politics. Nonetheless, he recognized that "achieving sagehood is an endless process."[2] Politics (including law) must, therefore, be independent from morality, or else it, too, would be endlessly unfinished and inadequately protective. Mou thus found himself advocating a position that fell between liberal right-based theories and traditional Confucian (or communist) good-based theories. Unlike the liberals, Mou held that moral and political value must retain continuity, lest politics be unmoored from the underlying source of all value, in which case we would have no reason for confidence that the outcomes of our political processes were ultimately aimed at making our lives better. Unlike the communists and earlier Confucians, however, politics and law must nonetheless stand on their own, independent of morality. In other words, Mou rejected both a direct connection between morality and politics, and a lack of connection. His alternative is an indirect connection. Political value, he says, emerges out of morality, but achieves an independent status because the further development of moral value requires what he terms "self-restriction" (*ziwo kanxian* 自我坎陷).[3]

I am persuaded by Mou that self-restriction is critical to a fruitful contemporary Confucian development of political philosophy. However, let me make clear from the outset that my explication of this idea differs in some crucial ways from Mou's, and the "Progressive Confucianism" that I develop goes well beyond any of Mou's explicit arguments. Self-restriction plays key roles in at least three areas of Mou's philosophy. It explains how cognition of the empirical world is possible for creatures whose moral heartminds also respond to the lifeworld in a nonempirical way; it explains how and to what degree scientific norms can govern our activities, at least partly independently from morality, and it explains how laws and rights can structure our political lives without being overridden by individual claims to better moral insight. In each case, Mou argues that what is being "restricted" is the direct, intuitive grasping of moral reality by the moral heartmind. Understanding this latter idea, which he frequently terms "intellectual intuition," is critical to a full account of Mou's theory of self-restriction. With some reinterpretation, however, we can detach the idea of self-restriction from the rest of Mou's "moral metaphysics" without losing its significance for political philosophy. Self-restriction must certainly be grounded in an account of ethical value, but a range of views can fit into the following general sketch of Confucian ethics:

- Humans are capable of developing our attunement to and care for all aspects of our social and natural environment, which most centrally involves those people with whom we have particular relationships.

- Our care for distinct dimensions of value in our environments (e.g., family responsibilities, the well-being of strangers for whom we are responsible, and concern for our friends) must be harmonized.

- Well-lived human lives and the flourishing of our communities both depend on people successfully developing the aforementioned capacities to significant degrees.

- These capacities can be usefully explained through reference to individual virtues such as humaneness and propriety, although these virtues are at least somewhat interrelated (and perhaps, depending on the specific account, ultimately just different aspects of a single capacity), and the ultimate goal of Confucian ethics is the full development of these virtues on the part of all people.

In order to concentrate on Confucian political philosophy, I will not defend this picture of Confucian ethics here.[4] I will use some of Mou's specific discussions of self-restriction as my point of departure, and in fact I believe that Mou would accept virtually everything I say here about self-restriction. But we do not need to take on board all of Mou's system in order to see the value of self-restriction, and this approach opens it up to a much wider audience.

Mou himself glosses "self-restriction" as meaning "self-negation" (*ziwo fouding*) in a Hegelian sense: that is, the limitation of one thing by something else of a fundamentally distinct kind.[5] This is a good start on its meaning, but before pursuing that further, attending to the term *ziwo kanxian* itself, which is unusual and which Mou invented, is worthwhile. "Self-restriction" is formed by combining the common noun "self" (*ziwo*) and the decidedly uncommon verb "*kanxian*," which Mou constructs from two related terms from the *Book of Changes*. "Kan" is one of the eight trigrams out of which the sixty-four hexagrams of the *Changes* are composed. Its bottom and top lines are broken or *yin* lines; the middle line is a solid, *yang* line. Contemporary scholar Richard John Lynn gives "sink hole" as its basic meaning, and as several early commentaries clearly show, it has the connotation of water flowing through it. One such commentary also associates *kan* with the "rain, by which things are moistened" (*run*). Flowing water and moistening are both positive sounding, despite the negative connotations of sink hole. In addition, two of the earliest commentaries define *kan* as "*xian*," or "pit."[6] With all this in mind, we should think of *kanxian* primarily as a lowering and limitation, like sinking into a pit. This justifies translating it as "restriction." However, its associations with water and especially with moistening are also crucial because Mou sees self-restriction ultimately to be a vital, positive stage in broader processes of cognition and moral growth.

Self-Restriction in Politics

As mentioned, Mou uses self-restriction in three distinct contexts: cognition, science, and politics. His earliest introduction of the term occurs in an effort to argue that Wang Yangming's (1472–1529) theory of moral cognition implicitly includes the idea of self-restriction.[7] Given the strategy outlined above, however, I will focus instead on Mou's most approachable account of self-restriction's function in politics and demonstrate that we can draw from it an idea of self-restriction that is compelling even when freed from Mou's other theoretical commitments. Key to Mou's discussion is a distinction between the functional presentations of ethical reasoning and the structural presentations of analytical reasoning. By the first of these pairs, he means an individual's particularist, situation-specific ethical judgments, which he sees as the core modality of Confucian ethics.[8] He understands these judgments to come from the properly cultivated moral heartmind, and in this sense to be subjective; he also puts this in terms of the individual's virtuous character.[9] The structural presentation of analytic reasoning, on the other hand, refers to general, objective rules or frameworks. With this in mind, here is Mou:

> A democratic political structure is something that emerges from the conscious decisions people make in their political lives; based on this clue, we can connect it to ethical reasoning. But such political structures are objective frameworks belonging to objective practice, and thus cannot be completed by the functional presentation of ethical reason. The inner logic of the political structure itself is a manifestation of the structural presentation of reasoning; this reasoning temporarily cannot be thought of in terms of individual virtue or practical reasoning, but has shifted into analytic reasoning without ethical meaning. . . . But this overall political structure itself is something desired by ethical

> reasoning. In other words, the realization of this political structure is also the realization of a highest ethical value. This shows that in order to realize this ethical value, ethical reasoning must [come] from within the midst of its functional presentation restrict itself (*ziwo kanxian*), step back a pace, and shift into the structural presentation of analytical reasoning. Observed from within this structural presentation of reason, politics has its independent significance, forms its own, independent realm of value, and has temporarily left ethics behind; it seemingly has no connection with ethics. From within the structural presentation, the various aspects of this political structure—like the organization of power and the definition of rights and duties—are all on par with one another, and thus can be the subjects of an independent political science. People can discuss these aspects using pure political discussion, striving to clearly establish a reasonable, impartial framework (*heli gongdao* 合理公道).[10]

As we can see, for Mou that which restricts itself is a certain kind of reasoning in favor of a different modality of reasoning. From elsewhere in Mou's writings, though, the difference between ethical and analytic reasoning is clearly more dramatic than I have indicated. He really has in mind two fundamentally different kinds of consciousness: an innate moral consciousness that has the ability to directly intuit the basic moral nature of the cosmos, and a cognitive, analytical consciousness that works by distinguishing subject from object.[11] One key to my appropriation of Mou is to realize that self-restriction still makes sense if we give a much less metaphysically charged interpretation of the two forms of reasoning. As noted earlier, Mou takes "the virtue of one's moral character" (*renge zhong de dexing* 人格中的德性) to be roughly equivalent to the deliverances of one's moral heartmind; I propose simply to see ethical reasoning in terms of the perceptions and reactions of virtuous character to particular situations. This is consistent with Mou's more elaborate story, but does not require that we follow Mou in all the specifics. Furthermore, my version still provides a solid (and solidly Confucian) normative grounding for ethics, based in the general framework of Confucian ethics sketched earlier.[12]

What about the reasoning that takes place within the political realm? How is this different from ethical reasoning? I accept much of what Mou says: it is reasoning in terms of different values and in keeping with general, objective rules. Rather than basing one's judgment and behavior on one's own perception of the situation, one is bound by laws and works within political processes. Among other things, this means accepting the messiness and imperfections of the political process. As he succinctly states in one of his lectures: if a sage wants to be president, he must "observe the political rules."[13] I will not address right now some key questions about the nature of reasoning and judgment from within the political perspective—questions concerning the ways in which ethical reasoning might still make its presence felt within the political realm. Instead, let us take note of the first sentence from Mou's long quote: it is important that politics emerges out of the ethical activity of individuals as they merge in political life because Mou's basic picture is that a certain kind of political structure is ultimately needed as the indirect means to more complete ethical practice. Ethical reasoning "restricts itself" in order to more fully realize itself, and thereby allows for an independent realm of political value to exist. It is independent in the sense that it cannot, at least under normal circumstances, be overridden by an individual's claim to superior ethical insight. As Mou later states in the same book:

> No matter how great or spiritual the attainments of one's [virtuous] character, when manifested in politics, one cannot override the relevant limits (i.e., the highest principles of the political world), and in fact must devote one's august character to the realization of these limits. When one is able to successfully realize these limits, in ancient times one would be called a "sage-king"; in modern times, a "great statesperson." If one cannot, in ancient times one would be called a "hegemon," "tyrant," or "autocrat"; in modern times, a "totalitarian ruler" or "dictator."[14]

Mou ignores here the differences between ancient and modern politics; on his more considered account, even the best of ancient politics suffers from its lack of independence.

Let us take a step back. We need to understand two key things about self-restriction: what it is and why it is necessary. So far in this section we have made some progress toward understanding what it is, at least with respect to the relation between ethics and politics. Now let us focus on the justification of self-restriction (as it applies to ethics and politics). In brief, the argument is as follows: Our subjectively-felt, internalized morality implicitly points toward an ideal of full, sagely virtue. Full virtue must be realized in the public, political world. Without objective structures (such as laws), the public goals of full virtue are inaccessible. Since these objective structures restrict the ways in which our subjective moral feelings can be manifested, Mou concludes that the achievement of virtue requires self-restriction. Objective, public standards are thus not only related to inner virtue, but they are also distinct from one another. Before I unpack this argument, let me emphasize why it is important. Mou's idea, which I endorse, is not that a constitution, laws, and rights are merely *compatible* with Confucianism, but rather than these objective political structures are *required* by Confucianism if it is to realize its own goals. Mou's argument does not depend on an independent commitment to constitutional democracy, but is a critique internal to the Confucian tradition. The fact that he draws on Hegelian language does not change this fact, just as the ways in which earlier Confucians drew on Buddhist ideas does not render their critiques external to the tradition.

In any event, turn now to the argument itself, which has three premises: (1) we (Confucians) are committed to seeking full virtue; (2) full virtue must be realized in the public world; and (3) the public realization of full virtue requires objective structures that are independent from claims of virtue. The first premise should be uncontroversial: the pursuit of ethical self-improvement and the criticism of those who rest content with moral mediocrity are perennial themes in Confucian writings. Some writers over the last century have sought to resist the second premise, arguing that Confucianism can have a continued role in the modern world only if it confines its aspirations to the development of an inner virtue that has no necessary expression or influence in the outer world. We can see something of this attitude in Yu Dan's extraordinarily popular recent book on the *Analects*, and eminent scholar Yu Ying-shih has repeatedly made arguments to this effect.[15] However, absolutely central to the Confucian conception of virtue is that inner states and dispositions have an outer manifestation and influence. Indeed, this is one of the real insights of the tradition that we are now beginning to see confirmed by modern psychology. More certainly can be said about this premise, including its dependence on the lack of a firm distinction in the external between "private" (like family) and "public" (like political); on this score, Confucians and feminists find themselves both supporting the latter's slogan that "the personal is political." Still, the core of Mou's argument clearly comes in the third premise.

The premise that the public realization of full virtue requires objective structures can itself be distilled into three steps. First, publicly realized full virtue means that everyone is also and simultaneously realizing virtue; as we read in *Analects* 12:1, "If one day he can overcome himself and turn to humaneness, the world will turn to humaneness along with him."[16] Similarly, *Analects* 12:16 says that the good person "completes the good in others"; *Analects* 4:25 tells us that "virtue is not solitary; it must have neighbors." We can read these latter two statements in a narrow way, perhaps only including the elite stratum of society, but as I argue elsewhere, this tendency within early Confucianism is something that a contemporary Progressive Confucianism has good grounds for rejecting. The fundamental interrelationship of people on which these sayings from the *Analects* are based should include all people.

Second, the attainment of virtue by others must be their individual and active achievement. As Mou explains at one point (partly using Hegelian language), actual freedom requires self-awareness, which in turn requires struggle; each person must feel that he or she is an independent individual. This is connected to the pervasive Confucian commitment to "getting it for oneself" (*zi de* 自得); slightly later in *Analects* 12:1, the text continues: "To be humane comes from oneself; how could it come from others?"[17] Third, only when rights to exercise agency with respect to matters both large and small are guaranteed, via external political structures, can the possibility of individual, active engagement with one's own self-cultivation be assured. People need to have opportunities to take responsibility for various aspects of their world, including the possibility that they are most qualified to serve as the head of government.[18] Virtuous insight must therefore be restrained—restrict itself—by adherence to the objective structures that protect the rights of all. Only then is full virtue a possibility.

Is This Confucianism?

One of the persistent criticisms of Mou's theory of self-restriction is that it, and therefore the constitutional and democratic structures it purports to require, is not really Confucian. At its most extreme, this line of criticism alleges that self-restriction is a purposeful obfuscation designed to conceal the wholesale borrowing of Western political values. Although I am not adopting Mou's full theory, some of these same challenges are still relevant to my more minimal understanding of self-restriction, so we should consider them here. Mou believes that his self-restriction idea is necessary in order to preserve the value and relevance of Confucianism—as a whole—in the contemporary world. Even though Confucianism is not a single, systematic philosophical theory, but rather a more than two-millennia-long tradition of philosophical theorizing and practice, it still has recurrent and mutually reinforcing key parts that we can think of on the model of a single theory. If Mou is right that self-restriction is necessary to save the body of theory and practice that is Confucianism, then if adopting self-restriction is to abandon Confucianism, all hope for Confucianism would seem to be lost. This would have consequences both for people's identity as well as for the other ideas and values of Confucianism because if the theory as a whole is no longer tenable, each part of it is thereby called into question. Perhaps its several aspects might be combined with other ideas into a new whole; or perhaps their resonance will linger on in somewhat distinctive versions of Liberalism, socialism, and so on. But if Confucianism cannot be combined with self-restriction and if self-restriction is necessary, dramatic consequences surely follow.

Advocates of Confucianism thus have three strategies: (1) reject the idea that Confucianism today has distinctive challenges and hold that self-restriction has no problem to solve; (2) accept that Confucianism has challenges, but argue for a different solution to them; or (3) adopt something similar to Mou's approach. For example, the contemporary institutional Confucian thinker Jiang Qing shares Mou's concern about the contemporary challenges to Confucianism, but thinks both that a different solution is available and that self-restriction is deeply non-Confucian. I address the latter charge below. Jiang's own solution can be quickly sketched: he argues that the Confucian tradition has ample resources on which it can draw to develop a robust and successful contemporary politics. According to Jiang, Mou ignores these institutions because Mou is convinced that "outer kingship" must somehow emerge from "inner sagehood." That is, ethics (which Mou connects strongly with the inner moral heartmind) has priority in any theorizing. Jiang disagrees, and says that inner and outer are two parallel aspects of the tradition; their relation is structural rather than causal. He therefore urges that political philosophers set aside an obsession with the heartmind and focus on creatively adapting Confucian institutions to China's current situation.[19] Jiang also argues that Confucians should not take democracy to be an indispensable guide to their institutional innovation because this is to unjustifiably privilege a type of institution that happens to have been successful in the West, but has no universal validity. Jiang's idea that inner morality and outer politics are independent, parallel tracks is only tenable, however, if moral development does not depend on a particular political form. We will see that Mou lays the groundwork for me to argue to the contrary: political (and social) institutional forms do matter to moral development, and often matter enormously. This is why Confucians must advocate participatory politics and must critique oppression. This is not unjustifiably privileging "Western" democracy because to whatever degree Progressive Confucianism converges with Western models—and it is likely to be distinctive in several respects, as we will see—this follows from the internal logic of Progressive Confucianism, not from a desire to copy the West.

Mou himself sometimes argues that self-restriction is a plausible interpretation of what earlier Confucians, and especially Wang Yangming

(1472–1529), had in mind.[20] In other places, particularly when addressing politics and science, Mou does not read the idea of self-restriction back into the tradition. Instead, his argument—one instance of which he had already seen above—is that core Confucian commitments demand a certain kind of approach to political legitimacy and to scientific independence, even though this was never fully realized by historical Confucian philosophers.[21] The needed approach relies essentially on self-restriction. Mou does on occasion cite brief bits from Confucian classics when spelling out this kind of argument, but his point in these contexts does not claim that the need for self-restriction was already understood. Rather, we can see that Mou employs more subtle strategies. One of his goals is to show a resonance, or at least lack of contradiction, between self-restriction and the earlier Confucians' explicit statements.[22] Another tactic is to maintain that Confucians did largely grasp the inner spirit of legitimate (democratic) politics, even though they missed the crucial role of self-restriction in actually making a polity legitimate.[23] Finally, Mou argues rather plausibly that certain Confucians—he stresses Gu Yanwu (1613–1682) and Huang Zongxi (1610–1695) in particular—at least partly saw the need for a development of Confucianism in the direction that Mou now insists on, although they were not radical enough.[24]

What should we make of these various claims? First, it is hard not to agree with Jiang Qing when he says that a careful reading of Wang Yangming makes clear that (on Wang's account) good knowing "can only manifest (*chengxian* 呈現) itself, and cannot restrict itself (*kanxian*)."[25] Jiang shows that Wang repeatedly uses language calling for the direct manifestation of good knowing and never hints at the much more involved and indirect process that Mou has in mind.[26] I propose that we accept the idea that self-restriction is implausible as an interpretation of preexisting Confucian texts. However, the question of whether self-restriction is a creative development of Confucianism remains. Jiang argues that it is not, but instead amounts to abandoning Confucianism, reasoning as follows. First, as we have seen already, self-restriction cannot reasonably be seen as an interpretation of preexisting elements of the tradition. Second, Jiang canvasses the multiple foreign sources of Mou's idea of self-restriction: Hegel, Kant, Buddhism, and even Aristotle. From this he concludes that Mou has transformed his Confucian discourse into a fundamentally Western framework; Mou's so-called Third Era of Confucianism is actually "Western Learning (*xixue* 西學)."[27]

Jiang is mistaken in two key ways, both with respect to Mou's own version of self-restriction (which is of course Jiang's target) and with respect to my more generalized understanding of self-restriction. First, I agree with several other commentators who maintain that while Mou has indeed digested a wide range of inspirations, East and West, his fundamental goals and conclusions are Confucian, rather than Kantian, Hegelian, or Buddhist.[28] The entire structure of his philosophy, including the "New Politics" (*xin waiwang* 新外王), is designed to enable the realization of a Confucian socioethical vision. The issue is slightly different for my own account of self-restriction, which does not rely on a particular Buddhist- and Kantian-influenced version of Confucianism, but the same conclusion still applies. Second, Mou has argued that self-restriction is in fact *necessary* in order to realize the Confucian ideal of full virtue. This is a vital part of Mou's justification that Jiang neglects; it means that not only is Mou's (or my) approach to creatively developing Confucianism acceptable, it is actually required.

Progressive Confucianism

The core idea behind self-restriction is to provide an "indirect" connection between ethical and political values. Political values must be rooted in ethics, and yet independent from it; ethical values must be restricted within the political realm, yet ultimately served by this relationship. On Mou's understanding, politics emerges out of the ethical activity of individuals as they merge together in political life, and a certain kind of political structure is ultimately needed as the indirect means to more complete ethical practice. Underlying this relationship are two key thoughts: that the emergence of political norms depends on the actual interaction of ethical agents seeking to better realize their ends, and that any actual set of political norms can be assessed in light of its contribution to furthering ethical development. This latter point is particularly important because it leads to what might be called a legitimacy constraint on political norms—that is, a perspective from which the actual results of political construction can be criticized. To what degree does the resulting framework enable individuals in all groups to develop ethically? Insofar as barriers are placed in front of any group's capacity for moral growth, the legal, political, or social framework should be subject to Confucian criticism.

My reasons for terming the resulting approach "Progressive Confucianism" can now be made clear. It is progressive in two senses: it is committed to both individual and social progress, as measured by the development of the virtues at the heart of Confucian ethics, and it shares with other "progressive" political movements a stress on overcoming oppression. For example, elsewhere I have argued that since Confucians rightly recognize the importance of situational factors to ethics and to ethical development, once they recognize the ways that social situations can systematically undermine or limit the capacity of some individuals to develop virtue, Confucians should have a strong motive to criticize and reform their societies.[29] Admittedly, traditional Confucianism did not often follow this path. Instead, we find ample evidence that social distinctions of the kinds that can be oppressive were regularly endorsed. Note that people do not have to be, or understand themselves to be, passive victims to be correctly characterized as subject to oppression. The key is the constraints: oppression is about structural limitations on the ways in which a group can flourish or develop. While both the historical and theoretical cases are complicated, I have argued that aspects of Confucian views (like the call for "distinction" between husbands and wives) lent themselves to the support of an oppressive social system and that Confucians did not do enough to criticize the system's various incarnations of the centuries. If these arguments and the general framework of Progressive Confucianism are sound, however, the result is that Confucians today are well-placed both to build on their traditions and—in so doing—to critique oppressive aspects of their societies. By understanding the role of ethical values as indirectly grounding our political norms, contemporary Confucian political philosophers can make important contributions both to broader discussion of political theory and to the well-being of their fellow citizens.[30]

Notes

Author's note: An earlier version of this chapter was presented at the University at Buffalo's Conference on New Confucianism, and subsequently at the National Central University (Taiwan) Conference on the International Dimensions of Neo-Confucianism. I thank participants in both conferences for their constructive suggestions. This chapter draws extensively on material in chapters 1 and 2 of my book, *Contemporary Confucian Political Philosophy: Toward Progressive Confucianism* (Cambridge, UK: Polity Press 2012).

    1. Mou Zongsan, *Zhengdao yu zhidao* 政道與治道 [Authority and governance] (Taipei: Xuesheng Shuju, 1991), 140.

    2. Ibid., 127.

    3. Ibid., 59. David Elstein first used this translation of *ziwo kanxian*; see Elstein, "Mou Zongsan's New Confucian Democracy," *Contemporary Political Theory* 11, no. 2 (May 2012): 192–210. In my book *Sagehood: The Contemporary Significance of Neo-Confucian Philosophy* (New York: Oxford University Press, 2009), I translated *ziwo kanxian* as "self-negation," following Mou Zongsan's own lead: see Mou, *Zhongguo zhexue shiqiu jiang* 中國哲學十九講 [Nineteen lectures on Chinese philosophy] (Taipei: Xuesheng Shuju, 1983), 278. However, given that Mou uses the explicitly Hegelian language of "negation" (rendered into Chinese as *fouding*) in order to explain what *kanxian* means, it now seems wiser to follow Elstein's more literal translation. See also below on the justification of "restriction."

4. One controversial dimension of my picture is the central role virtues play; for extensive discussion of different approaches to these matters, see my book chapter "The Analects and Moral Theory," in *The Dao Companion to the Analects*, edited by Amy Olberding (Dordrecht: Springer, 2013), 225–257.

5. Mou Zongsan, *Xianxiang yu wuzishen* 現象與物自身 [Phenomena and Things-in-Themselves] (Taipei: Xuesheng Shuju, 1975), 122.

6. See Shuogua, "Explaining the Trigrams," in *The Classic of Changes: A New Translation of the I Ching, as Interpreted by Wang Bi*, edited by Richard John Lynn (New York: Columbia University Press, 1994), 121, 123; and Xugua, "Providing the Sequence of Hexagrams," in *The Classic of Changes*, 105. The former text adds that "*Kan* is water, is the drains and the ditches, is that which lies low, is the now-straightening and now-bending, and is the bow [and] the wheel," Xugua, "Providing the Sequence of Hexagrams," 124. For some helpful discussion, see Tang Zhonggang 汤忠钢, *Dexing yu zhengzhi: Mou Zongsan xianrujia zhengzhi zhexue yanjiu* 德性与政治: 牟宗三新儒家政治哲学研究 [Virtue and politics: Research on Mou Zongsan's New Confucian political philosophy] (Beijing: Zhongguo Yanshi chubanshe, 2008), 121.

7. See Mou Zongsan, *Wang Yangming zhiliangzhi jiao* 王陽明致良知教 [Wang Yangming's teaching of extending good knowing] (Taipei: Zhongguo wenhus shuju, 1954), 27–28. The book was first published in 1947 as two separate journal articles; for details, see Ming-huei Lee, "Wang Yangming's Philosophy and Modern Theories of Democracy: A Reconstructive Interpretation," *Dao: A Journal of Comparative Philosophy* 7, no. 3 (2008): 287n6. As N. S. Chan notes, he also uses *kanxian* in his book *A Critique of the Cognitive Mind*, which he completed writing in 1949; See Chan, *The Thought of Mou Zongsan* (Leiden: Brill, 2011), 118.

8. Mou, *Zhengdao yu zhidao*, 46–48.

9. Ibid., 47.

10. Ibid., 58–59.

11. One of Mou's most controversial doctrines is that through the former consciousness, humans are capable of "intellectual intuition." For some background and discussion of these ideas, see N. S. Chan, *The Thought of Mou Zongsan*, esp. 142–150; Sébastien Billioud, *Thinking through Confucian Modernity: A Study of Mou Zongsan's Moral Metaphysics* (Leiden: Brill, 2012); and Nicholas Bunnin, "God's Knowledge and Ours: Kant and Mou Zongsan on Intellectual Intuition," *Journal of Chinese Philosophy* 35, no. 4 (2008): 613–624.

12. Of course more is to be said about what counts as a virtuous perception or reaction, how this relates to the attunement and care that I mentioned above, how these individual reactions to particular circumstances harmonize with one another and with multiple dimensions of value, and so on. Mou offers one kind of answer based around his idea of intellectual intuition; I offer a different answer in my book *Sagehood*, and other Confucian philosophers have developed still other alternatives.

13. Mou, *Zhongguo zhexue shiqiu jiang*, 278.

14. Ibid., 128.

15. See Yu Ying-Shih 余英時, *Xiandai ruxue de huigu yu zhanwang* 現代儒学的回顾与展望 [Review of and prospects for contemporary Confucianism] (Beijing:

Sanlian shudian, 2004), 132–186. I discuss Yu Ying-shih's arguments in chap. 10 of my book *Sagehood*.

16. Adapted from by E. Bruce Brooks and A. Taeko Brooks, *The Original Analects* (New York: Columbia University Press, 2001), 89.

17. Theodore de Bary has particularly emphasized the idea of "getting it for oneself" in his many writings on Neo-Confucianism; see, e.g., *The Message of the Mind in Neo-Confucianism* (New York: Columbia University Press, 1989).

18. These ideas are not explicit in Mou's writings, but I take them to follow from and fill out his position. They are partly alluded to in the famous 1958 "Manifesto to the World's People on Behalf of Chinese Culture," of which Mou was a coauthor. For an English translation of the 1959 Manifesto, see Carsun Chang, *The Development of Neo-Confucian Thought* (New York: Bookman Associates, 1962), 472.

19. Jiang Qing 蒋庆, *Zhengzhi ruxue: Dandai ruxue de zhuanxiang tezhi yu fazhan* 政治儒学: 当代儒学的转向, 特质与发展 [Political Confucianism: The changing direction, particularities, and development of contemporary Confucianism] (Beijing: Sanlian, 2003), 46–52.

20. In a 1954 monograph on Wang Yangming's theory of innate good knowing (*liangzhi*), Mou argues at length for an interpretation of Wang's notion of "extending" (*zhi*) one's good knowing according to which as part of this process, one provisionally restricts one's good knowing in order to know objects, thus grasping how to control them. This cognitive knowledge is then subsumed into the good-knowing response to a situation, such that—if one's good knowing is not obscured by selfishness—one's response cannot help but be correct. The key for now is that Mou clearly is offering this as an interpretation of Wang's teaching; Mou, *Wang Yangming zhiliangzhi jiao*, 27–28. Mou offers his interpretation as a gloss or commentary (*an*) to two passages from Wang's *Record for Practice*: Wang 1983, 37 (§6) and 182 (§139). We see the same thing in Mou's much later, explicitly Kantian-influenced account of cognition in Phenomena and Things-In-Themselves. Mou claims to find in a brief passage from the "Great Commentary" to the *Book of Changes* the idea that the moral heart-mind "extends itself dialectically," via self-restriction, in order to appropriately handle the objects in situations it encounters; Mou, *Xianxiang yu wuzishen*, 122–123. The passage Mou cites is: "*Qian* is the strongest thing in the entire world, so it should always be easy to put its virtue into practice. Thus one knows whether or not there is going to be danger. *Kun* is the most compliant thing in the entire world, so it should always be simple to put its virtue into practice. Thus one knows whether or not there are going to be obstacles"; Lynn, *The Classic of Changes*, 93–99. Mou's stress is on the idea of knowing "dangers" and "obstacles."

21. Mou, *Zhengdao yu zhidao*.

22. One example of this is when he cites Confucius's statement that "To love knowledge without loving learning has the defect of diffuseness"; *Analects* 17:8 by way of illustrating the problems that come when one denies the importance of self-restriction and thus denies room for independent scientific inquiry; ibid., 58.

23. Ibid., 141.

24. Ibid., chap. 9.

25. Jiang Qing, *Zhengzhi rujia*, 84.

26. Jiang also points out that Wang's political solution to the issues of his day, which involves relying on the good knowing of heroic sages, differs dramatically from Mou's democratic politics; Jiang, *Zhengzhi rujia*, 86. While true, this is less relevant to the immediate question because I am already granting that in the case of political uses of *kanxian*, Mou acknowledges his departure from earlier voices in the tradition. While Jiang does not consider it explicitly, the same can be said for Mou's later references to the *Book of Changes*; see n. 20 above.

27. See Jiang, *Zhengzhi rujia*, 66–72.

28. See, in particular, Zheng Jiadong 郑家栋, *Mou Zongsan* 牟宗三 [Mou Zongsan] (Taipei: Dongda tushu gongsi, 2000), 87. Even Tang Zhonggang, who is in many ways critical of Mou, would agree that notwithstanding his uses of Western philosophy, Mou remains fundamentally a Confucian. See Tang Zhonggang 汤忠钢, *Dexing yu zhengzhi: Mou Zongsan xin rujia zhengzhi zhexue yanjiu* 德性与政治: 牟宗三新儒家政治哲学研究 [Virtue and politics: Research on Mou Zongsan's New Confucian political philosophy] (Beijing: Zhongguo Yanshi chubanshe 2008). For a particularly clear discussion of Buddhist influence on the idea of self-restriction, see Jason Clower, *The Unlikely Buddhologist: Tiantai Buddhism in Mou Zongsan's New Confucianism* (Leiden: Brill, 2010), 119 n. 90.

29. See chap. 7 of my book *Contemporary Confucian Political Philosophy*.

30. Though for reasons of space I cannot expand on the similarities here, my approach to contemporary Confucian political philosophy, not surprisingly, overlaps in certain ways with the work of others who also build on the legacy of Mou Zongsan, such as the Kantian New Confucianism of Ming-huei Lee or the Critical New Confucianism of An-wu Lin.

7

Confucianism and Civil Society

The New Meanings of "Inner Sage" and "Outer King"

An-wu Lin

TRANSLATED FROM THE CHINESE BY TZE-KI HON

Since the mid-1990s, in view of the momentous changes after the end of the Cold War, I have repeatedly made a distinction between "New Confucianism" and "Post–New Confucianism."[1] The distinction is intended to underscore the fact that a new approach is needed to make Confucianism relevant to contemporary pluralistic society. My view is that whereas New Confucianism (*xin rujia*) focuses on building a democracy through the moral awakening of individuals, Post–New Confucianism (*hou xin rujia*) concerns itself with sustaining a fair and open society by training responsible citizens. Thus, the difference between the two New Confucianisms lies not in moral philosophy but in how to ensure justice in our contemporary society.[2]

To a great extent, Post–New Confucianism builds on the New Confucian project to bring science and democracy to China. But it goes beyond New Confucianism by directly addressing the three social injustices in traditional Chinese society, namely, imperial autocracy, elitism, and patriarchy. In order to eliminate these three social injustices, Post–New Confucianism promotes what Jürgen Habermas calls "civil society," in which citizens— old or young, male or female, powerful or powerless—are free to participate in public discourse. Unlike New Confucianism, which emphasizes the development of personal morality as the foundation of a democratic society, Post–New Confucianism views the public and private domains as a dynamic totality that drives a deliberative democracy forward through consultation and collaboration among citizens.

For this reason, Post–New Confucianism can be called "Civil Confucianism" (*gongmin ruxue* 公民儒學) because its goal is to support a civil society in which public discourse will freely take place to guide political decision.³ As Habermas has pointed out, a major characteristic of civil society is the occurrence of communicative acts in the public sphere, which are possible only when all citizens follow the rule of law and control their private interests for the sake of the public interest. To achieve a balance between the public and private interests, the starting point of Civil Confucianism must be learning to be an "outer king" (*waiwang*) rather than an "inner sage" (*neisheng*), although both are needed to sustain a civil society. The emphasis on the outer king is not intended to privilege rulers over citizens. The emphasis is necessary, rather, to ensure that the sociopolitical infrastructure for a deliberative democracy is in place. This reversal in the relationship between the outer king and the inner sage is precisely what distinguishes Post–New Confucianism from New Confucianism.

The Third Epoch

As is well known, New Confucianism is the third epoch in the development of Confucianism. During the first epoch (Zhou dynasty, 1046–256 BCE), Confucius promoted social mobility by transforming the concept of *junzi* (the gentlemen, the great man). By making *junzi* a moral category with which to measure the moral achievement of a learned person, Confucius turned moral cultivation into a social marker comparable to being descended from an aristocratic family or holding office in the government.⁴

During the second epoch (from the Qin to the Qing dynasties), the Confucian thinkers of the Imperial Age reinterpreted Confucianism to lend legitimacy to the imperial throne. To support imperial autocracy, they restructured Confucian learning such that attention was no longer paid to the Five Relationships that centered on bloodline and kinship, but rather to the Three Bonds that promoted loyalty to the emperor, obedience to parents, and subservience of wives to husbands.⁵ This shift to the Three Bonds gave rise to long-standing injustice in Chinese society wherein those in power bullied those who had no power, the older victimized the younger, and the men mistreated the women. As a result, for centuries Confucianism was intimately linked to authoritarianism, elitism, and patriarchy.

During the third epoch (from 1911 to the present), the goal of New Confucianism has been to bring science and democracy to China. More specifically, it aims to eliminate the Three Bonds: the imperial system, the patrilineal family structure, and patriarchal social practices. Certainly, the success of the 1911 Revolution ended the imperial system. But the revolution did not create a stable sociopolitical order in which to develop constitutional democracy and civil society. Worse still, from the 1920s to the present, the focus of New Confucianism has been limited to self-cultivation, privileging the development of the inner sage over the perfection of the outer king. Today we need a change in priority that focuses on social justice rather than on moral metaphysics, on civil rights rather than on ethics, and on citizenship rather than on sagehood.[6]

In this regard, what I call Post–New Confucianism is both a continuation and an expansion of New Confucianism. It continues the New Confucian project of introducing Western science and democracy to China, and it is part of the third epoch of Confucianism that aims to create a fair and just society in China by eradicating the Three Bonds. On the other hand, Post–New Confucianism goes beyond New Confucianism by attempting to strike a balance between the inner and outer domains, the private and public interests, the individual and social roles. By viewing the inner sage and the outer king as a dynamic totality, Post–New Confucianism supports diversity and pluralism in society without losing sight of equity and equality. By connecting individual interests and social interests, Post–New Confucianism emphasizes social justice and civil governance without ignoring individual freedom and personal interest. And above all, by linking individuals to society, Post–New Confucianism builds a civil society in which human relationships are multiple and malleable and yet are regulated by the rule of law. As such, Post–New Confucianism directly addresses the modern proclivity for privacy and individual rights while at the same time building on the core ideas of Classical Confucianism, such as reciprocity, free will, and moral perfection.

In short, Post–New Confucianism is designed for the twenty-first century, an era when plurality, ambiguity, and mobility are the norms and civil governance is based on reaching consensus in the public sphere. When rendered in philosophical terms, Post–New Confucianism can be described as building on the mutual dependence between *xin* (mind and heart) and *shen* (body). On the one hand, *xin* is rooted in *shen* when the human mind guides the person to make right decisions in daily life. On the other hand, *shen* is rooted in *xin* when the concrete reality of everyday experience triggers a person to search inwardly for moral guidance. In the former case, the universal principle of human goodness finds an expression in the particular circumstances of one's life; in the latter, one's particular viewpoint manifests the universal principle of human goodness. Regardless of whether it is from the universal to the particular or from the particular to the universal, we must activate the same innate human goodness to guide our actions. No matter whether we start from the outside or the inside, the key point is that we must find a way to manifest our innate human goodness in daily practices. Ultimately, it is the interconnection between the outer and the inner, the private and the public, and the individual and the community that makes civil society possible.[7]

Three Intellectual Sources

In retrospect, three intellectual sources undergird my thinking about Confucianism's role in civil society. First is Mou Zongsan's moral metaphysics. According to Mou, human goodness is not only innate, something that every human being inherits from nature, but it is also an intuition that gives each person the ability to separate good from evil, right from wrong.[8] To me, this "intellectual intuition" (*zhide zhijue* 智的直覺) is the driving force of the Chinese Enlightenment that began in the 1911 Revolution and continues in the present day. The goal of the Chinese Enlightenment is to end the Three Bonds and to build a pluralistic and law-abiding civil society in China. Even though the Chinese Enlightenment is about political and social change, it is intrinsically a moral enterprise that invites individual Chinese citizens to participate in changing China after moral awakening.

While Mou Zongsan elucidates the metaphysical roots of moral behavior, he does not explain how human goodness can be translated into political action. On this score, I find Xiong Shili's discussion about the inseparability of "substance" (*ti* 體) and "function" (*yong* 用) illuminating. According to Xiong, cosmic transformation is a constant process of generation and regeneration, with no clear distinction between self and other, between inner and outer, between part and whole. In particular, Xiong emphasizes the concept of *zaohua* (造化, creation and transformation) that breaks down all dualities in philosophy. From the perspective of the self-renewal of the universe, Xiong argues, everything that exists is temporary and incomplete because the universe is a gigantic system made up of an infinite number of forces. To me, Xiong's concept of *zaohua* complements Mou's moral metaphysics, highlighting the fact that while "moral intuition" is a driving force of the Chinese Enlightenment, it is only one of many factors in building a civil society.[9]

Finally, Wang Fuzhi (1619–1692) helps me understand the reciprocity between the inner sage and the outer king. If indeed, as according to Xiong, the universe is a gigantic system made of many different, competing forces, then the same is true of building a civil society. The process must be multicausal rather than monocausal. To borrow a metaphor from Wang Fuzhi, the process of building a civil society must be "a unity of opposites" (*liangduan er yizhi* 兩端而一致). Certainly, for Wang Fuzhi, the two opposites are cosmic and metaphysical concepts such as *dao* (the way) and *qi* (material force), *li* (principle) and *yu* (desires). But in the political practice of the twenty-first century, the opposites can be understood as the inner and the outer, the private and the public, the individual and the community. If translated into New Confucian terminology, the opposites are the inner sage and the outer king.[10]

For me, Wang Fuzhi's concept of the unity of opposites shows the possibility of thinking about contemporary political practice as a kind of *zaohua*, generation and regeneration. What is being generated and regenerated is the communicative act in the public sphere wherein citizens constantly engage in public debates to reach a consensus. In our time, it is not enough to focus only on one's "inner sagehood," no matter how important it is to cultivate oneself morally to participate in public affairs. Rather, it must be a double process: developing one's moral principles to guide one's political actions on the one hand and actively participating in public discourse to sharpen one's moral sensibility on the other. Through this constant interplay between the inner and the outer, the self and the other, the private and the public, communicative acts occur in the public sphere.

A New Morality

More importantly, this reciprocity between the inner and the outer reveals a new approach to morality. Rather than viewing morality as an abstract philosophy about the metaphysical roots of moral practices, the new approach takes seriously the complexity of contemporary political life. Being moral in the twenty-first century is to involve oneself in political activities, to improve the community, and to bring justice to society, while remaining fully aware of the danger of politics. Unlike morality in the Imperial Age, morality in the twenty-first century cannot be limited to self-cultivation. It must be part of the daily struggle against corruption in the political system and against injustice in society.

In specific terms, the Confucian moral practice of the twenty-first century must begin with a new understanding of the inner sage and the outer king. First, the two concepts must be separated from the long history of authoritarianism, elitism, and patriarchy in imperial China. Second, they must directly address the two fundamental concerns of our modern era: equality and plurality. The inner sage, for instance, must affirm individual subjectivity and self-transformative power. He or she must have a curious mind and devote it to objective, unbiased, fact-based learning. By the same token, the outer king must contribute to creation of a fair and just society. He or she must find ways to ensure that all citizens, regardless of backgrounds and abilities, will be protected by democratic institutions and the rule of law. Together, the inner sage and the outer king must create an environment that allows everyone—young and old, rich and poor, male and female, powerful and powerless, educated and uneducated, mainstream and minorities—to participate in the collective enterprise of sustaining a fair and just society.[11]

In addition, both the inner sage and the outer king must direct attention to the multiple voices and resources within the Confucian tradition. While I agree with scholars that we should adopt the Weberian notion of "ideal type" to identify the main characteristics of the Confucian tradition, I am acutely aware of the danger of reducing the complex Chinese tradition into a few simple formulas. To me, a search for an ideal type should not be an excuse for reductionism. Rather, it is only a point of departure from which to find diverse trends and multiple alternatives in the long history of the Confucian tradition.[12]

Confucianism and Civil Society

In the final analysis, contemporary Confucianism must serve the needs of civil society. Originally, Classical Confucianism might have promoted rule by virtuous persons. But throughout the history of imperial China, Confucianism had been used to support imperial autocracy, elitism, and patriarchy. Its teaching was intimately linked to the power of kings, patriarchs, and self-appointed sages. Because of this "misplaced Dao" (*dao de cuozhi* 道的錯置), Confucianism became an oppressive ideology, supporting the rulers and suppressing the ruled. For the rulers, Confucianism justified their authoritarian rule by honoring them as sages who possessed the virtue to rule the world; for the ruled, Confucianism kept them in place by asking them to accept the status quo. In the former instance, the notion of "innate human goodness" (*liangzhi* 良知) legitimized authoritarian rule; in the latter, it perpetuated social injustice. Worse still, over centuries, the Chinese developed a fatalistic view on politics because of the misplaced Dao. The Chinese believed that either they would be in power to bully the powerless or they would be powerless and suffer under authoritarian rule. Gone were the optimism and activism present when Classical Confucian thinkers coined the terms "inner sage" and "outer king."[13]

In our times, the first thing we must do is to bring back the optimism and activism of Classical Confucianism. More importantly, we must give new meanings to the terms "inner sage" and "outer king" to serve the needs of contemporary society. The term "outer king" does not imply a return to imperial rule. Rather, it means building the sociopolitical infrastructure to support a civil society, such as creating a "social contract" between citizens and the state, establishing the rule of law to protect individual liberty, and providing social space for public discourse. These social and political structures are essential to providing a safe environment for citizens to assert their rights, and they are the key elements that separate modern "civil society" (*gongmin shehui* 公民社會) from premodern "kinship society" (*jiazu shehui* 家族社會).[14]

The term "inner sage" no longer relates to perfecting oneself morally by supporting the Five Relationships and the Three Bonds. On the contrary, the inner sage now implies the performance of the duties and functions of a citizen. Specifically, it means that the inner sage must know his or her rights; at the same time, the inner sage must balance his or her private rights with the public interest. In short, the inner sage of contemporary society must always ponder the following three questions. First, how can he or she find ways to balance the individual needs for privacy and autonomy with the public needs for equity and equality? Second, how can he or she apply the notion of filial piety in a civil society, knowing that filial piety originates in a patrilineal family system? Third, how can he or she temper functional rationalism with morality when building a fair and just society requires planning, management, and cost-benefit analysis?[15]

In the end, the answers to these questions will lead to a paradox: "wholeheartedly serving the public interest without sacrificing one's private interest" (*dagong yousi* 大公有私). Unlike the *junzi* in imperial times who could claim to "wholeheartedly serve the public interest with no care for private interest" (*dagong wusi* 大公無私), the inner sage in a contemporary society must be a citizen who is constantly looking for ways to bridge the inner and the outer, the private and the public.

Notes

1. Over the past two decades, I have published many articles and books distinguishing between New Confucianism and Post–New Confucianism. For a summary of my view, please read my book *Ruxue geminglun: Hou xin rujia zhexue de wenti xiangdu* 儒學革命論: 後新儒家哲學的問題向度 [Revolution in Confucianism: On the philosophy of Post–New Confucianism] (Taipei: Taiwan xuesheng shuju, 1998), esp. chap. 3.

2. For a list of differences between New Confucianism and Post–New Confucianism, see my article "Xin rujia, hou xinrujia, xiandai, yu houxiandai: Zuijin shinianlai de xingcha yu sikao zhi yiban" 「新儒學」, 「後新儒學」, 「現代」與「後現代」——最近十年來的省察與思考之一斑 ["New Confucianism," "Post–New Confucianism," "Modernity," and "Postmodernity": My views and thoughts in the last ten years], *Ehu* 鵝湖 30, no. 12 (June 2005): 8–21.

3. Elsewhere I explain this view in detail. See *Rujia zhuanxiang: Cong xin ruxue dao hou xinruxue de guodu* 儒學轉向: 從「新儒學」到「後新儒學」的過渡 [A change of direction in Confucianism: The transition from New Confucianism to Post–New Confucianism] (Taipei: Taiwan xuesheng shuju, 2006).

4. Elsewhere I explain the social and political implications in this change from a focus on the Five Relationships to a focus on the Three Bonds. See my book *Rujia yu Zhongguo chuantong shehui zhi zhexue xingcha* 儒家與中國傳統社會之哲學省察 [A philosophical critique of Confucianism and Chinese traditional society] (Taipei: Youshi wenhua shiye, 1996).

5. For a detailed discussion of this change, see my book *Dao de cuozhi: Zhongguo zhengzhi chuantong de genben kunjie* 道的錯置: 中國政治傳統的根本困結 [Misplaced Dao: The essential problem of Chinese political thought] (Taipei: Taiwan xuesheng shuju, 2003).

6. For the significance of this change, see my book *Rujia lunli yu shehui zhengyi* 儒家倫理與社會正義 [Confucian ethics and social justice] (Beijing: Zhongguo yanshi chubanshe, 2005).

7. For a detailed discussion on the relation between xin and shen, see my article "Cong 'yixin kongshen' dao—'shenxin yiru': Yi Wang Fuzhi zhexue wei hexin jianji yu Cheng-Zhu, Lu-Wang de taolun" 從「以心控身」到「身心一如」: 以王夫之哲學為核心兼及於程朱, 陸王的討論 [From "controlling the body by the mind" to "the combination of body and mind": A study of Wang Fuzhi's philosophy and the debate between the Cheng-Zhu and Lu-Wang schools], *Guowen xuebao* 國文學報 30 (June 2001): 77–96.

8. On the significance of Mou Zongsan's philosophy, see my article "Yingjie hou Mou Zongsan shidai de lailin: Mou Zongsan quanji chuban ganji" 迎接「後牟宗三時代」的來臨—《牟宗三先生全集》出版感紀 [Welcome the arrival of the Post–Mou Zongsan era: Thoughts on the publication of *The Complete Works of Mou Zongsan*], *Ehu* 鵝湖 28, no. 9 (May 2003): 1.

9. For my view of Xiong Shili's philosophy, see my book *Mou Zongsan qianhou: Dangdai xin rujia zhexue sixiang shilun* 牟宗三前後: 當代新儒家哲學思想史論 [Before and after Mou Zongsan: A historical account of the philosophical thoughts of Contemporary New Confucians] (Taipei: Taiwan xuesheng shuju, 2011), chap. 14.

10. For Wang Fuzhi's philosophy, see my book *Wang Chuanshan renxingshi zhexue zhi yanjiu* 王船山人性史哲學之研究) [A study of Wang Chuanshan's philosophy on humanistic history] (Taipei: Dongda tushu gongsi, 1987).

11. For a detailed discussion of the relation between the inner sage and the outer king, see my article "Cong waiwang dao neisheng: Hou xin ruxue de xin

sikao" 從「外王」到「內聖」：後新儒學的新思考 [From the outer king to the inner sage: The new thought of Post–New Confucianism], *Ehu* 鵝湖 30, no. 2 (Aug. 2004): 16–25.

12. I further develop my argument on the Weberian ideal type and contemporary civil society in my article "Hou xinruxue de shehui zhexue: Qiyue, zeren yu 'yiti zhiren'—maixiang yi shehui zhengyilun wei hexin de ruxue sikao" 後新儒學的社會哲學：契約，責任與「一體之仁」—邁向以社會正義論為核心的儒學思考 [The social philosophy of Post–New Confucianism: Contracts, duties, and the one body of humanity—Confucian thought on social justice), *Si yu yan* [Thoughts and words] 思與言 39, no. 4 (2001): 57–82.

13. I discuss the consequences of this misplaced priority in Confucian morality in *Rujia yu Zhongguo chuantong shehui zhi zhexue xingcha*.

14. For the differences between civil society and kinship society, see *Rujia yu Zhongguo chuantong shehui zhi zhexue xingcha*, esp. conclusion.

15. Elsewhere I discuss the social implications of the inner sage being a responsive and responsible citizen. See my book *Rujia lunli yu shehui zhengy*.

8

A Mission Impossible?

*Mou Zongsan's Attempt to
Rebuild Morality in the Modern Age*

Ke Sheng

In discussing morality in our modern time, the renowned Scottish philosopher Alasdair MacIntyre argues that discussing moral principles in a secular world driven by global trade and industrial production is fruitless. He asserts that although many attempts have been made to construct a moral code for the modern age, they are doomed to fail because of the amoral nature of the modern society. To make his point, MacIntyre writes:

> Thus all these writers share in the project of constructing valid arguments which will move from premises concerning human nature as they understand it to be to conclusions about the authority of moral rules and precepts. I want to argue that any project of this form was bound to fail, because of an ineradicable discrepancy between their shared conception of moral rules and precepts on the one hand and what was shared—despite much larger divergences—in their conception of human nature on the other. Both conceptions have a history and their relationship can only be made intelligible in the light of that history.[1]

MacIntyre emphasizes the historical background of the emergence and practice of morality, and he points out that morality cannot be separated from its social context. So what we call moral virtues, such as justice and bravery, are derived from a particular understanding of human nature at a particular moment in time. In addition, MacIntyre believes that one of the most important results of modernization is individualism. This new human identity separates an individual from his or her role in society, and each person only looks after his or her own interest. In modern society, MacIntyre asserts, human beings treat one another as equal because they are all rational beings seeking to maximize their personal interests. This chapter maintains that, like other modern philosophers, Contemporary New Confucians have to confront all the modern predicaments that MacIntyre diagnoses, and yet, contrary to MacIntyre's bleak prognosis, they try to develop a moral mission to give meaning to modern life.

The Mission of Contemporary New Confucianism

Contemporary New Confucianism emerged in response to the May Fourth Movement (1915–1923). Professor Lin Yüsheng uses the term "totalistic antitraditionalism" to describe the characteristic of the New Culture Movement that viewed Confucianism as a stumbling block to China's modernization.[2] According to Lin, the fierce critique of the Confucian tradition made the May Fourth Movement a unique historical phenomenon in which all Confucian moral values were under attack.

The impact of the critique can be seen in three areas. First, the authority of Confucius was discredited. Confucius, the key figure of the Confucian tradition for more than 2,000 years, lost his sanctity in the minds of the Chinese people. This loss of authority reminds us of MacIntyre's analysis of the failure of all the projects to rebuild morality in the modern age. For MacIntyre, before the Renaissance an external authority provided a guarantee for traditional morality in Europe. But after that, with the decline of the authority of the Church, morality lost its external basis. Without this external authority, God and God's agent the Church, people no longer had reason to adhere to morality. What modern philosophers intend to do is to highlight the importance and usefulness of morality in a secular world.

Anyone in China who wants to save the old Confucian morality faces a challenge similar to that of moral philosophers in the West: to show its usefulness and significance in a secular society that is founded on commerce and industrial production. Like the philosophers in the West, Contemporary New Confucians cannot rely on tradition to discuss morality. They must build a moral system based on reason.

Second, the May Fourth iconoclasts also attacked Confucian rituals. They saw Confucian rituals as part of the system of oppression the ruling class used. As a result, Contemporary New Confucians of the time could no longer advocate the Confucian rituals. This first generation of Contemporary New Confucians consciously rejected Confucian rituals and tried to separate the two components, Confucian rituals and Confucian ideas. They wanted to save Confucianism by preserving the Confucian ideology without any ritual.

Third, in many regards, the New Culture Movement gave rise to individualism in modern China. Individualism emerged along with the totalistic antitraditionalism and was the result of a gradual process of modernization. The main characteristics of modern Chinese individualism are similar to what MacIntyre describes in Western society. He argues that morality in Western society is no longer grounded in universal principles, and therefore individuals must establish their own personal standards to judge their actions.[3] Similarly, Contemporary New Confucians develop their philosophy in response to the cultural iconoclasm of the May Fourth Movement. They accept the May Fourth critique because they know that modern China must be fundamentally different from imperial China. Additionally, they know that they cannot avoid the challenge of modernity that MacIntyre describes, namely, how to give moral meaning to a secular life dictated by commercial and industrial production.

Seemingly embarking on an impossible mission, Contemporary New Confucians find ways to discuss morality in modern society. As mentioned earlier, the first generation of Contemporary New Confucians, such as Xiong Shili, were deeply influenced by the New Culture Movement. As for the successors of Xiong Shili, such as Mou Zongsan, Tang Junyi, and Xu Fuguan, they were also tremendously affected by the New Culture Movement. For example, like the May Fourth iconoclasts, they promoted science and democracy, as shown in their 1958 Declaration.[4] Thus, when analyzing the historical and social context in which the Contemporary New Confucians work, we must pay attention both to their relationship to the New Culture Movement and to their creative interpretation of Song-Ming Neo-Confucianism. Of course, the latter is a major resource of their philosophy because they accept the fundamental philosophical argument of Neo-Confucians. And in one sense they have a similar task in mind, that is, reviving Confucianism in a new epoch.

Beginning in the Song dynasty (roughly the eleventh century), the Neo-Confucians began to revive Confucian morality by creating a philosophical system of moral-metaphysics that connected the cosmos and humanity. And in this moral-metaphysics, morality is valid only because moral principle is the same as the principle of the universe, commonly known as *tiandao, taiji, tianli*. Because of this, morality is not only cosmologically rooted but also a representation of the principle of the natural world. In late imperial China, Neo-Confucians could employ two measures to support a moral system: the authority of Confucius and the Confucian rituals. Of course, these two measures presented a particular understanding of human nature from the Confucian notion of *ren* (humanness). In modern times, however, both of these measures have lost their effectiveness in the aftermath of the New Culture Movement. The "totalistic antitraditionalism" of the May Fourth iconoclasts discredited the Confucian tradition and the Confucian rituals. Since Contemporary New Confucians still want to promote Confucian morality in modern society, they have to face the challenge MacIntyre posed: How can we establish morality in a secular society based solely on reason?

The early Contemporary New Confucians may not have understood the magnitude of the challenge they confronted, which had never happened so violently in Chinese history. They still insisted on their faith in Confucianism and the universality of it. But the world was totally different; it was the modern world. Here we can see a dilemma that the New Confucians have to face but are not clearly aware of. What they want to do is to maintain a Confucian morality that inherits its contents from the tradition. But the method they try to use is a modern one that relies on human rationality. So a dilemma emerges over using modern means to achieve traditional ends. In addition to this "ends-means dilemma," Contemporary New Confucianism must deal with another issue: the "particularity-universality dilemma." The latter dilemma also originates from the historical background of morality, although in a slightly different way. It is related to the great target and the puzzle Contemporary New Confucians are working with. It profoundly influences the formation of their philosophy. For better understanding, we must go further with MacIntyre's argument.

After his criticism of modern morality, MacIntyre goes back to Aristotle to seek help and advocates the theory of virtue. Virtue ethics, according to MacIntyre, means that all the virtues that we need in human life cannot be understood without their particular context. Here the particular context refers to the historical situation, the social relations, and the comprehension of the goal of human being. So he indicates that the theory of virtue should begin from practice. In his works, *practice* is a complicated and primary concept. He writes:

> By a "practice" I am going to mean any coherent and complex form of socially established cooperative human activity through which goods internal to that form of activity are realized in the course of trying to achieve those standards of excellence which are appropriate to, and partially definitive of, that form of activity,

with the result that human powers to achieve excellence, and human conception of the ends and goods involved, are systematically extended. . . . In the ancient and medieval worlds the creation and sustaining of human communities of households, cities, [and] nations is generally taken to be a practice in the sense in which I have defined it.[5]

Virtues can come only from the practice of human beings in the process of trying to achieve standards of excellence. In emphasizing the concept of practice, MacIntyre's purpose is to connect virtues with human activities. Virtue, then, is not something with fixed meaning, but something constantly changing with history and varying in different traditions. And thus, there is no universal morality, but only particular moralities. Each is legitimate in its own way. But, surprisingly, Contemporary New Confucians do not take MacIntyre's position. On the contrary, they promote Confucian morality as a universal system. For them, when facing the attack that Confucianism was an ancient ideology unsuitable for the modern society, the universality of Confucianism is the only, or at least a major, reason for its relevance in the twenty-first century. For example, Mou Zongsan always noticed the universality of Confucianism in his speech as the main reason for advocating the significance of Confucianism in industrial society. He preferred to use "eternal principle" (常道) to refer to Confucianism. For Mou, "eternal principle" appropriately expresses the universality of Confucianism in two ways. He writes: "Chinese people prefer to call it 'eternal principle,' which can be understood in two ways: one is its permanence, which means the diachronic universality; the other is that it can be adopted by everyone. This means the synchronic universality of it and that Confucianism can be adopted by all the people in the world."[6] The diachronic universality shows that Confucianism would not change in different historical situations, the synchronic universality that Confucianism is beyond culture, tradition, and race. Almost all the Contemporary New Confucians share this position. The crucial point is that they promote Confucian morality simply because it is universal and it is the only way that human beings should choose.

Here we can compare this position with other Confucian scholars in mainland China, especially during the last decade. In recent years in mainland China, some scholars who would like to be regarded as Confucians become increasingly active. Of course they have different points and approaches for renewing the authority of Confucianism in mainland China, but some commonalities do exist among them. One of these is that they all take the political aspects of Confucianism more seriously than the Contemporary New Confucians, who pay more attention to the philosophical character of Confucianism. This difference has some important consequences, and in what follows I discuss one of them. In their new book, *What Is Universality? Whose Value?*, the new generation of Confucians in mainland China justifies the validity of Confucianism by pointing out that Confucianism is *our* tradition and culture, for we Chinese are all shaped by it and there is no other choice.[7] It seems that they take a different position from the New Confucians because they are more relativistic and less ambitious about Confucianism. They only intend to demonstrate that it is a regional, historical, and special tradition, not a universal truth. Perhaps this change stems from the change of the environment of China in the last fifty years, particularly the last two decades. Perhaps we can say that while the new generation has more self-confidence than the older generation, such as Mou Zongsan, they show less confidence on Confucianism. Their argument for the validity of Confucianism is based on cultural particularity, not universality. That means that the usefulness of Confucianism is not based on the commitment that it is universally right, but only because it is suitable for the Chinese.

Here I am not interested in making a judgment on which way is right. But apparently the Contemporary New Confucians half a century ago had a bigger dream. What they wanted to prove was that Confucianism is right and true not only for the Chinese but also for peoples around the world. This may be an idealistic project for the Confucians. To achieve it, the new generation of Contemporary New Confucians cannot avoid the two dilemmas indicated above. A formidable mission is now before Contemporary New Confucians, and it seems impossible to complete. On the one hand, they are deeply disturbed by the social issues of modernization. Because of this, they see Confucian morality as a universal system based on human reason. On the other hand, they do not agree with the solution of virtue ethics that MacIntyre offered for the secular society because they all firmly believe in the universality of Confucianism.

Mou Zongsan's Endeavor

Among the Contemporary New Confucians, Mou Zongsan is the most systematic and creative philosopher. Particularly, he offers a solution to the New Confucian dilemma by creatively reinterpreting the Song-Ming Neo-Confucianism in two areas. First, in discussing morality, Mou focuses his attention on the individual's innate ability, rather than on social norms and behavioral code. Second, on the basis of the Confucian moral metaphysics, Mou develops a moral philosophy that highlights the cosmological roots of daily life.

To develop these two points, Mou Zongsan finds inspirations from the Ming philosopher, Wang Yangming (1472–1529). Mou adopts Wang's concepts *liangzhi* (human consciousness 良知) or *zhi de zhique* (intellectual intuition 智的直覺) to describe the metaphysical foundation of his moral system. For him, *liangzhi*, coming from one's inner heart and without any positive definition, is the basis of morality. Here *liangzhi* plays two interrelated roles in his moral theory. On the one hand, it is understood as the essence of morality, which in Confucian tradition means the essence of human beings.[8] In other words, *liangzhi* determines that the human being "must" be a moral being because the only way a person can find meaning in his life is to follow *liangzhi*. On the other hand, *langzhi* distinguishes good and evil, thereby separating public interest from private desire.

On closer inspection, however, Mou Zongsan's *liangzhi* is different from Wang Yangming's. Wang Yangming always considers *liangzhi* in a social setting, especially when he uses the concept to denote the ability of distinguishing good from evil. Although initially Wang's *liangzhi* seems to refer to the inner ability of a human being, if we investigate his writings more carefully, we find they are always accompanied by the role of person.[9] For example, when his student asks him, "How does *liangzhi* inform us what to do in everyday life," Wang Yangming answers: "Knowing is the substance of one's heart. One's own heart will know how to act spontaneously. When one meets his father, it (*liangzhi*) knows that one should be filial; when one meets his brother, it knows that one should love and respect his elder brother. If someone finds that a child is going to fall into a well, he cannot help but have a feeling of alarm and commiseration. This is called *liangzhi*. It is self-sufficient and needs no other help."[10] Of course, in Wang Yangming's work we can find a tendency to go beyond the concrete historical and social limits.[11] But here the relationship between father and son, elder brother and younger brother, forms the context for understanding the function of *liangzhi*. According to Wang Yangming, the love of one's own parents is the root of all morality. Here, the relationship between children and parents is regarded as primordial and therefore the most important. Man is understood as someone who must fulfill his social role.

In contrast to Wang Yangming, Mou Zongsan goes in a different direction when discussing the foundation of morality. According to Mou, the source of morality comes from the innate nature of human beings, which is known as the feeling of alarm and commiseration (as Mencius said).[12] Mou describes the inner moral essence of human beings as "the nature of the entire person that will feel uncomfortable to degenerate and fall to crime."[13] Here the discomfort with immoral behavior is a revelation of moral consciousness. And for Mou, this revelation does not come from the intellect, but from an intuition. To describe this intuition, Mou uses the category *nijue tizheng* (an existential affirmation of intuitive feeling 逆覺體證)[14] to explain this experience:

> When someone is eager to expect the emergence of a truly moral activity, and at the same time feels uneasy about degeneration, this uneasiness is just the representation of his inner moral heart. At this moment, the person must hold up this uneasiness and keep away from sliding with desire. The person must stop the slide. And this stop means to go back to your inner moral heart. Please be silent and not exigent. Stop and go back. This feeling of uneasiness will make itself manifest, will present itself, and will not disappear again. We, human beings, must follow it and affirm it after it reveals itself. And this is our innate moral heart/consciousness which makes our moral activity possible. This feeling is what we call *nijue tizheng* (逆覺體證).[15]

For Mou, moral decision is not determined by social roles and obligations (as in Wang Yangming's model); rather, it develops from an inner intuition rooted in one's heart and mind. In adopting this view, Mou completely modifies the traditional Confucian understanding of inner morality, which is founded on the basis of blood relationship (kinship) and connects human morality directly to the natural principle of the cosmos. In addition, for Mou, the revelation of the innate human goodness does not have to take place in familial and social relationships. Instead, it can emerge in the action of an individual who sees moral cultivation as an individual quest for self-discovery and self-fulfillment. Based on such an understanding, Mou modifies the traditional way of defining the essence of an individual within social relationships and turns moral cultivation into an occasion for achieving modern individualism.

To prove his point, Mou refers to Mencius's parable of a child falling into a well.[16] In his interpretation of the parable, Mou focuses on the role of human emotions in making moral decisions. For Mou, the emotion of sympathy toward the child emerges not because we care about it as a member of our family, but because we care about it as a living being in the universe. We save the baby because she is a precious life that must be saved, not because she is related to us in blood or in kinship.

If Mou uses this approach to reply to the first dilemma, he uses a modern means to guarantee the origin of traditional Confucian virtues. Now he must prove the universality of Confucianism, which constitutes the second dilemma.

To do this, as discussed earlier, Mou cannot merely use rationality to solve the problem any longer. Instead, he turns from rationalism to existentialism. He tries to go back to the original experience of a human being in his life-world. In this sense, the task for him is not to prove or to explain, but to "show." In many ways, Mou's existential turn is shaped by his understanding of the Chinese tradition. The substance of Confucianism cannot be seen or grasped as something really "there." It can only be grasped by action or existence. On the basis of this understanding, Mou proceeds to show that we can reveal *liangzhi* in action, particularly in dealing with problems in daily life.

We can see this through Mou's interpretation of Neo-Confucianism. For Mou, Neo-Confucianism designs two approaches to present the unity of the Way of Heaven (*tiandao*) and Human Nature (*renxing*). One is top-down, starting from the Way of Heaven to Human Nature, from the transcendent substance to the concrete existent human being, as outlined in the *Doctrine of the Mean*.[17] But since the Way of Heaven, the transcendent substance, cannot be recognized by human beings, Mou believes that this approach is merely a hypothesis. And the opposite way is bottom-up, starting from the human heart to the Way of Heaven. This approach is the only possible way to present a foundation for morality.

In this way, Mou's existentialist solution provides an ingenious answer to the two dilemmas discussed in the second section. For the first dilemma, he uses existential experiences, not human rationality, to prove the possibility of modern morality. Existential experiences do not need any rational explanation and demonstration. It is just what it presents there. So morality, which is no longer based on any rational construction, can still be accepted because it comes from the daily experiences of human beings. For the second dilemma, since existential experiences are universal, there will be the same reaction when people are put into the same situation in spite of the difference between traditions and nations. According to this, Contemporary New Confucians can claim that Confucian morality is not a special inheritance for Chinese but a universal one.

But is this existentialism sufficient to establish morality in the modern epoch? Since MacIntyre has already criticized Sartre's existentialism, we have to ask what the difference is between Sartre and Mou. In his book, *Moral Idealism,* Mou also criticizes Sartre: "Today's existentialists, such as

Sartre, Heidegger, and so forth, want to investigate our real life without the definition of logic. This is certainly right. But if we follow Sartre's philosophy (Heidegger is different), we have to deny human nature, and take human nature as undefinable."[18]

For Mou, Sartre's view that man's existence precedes his essence results in the denial of the existence of human nature. But in Chinese philosophy in general and in Mou in particular, human nature is eternal, and this eternity lies in man's internal moral subjectivity. We find this criticism of existentialism is familiar to MacIntyre. When he talks about the philosophical obstacles, MacIntyre refers to existentialism. According to MacIntyre, Sartrian mode, as an instance of existentialism, is one of the chief obstacles because "a self separated from its roles in the Sartrian mode loses that arena of social relationships in which the Aristotelian virtues function if they function at all."[19] For Mou, however, the existential method is good because it offers an alternative way besides logical analysis to describe the original experience, which is the foundation of Confucian morality. But the conclusion of existentialism cannot be accepted because it lacks moral idealism. Here the moral idealism means the faith of Confucianism's virtues and the moral subjectivity. In other words, when we use the category, Mou's existentialism only means that he uses the method to describe the very original experience, not that he draws the same conclusion of modern existentialism.

Then, the moral subject, as we have found above, can appear only in existential experience and cannot become the object of rational cognition, known or described by reason.

Here we come to the limitation of Mou's existentialism; that is, Mou does not develop his existentialism to its logical end. If we follow his thinking, then the next problem will be more difficult: How can we establish morality only with the existential experience? Or in other words, how can we find moral values in the original experience? This is a more difficult task. And just on this problem, Mou backs off and seeks help from the traditional dogma by declaring that the moral nature of human beings cannot be empirically demonstrated. Manifest in his philosophy is the declaration of the intellectual intuition of human being, which sounds rather arbitrary. Of course I am not against Mou's philosophy. Perhaps we still have opportunity to further develop his existentialist approach.

Conclusion

I agree with Mou that modern Chinese philosophy, particularly with respect to morality, must be linked to an individual's existential situation. But can the metaphysical underpinning of moral behavior be manifested in the life-world, in individuals' existential experience, when it is abstracted from historical environment? Does a universal human nature transcend conventional boundaries, such as nation, tradition, and culture?

As discussed above, at least beginning in the Song dynasty, Neo-Confucians began to reconstruct Confucian morality on a new foundation. And Contemporary New Confucianism can be seen as their successors with respect to building a new moral philosophy based on the Confucian notion of *ren*. Mou, for one, creates a moral philosophy that emphasizes the existential experience of innate human goodness. In a nutshell, Mou's moral philosophy is a reaffirmation of the old Confucian position about "the superior man not being a vessel" (君子不器). It is said that Confucian morality will not prescribe any specific principles as to what man should do. Instead, a moral person must make the right choice in various situations because life is complicated and full of options.

Situational ethics had been practiced in China for thousands of years until the modern times. In the past, the moral tradition worked because it was supported by an elaborate system of etiquette rituals. Thus, Confucians need not define what human beings should or should not do because each person could find guidance in Confucian rituals. In modern China, however, Confucian rituals are abandoned due to totalistic antitraditionalism. As a result, people often do not know what to do in concrete situations. Is Mou's creative transformation of Confucian morality, then, sufficient to establish morality in modern China—or is it another mission impossible? This is something that we need to discover.

Notes

Author's note: I would like to thank Professor Hon Tze-ki and Professor Liu Wei for their extremely helpful comments on earlier versions of this chapter. This chapter is supported by Youth Innovative Research Team of Capital Normal University.

    1. Alasdair MacIntyre, *After Virtue* (Notre Dame, IN: University of Notre Dame Press, 2007), 52.

    2. See Lin Yüsheng, *The Crisis of Chinese Consciousness: Radical Antitraditionalism in the May Fourth Era* (Madison: University of Wisconsin Press, 1979), 4.

    3. MacIntyre, *After Virtue*, 33.

    4. See Mou Zongsan, Carsun Chang, Tang Junyi, and Xu Fuguan, "A Manifesto for a Re-Appraisal of Sinology and Reconstruction of Chinese Culture," in *The Development of Neo-Confucian Thought* (New York: Bookman, 1962), 455–483.

    5. MacIntyre, *After Virtue*, 187.

6. See Mou Zongsan, "Shidai yu ganshou" 時代與感受 [Feelings of the times], in *Mou Zongsan quanji* 牟宗三全集, vol. 23 (Taibei: Lianjing chubanshe, 2003), 323.

7. Zeng Yi 曾亦 and Guo Xiaodong 郭曉东, eds., *Hewei bushi? Shuizhi jiezhi?* 何谓普世？谁之价值？ [What is universality? Whose value?] (Shanghai: East China Normal University Press, 2013).

8. Here, the word "essence" is not used in the sense of Essentialism. I use it only to describe a certain understanding of human nature in Chinese tradition.

9. Wang Yangming used *liangzhi* in two ways. One focuses on its moral feature and the other on its ontological feature. For the latter, *liangzhi* is understood as the noumenon of human consciousness, beings of the world, and so on. For the former, which is more relevant for our present purpose, Wang Yangming uses it to indicate the moral nature of human beings. And at this point, when talking about how to recognize it in our daily life, he always uses the examples of father and son or emperor and officials. For example, when Xu Ai, his student, asked him whether finding the moral principle only in our minds was enough, Wang Yangming said finding the moral principle in the object rather than in our minds was impossible. When you want to take care of your father, you should find the motivation in yourself, not your father. And the same should happen with regard to the relationship between brothers and friends. See Wang Yangming, *The Complete Works of Wang Yangming* (Shanghai: Shanghai Guji Press, 2009), 2.

10. 又曰：「知是心之本體，心自然會知：見父自然知孝，見兄自然知弟，見孺子入井自然知惻隱，此便是良知，不假外求。」*The Complete Works of Wang Yangming*, 6.

11. See Tu Wei-ming, *Neo-Confucian Thought in Action: Wang Yang-ming's Youth (1472–1509)* (Berkeley: University of California Press, 1976).

12. Mencius, Gongsun Chou: "所以謂人皆有不忍人之心者，今人乍見孺子將入於井，皆有怵惕惻隱之心 . . . ." *Mengzi Zhengyi* (Beijing: Zhonghua shuju, 1987).

13. "人皆有不安於下墮而致淪落的本性，不安於下墮於罪的本性便是道德性." Mou Zongsan, "Zhongguo zhexue de tezhi" 中國哲學的特質 [Characteristics of Chinese philosophy], in *Mou Zongsan quanji*, vol. 28 (Taibei: Lianjing chubanshe, 2003), 68.

14. Sébastien Billioud translates this category as "retrospective verification" in his book *Thinking through Confucian Modernity: A Study of Mou Zongsan's Moral Metaphysics* (Leiden: Brill, 2011).

15. Mou Zongsan, *Xinti yu xingti* 心體與性體 [The metaphysical principle of the mind and the metaphysical principle of nature] (Taipei: Zhengzhong shuju, 2002), vol. 3, 338.

16. Mencius, Gongsun Chou, *Mengzi Zhengyi* (Beijing: Zhonghua shuju, 1987), 2.20.

17. "It is the principle of heaven that makes the nature of human beings" (天命之謂性), *Zhongyong* 中庸 [The doctrine of the mean], chap. 1.

18. "如薩特利, 海德格, 等, 都是想在邏輯定義以外而另行考察真實的人生. 這是對的. 然如薩特利那樣, (海德格不如此), 必否決人性, 必以為人性不可定義, 則輕浮而悖矣." Mou Zongsan, *Daode di lixiang zhuyi* 道德的理想主義 [Moral idealism] (Taipei: Xuesheng shuju, 2000), 124.

19. Ibid., 205.

9

The Challenge of Totalitarianism

Lessons from Tang Junyi's Political Philosophy

THOMAS FRÖHLICH

Intellectual aspirations to reclaim "Confucianism" as a resource for critical reflection about political democracy date back to the first half of the twentieth century and gained momentum in exilic circles outside the People's Republic of China in the 1950s. On the Chinese mainland, the issue of relating Confucian intellectual and political traditions to democratic thought experienced a resurgence in the 1990s. During these historically eventful periods widely different meanings were ascribed to Confucianism and to democracy. We accordingly find a broad range of explicitly "Confucian" positions that responded affirmatively, critically, or outright negatively to what was perceived as Western types of (liberal) democracy, while sometimes attempting to fathom the outlines of a future "Confucian democracy" in China.[1] Although introducing the plural form of "Confucianisms" here would be more precise, we can still detect several basic features most Confucian references share. For one, most proponents of Confucianism favor some form of democratic government, while suggesting that an infusion of Confucian ideas and traditions might considerably enhance existing systems of liberal democracy. Such expectations usually pertain to the implementation of social justice, the meritocratic efficiency of government agencies, and a general willingness to uphold personal virtues and ethical values in politics. In contrast, explicit affirmations of antidemocratic ideas based on "Confucianism" have become the exception in international debates—that is, if one decides to look past those, such as Lee Kuan Yew in Singapore, who subsume Confucianism within "Asian values" in order to deflect criticism of governments lacking democratic legitimation.

Additionally, references to Confucianism in discussions about democracy further share the feature that even though they often bemoan the dubious record of "Confucianism" with respect to democracy, they seldom analyze it in detail.[2] As a result of this oversight, "Confucianism," or the adjective "Confucian," is often used as a vague denominator for a stockpile of political ideas and practices that apparently can serve to justify democratic, nondemocratic, and even antidemocratic thought and institutions alike. There is a tendency to downplay the entanglement of Confucian ideas and practices with nondemocratic forms of government before and after the founding of the Republic of China in 1912. This is particularly unsatisfying when an allegedly novel, non-Western critique of Western-style democracies—or even a superior concept of a future democracy—is presented in the name of Confucianism. Merely examining the Confucian classics in a highly selective manner in order to detect protodemocratic ideas, however, is not enough. Neither are arbitrary identifications of long-standing Chinese ideas and government institutions as ostensible "Confucian" achievements convincing, regardless whether they pertain to the civil service examinations, the ideal of the equal dignity of the emperor and chancellor, or the complex or "meritocratic" rules for the promotion and demotion of government officials. Unfortunately, political ideas and practices like these evolved over long periods of time and often without any close connection at all to the "classical" works of Confucianism. Apart from the tendency to overstate the impact of Confucian thought at the expense of other intellectual strands of political traditions present in other "classical" works (e.g., from the Legalist and Mohist canon) and in less prestigious but in fact highly influential writings (such as manuals for imperial officials, legal texts, etc.), there is a real risk of committing anachronistic distortions. Imposing democratic concerns on "Confucian" writings, which stem from an unrelated historical context, can be utterly misleading.

Even if we were to grant that one might succeed in retrieving the vestiges of protodemocratic ideas and practices from the traditions of Confucianism, the shift to the political discourses of the twentieth century and beyond would still entail a major challenge. Unless Confucian traditions prove effective with respect not only to a critique of shortcomings in contemporary democratic government but also, and equally importantly, to a critique of nondemocratic or antidemocratic currents in modern societies, they must remain a dubious fellow traveler of modern democratic thought. By the same token, a Confucian "renewal" that limits itself to explanations for the past failure of Confucianism to establish political democracy in China does not suffice. If a reconstructed or "renewed" Confucianism is to function in a comprehensive way as an intellectual resource of democratic theory and ideas, it will have to prove its ability to address fundamental challenges to political democracy. Among these we find, first and foremost, the totalitarian and authoritarian challenges that emerged in the twentieth century. Inasmuch as a renewal of Confucianism remains oblivious to such challenges, its critique (or affirmation) of liberal democracies must not only remain aloof to reality but also lack the theoretical tools for delimiting democracy. Besides this, given that the convergence of Confucianism and democracy is fairly recent and was accompanied throughout the twentieth century by competing nondemocratic "Confucian" claims (ranging from early Republican calls to establish Confucianism as a state religion to later justifications of authoritarian rule in terms of Confucian traditions and values in Taiwan, Singapore, and South Korea), it seems even more important to grasp the nondemocratic or even antidemocratic undercurrents of Confucianism. This is not to say that one necessarily needs to suggest that modern Confucianism was vulnerable to being absorbed by totalitarian ideologies or that it even contained prototypicalitarian elements.[3] Unfortunately, however, contemporary advocates of Confucianism often take very little interest in analyzing the antidemocratic challenges that still prevail in today's world. Additionally, many of these advocates completely neglect the legacy of their predecessors who in the mid-twentieth century did in fact take totalitarian and authoritarian challenges to democracy seriously.

Among the proponents of a modern Confucianism who addressed the topic of totalitarianism, the political thought of the philosopher Tang Junyi (1909–1978) stands out. Indeed, from the early 1950s onward, Tang reflected on totalitarianism more comprehensively than the vast majority of his fellow Confucian thinkers.[4] In this respect, Tang Junyi's modern Confucianism may be considered "practical" in an emphatic sense. This is not the case with many recent attempts to invoke a renewal of Confucianism, even though they claim that contemporary Confucianism now has a heightened interest in "practical" matters. There is, thus, the impression that contemporary Confucianism tends to brush aside the need to reflect on the challenges of authoritarianism and totalitarianism, while still trying to convey the image of Confucianism as a repository for critical thought about democratic theory and practice.

Against this backdrop, a critical reflection on Tang Junyi's intellectual struggle with totalitarian challenges, which has so far received only scant attention, might serve to forward the question of how to relate Confucian political thought to the global experience of totalitarian systems. What is at stake here is the credibility of Confucianism with respect to liberal democracy. The dubiousness of modern Confucianism pertains not only to its stance vis-à-vis totalitarian ideas, which amounts to a radical exclusion of liberal democracy, but also to claims that a Confucian renaissance will be beneficial to the contemporary world. Such claims have been repeated again and again since the end of the World War II,[5] but the ever-looming question of totalitarianism has so far been largely sidelined in international debates on the Confucian renewal. As long as attempts at Confucian revivals and reconstructions of Confucian humanism remain flawed through their neglect of the darkest periods of the twentieth century, they will continue to cause uneasiness with regard to the historical memory of (Western) postwar democracies. The fact that the Confucian revivals are currently flourishing on the Chinese mainland, where the public memory of foreign and Chinese totalitarianism remains highly constricted by official ideological standards, only adds to this uneasiness. The same may be said of another large-scale revival of Confucianism that occurred in postwar Taiwan, again under conditions of an ideologically confined memory culture. It began in the 1950s and intensified during the so-called renaissance of Chinese culture movement (*Zhongguo wenhua fuxing yundong* 中國文化復興運動) from the mid-1960s onward. Those who consider maintaining an awareness of the dangers of totalitarianism in contemporary democratic societies crucial might indeed find difficulty in approving the current agenda of a Confucian revival.

In order to address these issues, an inquiry into Tang Junyi's political philosophy proves especially illuminating. Tang produced numerous writings that reflected on totalitarianism, and he did so, tellingly, while living in Hong Kong—that is, outside of the ideological restrictions of the party-states on both sides of the Taiwan Strait. He did not, however, present a full-fledged examination of Western and Chinese totalitarian governments, let alone a theory of totalitarianism. Tang Junyi applied "totalitarianism," as will be shown, in a very broad sense but was hardly interested in National Socialism and Soviet Stalinism, focusing instead on the Stalinist-like system that emerged in China after 1949. Therefore we must include in our analysis Tang's writings in which he discussed topics related to totalitarianism, namely his concept of modernization and his speculative thoughts on history with their distinctly optimistic outlook. To conclude, we take Tang's own claim regarding the global significance of modern Confucianism at face value. In doing so, we relate it to non-Chinese societies by asking how and to what effect it might address a cataclysmic core experience of the modern West that was brought about by a totalitarian regime: the Holocaust.[6]

Modernization and Human Agency from a Confucian Perspective

Tang Junyi's philosophy is marked by the highly ambitious goal of establishing a normative theory of a worldwide process of modernity covering all spheres of society as well as the dimension of human subjectivity in the context of the modern world. This agenda is arguably a defining feature not only of Tang's modern Confucianism but also of mainstream Confucian thought since the twentieth century. An adequate appraisal of the related philosophical projects must therefore take into consideration the strong assumptions about human "history" that permeate attempts to "reconstruct" a *modern* Confucianism. After all, there is no doubt that for Tang "the revival of Confucianism in a new form, i.e., a reconstruction of Confucianism, is a necessary condition for keeping such a [historical] continuity in some East Asian countries."⁷ Apart from generating continuity, this reconstruction served another purpose, namely that of uncovering a broad range of social, cultural, and political ideas, principles, values, and norms that will have a positive impact on Chinese modernization.

Even though Tang never claimed that modernization as a whole could be guided by holistic social planning, he was convinced that modernizing communities could exert a considerable measure of control over the process of modernity. He believed that "modernization" (*xiandaihua* 現代化) on a global scale would, in the long run, lead to the establishment of modern nation-states with democratic and constitutional governments and to pluralistic, industrialized, and scientifically progressive societies.⁸ According to Tang, modernity was thus not characterized by a forceful nature, as it was depicted, for example, in Max Weber's image of an "iron cage of dependence," which consists of the anonymous coercive power of bureaucratic and economic structures and processes that tend to subdue the individual and collective will of human agents. Tang rejected such bleak prospects. His normative theory of modernization claims that human collectivities may retain the power of consciously choosing and opting for a specific type of modernity in terms of a *project*—a claim that pertains also to the reconstruction of Confucianism in the context of modernity: ". . . we have to acknowledge that there are some new ideas and new spirits which are missing in traditional Confucianism. If we do not want to keep Confucianism backward of age, we have to look forward and plan a reconstruction of the Confucian spirit to meet the modern need."⁹

Confucian concepts of "modernization" thus hold the promise that the project of modernity will produce an overall betterment of Chinese society and, eventually, also of non-Chinese societies. In this vision of modern Confucianism, the fact that China arrived belatedly to a modernizing world of nation-states does not take away the hope of "catching up" in terms of modernization. The notion of progress refers here to a willful collective effort that involves "learning" from historical experience, good or bad, Chinese or foreign. One striking example (among many) of this line of thought can be found in the passage where Tang elaborates on the economic backwardness of contemporary China. In a highly optimistic manner, he perceives this backwardness as a fortunate break that will provide China with an opportunity to avoid the consumerism and cultural-spiritual shallowness that has afflicted modernizing Western countries such as the United States, where in the eyes of Tang the reification of modern man was particularly severe.[10]

The expectation that China's project to catch up in terms of modernization is, essentially, manageable by a Chinese community whose members agree on the goals and means of modernization and are able to contain its side effects is reminiscent of German theories of a "*Sonderweg*" (special path) in the modern world. These theories, which emerged in Germany at the end of the nineteenth century, placed equal emphasis on belated efforts in nation-building, industrialization, and technological progress. These theories, which served different purposes, are sometimes critically depicted as causes for Germany's involvement in two world wars. Before World War II, they were applied in an affirmative manner and centered on the assumption that Germany's alleged ability to refute "Western" rationalism and adhere to its own superior cultural spirit was actually beneficial.[11] Tang's depiction of China's path to modernity and his project of a Confucian renewal within modernization efforts is, *mutatis mutandis*, in line with the main thrust of *Sonderweg* theories that affirm cultural particularity. The core element here is the anticipation of a superior social modernity guided by humanistic values and ideas that are gleaned from a reinterpretation of China's "unique" culture and history. On the basis of such reinterpretation, an effort to "learn" from achievements and failures in Western modernization shall take place.

The optimistic expectation of implementing social modernization through a "learning" mode was widespread in twentieth-century Chinese ideas of modernity.[12] Tang relates the topic of "learning" not only to the sphere of collective action by the state and certain social agents but also to how individuals conduct their lives. In a particularly striking statement from 1974, he muses about the "beautiful virtues" of the "Chinese," which he says are still observable in the Taiwanese countryside. In contrast, he asserts that most city dwellers in Taiwan and Hong Kong are under the "negative" influence of "Western culture." Tang was convinced that "we just need the resolve to change customs, which will not be difficult [to do]," given that these negative customs came from "outside" and were thus not deep-rooted. If one really wants to change them, he adds, it can be done right away. He provides a disturbing example of this by claiming that the Chinese Communist Party (CCP) managed to rid Shanghai of lavishness and corruption after 1949.[13] But Tang's point here was not a vindication of communist measures to implement social change, and he certainly had no intention of advocating the CCP's actions in Shanghai as a model for modernization. Still, the prospect of reining in the woes of modernization in a willful collective effort obviously fascinated him.

Tang considered the negative effects of the progressive division of labor in modern societies in a similar manner. He points out that this is a crucial matter in Western countries, and particularly in the United States, because the increasing division of labor creates a social situation in which individuals can no longer estimate the intrinsic value of their labor.[14] This problem concerns not only the economic sphere but also phenomena such as the increasing "professionalization" in other social spheres, including academic life. Tang relates these observations to an ongoing submission of "cultural forces" to political and economic "forces" resulting in general tendencies of "reification" and cultural "degeneration."[15] He claims that purposeful "change" in the "forms" of social and cultural activities might prevent these tendencies from spreading further into the social realm. What he had in mind here was a renewal and rejuvenating of traditional Chinese associations on the level of communities.[16] In these communal contexts, human beings might truly interact with each other as individuals and hence break up the uniform standards of instrumental values on the basis of their individualized value-consciousness. Significantly, Tang focuses here on the "forms" of these tradition-inspired associations and interactions and not on specific contents and values. He thus ascertains in very general terms that the implementation of noninstrumental forms of mutual associations and interaction hinges on a revival of a "classical kind of spirit" in society, politics, and ethics, thereby relying on a certain "value-consciousness." The individuals would learn to interact with each other by evaluating their respective accomplishments and knowledge within a broad range of intellectual or artistic activities, as well as other forms of individual "effort" (*gongfu* 功夫). However, Tang did not naïvely believe that the workings of instrumental rationality might be completely dissolved in modern societies, but instead he expected that they could be confined to their appropriate areas, such as the economic sphere. This might result in a foil for modern society in which the "lines of latitude" could be calculated according to the "spirit of societies based on the division of labor of the modern type" and the "lines of longitude" according to a classical spirit.[17] With regard to the prospects of societies that had recently begun to modernize, Tang was certainly convinced that East Asian societies, due to their particular cultural traditions, were in an excellent position to create these foils of social modernity. Yet at that time Japan was the only country in the region that pursued such a course of modernization.[18]

To conclude, there can be no doubt that Tang deemed ideational and normative factors crucial for solving "global" problems of modernity. He therefore highlighted a critical awareness of cultural traditions that strengthen social cohesion. According to Tang, such an endeavor would involve a broad range of humanistic cultural activities, including intellectual, spiritual, and aesthetic "efforts" of individuals to "overcome themselves," for example, by engaging in Confucian scholarship, Chinese arts, Indian Yoga, Buddhism, or Christian devotion.[19]

The main trajectory for propelling normative inputs in the course of modernization was, as Tang saw it, state action. Accordingly, he refrained from depicting the process of modernity as an increasing decay of the state's capacity to dominate societal development. On the contrary, the idea of an evolving modern Chinese state, still in the making, assumes an orienting function for modernization in Tang's modern Confucian project. In spite of the experience of a misappropriation of state coercive power in the dictatorial party states in China before and after 1949, the idea of statehood still looms large in Tang's concept of modernization. Even so, he repeatedly expressed his conviction that all Chinese states had failed so far to give authentic expression to the normative resources of the Confucian "main current" of China's national culture.[20] These states could therefore not claim to constitute the equivalent of the new political form, that is, the constitutional, democratic government to which modern Confucianism aspired. Because Tang believed that a modernizing Chinese state would evolve as an emanation from the normative resources of a renewed Confucian "main current," he rejected the idea that such a state could be founded by a combination of revolutionary ideology and military force. The extant party-states of the CCP and Guomindang (GMD) were therefore not what Tang had in mind.

In giving thought to the formation of the modern state, Tang drew selectively from Hegel's concept of a state of ethical nature. But he was clearly not a Hegelian theoretician of state, and he accordingly refrained from applying the speculative framework of Hegelian philosophy of history to his own concept of state. As a consequence, he never referred to the historical manifestation of a "world spirit" in this context. Tang also differs from Hegel in that he envisioned the ideal form of the modern state as an *immediate* emanation of the human (ethical) will to the state and thus designated the state to be the highest, direct manifestation of *human* reason in history—and not, as Hegel would have it, as the manifestation of a "cunning of reason" that remains aloof from concerted human action: "This may be called the *cunning of reason*—that it sets the passions to work for itself, while that which develops its existence through such impulsion pays the penalty, and suffers loss."[21] Tang bolsters his departure from the Hegelian theory of the state by criticizing Hegel for failing to clarify that the state, although it is a "manifestation of the objective spirit," cannot detach itself from the striving of "the subjective spirit which exists for itself," that is, a striving resulting "spontaneously" from the "rational self" and the moral will of individuals.[22]

Foundations of Historical Optimism

Against this backdrop, Tang developed an optimistic vision of the process of modernity as ongoing civilizational progress on a global scale that is accessible for "China." Given a successful "reconstruction" of the Confucian "main current," China would be able to partake in global progress by implementing its own type of guided and controlled social modernization. The general direction of this modernization is foreseeable, according to Tang because it is part of a process of global modernity that tends toward democracy and constitutional government, scientific and technological progress, industrialization, and an open, pluralistic society. For modern Confucianism, modernity is thus not turning into a lost cause of humanity. It carries, on the contrary, a promise to empower human agency to the point where it becomes the master of its own fate.

Pessimistic notions of modernity as an inescapable historical fate or as a process beyond any measure of control by human agents therefore fundamentally contradict the modern Confucian notion of human agency asserting itself in the process of modernization. From the perspective of Tang's Confucian project, these pessimistic notions entail the danger of self-fulfilling prophecies, and the same may be said of diagnoses of modernity such as Max Weber's, which assume that human agency becomes disempowered in the course of instrumental modernity. Tellingly, Tang bluntly rejects, in his late work, Western theories that undermine a firm belief in the effectiveness of "holy values," such as existentialism and the Freudian psychology of the unconscious, along with Western notions of human history as an inevitably chaotic process characterized by contingent events.[23] Even though he was apprehensive of human agency suffering from reification and alienation—a modern threat causing individuals to become oblivious to the dangers of modernity—Tang overall disagreed with an overall pessimistic vision of modernity.[24]

Tang's belief in the dominant role of human agency in the process of modernity is based on assumptions about human nature and the human being, which he obtained from his interpretations of Confucian thought. Two perspectives are particularly relevant in this regard: First, his modern Confucianism asserts that the perfectibility of the human being as a "sage" (*sheng* 聖 or *shengren* 聖人) is a historical reality, but this is so only in terms of a positive, orientating limit-concept. According to Tang, modern man should strive for sagehood, yet such sagehood may at best be attained in a fleeting moment of moral intuition.[25] Sagehood is neither a permanent state of mind nor an individual's way of life, nor can it be realized by whole collectivities of human agents, such as congregations, nations, and classes. A revolution of human society in the name of establishing a community of sages is consequently absent from the agenda of Tang's modern Confucianism, as is the idea of the collective human will totally dominating history; but the opposite notion is also absent, namely, the idea of human beings subdued by the process of modernity.[26] In other words, the perfection of the human being is said to be attainable in an instantaneous, immediate realization of moral intuition that marks a moment in which the human mind breaks free from its own embedment in history. Accordingly, modern Confucianism conceives of the "sage" as the symbol of the individual's perfection, but not in terms of a sage who is confined, so to speak, to a historical dimension. That nowhere in the modern Confucian discourses do we find the assumption that the very mode of an ahistorical, immediate presentification of "sagehood" itself could be subject to historical change or even "renewal" (*xin* 新) is no coincidence. Additionally, by relating the notion of human nature to the assumption of an inborn human capability to attain such "inner sagehood," modern Confucianism establishes a notion of the intangibility of human nature, and consequently the human being, vis-à-vis the modern world in its historical dimension. This, in turn, is the religious-anthropological basis for the Confucian insistence on the stronghold of human agency in history, including the process of modernity.

Second, Tang's modern Confucianism clearly refrains from claiming that human beings are perfectible as a *species*. Even if one were to believe that at one point in history a community of sages might be realized, their offspring neither would be born as sages, nor would the institutions and structures of such a community perforce lead every human being to perfection. The perfectibility of the human being evidently pertains to the individual, not to the species, and as individual human beings retain the freedom to strive for sagehood—or not to strive for it—or to strive and fail along the way. As a consequence, there will be no "end" of history brought about as the victory of sagely inwardness over all "outer," alienated formations of modernity. Tang's Confucian thought does not offer the consolation of an idyllic modern world that is free from alienation. But even though "objective" constellations of alienation will persist, the Confucian individuals will be spared the distress of experiencing them solely as "outer" obstacles. Instead, they may perceive and thus mitigate them as conditions of their individual quest for sagely inwardness, which, after all, will be attained in the course of participating in and struggling with the world.

The religious-anthropological notion of the intangibility of human nature marks one of the main ideational rifts between Tang's modern Confucianism and Marxism. While both tend to emphasize the importance of the role of human agency with respect to the course of history, Marxism does so by positing that the human being should be considered the product of a historical and social formation. A purposeful transformation of human collectivities through generating the conditions for the emergence of a "new man" within a perfected society is thus feasible according to the Marxist scheme. In contrast, modern Confucianism assumes that the "nature" (*xing*) of the human being is not subject to change and remains essentially out of reach of any attempt to objectify or manipulate it. What is subject to change is indeed not the human being itself, but only its symbolic representations, which might find their "true" cultural expression in the humanistic "main current" of the Chinese nation. This Confucian outlook had to be defended not only against Marxism but also against those theories of historical research that Tang criticized because of their positivistic approach. Such positivism entailed the reduction of history to a mere "object" of research, and it implied the depletion of subjectivity by stripping the human subject of its historical dimensions, thereby reducing it to a putatively pure subject of cognition.[27] Vis-à-vis these challenges, modern Confucianism was to provide individuals with the conviction that they could contribute—even in the face of their vain efforts to attain sagehood—to a gradual betterment of their community.

Delimiting a "Philosophy of History"

Tang Junyi's speculation about history defies a clear-cut classification as philosophy of history, theology of history, or philosophic-historical anthropology. These difficulties of classification partially stem from the fact that Tang was not a historian, either by professional training or by the thrust of his work. He referred to this speculation as a "philosophy of history" (*lishi zhexue* 歷史哲學), yet this may lead, if taken at face value, to considerable misunderstandings.[28] Instead of regarding Tang's "philosophy of history" as an offshoot of European philosophies of history, it is more apt to delineate it in a much broader conceptual framework—so broad that it even includes references to German historicism from the nineteenth century.[29]

Tang understands the individual's subjectivity and how the individual is related to his or her "true" nature, that is, sagehood, in accordance with the assumption that the interpretation of history serves the individual's insight into personhood and the nature of man. Because of such proximity to historicism Tang's *lishi zhexue* is clearly set apart from Hegelian philosophy of history—in spite of his otherwise sustained interest in Hegelian philosophy. After all, what Tang denotes as *lishi zhexue* is not a historical-philosophical enterprise of detecting the self-realization of reason in history, as Hegel's philosophy of history claimed to do by retracing the manifestations of the "world spirit" in human history. In contrast, Tang posits that whereas the cosmic unity, the "mind of Heaven," may manifest itself in the subjective human mind, it does not permeate human history as a force. Consequently, he developed no idea of a world spirit present in history,[30] and he criticized Hegel's philosophy of history for its assumption that "all cultural affairs and heroic personalities" were mere vehicles for the self-manifestation of "absolute mind." Tang believed that Hegel failed to acknowledge that the human being could indeed firmly establish its cultural activities and its individual personality as its own "inherent goals."[31] Accordingly, Tang measures reality against the religious-anthropological assumption that human beings are destined to realize their natural ability to attain sagehood. The general course of history thus appears to be imbued with "reason" to the degree to which historical conditions as a whole are conducive to individuals' self-perfection in sagehood.

Tang's modern Confucianism conveys an overall optimistic outlook on history by depicting the course of history as pointing to an increasing formation of political, social, and cultural conditions that are favorable to individuals' efforts of self-perfection. This optimism also pertains, as we have seen, to the process of modernity. Even though Tang does not elaborate in detail on the question of whether fully modernized societies will be identical in an "ideal humanistic world,"[32] he leaves no doubt that modernization can amount to historical progress in terms of individual and collective life (e.g., by fostering the "authentic" political expression of Confucianism in the form of a liberal democracy).[33] In taking a global view of the twentieth century, Tang expresses his expectation that the formations of humanism,[34] can play a crucial role by reining in the woes of social modernity. He thus states the following with utterly optimistic conviction:

> What we are awaiting is merely the self-consciousness of all humanity, in which it will seek a common goal and then take up common endeavors. As for this common goal, one can talk about it from two perspectives: (1) It is indispensable to liberate "culture" from the heavy pressure of "politics" and "economics" and to do the utmost to have the "cultural powers" surpass the "political powers" and the "economic powers" (this is "humanism"). (2) Whatever the new social ideal is, those who make a great effort to realize this ideal must, at the same time, engage in self-reflection and clearly recognize in advance the potential abuses so as to prevent them in time (here, we must wait for those of great insight and wisdom).[35]

But Tang did not bolster such optimism with a claim to reveal a historical "plan" or a "law" that would explain the inevitable sequence of certain periods or epochs in history. Nor did his "philosophy of history" entail the teleological idea of human history generally moving toward a final goal or purpose, such as the ultimate realization of freedom and emancipation. Even if the "ideal humanistic world" could be realized in history, neither would it mark a final stage of history nor would the forms of individual and collective freedom realized in such a society be the pinnacle of human freedom. After all, the perfectibility of the human being—even if it is momentarily realized in the world—is not a matter of *historical* subjectivity. It rather entails a transgression of the totality of historical conditions:[36] in realizing self-perfection in the highest form, human beings lift themselves beyond their historical existence to attain "inner sagehood." Accordingly, modern Confucianism does not speculate about the final realization of human emancipation in history nor does it speculate about a final, apocalyptical crisis of humanity. This absence of eschatological elements is indeed characteristic of Tang's philosophy of history.[37]

On the Totalitarian Challenge

At first glance, Tang Junyi seems to be in an awkward position to examine the formation and various manifestations of totalitarianism because he hardly takes account of speculative ingredients that are often considered fundamental to totalitarian ideologies. Among these are secularized eschatologies stemming from philosophies of history, complete with ideas about a struggle of humanity against its enemies, and the accompanying belief in the final, this-worldly elimination of all antinomies. It is thus not surprising that in his analysis of totalitarianism he does not attempt to explore the ideological foundations of Western forms of totalitarianism in a comprehensive manner. Yet he apparently felt that to remain silent on totalitarianism was not an option. Given the experience of European fascism, National Socialism, Stalinism, the communist takeover of the Chinese mainland, and the tensions of the Cold War period, the need to examine totalitarianism was compelling, even more so because Tang was convinced by the early 1950s that the government of the People's Republic of China was in fact a totalitarian regime (see below).

Apart from the harsh experience of civil wars and world wars leading up to the mid-twentieth century, other issues engendered Tang's interest in totalitarianism. Most of all, his optimistic outlook on human history in general and on the global course of modernity in particular was at stake. If an analysis of totalitarianism would show that totalitarian societies were as likely to be the outcome of modernization as democratic societies, then Tang's optimism would have been shattered. Additionally, the renewal of "humanism" that was at the core of modern Confucianism had to measure up to the catastrophic experience of totalitarianism if it was to avoid the criticism of being a mere reverie of an idyllic world or, worse still, a naïve escapism that curtails critical thought. The following shows that Tang addressed these challenges in his reflections on history, modernity, progress, and totalitarianism, but he did so in a highly selective manner when it came to include the history of non-Chinese totalitarianism. Far from leaping into such reverie, Tang assumed that totalitarianism was neither nonmodern nor antimodern, nor a mere aberration that occurred as a singular event in the course of Western-induced modernity.

Tang probably first dealt with the problem of totalitarianism in 1951 when he wrote an article for the *Democratic Review* (*Minzhu pinglun* 民主評論) about repressive and violent measures by the communist regime on the mainland.[38] His choice to publish this text in the *Democratic Review* set a precedent for the following decades, and he continued to publish articles on totalitarianism in journals that appealed to a broad readership. Whereas the historical contexts of Tang's interest in analyzing totalitarian rule can be readily discerned, we can only speculate about the theoretical inputs he had absorbed. In the early 1950s he was most likely aware of discussions in the United States about totalitarianism that had begun in the mid-1930s. On the whole, Tang's analyses are to some degree in line with conservative critics from the *Review of Politics*: these critics had assumed that a totalitarian reaction was triggered by a fatal crisis of Western civilization, complete with an equally disastrous crisis of capitalism, which entailed unrestrained materialism, rampant individualism, and a widespread spiritual void in modern

Western societies. Consequently, some of these conservative thinkers identified an ethical renewal of society as the essential antidote to totalitarianism.[39]

Tang neither devised a theory of totalitarianism nor presented a comprehensive analysis of totalitarian ideologies or totalitarian regimes. This is, however, not surprising given the state of international studies on totalitarianism on which one commentator recently concluded: " 'Totalitarianism' remains as ambiguous today as ever: as a historical concept it is insecure and contested, as memory it is geographically promiscuous and unstable, and nebulous; only as a semantic marker of new political constellations, identities, and ideological alliances is it, as ever, indisputable."[40] As for Tang Junyi's writings on totalitarianism, we find no comparative analysis of the inner workings of totalitarian regimes of the twentieth century, even though Tang conceptualized totalitarianism to include Italian Fascism, National Socialism, Stalinism, and Chinese communism. Nor did he analyze ideological components of totalitarianism such as fascism, racist ideologies or anti-Semitism. Overall, he applied the label of totalitarianism in a very loose, sometimes polemical manner.

With regard to the system of Chinese communism, Tang did not examine it in a comprehensive manner, but rather presented detailed observations about its workings and inscribed these into a larger theoretical framework of "totalitarianism[s]." From the 1950s to the 1970s he used the terms "totalitarianism" (*jiquanzhuyi* 極權主義), "totalitarian world" (*jiquan shijie* 極權世界), "totalitarian system" (*jiquan zhidu* 極權制度), "totalitarian society" (*jiquan de shehui* 極權的社會), and "totalitarian politics" (*jiquan de zhengzhi* 極權的政治) to refer to Chinese "totalitarianism from Qin Shihuang up to the contemporary Qin Shihuang-ism of Mao Zedong,"[41] to the European "Fascists" Mussolini and Hitler, and to the Russian "communists" Lenin and Stalin.[42] Whether Tang's use of "totalitarianism" includes GMD rule, which he believed was "fascist" during the period from the dissolution of the first united front in the mid-1920s until the end of World War II, is not entirely clear.[43] Nevertheless, Tang gives the concept of "totalitarianism" a very broad extension, which comprises even the dynastic rule of the Qin as well as czarist Russia.[44]

That Tang did not substantiate this extensive use of "totalitarianism" is deplorable. Whether he actually believed that totalitarianism had intellectual or institutional roots reaching back to the Qin Dynasty and whether he, therefore, agreed with Xu Fuguan's diagnosis of Chinese despotism, remains doubtful.[45] Additionally, Xu Fuguan polemicized in the early 1950s against Tang and Mou Zongsan by claiming that their project of modern Confucianism was not immune to an absorption by totalitarian ideas.[46] In countering Xu's criticism, Tang presented a conceptual argument as well as a historical interpretation. On the conceptual level, he proposed a definition of "politics" that placed the emphasis on the need to confine "politics" to an institutional "realm" without imposing it on other spheres within society. Politics, according to Tang, had to be functionally limited to the task of *indirectly* supporting the realization of social and cultural values by safeguarding the organizational and institutional framework.[47] Aside from these systematic considerations, Tang reacted to Xu Fuguan's criticism with an attempt to discern intellectual currents in Chinese history that are characterized, to some degree, by an affinity to totalitarianism. This approach is typical of Tang's profound skepticism toward the *political* traditions of Confucianism, which in fact exceeds Xu Fuguan's critique of the Confucian tradition. As Tang sees it, the Confucians of the past had tried to endow their doctrines with immediate ruling power by propagating the idea that the ruler (*jun* 君) and the (highest) "teacher" (*shi* 師) should be one and the same person.[48]

Tang detects similar tendencies of infusing politics with totalizing, doctrinal claims to truth in strands of Buddhism, Daoism, and "original" Christianity,[49] but he primarily targets the twentieth-century New Culture Movement, insinuating strong affinities to totalitarian thought. He assumes that these affinities become manifest in the conviction of New Culture advocates that the totality of extant drawbacks in Chinese society can be removed by implementing a new, antitraditional and antimetaphysical culture in a surgical manner. Accordingly, the totalizing notion of a "new culture" promised to eliminate all the remnants of Confucianism, including the familial virtue of filial piety, and to replace the social significance of religions altogether with "science and democracy." In his criticism of such a belief in the salutary conflation of politics and true doctrines, Tang arrived at the drastic conclusion that the New Culture Movement on the whole played a crucial role in facilitating the spread of communism in China.[50]

Given Tang's very broad conceptual extension of "totalitarianism," we should not be surprised that he did not present a clear-cut definition of totalitarianism but instead contented himself with elucidating certain characteristics and mechanisms of totalitarian rule and ideologies. Tellingly, he did so by focusing on communist rule in China and not on Soviet Stalinism or National Socialism. In 1951, on the occasion of writing about trials and killings in communist China that involved incidents of children being encouraged to expose crimes their parents allegedly committed, he deemed these incidents to be "unbearable," adding that Chinese communists' "massacres" and repressive propaganda could not be fully comprehended by solely analyzing some specific political or other reasons for such actions.[51] The communist concept of politics, according to which "politics" was to rule and control every aspect of human life, and which allowed only for a single distinction—the one between a "we"-group and an enemy who must be eliminated—had to be taken into account. The involvement of children's accusations in the execution of their parents was, as Tang assumed, to serve the purpose of eliminating the very root of "humaneness" in human beings, namely by eradicating the sphere of intimate feeling for one's parents as the human being's initial expression of humaneness.[52] What he suggests here is that the totalitarian "politics" of Chinese communism did not aim only at dehumanizing the enemy, but it also served to create a "we"-group whose members are similarly incriminated and entangled in dehumanizing acts of breaking taboos that amount to a fundamental denial of humaneness. Tang hence called Chinese communism an ideology of "negating everything (*fouding yiqie* 否定一切)," which thereby attained the intensity of a "new religion." By reifying the human being to the point of dehumanization, the ideology of Chinese communism was truly "satanic."[53]

We can draw two conclusions from Tang's observations here: First, the communist campaign to systematically dissolve familial ties might be understood, from a Confucian perspective, as an attempt to destroy those social and ethical relations that play an important role in the formation of an individual's personal identity. Second, mechanisms of totalitarian rule function to categorize the victims under anonymous, deindividualized labels, thereby facilitating a decrease of solidarity and a growing indifference on the part of bystanders. With respect to incriminating the "we"-group into the acts of the perpetrators, the term "satanic" is relevant because it links Tang's analysis to his reflection on the human lust for power and inclination toward cruelty.[54] It is implied here that the totalitarian mechanisms of Chinese communism radically dissolve ethical relations and social contexts of humanistic culture and hence serve to expose the individuals to their own self-consuming lust for power.[55] Incriminated, exposed, and deindividualized human beings would now be ready to participate in the violent tearing down of the old order. Tang alludes to this aspect of totalitarian ideology in his sharp rejection of revolutionary morality:

> The communists' acclamation of revolutionary morality as the highest morality of man is one type of pan-moralism which is morality perverted for a political purpose. The ideology of such a pan-moralism can strip a man of all his cultural garments and sacrifice him naked on the altar of political revolution. Such an attitude, be it admitted, is not without moral sentiment originating from within. But, nonetheless, when the naked moral being of a revolutionary hero is worshipped above all men, the

preservation of traditional human culture would be considered as of no essential importance, and barbarism among other things will come out from this very pan-moralism.[56]

However, totalitarian rule in communist China was ridden with inner contradictions, even regarding the treatment of familial ties. Tang recognized that the communist regime did not intend to dissolve these ties altogether but rather tried to make use of them in order to secure and exert power within the ruling circles. Two particularly striking cases were the ascendance to power of Mao's wife, Jiang Qing, and the Red Guards' intimate attachment to Mao that culminated in their fervent admiration of the "Great Helmsman." This was, according to Tang, clearly reminiscent of familial ties and was probably even inspired by Mao's earlier readings of late imperial novels such as *The Romance of the Three Kingdoms* and *Water Margin*.[57] Tang concludes that communist rule in China had to rely on such "traditional" measures to secure power because it was permanently faced with severe ideological contradictions. Among these, the ideological tensions between universal aspirations to world revolution and particular claims of Chinese nationalism that took shape in the rift between a pro-Soviet and an anti-Soviet camp within the CCP stand out. That Tang did not attempt to inscribe such detailed observations of the inner workings and mechanisms of totalitarian rule on the Chinese mainland into a systematic examination of Chinese totalitarianism is regrettable. Instead, he contented himself with detecting signs of contradictions within communism in China, never attempting to systematize his observations in the manner of Franz Neumann's *Behemoth* (1942/1944), which contains an analysis of the inner antagonisms, rampant contradictions, and chaotic aspects of National Socialism. Neither did Tang try to relate his observations about the Chinese communist state to an extensive examination of totalitarianism on the scale of Friedrich and Brzezinski's classical *Totalitarian Dictatorship and Autocracy* (1956), which he most likely had not studied.

Even though Tang did not present a comprehensive analysis of totalitarianism, he did try to uncover its sources. He thus discussed factors that were conducive to the emergence of totalitarian rule, however, without claiming to identify all the compelling causes that lead to totalitarianism. This approach is loosely similar to Hannah Arendt's in The Origins of Totalitarianism from 1951. Such an approach involves vastly different elements and layers. With respect to the question of why individuals show inclinations toward totalitarianism, Tang turned to habitual attitudes. He identified a specific "attitude of thinking" that is best described as a "passive state" in which individuals "habitually conform to opinions that they themselves have naturally formed." Due to a lack of intellectual alertness and reflection, individuals are said to be particularly prone to fall victim to political, religious, and social propaganda that aims to make them readily conform to a "totalitarian system." In a pessimistic diagnosis, Tang ascertained that these attitudes are very difficult to alter.[58] One effect of such habitual passiveness can even be seen, he believed, in the United States, where many people strove solely for their own personal gain while trying to minimize their losses vis-à-vis their government. Similarly, many overseas emigrants from China became increasingly unwilling to actively resist totalitarianism the longer they lived in the "free world" (*ziyou shijie* 自由世界).[59]

On a different level of analysis, Tang diagnosed the decline of the individual in modernity and related this development to the rise of totalitarianism. He depicted modern societies as characterized by the excessive spread of instrumental rationality throughout the political, social, cultural, and economic sphere. As a consequence, the individuals understand, evaluate, and organize their own lifeworld, including their mutual relations and their self-conceptions, solely in consideration of efficiency and utility, thereby reifying the human being itself. The objectified human being is thus put at the disposition of the alleged overall progress of society. The quintessence of Tang's diagnosis of modernity is evident from his conclusion that there is a potential convergence between totalitarian and liberal societies in the common degeneration of the individual: Both totalitarian societies and societies of "laissez-faire individualism" comprise individuals who are closely enmeshed in an unrestrained quest for wealth, power, and prestige that eventually leads to the individual's loss of a "feeling of authentic existence" (*zhenshi cunzai gan* 真實存在感).[60] The decline of the "authentic self" in turn gives rise to the formation of an isolated and alienated self in the spheres of politics, society, and "academic culture." This atomistic self is particularly prone, according to Tang, to the lures of totalitarianism.[61] In this context, Tang turned to the global ascension of a Janus-faced scientific civilization that is crucial to "free and democratic societies" but that may also function as a trajectory for the reification of modern man: "If man is regarded merely as an object in the external world, then like other external objects he has no reason not to be used, controlled and manufactured. The totalitarian states do in fact use scientific knowledge and techniques to remold men for political purposes, degrading their dignity and condemning their soul. Here we can again see the need for Confucian teachings, which respect scientific study on the one hand, and hold sacred the transcendental subjectivity of man on the other."[62] Without critical reflection on the mixed blessing of the modern advancement of science and technology, a failure of the project of modernity is looming. The reconstruction of Confucianism was to serve as a bulwark against such danger. Tang repeatedly warned that the totalizing reification of the human being in modern societies resembles that of totalitarian societies, which also makes comprehensive use of modern science and technology. Here he draws a parallel between the repressive regimes of Nazi Germany and Stalinist Soviet Union: "For example, Hitler and Stalin and other dictators all made use of scientific and technological methods to build a human society. But what kind of society did they actually build? They applied scientific and technological methods to control and enchain the freedom of humanity, form autocratic and dictatorial politics, and destroy democratic institutions. [This] was evidently even more effective than not using scientific and technological methods."[63] Another layer of origins of Chinese totalitarianism that Tang detected pertains to the peculiar historical conditions under which communism took hold in China. In Tang's view, "Marxism-Leninism" became accepted in China in the context of widespread anxieties among the Chinese about the survival of their nation amid imperialistic threats foreign nation-states posed since the mid-nineteenth century. Communism was thus seen as a powerful weapon to resist imperialistic intrusions and also as a tool to strengthen the Chinese nation.[64] This perception certainly fit the popular view that the whole Chinese nation had become a "proletarian class" at the hands of "capitalist states of the West." Additionally, the fact that "Marxism-Leninism" was "anti-Western Western thought" decisively enhanced, according to Tang, its attractiveness in the Chinese world.[65] Whether Tang himself subscribed to this diagnosis is open to discussion. He did not, after all, clarify the meaning of "capitalism" nor its relation to "imperialism" and "colonialism." In his analysis of Western imperialism, he maintains, however, that socioeconomic groups and organizations within Western nation-states were the driving agents propelling imperialistic politics.[66] Tang was convinced that the submission of the nation-state to forces from the socioeconomic sphere was a crucial prerequisite for imperialistic action, which in turn effected a totalitarian backlash in the victimized countries. He consequently insisted on the need to establish strong nation-states in order to contain totalitarianism. Only within the institutional setting of democratic nation-states would the societal sphere with its capitalist dynamic be reined in, thereby preventing a totalitarian backlash. Tang thus identifies the nation-state in its political form of liberal democracy as a bulwark against totalitarianism, and its absence in China had particularly disastrous consequences.

Perhaps because of this diagnosis Tang never considered the quest for a strong nation-state as a potential origin of Chinese totalitarianism. He instead bolstered his analysis by drawing his readers' attention to the fact that Mussolini, Hitler, Lenin, and Stalin all proclaimed their determination to resist "inequality and crimes in the capitalist societies of the modern West" when they successfully mobilized the masses.[67] Here, Tang's analysis is highly problematic, not only because the generalizing equation of Italian Fascism, National Socialism, Leninism, and Stalinism is misleading from a historical point of view, but also equally disturbing is the implicit vindication of totalitarianism as a form of self-defensive reaction against severe capitalist or imperialistic threats to one's nation.

Overcoming Totalitarianism?

The strengthening of (democratic) nation-states vis-à-vis transnational socioeconomic aspirations of imperialistic expansion is not the only means of curbing the danger of totalitarianism that Tang discussed. He also deemed it imperative, as we have seen, to initiate a renewal of humanistic thought and values (e.g., as a renewal of a "classical spirit") within a liberal democracy. He related this agenda explicitly to the struggle of the "free world" against the "totalitarian world," which he saw unfolding in the 1950s as a struggle that should involve the "reconstruction" of a "democratic spirit."[68] The notion "democratic spirit" refers to Tang's conviction that the stability of democratic government requires the social diffusion of a humanistic culture.[69] In a 1974 interview, he thus warned that because "democracy" was abused by totalitarianism in the twentieth century, establishing a kind of "education and culture" that generates common knowledge about "true democratic political institutions" was now necessary.[70] When seen from this perspective, the modern Confucian project to interweave the renewal of China's humanistic "main current" with the adoption of a democratic political form is also an attempt to fend off totalitarianism.

Tang's modern Confucianism entails, if not a detailed prediction about the future of Chinese totalitarianism, then at least the general prediction that totalitarianism is bound to eventually collapse in China primarily because of its antagonistic stance toward the "main current" of China's "national culture." In the 1958 Manifesto, Tang and his coauthors expect that Chinese Marxism-Leninism will falter due to the self-destructive power struggles within its ruling elite, but most of all because of its erroneous concepts of human nature and culture that are fixed to the "standpoint of class." These concepts are said to run counter to globally shared "principles" of "higher culture" as well as to China's "cultural thought" of several millennia, which refers to the "[human] mind" and "human nature" in order to establish the "moral subject."[71] The tautology of the prognosis asserts, in essence, that totalitarianism is not entrenched in the cultural "main current" of the

Chinese nation, whereas the democratic nation-state is indeed its authentic political form. According to Tang, there is thus no historical "necessity" for the victory of totalitarianism (i.e., "Marxism-Leninism") in China. Establishing a democratic nation-state, on the other hand, will eventually occur, as "evidenced" by the fact that it is in accordance with the "main current" that shapes the course of Chinese history.[72]

However, as we have seen, Tang does not conceptualize this development as a result of linear, planned human action. The individuals are unburdened, in Tang's theory of state, from the need to unreservedly identify themselves with factual efforts of nation-state building. Similar to the so-called Hegelian Left, Tang's political hermeneutics distinguish clearly between the truth claims of the state in historical reality and the truth of the concept or the idea of the state: the "idea of the state" (*guojia zhi linian* 國家之理念) is a "purely spiritual idea" (*chuncui jingshen de linian* 純粹精神的理念).[73] The historical reality of the state, in other words, is not to be considered an *immediate* manifestation of reason.[74] In a somber mood, Tang drew the distinction, in 1955, between the "Republic of China" as the label for a pending effort of state building on the one hand and as the denominator for the contemporary, unsatisfying reality represented by the current state of the Chinese Republic on the other:

> Although today's national government has retreated to Taiwan, the question about its achievements in carrying out democratic, constitutional politics is another matter altogether. But nothing will ultimately be able to obstruct the Chinese nation from proceeding along this path, in order for the Republic of China to make a name for itself and conform, in actuality, to [the concept of the] Republic of China.... The outer impediments consist, of course, in the Communist Party, which completely disagrees with the spirit of the Chinese Republic striving for the construction of a "Chinese, national, democratic state," and [instead] solely believes in Marxism-Leninism, one-sidedly [establishing] an autocracy of one party and one class.[75]

Furthermore, Tang did not assume that the *concept* of the state wields such power over historical reality as to enforce its own implementation by prefiguring and anticipating actual political and social movements.[76] In accordance with this conceptual delimitation of the theory of the state, Tang repudiated Kang Youwei's vision of a limitless world of "great uniformity" in which all extant legal, political, social, and cultural "boundaries" (*jie* 界) and institutions would eventually dissolve:

> If we again imagine that in an ideal world everybody would generally have only one [way of] thinking, one [single] will, one [way of] feeling, and would lead the same cultural life, again without any difference, then the interchange of human thought would no longer exist, and neither would affectionate mutual concern.... This would amount solely to the death of the humanistic world.... Our ideal world is thus not a world of identity in which there is no difference between human beings.... We therefore do not call our ideal world a world of great uniformity (*da tong* 大同), but rather a world of grand harmony (*tai he* 太和). The difference between harmony (*he* 和) and commonweal (*tong* 同) is something that we must urgently recognize.[77]

We may conclude from Tang's critique that such visions of a great uniformity are totalitarian in essence, not only because they applaud a totalitarian future but also because the visionaries ascribe to their own ideas a totalizing, reality-consuming power. The danger, then, lies in the assumption that the respective "ideals" wield total power over historical reality. Tang tries to hold this totalitarian implication at bay when he pins down "ideals" by introducing notions of sagehood and *liang zhi* as *limit-concepts*, as we have seen.

Given this astute awareness of the ideological aberration of totalitarianism, it may seem perplexing that Tang, for all his astute criticism of the downsides of Western types of modernity and modernization, refrained from linking the critique of modernity/modernization more closely with a diagnosis of Western types of totalitarianism. As for the mainstream of contemporary Confucian thought, an even more perplexing image emerges. That Confucian critics of "Western modernity" generally stop short of tapping into those intense Western debates about modernity that take up the issue of the project of modern, "Western" enlightenment reverting into a totalitarian collapse of civilization is indeed ironic. By abstaining from these debates, the Confucian reflection on modernity evades disturbing questions and unsettling perspectives, above all the acknowledgment of "the gnawing suspicion" that Zygmunt Bauman expressed, namely "that the Holocaust could be more than an aberration . . . from the otherwise straight path of progress. . . . We suspect (even if we refuse to admit it) that the Holocaust could merely have uncovered another face of the same modern society whose other, more familiar, face we so admire."[78] Such a somber assessment adds additional weight to the question of why the Holocaust—as well as the Soviet Gulag—plays such a marginal role in modern Confucianism's critical reflections on modernity.

In the case of Tang Junyi, although he mentions National Socialism and Stalinism in the context of "totalitarianism," that he does so only in passing and without attempting to explore the implications of the Holocaust and the Gulag is remarkable. Trying to provide a comprehensive explanation for Tang's reservations in this regard would be tedious, perhaps even futile. Without a doubt, one would have to take into account the fact that by the 1950s and early 1960s, Tang's most immediate concern about totalitarianism was its Chinese manifestation, which he was quite literally facing from his home in Hong Kong. It was therefore a particularly pressing topic, even more so in the general context of the Cold War period. To avoid an anachronistic default in intellectual history, one would moreover have to consider the international discussions and debates as well as the media coverage about the Holocaust up to the 1970s (in Tang's case) and take into account the reception of these in the Chinese-speaking world. Even though there is a severe lack of research on this topic, we may safely say that Adorno and Arendt, for example—two of the most prominent thinkers of the immediate postwar period to reflect on the Holocaust as the other side of the modern society's coin—were largely unknown in Chinese circles in the 1950s and 1960s.

Given these qualifications and constraints, simply brushing aside the topic with respect to Confucian critics seems prudent. However, the whole issue has a sting to it because, for one, modern Confucianism emphatically insists on its responsibility to address an international public, and not solely the Chinese audience. This, if nothing else, validates the concern of examining Confucian reflections on the Holocaust—or rather, the lack thereof. This concern would arguably not need such validation in the first place. Be that as it may, instead of asking why modern Confucianism continues to marginalize the Holocaust, one might rather be inclined to think about the upshot of overcoming such neglect. This would be, in other words, a matter of pondering the consequences for modern Confucianism if it were *"to treat the Holocaust as a rare, yet significant and reliable, test of the hidden possibilities of modern society"*[79] and hence share ". . . . the [disturbing] awareness that 'if it could happen on such a massive scale elsewhere, then it can happen anywhere; it is all within the range of human possibility. . . .' "[80]

From such a perspective, serious doubts might be raised about modern Confucianism's optimistic assumption that modernity-as-modernization is, on the whole, a process leading to the betterment of human society. This assumption rests, after all, on the conviction that the dangerous excesses of modernization coupled with instrumental rationality may be swiftly contained by a collective effort based on commonly shared humanistic concerns and values. In this context, modern Confucianism depicts the threat of the human being's reification in societies undergoing rapid economic and technological transformation as pertaining to the "authenticity" of the individual's way of life. But the lethal threat industrialized "reification" posed in death camps is met with silence. By neglecting this terminal point of *"the hidden possibilities of modern society,"* modern Confucianism misjudges the real danger of "reification." It also disregards the fact that the genocide on the scale of the Holocaust involved highly advanced, modern bureaucratic procedures, technological achievements, industrial organization, and pseudoscientific theories.

Moreover, whether modern Confucianism is prepared to reflect on the fact that as the Holocaust moved forward its bureaucratic routinization and industrial mechanisms established assiduous functional patterns and structures on the basis of which perpetrators and sympathizers cast aside moral concerns is doubtful. When applying a "Confucian" approach that essentially relies on a normative juxtaposition of instrumental and moral rationality, the Holocaust cannot be adequately described, let alone analyzed. The same holds true for attempts to grasp the mindset of the bystanders: simply describing them as morally degenerate individuals or as a mass of people who were cut off from ethical relations and deprived of a humanistic education would be incorrect. The Holocaust resulted, in other words, not just from a temporary absence or weakness of moral rationality, humanistic culture, and ethics vis-à-vis instrumental rationality, but *". . . was born and executed in our modern rational society, at the high stage of our civilization and at the peak of human cultural achievement. . . ."*[81] When seen from this perspective, it is questionable whether the Confucian vision of modernity, with its highly optimistic expectation of a modernization guided by a renewed humanistic culture, may apprehend ". . . the most terrifying, and still most topical, aspect of the 'Holocaust experience': that in our modern society people who are neither morally corrupt nor prejudiced may also still partake with vigour and dedication in the destruction of targeted categories of human beings. . . . This is by far the most important lesson of the Holocaust."[82]

This "lesson" seems to thwart depictions of totalitarianism as an epiphenomenon of modernity that a Confucian renewal may eliminate. The reflection on the Holocaust sobers optimistic outlooks on modernity. Two conclusions may be drawn here: First, the analytical and conceptual resources of modern Confucianism provide an inadequate basis for reflecting on the process of modernity as entailing the possibility of a Holocaust. Second, keeping the reflection about the Holocaust at bay is indeed a precondition for preserving the kind of historical optimism that characterizes the vision of a superior, Confucianized project of modernization. This belief in the superiority of a modernization Confucianism informs thus comes at a considerable price, and its claim to establish a renewed humanism of global dimensions remains dubious.

However, Hannah Arendt raises another concern about the Holocaust in her controversial book *Eichmann in Jerusalem*, which Tang Junyi's moral philosophy may address:

> What we have demanded in these trials . . . is that human beings be capable of telling right from wrong even when all they have to guide them is their own judgment, which, moreover, happens to be completely at odds with what they must regard as the unanimous opinion of all those around them. . . . These few who were still able to tell right from wrong went really only by their own judgments, and they did so freely; there were no rules to be abided by, under which the particular cases with which they were confronted could be subsumed. They had to decide each instance as it arose, because no rules existed for the unprecedented.[83]

Arendt reflects here on a social situation in which all conventionally authorized moral wisdom, established ethical rules, and religious authorities fail, without exception, to provide individuals with sound moral judgments. The problem that arises in such a situation not only concerns the correctness of moral judgments as such, but also alternative sources for moral judgments that individuals might tap into in order to acquire (or preserve) the ability to tell right from wrong. This latter issue echoes in Tang's thought. His moral philosophy, as an integral element of the whole modern Confucian project, is a response to the deplorable state of China in the mid-twentieth century: according to Tang, China was deprived of reliable moral standards by the 1950s—on the mainland under communist control, as well as in Taiwan under the authoritarian regime of the GMD. Modern Confucianism was thus confronted with the issue of identifying reliable sources of correct moral judgment. However, Tang and other Confucian intellectuals did not address this issue by relating it to totalitarianism in as straightforward manner as Hannah Arendt did.

Still, Tang was evidently convinced that propagating Confucian moral values and virtues in societies totalitarianism threatened—no matter how diligently this was done—would not suffice to secure correct moral judgments, let alone prevent totalitarian takeovers. Nor would it effectively reduce the spread of indifference and passiveness on the part of the bystanders once the shift to a regime of terror had begun. As a matter of fact,

Tang remained skeptical with respect to the moral impact of Confucianism in modernizing societies, even if those societies were not immediately endangered by totalitarianism. In 1965 he expressed his skepticism thusly:

> . . . the modern industrialized community is highly departmentalized in its structure by the division of labor. Here man must particularize in something, has his special profession, and consequently has his special social position in a corner of the complicated structure. Man's moral practice as demanded by the modern community is just to be loyal to his special profession and not feel ashamed of his special position. Here the Confucian idea of the whole man as a cultural and moral being seems inadequate to be the spiritual ground for the establishment of modern community and modern vocational morality.[84]

Tang consequently refrained from turning his moral thought into a search for allegedly superior moral values and virtues or ethical practices. His reflection on a Confucian concept of morality and ethics did not lend itself to practical concerns in such an immediate, yet insufficiently complex, manner. Instead, his moral thought is best described as centering on the issue of the self-image of individuals. What is at stake here is the capacity of individuals to conceive of themselves as solitary moral authorities, namely as "sages" capable of moral intuition. Such a self-depiction can be considered, in accordance with Tang, as an intrinsic requirement for the individual's ability to make autonomous moral judgments. With its core concept of *liang zhi*, Tang's Confucianism unfolds a moral theory that describes the individual as having immediate access to an innate source of judgments about right and wrong. This entails a tendency to deemphasize the role of society as the producer of morality. Accordingly, the individual is seen as not bound by conventionally sanctioned moral rules in realizing his or her capacity for moral intuition. Tang's Confucian thought addresses, in other words, "the question of *moral responsibility for resisting socialization*"[85]—and hence a problem that belongs to the reflection on the Holocaust.

But it does not belong there exclusively: notions of *liang zhi*, after all, also proved attractive to Chiang Kai-shek and his followers, as well as to twentieth-century Japanese militarists. The notion of *liang zhi* has, seemingly, an inevitable ambiguity. Given the idea of an intuitive enlightenment that is quintessentially aloof in its immediacy from any symbolic prefiguration and representation, any attempt to attach such enlightenment firmly to certain normative choices amounts to a precarious undertaking. Faced with such a dilemma, Tang inscribed his moral intuitionism into an ethics that stressed the individual's social responsibility. The Confucian individual was not to withdraw into the irrationality of purely spiritual inwardness, but rather called on to bear the tension between the requirements of social life and the continuous effort to realize the self-image of becoming the sole mediator of the "inner sage."

Notes

1. See Fröhlich, "'Confucian Democracy' and Its Confucian Critics: Mou Zongsan and Tang Junyi on the Limits of Confucianism," *Oriens Extremus* 49 (2010): 167–200, esp. 168–174.

2. As a matter of fact, some intellectuals from the so-called second generation of modern Confucianism such as Tang Junyi, Mou Zongsan, and Xu Fuguan addressed this problem in a profound manner. On Tang and Mou, see Fröhlich, "'Confucian Democracy' and Its Confucian Critics," 174–194. Wei Zhengtong 韋政通 is one of the few critics of modern Confucianism who went into some detail on this topic; see, e.g., Wei Zhengtong, *Rujia yu xiandaihua* 儒家與現代化 [Confucianism and Modernization] (Taibei: Shuiniu chubanshe, 1989), 95–107. For a mainland Chinese and typically brief rejection of the alleged "antidemocratic" orientation of modern Confucianism, see Qi Liang 启良, "Zou chu zhengzhi ruxue 走出政治儒学" [Going beyond political Confucianism], in *21 shiji Zhongguo zhexue zouxiang—Di 12 jie guoji Zhongguo zhexue da hui. Lunwen ji zhi yi.* 21 世纪中国哲学走向—第 12 届国际中国哲学大会. 论文集之一 [Trends in Chinese philosophy of the twenty-first century—The twelfth International Plenary Session on Chinese Philosophy. Collected writings, part 1], edited by Fang Keli 方克立 (Beijing: Shangwu yinshuguan, 2003), 438–440.

3. Gan Yang assumed that there are continuities between "traditional societies" and "socialist states" (which evolved, according to Gan, in precapitalist, traditional societies) that become manifest in the persistence of totalitarianism and (totalizing) moral idealism. He ascribed to Confucianism strong moral-idealist tendencies and called on modern Confucianism to finally learn its historical lesson. See Gan Yang 甘陽, "Ruxue yu xiandai—jian lun ruxue yu dangdai Zhongguo" 儒學與現代—兼論儒學與當代中國 [Confucianism and the modern age: Including a discussion of the role of Confucianism in modern China], in *Ruxue fazhan de hongguan toushi. Xinjiapo 1988 nian ruxue qunyinghui ji shi* 儒學發展的宏觀透視 [A macro-view of the development of Confucianism], edited by Tu Wei-ming 杜維明 (Taibei: Zhengzhong shuju, 1997), 607, 613–614. Xu Fuguan raised a similar criticism of Tang Junyi's and Mou Zongsan's modern Confucianism in the early 1950s (see below); more recently, Thomas Metzger presupposes, with respect to modern China, that what he calls "the four ideologies" (i.e., modern Confucian humanism, Chinese Marxism, Chinese Liberalism, Sunism) were characterized by an "epistemological optimism." He then suggests ". . . that the structure of authority in China is closely connected to a tradition-rooted, pervasive form of epistemological optimism

contrasting with a much more pessimistic epistemology in Western liberal democracies meshes with Charles E. Lindblom's view regarding the contrast between the epistemology of the latter societies and that of the U.S.S.R."; see Thomas Metzger, *A Cloud across the Pacific: Essays on the Clash between Chinese and Western Political Theories Today* (Hong Kong: Chinese University Press, 2005), 175, 182.

4. For example, Zhang Junmai commented extensively on international communism and Chinese communism after World War II. See Zhang's articles in *Zhang Junmai yanlun ji: Yijiusijiu nian yihou* 張君勱言論集: 1949年以後 [Zhang Junmai's speeches and talks after 1949] (Taibei: Maitian chubanshe, 1989), vol. 2, 3, 4. In the 1930s he had written a book about the Soviet Union under Stalin, covering the years 1928 to 1933 (史泰林治下之蘇俄 [The Soviet Union under Stalin], 1933), and published a brief comparison of the dictatorships in the Soviet Union, Nazi Germany, and Fascist Italy (in his 立國之道 [The way to establish the state], 1938), using terms such as "fascist" or "autocracy," but not "totalitarianism."

5. See, e.g., the 1958 Manifesto drafted by Tang Junyi and signed by Tang, Zhang Junmai, Mou Zongsan, and Xu Fuguan ("Wei Zhongguo wenhua jinggao shijie renshi xuanyan—women dui Zhongguo xueshu yanjiu ji Zhongguo wenhua yu shijie wenhua qiantu zhi gongtong renshi 為中國文化敬告世界人士宣言—我們對中國學術研究及中國文化與世界文化前途之共同認識," *Minzhu Pinglun* 民主評論 [Democratic critique] 9, no. 1 [Jan. 1,1958]: 2–21). More recently, Tu Wei-ming prominently raises similar claims to global significance of a renewed Confucianism/Confucian humanism; e.g., Tu, "Multiple Modernities—Implications of the Rise of 'Confucian' East Asia," in *Chinese Ethics in a Global Context: Moral Bases of Contemporary Societies*, edited by Karl-Heinz Pohl and Anselm W. Müller (Leiden: Brill, 2002), 55–77, esp. 60, 66–67.

6. That the concept of totalitarianism is highly problematic and gave rise to prolonged controversies in academic circles as well as in public discussions is well known, not the least because it seems to imply a conceptual, functional, or otherwise retraceable equation of National Socialism and Stalinist communism. Comparisons pertaining to the nature and function of death camps, to the ontological status of "class struggle" as compared to "racial struggle," to the organizational structure of the regimes, and to the "difference between a state that commits genocide and a genocidal state" are still, and will most likely continue to be, controversial issues. In a review article, Anson Rabinbach sums up this state of research by noting that ". . . until recently, few systematic comparisons on the current state of historical research have actually been undertaken." See Rabinbach, "Moments of Totalitarianism" (review article), *History and Theory* 45 (Feb. 2006): 72–100 (above quotations, see 77–78, 85). Advocates of modern Confucianism did not take note of these controversies surrounding "totalitarianism."

7. Tang Junyi, "The Reconstruction of Confucianism and the Modernization of Asia," Report of International Conference on the Problems of Modernization in Asia (July 1965, Seoul), *Tang Junyi quanji juan shijiu* 唐君毅全集 [Collected works of Tang Junyi] (Taipei: Xuesheng shuju, 1988), vol. 19, 361.

8. Ibid.

9. Ibid., 369.

10. Tang Junyi, "Zhonghua renwen yu dangjin shijie (xia)" 中華人文與當今世界上, 下 [Chinese humanism and the world of today, part 2], in *Tang Junyi quanji juan*, vol. 8, 135.

11. For a concise introduction to theories of a German "*Sonderweg,*" see Henning Ottmann, *Geschichte des politischen Denkens. Das 20. Jahrhundert. Der Totalitarismus und seine Überwindung*, vol. 4/1 (Stuttgart: Metzler, 2010), 335–338.

12. See Fröhlich, "Regulating, Governing, and Pacifying the Modern World: Optimism Regarding Progress in Chinese Interpretations of the *Great Learning*," in *Lectures et usages de la Grande Étude. Sous la direction de Anne Cheng*, edited by Damien Morier-Genoud (Paris: Collège de France Institut des Hautes Études Chinoises, 2015), 387–413.

13. Tang, "Zhonghua renwen yu dangjin shijie," *Tang Junyi quanji*, vol. 8, 324.

14. Ibid., 115.

15. Tang, "Zhonghua renwen yu dangjin shijie bubian (xia)" 中華人文與當今世界補編上, 下 [Chinese humanism and the world of today, supplements], *Tang Junyi quanji*, vol. 10, 392.

16. Tang, "Zhongguo renwen jingshen zhi fazhan" 中國人文精神之發展 [The development of the Chinese humanistic spirit], *Tang Junyi quanji*, vol. 6, 193, 206. Tang refers here to communal associations whose members meet each other "immediately" and on grounds of shared ethical values or territorial, familial, or emotional ties—that is, without the intermediation of "outer" purposes like common economic interests. Chinese communities typically include, according to Tang, organizations of family or clan members, but also alumni, members from the same birthplace, academics, participants in "poetry and wine gatherings," and even secret societies. These quasi-natural associations were, in Tang's view, more common in China than in the West, and this heritage might serve as an important reference for individual self-realization in modernizing societies.

17. Tang, "Zhonghua renwen yu dangjin shijie," *Tang Junyi quanji*, vol. 8, 115–118, 123, 125, 129. In this context, see also the following passage in which Tang rhetorically asks: "How can an individual spiritual being really be an individual, if his religious, moral, and cultural life is not integrated into a unity as a genuine Confucian aspires to?"; Tang, "The Reconstruction of Confucianism and the Modernization of Asia," *Tang Junyi quanji*, vol. 19. 365.

18. At times, Tang's confidence in the success of Japan's modernization was shattered, leaving him to express his hope that the Japanese would not define Japan's progress in industrialization solely in terms of an increase in industrial production alone, but also with respect to the benefits of cultural life; see Tang, "Zhonghua renwen yu dangjin shijie," *Tang Junyi quanji*, vol. 8, 211. Whether Tang's topical way of thinking in longitudes and latitudes is inspired by topical thinking as prevalent in the philosophy of the Kyoto school is difficult to determine. Be that as it may, Tang obviously shared with the Kyoto school, and with influential European and U.S. intellectual trends of the mid-twentieth century, the apprehension that the process

of modernity and rationalization might entail strong tendencies of massification and deterioration of cultural standards.

19. Tang, "Zhonghua renwen yu dangjin shijie," *Tang Junyi quanji*, vol. 8, 56–57.

20. According to the concept of a "main current" (*zhu liu* 主流), China's national culture contains a spiritual/ideational "core" (*hexin* 核心) or "essence" (*benzhi* 本質) that finds its most authentic expression in the so-called Confucian study of mind and (human) nature (*xin xing zhi xue* 心性之學). Tang and his coauthors of the 1958 Manifesto believed that the survival of national culture hinged on the continuing reinterpretation and reenactment of the Confucian "main current," which comprised philosophical and religious elements. However, the concept of "main current" does not amount here to a traditionalist insistence on an unchanging normative validity of the national culture in modernity, nor is it a case of a rigid essentialist view of an ahistorical core of national culture. For a detailed discussion of Tang's concept of main current see Fröhlich, "The Exilic Prism of Modernity: New Perspectives on the Post-War Philosophy of Tang Junyi," *Oriens Extremus* 52 (2013): 37–82.

21. Georg Wilhelm Friedrich Hegel, *The Philosophy of History* (Kitchener, ON: Batoche Books, 2001), 47.

22. Tang, "Wenhua yishi yu daode lixing" 文化意識與道德理性 [Cultural consciousness and moral reason], *Tang Junyi quanji*, vol. 20, 262.

23. Tang, "Shengming cunzai yu xinling jingjie (xia)" 生命存在與心靈境界. 上, 下 [The existence of life and the horizons of spiritual potency], *Tang Junyi quanji*, vol. 24, 461–462. Tang elucidates in this context the historical development of the "victory of Marxism" in China mostly in terms of a general loss of faith in "traditional" values of Chinese and Western cultures: ibid., 464. His skepticism toward existentialism dates back at least to the late 1950s; see his criticism of existentialism's inability to "actively" seek a solution for humanity's spiritual crises in the modern world: Tang, "Zhonghua renwen yu dangjin shijie," *Tang Junyi quanji*, vol. 8, 57.

24. See, e.g., Tang, "Zhonghua renwen yu dangjin shijie," *Tang Junyi quanji*, vol. 8, 127.

25. In his theological-metaphysical reinterpretation of the concepts of *liang zhi* 良知 ("innate knowing") and *sheng ren*, Tang essentially posits that "Heaven" (*tian* 天) might manifest itself in the mind of the human being who apprehends in a (moral) intuition in actu (i.e., *liang zhi*) the ultimate principles of reality (i.e., the "principles of Heaven" *tian li* 天理), thereby momentarily turning into a "sage"; e.g., Tang, "Renwen jingshen zhi chongjian," *Tang Junyi quanji*, vol. 5, 588–589; Tang, "Zhongguo renwen jingshen zhi fazhan," *Tang Junyi quanji*, vol. 6, 363–371; Tang, "Wenhua yishi yu daode lixing, *Tang Junyi quanji*, vol. 20, 369.

26. As mentioned above, Thomas Metzger subsumes Tang Junyi's modern Confucianism into the category of an "epistemological optimism" that is characterized by the assumption that the "ultimate reality" of all phenomena is detectable and describable by human beings. Yet with respect to Tang's philosophy, the idea of the

human being's insight into the absolute truth of the "Heavenly principles," we should note, cannot be detached from the assumption that such an insight is attainable only in an ephemeral moment of intuition and only by individuals, never by whole (political) collectivities. As a consequence, the intuitive insight never amounts to a permanent, *political* state of existence. Claims to absolute truth, together with their totalitarian repercussions, are therefore not supported by Tang's political thought; see Metzger, *A Cloud across the Pacific*, 21–31, 171–182 [n. 138], 220, 672–676. On Tang's concept of intuition, see Fröhlich, "Confucian Philosophy Reconsidered."

27. On Tang's criticism of positivism in the context of historical research see, e.g., Tang, "Zhonghua renwen yu dangjin shijie," *Tang Junyi quanji*, vol. 7, 165, 167; for a discussion of this issue, see Fröhlich, "The Exilic Prism of Modernity."

28. The fact that Tang conceives of *lishi zhexue* not simply as a philosophy of history in the European tradition becomes evident when he agrees with Mou Zongsan that the *Spring and Autumn Annals* (*Chunqiu* 春秋) are the pioneering works of Chinese "*lishi zhexue*"; see Tang's article "A Philosophical Inquiry of Chinese History," published in *Rensheng* 120 (Nov. 1955); Tang, "Zhonghua renwen yu dangjin shijie," *Tang Junyi quanji*, vol. 7, 178.

29. I will analyze Tang's speculation about history in more detail in a forthcoming monograph on Tang Junyi's philosophy.

30. See also Huang Zhaoqiang 黃兆強, *Xueshu yu jingshi—Tang Junyi de lishi zhexue ji qi zhongji guanhuai* 學術與經世—唐君毅的歷史哲學及其終極關懷 [Learning and statecraft—The philosophy of history and ultimate concerns of Tang Junyi] (Taipei: Xuesheng shuju, 2010), 27, 54–55, 61–62.

31. Tang, *Zhongguo wenhua zhi jingshen jiazhi* 中國文化之精神價值 [The spiritual values of Chinese philosophy] (Taipei: Zhengzhong shuju, 1997), 231.

32. On Tang's discussion of the "ideal humanistic world," see the following texts: Tang, "The ideal humanistic world," first published in *Minzhu Pinglun* [Democratic review] 1, no. 2 (July 1949); reprinted in Tang, *Renwen jingshen zhi chongjian* 人文精神之重建 [The reconstruction of the humanistic spirit] (Hong Kong: Xin shuyuan, 1974), 59–72; "Basic knowledge about humanistic culture and democracy," first published in *Minzhu Pinglun* 3, no. 24 (Dec. 1952), and reprinted in Tang, *Renwen jingshen zhi chongjian*, 388–401; "Social humanism and the spirit of democracy in China and the West," first published in *Minzhu Pinglun* 4, no. 4 (Jan. 1953); reprinted in Tang, *Renwen jingshen zhi chongjian*, 402–425.

33. Tang, "Zhongguo renwen jingshen zhi fazhan," *Tang Junyi quanji*, vol. 6, 175–176; 1958 Manifesto, 39.

34. On Tang's concept of "humanism" (*renwenzhuyi* 人文主義, or just *renwen* 人文) see, e.g., Tang, "Renwen jingshen zhi chongjian," 592–597. Tang strongly emphasized that a Confucian-based humanism would not contradict religious teachings but would serve to accommodate non-Confucian religions and uphold its own interest in a transcendental realm; in this sense Tang suggested labeling Confucian humanism an "idealistic humanism" or "humanistic idealism."

35. Tang, "Zhonghua renwen yu dangjin shijie bubian," *Tang Junyi quanji*, vol. 10, 393.

36. With respect to European philosophies of history, Marquard deems the notion of the human being's perfectibility *within* history to be a tenet of the historical-philosophical conception of history as the progressive development of human emancipation; see Odo Marquard, *Schwierigkeiten mit der Geschichtsphilosophie. Aufsätze*, 4th ed. (Frankfurt: Suhrkamp, 1997), 67–68.

37. Significantly, Tang takes little if any interest in the eschatological implications of European philosophies of history, and he does not reflect on the thesis that philosophies of history evolved out of a secularization of earlier theological speculations about history. For the European context of this, see Marquard, *Schwierigkeiten mit der Geschichtsphilosophie*, 15–16.

38. The article "Is a Human Being a Human Being after All?" was published in *Minzhu Pinglun*. 2, no. 24 (June 1951); see Tang, "Zhonghua renwen yu dangjin shijie bubian," *Tang Junyi quanji*, vol. 10, 131–137.

39. On the early American debate about totalitarianism, see Wolfgang Knöbl, *Spielräume der Modernisierung. Das Ende der Eindeutigkeit* (Weilerswist: Velbrück Wissenschaft, 2001), 116–120. The *Review of Politics* was founded in a Catholic milieu. John Nef, an economic historian from the University of Chicago, warned about the detrimental effects of unrestrained materialism and the crisis of capitalism in Western societies, including the United States, in 1940; ibid., 119. American public and academic debates about totalitarianism date back to the 1930s and over time comprised a broad intellectual and political spectrum, at one time bringing together socialists, liberals, and conservatives in the "Committee for Cultural Freedom" founded by philosophers Sidney Hook and John Dewey in 1939. The scope of "totalitarianism" was contested throughout, and discussions responded to shifts in international politics, from the Hitler-Stalin Pact to U.S. cooperation with the Soviet Union in the war against Nazi Germany and to the subsequent rift in the Cold War period, which led to a revival of studies on totalitarianism in the 1950s; see Rabinbach, "Moments of Totalitarianism," 89–93; A. James Gregor, *Marxism, Fascism, and Totalitarianism: Chapters in the Intellectual History of Radicalism* (Stanford, CA: Stanford University Press, 2009), 12–14.

40. Rabinbach, "Moments of Totalitarianism," 100. In the same vein, in *Marxism, Fascism, and Totalitarianism*, A. James Gregor states that "[w]hat 'totalitarianism' is not is a 'theory.' . . . It is not clear that all members of the class share all its defining traits—nor is it clear how many of those defining traits, or in what measure, are required for entry into the class" (17).

41. See a 1974 article by Tang in *Mingbao* 明報: Tang, "Zhonghua renwen yu dangjin shijie," *Tang Junyi quanji*, vol. 8, 428. The reference to Mao Zedong pertains to Chinese communism of the early 1950s; see Tang, "Zhonghua renwen yu dangjin shijie bubian," *Tang Junyi quanji*, vol. 10, 136.

42. Tang, "Zhonghua renwen yu dangjin shijie," *Tang Junyi quanji*, vol. 8, 331.

43. For Tang's diagnosis of GMD fascist tendencies, see Tang, "Zhonghua renwen yu dangjin shijie bubian," *Tang Junyi quanji*, vol. 10, 157–158.

44. Tang, "Zhonghua renwen yu dangjin shijie," *Tang Junyi quanji*, vol. 8, 318–319.

45. As Liu Honghe points out, Xu Fuguan assumed in his study of centralized, bureaucratic rule in imperial China that a "totalitarian" type of despotism evolved in the Qin and Han Dynasties and persisted, in various forms, throughout imperial China; see Liu, *Confucianism in the Eyes of a Confucian Liberal: Hsu Fu-kuan's Critical Examination of the Confucian Political Tradition* (New York: Lang, 2001), 111–112.

46. Tang, "Zhonghua renwen yu dangjin shijie bubian," *Tang Junyi quanji*, vol. 10, 226–227.

47. Ibid., 226–237, 236–237; Tang, *Renwen jingshen zhi chongjian*, 389–391; on Tang's concept of politics, see Fröhlich, "Tang Junyi, Max Weber und die Mächte des Dämonischen: Zum Politikverständnis eines modernen Konfuzianers," *Asiatische Studien/Etudes Asiatiques* 57, no. 4 (2003): 813–848.

48. Tang, "Zhonghua renwen yu dangjin shijie bubian," *Tang Junyi quanji*, vol. 10, 235.

49. Ibid.

50. Ibid., 237.

51. Ibid., 131–132, 134.

52. Ibid., 132–133.

53. Ibid., 136. Arguably, Tang comes close to a concept of "political religion" in his analysis of totalitarian ideologies.

54. For a discussion of Tang's analysis of the human lust for power, see Fröhlich, "Tang Junyi, Max Weber und die Mächte des Dämonischen. Zum Politikverständnis eines modernen Konfuzianers," 828–833; on Tang's reflection about human cruelty, see Tang, *Wenhua yishi yu daode lixing*, 564–565.

55. Tang explicitly states that in the world of Marxism-Leninism, human beings are deprived of opportunities to rely on a moral or cultural way of life in order to rein in their lust for power. He adds that for the Communist Party, the existence of political power is identical with the existence of human life; see the 1972 unpublished manuscript, "On the Contradiction between Chinese Nationalism and Marxism-Leninism, and on the Road of China," reprinted in Tang, "Zhonghua renwen yu dangjin shijie bubian," *Tang Junyi quanji*, vol. 10, 422. See also Tang's diagnosis of the totalitarian politicization, and hence destruction, of the humanistic realm in the People's Republic of China: Tang, *Renwen jingshen zhi chongian*, 65, 388.

56. Tang, "The Reconstruction of Confucianism and the Modernization of Asia," 368.

57. Tang, "Zhonghua renwen yu dangjin shijie bubian," *Tang Junyi quanji*, vol. 10, 427–429 (unpublished manuscript).

58. Tang, "Renwen jingshen zhi chongjian," 572–573.

59. See Tang's 1958 article in *Zuguo Zhoukan*, vol. 28, no. 3–5, and reprinted in Tang, "Zhonghua renwen yu dangjin shijie," *Tang Junyi quanji*, vol. 8, 110.

60. Tang, "Zhonghua renwen yu dangjin shijie," *Tang Junyi quanji*, vol. 8, 424–425. Tang states, in the manner of Western mainstream criticisms of reifying effects of modernity: ". . . modern man, who sees and does nothing other than what his profession demands of him, leads a way of life more or less like a bee or an ant,

thus degrading the human spirit"; see Tang, "The Reconstruction of Confucianism and the Modernization of Asia," 370.

61. Tang, "Zhonghua renwen yu dangjin shijie," *Tang Junyi quanji*, vol. 8, 428. Tang is here referring, among others, to Jaspers, Buber, and Sartre as philosophers who warned that the basic problem of human existence in the twentieth century, in capitalist as well as socialist societies, was not so much one of material life as one of a deepening isolation and solitude on the part of the individual, which runs counter to an "authentic" mode of life; see Tang, "Zhonghua renwen yu dangjin shijie bubian," *Tang Junyi quanji*, vol. 10, 435 (unpublished manuscript).

62. Tang, "The Reconstruction of Confucianism and the Modernization of Asia," 367.

63. See Tang's 1959 article "World Humanism and Chinese Humanism," reprinted in Tang, "Zhonghua renwen yu dangjin shijie," *Tang Junyi quanji*, vol. 8, 49.

64. Tang, "Zhonghua renwen yu dangjin shijie bubian," *Tang Junyi quanji*, vol. 10, 445 (unpublished manuscript).

65. See a 1974 interview with Tang in *Mingbao*, reprinted in Tang, "Zhonghua renwen yu dangjin shijie," *Tang Junji quanji*, vol. 8, 318–319.

66. See, e.g., Tang, "Zhongguo renwen jingshen zhi fazhan," 223–224; Tang, *Wenhua yishi yu daode lixing*, 300.

67. See a 1974 interview with Tang in *Mingbao* (Hong Kong), reprinted in Tang, "Zhongguo wenhua yu dangdai shijie," *Tang Junyi quanji*, vol. 8, 331.

68. Tang, "Zhonghua renwen yu dangjin shijie," *Tang Junyi quanji*, vol. 8, 104.

69. See, e.g., Tang, *Renwen jingshen zhi chongjian*, 403, 409–410, 416, 423–424.

70. Tang, "Zhonghua renwen yu dangjin shijie," *Tang Junyi quanji*, vol. 8, 331. He had already claimed in 1951 that the problem of "Chinese communism" was in fact not a problem that was primarily related to certain political parties or to certain political systems but rather a problem of "culture" and "mind and (human) nature"; see Tang, "Zhonghua renwen yu dangjin shijie bubian," *Tang Junyi quanji*, vol. 10, 136.

71. Zhang, *Zhongguo wenhua yu shijie*, p. 44.

72. Tang, "Zhonghua renwen yu dangjin shijie," *Tang Junyi quanji*, vol. 8, 318–319; see also Tang, "Zhonghua renwen yu dangjin shijie bubian," *Tang Junyi quanji*, vol. 10, 445–446 (unpublished manuscript); Zhang, *Zhongguo wenhua yu shijie*, 44–45. In the same vein, Tang made retrospective prognostications in the form of historical diagnoses. Among these, we find his highly questionable dictum that contemporary Russia, due to its "totalitarian" tradition of czarism, was far more likely to witness a prolonged totalitarian era than China, whose "totalitarian" past had merely lasted for the very short period of the Qin dynasty; see Tang, "Zhonghua renwen yu dangjin shijie," *Tang Junyi quanji*, vol. 8, 318–319.

73. Tang, *Renwen jingshen zhi chongjian*, 392–393.

74. The so-called Hegelian Right in Germany is often said to have considered the factual state as the rational state, whereas the Hegelian Left attempted to conceptualize a *future* human community in which alienation and the institutions of

the state would have ceased to exist; see Ernest Vollrath, *Grundlegung einer philosophischen Theorie des Politischen* (Würzburg: Königshausen and Neumann, 1987), 128.

75. Tang, *Zhongguo renwen jingshen zhi fazhan*, 175–176; this article was first published in *Zuguo Zhoukan* 12, no. 7 (Nov. 1955).

76. Reinhart Koselleck called this latter type of concept, which gained wide currency after the French Revolution, "collective and motivating concepts capable of reordering and mobilizing anew the masses." These concepts, many of which were "–isms," aided political mobilization and were (and still are) used not only in academic contexts but also as political watchwords; see Koselleck, *Futures Past: On the Semantics of Historical Time* (New York: Columbia University Press, 2004 [1985]), 80.

77. Tang, *Renwen jingshen zhi chongjian*, 71–72; this article was published in *Minzhu Pinglun* 1, no. 2 (July 1949).

78. Zygmunt Bauman, *Modernity and the Holocaust* (Ithaca, NY: Cornell University Press, 2000 [1989]), 7.

79. Ibid., 12.

80. Ibid., 11.

81. Ibid., x. With respect to instrumental rationality, Bauman cogently analyzes: "This is not to suggest that the incidence of the Holocaust was *determined* by modern bureaucracy or the culture of instrumental rationality it epitomizes; much less still, that modern bureaucracy *must* result in Holocaust-style phenomena. I do suggest, however, that the rules of instrumental rationality are singularly incapable of preventing such phenomena; that there is nothing in those rules which disqualifies the Holocaust-style methods of 'social engineering' as improper . . . " (ibid., 17–18).

82. Ibid., 250.

83. Hannah Arendt, *Eichmann in Jerusalem: A Report on the Banality of Evil* (New York: Viking Press, 1964), 294–295, quoted from Bauman, *Modernity and the Holocaust*, 177.

84. Tang, "The Reconstruction of Confucianism and the Modernization of Asia," 368.

85. Bauman, *Modernity and the Holocaust*, 177.

10

A Critique of Colonialism and Capitalism

Tang Junyi's Views on Plurality and Openness

Hok Yin Chan

Like many Chinese refugees who fled to Hong Kong in 1949, Tang Junyi was ambivalent about the British colony. On the one hand, he found a home in Hong Kong after escaping from communist China. As an immigrant, he was free to do whatever he liked there as long as he followed the laws and paid taxes. From a safe distance, he could observe changes in China without the danger of being harmed by its endless political campaigns. On the other hand, he found the British colony a strange place. Geographically it was close to the mainland and not far from Taiwan, which the Guomindang (GMD) controlled. And yet, culturally it was a foreign land where the top officials were British and the dominant language was English. Under the Union Jack, the residents of Hong Kong (expatriates and locals alike) acted as if they were living in Great Britain. They conducted their business according to the British laws, held social conversation in English, and enjoyed the niceties of high tea.

For Tang Junyi, who was born and raised in Sichuan, his sojourn in the British colony was a self-imposed exile; he made the choice freely but had to endure the consequences. In the early 1970s, in a speech he delivered at a ceremony marking his retirement from the Chinese University of Hong Kong (CUHK), he made clear his refugee identity: "Hong Kong is a British colony. It is not a Chinese land, nor are its people Chinese. Only my friends and students who gather here are culturally Chinese. While our hopes and dreams are tied to China, we have no choice but to find shelter in this land."[1] On another occasion, Tang Junyi reflected on his experiences in Hong Kong. After spending twenty-some years in the colony, he still considered himself a person in exile, torn between his imagined homeland and his place of residence. He wrote: "In the 1950s and 1960s, we paid little attention to the problems in the Hong Kong colonial government because we were refugees. At that time, we focused on events related to China, rather than on Hong Kong."[2] In fact, Tang Junyi was not alone in feeling torn between homeland and place of residence. The other two New Confucian masters, Mou Zongsan and Xu Fuguan, were in similar situations. Mou Zongsan, for instance, affirmed his refugee identity by refusing to buy property in the Crown Colony. Xu Fuguan moved back and forth between Hong Kong and Taiwan, and in the end he chose to die in Taiwan.

Current scholarship tells us a great deal about Tang's moral metaphysics and his interpretation of Chinese thought, but we learn very little about him as an exile coping with alienation while living in a foreign land. This chapter redresses this imbalance by highlighting the significance of Tang Junyi's refugee identity in shaping his thoughts. To do so, I focus on how he, as a sensitive soul, came to terms with injustice in the British colony, and how he, as a thinker, built a philosophical system to express his yearning for an open and pluralistic society. We have much to learn from Tang Junyi about the complexity and cruelty of colonialism and capitalism. After all, Tang was a thinker who lived in an interesting time: China was undergoing massive political campaigns to build socialism, and Hong Kong and other parts of the Western world were expanding the market economy by increasing production and consumption. In this polarized world of the Cold War—divided by the ideological competition between communism and capitalism—Tang became an exile and a philosopher with a global perspective.

Contextualizing Tang's Humanism

In recent years, critics of Tang Junyi have often focused on his "humanism" (*renwen zhuyi* 人文主義). By humanism they mean Tang's efforts at finding a common ground among competing perspectives. Certainly, even Tang's fiercest critics admire his global vision of a universal framework built to bring together the different cultures, religions, and beliefs of this world. Yet his preoccupation with finding common ground has created confusion among his friends and foes.

For his friends, his balanced approach makes him a less effective spokesman for New Confucianism. Unlike Mou Zongsan, who is not afraid to make sharp remarks, Tang is too soft, too yielding, too compromising. For this reason, while Mou Zongsan is often thought of as a rigorous philosopher who articulates in clear terms the differences between New Confucianism and other schools of thought, Tang is likened to a diplomat who is able to forge an alliance among enemies by avoiding their differences.

This caricature of Tang may be an exaggeration, but it points to the fact that Tang was keenest at dialogue, negotiation, and collaboration—a virtue that we deeply treasure today in an open and pluralistic society. But during Tang's time and even after his death, his interest in dialogue and negotiation was considered one of his major faults. To some people, his willingness to compromise makes him an uncritical, uninspiring scholar of the Confucian tradition, showing nothing but the similarities between Confucianism, Daoism, and Buddhism.[3] To others, his balanced approach to cultural comparison leads to misunderstanding of world civilizations, emphasizing their common features at the expense of their distinctive qualities.[4] To yet others, his desire for negotiation and collaboration makes him an idealist with no knowledge of the horrifying reality of political conflicts, especially those driven by racial and religious differences.[5]

While valid, these criticisms miss one crucial point: Tang's experience in British Hong Kong. To a great extent, Tang's humanism was a response to the injustice in the colony. For instance, his demand for plurality and openness was a political act against the dominance of the English language in Hong Kong, where the majority of residents were Chinese. Similarly, his desire for dialogue and negotiation was an antidote against racial hierarchy and Eurocentrism in the colony, where Chinese immigrants, even if they were highly educated and possessed specialized knowledge, had to be recertified and retrained in accordance with stringent British standards. By the same token, his balanced approach to cultural comparison was aimed at Westernization (*xihua*) in Hong Kong, where all residents were encouraged to adopt Western names, to convert to Christianity, and to follow a Western lifestyle. In short, Tang's humanism was framed as a cultural critique of British colonialism, which in Cold War Hong Kong was presented as a stabilizing force vis-à-vis the chaos and upheavals in communist China.

The paradox is that, while Tang deeply resented the British colonial rule, he found his voice as a philosopher in Hong Kong. Despite his hatred of the colonial system, the system provoked him to think more deeply about human nature, social structure, cultural systems, and above all, uneven power relations among peoples. For this reason, Tang's humanism, like his refugee identity, was full of tension. On the one hand, he was comfortable employing a balanced and moderate tone to convey his radical political view; on the other hand, he chose to express his political radicalism through a plea for dialogue, compromise, and openness. Although full of tension, Tang's humanism was aimed at concrete social and political problems in the Hong

Kong of the Cold War, and many of these problems originated in the global spread of capitalism during the twentieth century. For a full understanding of Tang's humanism, we must keep these local and global contexts in mind.

Education in Colonial Hong Kong

During his stay in Hong Kong, Tang spent most of his time as an administrator in higher education, a setting in which he came face to face with the colonial cultural hegemony. To him, two events were particularly revealing: the certification of New Asia College as a nonprofit institution and the creation of CUHK. In the former, he was puzzled that in the early 1950s when New Asia College was having financial difficulties, the Hong Kong government not only did not help but also created more problems for the college by ordering it to pay large registration fees to comply with commercial laws. Exacerbating matters, the Hong Kong government did not recognize the qualifications of New Asia graduates, rendering their education worthless when they entered the job market.

From Tang's perspective, the education policy of the Hong Kong government was contradictory. On the one hand, it allowed New Asia College to exist and to produce educated workers for the labor market; on the other hand, it deliberately limited its social impact by categorizing it as a commercial institution and denying its graduates their educational qualifications. To Tang, what seemed most absurd was the order to pay large registration fees. Certainly, in a capitalist society, someone has to pay. But the Hong Kong government expected those who wanted to promote adult education both to pay for improvement of higher education in the colony and to provide revenue to support the government.[6]

This hypocrisy of colonial rule was further displayed with the 1963 founding of CUHK. First, Tang was upset that the administrators and faculty of Hong Kong University—at that time the only official institution of higher education in the colony—vehemently opposed the creation of another university, reasoning that each of the colonies under British rule had only one university. They implied that the existing cultural hierarchy in the colony could not be changed while the British continued to rule Hong Kong. To Tang, this objection to creating another university had little to do with education; rather, it was about preserving the power and privilege of the elites.[7]

Shortly after CUHK was established Tang was disturbed by the university's policy of using English as the official language. An immediate result of this policy was that scholars who did not know English (such as Qian

Mu) found they no longer had a role at CUHK. Soon these scholars had no alternative but to leave the university. For Tang, who knew English, the policy did not affect the security of his job, but it showed clearly the cultural hegemony of colonialism that forced the "barbaric people" to conform to the Eurocentric order. To express his anger over the English-only policy, he wrote many articles that discussed its absurdity and unfairness, describing his Chinese colleagues at CUHK as "shameless" when they insisted on speaking English in both public and private conversation.[8]

Another event that upset Tang was the university's decision to switch to a centralized system. On the surface, the change in the administrative system was undertaken to make CUHK more global and efficient. In effect, it eliminated the autonomy of the three formerly private colleges (New Asia College, Chung Chi College, and United College) that had joined the university. For Tang, the loss of autonomy of New Asia College was a big blow to his educational ambition. When it was founded in the early 1950s, New Asia College had as its goal to promote Chinese culture as a remedy to social fragmentations caused by commercialization, industrialization, and urbanization. To Tang's displeasure, a few years after the founding of CUHK, New Asia College existed only in name. It was no longer the educational institution to promote Chinese culture that its founders originally planned.[9]

Confucianism and Openness

To critique colonialism, Tang wrote fervently about Confucianism. To him, Confucianism was not only a subject of study, but also a source of cultural identity that gave him confidence and pride in facing adversity in life and injustice in society. For this reason, Tang's interpretation of Confucianism always had two levels of meaning. On the one hand, he gave a *descriptive* account of Confucianism by explaining its core concepts such as *ren* (human-relatedness), *zhong* (centrality), and *wulun* (Five Relationships). On the other hand, his interpretation of Confucianism was also *discursive* in the sense that he deliberately focused on areas that made Confucianism an antidote against the three pillars of colonialism: authoritarianism, elitism, and Eurocentrism.[10]

Take, for instance, his image of Confucius. In a series of articles criticizing the Hong Kong people for celebrating Christmas, Tang directly compared Confucius with Jesus, Buddha, and Muhammad. In the articles, he blamed the Hong Kong Chinese for adopting the name *sheng dan jie* 聖誕節 (literally, the festival for the sage's birthday) for Christmas, knowing full well that in the Chinese language the term "sage" (*sheng*) was reserved for Confucius. According to Tang, this use of *sheng dan jie* as the term for Christmas revealed a fundamental problem in colonial Hong Kong, where Westernized Chinese regarded Christianity as a universal religion that replaced all other religions. Similar to the English-only policy and the social homogenization based on British standards, calling Christmas *sheng dan jie* was a part of the civilizing mission to educate the "barbaric people." From the gaze of the colonists, local religions were the "other" that must be disciplined and suppressed.[11]

More importantly, in pointing out the linguistic error in calling Christmas *sheng dan jie*, Tang called attention to both the exclusivity of Christianity and the hypocrisy of colonialism. Just as Christianity excluded local religions based on monotheism, so, too, colonists suppressed local cultures on the grounds of achieving universal liberation. For Tang, the openness of Confucius was the exact opposite of religious and political intolerance. He wrote: "The compassion of Buddha, the redemption of Jesus, and the morality of Muhammad were indeed magnificent achievements in world religions. Yet the achievement of Confucius was even higher and broader: namely, he was willing to accept and recognize the magnificent achievements of other peoples."[12] At first glance, Tang seemed to be a nationalist who took pride in his own cultural hero. On closer inspection, however, Tang's Confucius was actually a symbol of tolerance and openness in contrast to the religious fanaticism that sparked attacks on and killings of members of other religions. For Tang, Confucius stood for the "virtue of yielding" (*rang de meide* 讓的美德), which taught that the truth is one but there are many ways to reach the same truth.[13] In Tang's view, religious pluralism was the only way to make the world free from religious conflicts and oppression.[14]

From today's perspective, we may question the accuracy of Tang's view on Christianity and other religions, but we cannot deny that he skillfully used Confucius as a symbol of tolerance to counter religious intolerance. Focusing on "yielding" (*rang*), he made Confucius the embodiment of openness to alternative religious viewpoints and practices. To make his point, Tang declared that because the Chinese practiced the Confucian virtue of yielding, they could accept all religions from around the world and yet cause no religious war.[15] While Tang's claim about Chinese religiosity is most likely an exaggeration, he had reason to promote religious tolerance because throughout history religious difference has been a major cause of war. For this reason, in his writings, Tang frequently reminded his readers of the cruelty of religious suppression and the horrifying destruction of religious wars.[16]

One of the characteristics of Tang is that he put his philosophy into practice. As a school administrator, he had had many opportunities to practice the virtue of yielding. For instance, in the 1950s when the Yale-China Association began to give financial assistance to New Asia College, Tang faced a crisis when some board members of the Yale-China Association demanded New Asia College be turned into a Christian college. Tang resisted the demand by arguing that the goal of New Asia College was to include all religions in the world. New Asia College did not oppose Christianity, he argued, but to become a Christian college would undermine its religious pluralism and its role as a facilitator of religious dialogue.[17] In the end, the board of directors accepted Tang's view and agreed to continue to support New Asia College.

Similarly, Tang showed his virtue of yielding in supporting Juliet Hollister's plan for building a Temple of Understanding in the United States. According to Hollister's plan, the Temple of Understanding would be a place for interfaith dialogue, where leaders of different religious faiths would gather in the same building to converse, to debate, and to develop a better understanding of one another. Hollister planned to build the Temple of Understanding in the shape of a hexagon to symbolize the union of six major world religions. For Tang, Hollister made an important contribution to world civilization by promoting religious tolerance through dialogue. Even though Hollister (who was a Protestant) did not use the term "virtue of yielding," Tang found that she was in effect promoting the virtue of yielding by providing a space for interfaith dialogue.[18]

China's Path to Modernization

In reviewing the history of modern China, however, Tang found that not many Chinese practiced the virtue of yielding. Instead of listening to opposing views, the Chinese were interested only in finding a simple answer. Worse still, the more simplistic the answer was, the more they were attracted to it. For Tang, the prime example of this quest for a simple answer was the May Fourth Movement (1915–1923). To him, there were two sides of the May Fourth Movement. On the one hand, it rightfully promoted China's modernization by introducing democracy and science; on the other hand, it erroneously dichotomized "tradition" and "modernity" by promoting totalistic antitraditionalism.[19] According to Tang, the cause of this binary view was the urge to find a simple answer: namely, viewing China's modernization as a replica of Europe's modernization. To describe this May Fourth mentality, he used the words *sui ren jiaogen* 隨人腳跟 (following another's footsteps).[20] The danger of this simplistic approach, Tang said, was the loss of Chinese subjectivity, *buneng ziji zuozhu shuli qilai* 不能自己作主樹立

起來 (not being able to establish oneself).[21] Not unlike Westernized Hong Kong Chinese who insisted on calling Christmas *sheng dan jie*, the May Fourth cultural iconoclasts displayed a "slave mentality" (*nuli yishi* 奴隸意識) by taking European experience as the universal standard and imposing it on the Chinese.[22] The difference between the two was that while Westernized Hong Kong Chinese were *colonized* after being subject to a long period of "civilizing," the May Fourth cultural iconoclasts were *self-colonized* and willingly gave up their cultural autonomy in the name of modernization.

For Tang, the problem with May Fourth cultural iconoclasm was not limited to self-colonization; it also included a conflation of modernization with Westernization. The conflation might give the Chinese a clear direction to modernize their country (i.e., following Europe's path), nevertheless it oversimplified the process of modernization, which included the creation of a set of political, social, and cultural systems to protect civic liberty, social justice, and a fair distribution of wealth and resources. In this regard, Tang agreed with the May Fourth thinkers that the Chinese must adopt democracy and science from Europe. He wrote: "In the West, there is a strong emphasis on the protection of human rights, academic freedom, religious freedom, and the freedom of speech. In addition, there has been valuable development in science, philosophy, religion, and fine arts. These splendid achievements must be separated from [the evils of] capitalism and colonialism. We must not confuse the two and deny the Europeans' contributions."[23] In short, Tang understood the problems of Chinese tradition. He also knew that Confucianism had long been associated with the imperial authority in support of autocracy, elitism, and patriarchy. For this reason, he did not oppose the May Fourth call for introducing democracy and science to end imperial autocracy, elitism, and patriarchy. What he opposed was totalistic antitraditionalism, which he thought was totally unnecessary. He wrote: "In the past, the Chinese did spend time thinking about humanism, democracy, freedom, and communitarianism. All these ideas were rooted in the traditional Chinese thoughts on society and human relations. Nevertheless, China did not develop an effective system to put those ideas into practice."[24] According to Tang, the problem with May Fourth cultural iconoclasm was that it denied the possibility of developing a modern system based on the past experience of the Chinese. That past experience, while parochial, was what characterized the Chinese as Chinese. More importantly, it was the basis for the Chinese path to modernization—a developmental model that followed the global pattern and yet was derived from and resonated with local experience and practices.

On many occasions, Tang explained this Chinese path to modernization. One occasion was the famous 1958 Declaration in which he (as one of the authors) discussed four types of subjectivity that were needed in a modern society: moral subjectivity, political subjectivity, cognitive subjectivity, and technological subjectivity.[25] Of these four types of subjectivity, the Chinese were stronger in some (e.g., morality) but weak in others (e.g., democracy, technology). Hence, Tang argued that the modernizing process in China must be a product of the virtue of yielding: namely, an open process of combining elements from different sources. Echoing the May Fourth call for the introduction of democracy and science, Tang saw the possibility of creating a Chinese humanistic culture based on the Western notions of liberty, equality, and freedom. He wrote: "To develop Chinese culture and learning, we must affirm the importance of academic freedom, religious freedom, etc. We should not see academic freedom, religious freedom, individual freedom, and independent spirit as luxuries. Nor should we just use them as slogans [and take no action to promote them]. Whether we affirm them or not is a critical issue in developing human character and human spirit [in the modern era]."[26] And yet, Tang did not think that China should single-mindedly follow the European example. On another occasion, he discussed what Europe could not offer. He wrote: "Today, in order to eliminate cultural prejudice and misunderstanding in this world, a perfect form of humanism must be a combination of elements from the East and the West. But we must first find a way to stand on our own before we can resist or eliminate cultural prejudice and misunderstanding."[27] The key point in this quote is "to stand on our own" (*li qi lai* 立起來). For Tang, adopting democracy and science is one thing, while having the determination to resist prejudice and misunderstanding is another thing. In the former, the Chinese will benefit from adopting European institutions that promote civic liberty, social justice, and a fair sharing of resources. In the latter, the Chinese must use their past experience to develop a moral system to fight against injustice and intolerance. What Tang is saying is that regardless how good the institutions are, they cannot guarantee fairness and justice unless the Chinese have the will to build a fair and just society. To Tang, altering the external circumstance is only half the means to changing society; the other half is a moral commitment that must be developed from the Chinese tradition.

Capitalism and Confucian Ethnics

To develop a moral commitment to justice and tolerance, Tang focused on the Confucian Five Relationships (emperor-official, father-son, husband-wife, older brother-younger brother, and friend-friend). For him, while capitalism had produced remarkable economic results—as shown by the rising living standards in Hong Kong, Japan, Taiwan, Europe, and the United States—it also created a fragmented society because of its emphasis on efficiency and productivity. Even worse, in order to boost production, capitalism encouraged a materialistic view of life: namely, every aspect of human life is linked to the satisfaction of individual material needs, such as buying a big house, having a large salary, and pursuing a lifestyle of conspicuous consumption. In his writings, Tang wrote fervently to criticize this materialism.[28]

At the same time, Tang also realized that, even with all its problems, capitalism is far better than communism, as evidenced by the huge human loss in the political campaigns of communist China.[29] Thus, Tang's critique of capitalism was always nuanced. It was not aimed at overturning the entire system (like some Marxist-Leninist critiques); rather, it was aimed at lessening the pain in a fragmented society under capitalism. One may say that Tang did not make a structural critique of capitalism because he did not question its fundamental assumption. Nevertheless, based on his experience, Tang discovered one of the problems of capitalism: the dehumanization of capitalists and laborers caused by chaining them to the constant circles of production and consumption. Given the fact that Tang was a refugee from communist China, he was extraordinarily daring and fair-minded in discussing the problems of capitalism while seeking shelter and fortune in capitalistic Hong Kong.

To mitigate the alienation in the fragmented society of capitalism, Tang promoted the Confucian Five Relationships. In contrast to the Three Bonds (submission of officials to emperor, submission of children to parents, and submission of wives to husbands), Tang viewed the Five Relationships as reciprocal rather than one-sided. They denoted *horizontal links* among groups of people rather than a *vertical hierarchy* between rulers and ruled.[30] To Tang, these five Confucian relationships could form the bedrock on which to build a pluralistic society by balancing individual freedom with family and civic duties.

The crux of the matter, Tang argued, was not whether these relationships were Chinese or Confucian but whether they could remedy the alienation and fragmentation in a capitalistic society.[31] On this score, he singled out the fifth relationship, that is, the relationship between a friend and a friend. He argued that this particular relationship was based on trust, and therefore he called it the "trust relationship" (*xin lun* 信倫).[32] This relationship could directly address the problem of alienation in capitalistic society when every human activity—private and public—became a means to accumulate more wealth or power. In the final analysis, Tang argued, modern life must be rebuilt on the basis of the reciprocity of "I and Thou," which means that every person must be treated as a person rather than as a tool for satisfying a materialistic interest.[33]

The Contemporary Significance of Tang Junyi

To this day, we find that Tang Junyi's writings resonate with our twenty-first-century life because many of the issues that he raised decades ago have not been resolved. In many respects, we are all exiles like Tang in this age of global capitalism in which capital and labor move across the globe freely and swiftly in search of a bigger profit. Whether we are "native born," "guest workers," or "expatriates," we have no roots in the place where we live and work. Every day we are torn between the ideal purity of an imagined homeland (e.g., the American Dream) and the frustration and alienation of daily life in our place of residence.

More significantly, the increased fragmentation of capitalistic society causes even more anxiety among those of us who have an insatiable desire for material goods. Today, the problems of individualism, materialism, and utilitarianism are more acute than they were in Tang's time. But unlike Tang, we seem to be ill-equipped to face the problems of injustice and intolerance. While we speak of building a pluralistic and open society in the age of global capitalism, in practice we tend to protect our own interests before we consider the interests of others.

Above all, thirty years after Tang's death, we have not been able to create a fiduciary community based on reciprocity and trust. Despite the affluence and high consumption in some parts of the world (e.g., London, New York, and Shanghai), we have not developed the trust relationship that Tang identifies as the most-needed remedy to our fragmented society. As today's global capitalism creates bigger gaps between the rich and poor, the haves and have-nots, we may want to heed Tang's advice that practicing the virtue of yielding is the best way to build a fair and caring society.

Notes

Author's note: I would like to thank Tze-ki Hon and Kristin Stapleton for their helpful comments and suggestions on an early draft of this chapter.

1. Tang Junyi, "Zhonghua minzu zhi huaguo piaoling" 中華民族之花果飄零 [The dispersion and relocation of the Chinese], in *Tang Junyi quanji* 唐君毅全集 [The collected works of Tang Junyi] (Taipei: Taiwan xuesheng shuju, 1989), vol. 7, part 1, 33.

2. Tang Junyi, "Zhongguo xiandai shehui zhengzhi wenhua sixiang zhi fangxiang, ji haiwai zhishi fenzi dui dangqian shidai zhi taidu" 中國現代社會政治文化思想之方向，及海外知識分子對當前時代之態度 [The direction of modern Chinese social-political thought and the attitude of overseas intellectuals toward the contemporary world], in *Tang Junyi quanji*, vol. 8, part 2, 232.

3. Lin Yüsheng 林毓生, "Miandui weilaide zhongji guanhuai: Tang Junyi quefa piping jingshen" 面對未來的終極關懷：唐君毅缺乏批評精神, *Zhongguo luntan* 中國論壇 15 (Aug. 1982): 23; Qi Liang 啟良, *Xin rujia pipan* 新儒學批判 [The critique of New Confucianism] (Shanghai: Sanlian shuju, 1995), 251–281; Wei Zhengtong 韋政通, "Xiandai rujia de cuozhe yu fuxing: Zhongxin sixiang de pipan" 現代儒家的挫折與復興——中心思想的批判 [The challenge and the revival of contemporary Confucianism: A critique of its central concept], in *Dangdai xinrujia* 當代新儒家 [Contemporary New Confucianism], edited by Feng Zusheng 封祖盛 (Beijing: Sanlian shudian, 1989), 120–136.

4. Thomas A. Metzger, *Escape from Predicament: Neo-Confucianism and China's Evolving Political Culture* (New York: Columbia University Press, 1977), 2, 39.

5. Jing Haifeng 景海峰, "Zongjiaohua de xinrujia: Lüelun Tang Junyi chongjian zhongguo renwen jingshen de quxiang" 宗教化的新儒家：略論唐君毅重建中國人文精神的取向 [Making New Confucianism a religion: A study of Tang Junyi's plan for rebuilding the Chinese humanistic spirit], in *Xiandai xinrujia yanjiu lunwenji* 現代新儒學研究論集 [Collected essays on contemporary New Confucianism], edited by Fang Keli 方克立 and Li Jinquan 李錦全 (Beijing: Zhongguo shehui kexue chubanshe, 1991), vol. 2, 226–243.

6. Tang Junyi, "Xinya shuyuan zhi yuanshi jingshen yu tongxue ying zimian zhishi" 新亞書院之原始精神與同學們應自勉之事 [The founding spirit of New Asia College and things that students must do], in *Tang Junyi quanji*, vol. 9, part 1, 489.

7. Tang Junyi identified two reasons that motivated the opposition of the University of Hong Kong faculty. One was financial, namely, the cost of funding a second university. See Tang Junyi, "Xinya yanjiusuo zhi cunzai yiji" 新亞研究所之存在意義 [The reasons for founding the New Asia Research Centre], in *Tang Junyi quanji*, vol. 9, 586. The second reason was the practice of having only one university in each colony. See Tang Junyi, "Xinya de guoqu xianzai yu jianglai" 新亞的過去，現在與將來 [The past, present, and future of New Asia College], in *Tang Junyi quanji*, vol. 9, 602.

8. Tang Junyi, "Zhonghua minzu zhi huaguo piaoling," in *Tang Junyi quanji*, vol. 7, part 1, 15.

9. Tang Junyi expressed his disappointment with the founding of CUHK in many of his articles. See, for instance, his article "Lixiang yu xianshi: Zhongwen daxue de jingshen zai nali?" 理想與現實——中文大學的精神在那裏？ [Ideals and reality: Where is the spirit of CUHK?], in *Tang Junyi quanji*, vol. 9, 574. See also "Tan xinya yu zhongda de jiaoyu lixiang: Da zhongda xuesheng bao" 談新亞與中大的教育理想——答《中大學生報》 [On the educational ideals of New Asia College and CUHK: A reply to the CUHK student newspaper], in *Tang Junyi quanji*, vol. 9, 589–591.

10. Tang Junyi, "Xiandai shijie wenhua jiaoliu zhi yiyi yu genju" 現代世界文化交流之意義與根據 [The meaning and the foundation of cultural exchange in the contemporary world], in *Tang Junyi quanji*, vol. 8, part 2, 425–428.

11. Tang Junyi, "Yesu shengdan zhengming" 耶穌聖誕正名 [On the correct name of the birthday of Jesus], in *Tang Junyi quanji*, vol. 10, part 2, 278–282.

12. Tang Junyi, "Kongdan jiaoshijie ji xinya shiliu zhounian xiaoqing dianli jiangci" 孔誕,教師節暨新亞十六周年校慶典禮講詞 [The birthday of Confucius, teachers' day, and the sixteenth anniversary of the founding of New Asia College], in *Tang Junyi quanji*, vol. 9, part 1, 537–538.

13. Tang Junyi, "Zhongguo renwen shijie zhi lirang jingshen: Zai fuli xingren hui di shiliu qi xueshu yanjiang hui jiangci" 中國人文世界之禮讓精神——在復禮興仁會第十六期學術演講會講詞 [The spirit of ritual and yielding in the Chinese humanistic world: A talk delivered at the sixteenth academic colloquium of the Association for Recovering Rituals and Revitalizing Human-relatedness], in *Tang Junyi quanji*, vol. 9, part 1, 231–232.

14. Tang Junyi, "Xiandai shijie wenhua jiaoliu zhi yiyi yu genju" 現代世界文化交流之意義與根據 [The meaning and the foundation of cultural exchange in contemporary world], in *Tang Junyi quanji*, vol. 8, part 2, 417.

15. Tang Junyi, "Zhongguo renwen shijie zhi lirang jingshen," 231–232.

16. Tang Junyi, "Rujia zhi xueyujiao zhi shuli ji zongjiao fenzheng zhi genjue" 儒家之學與教之樹立及宗教紛爭之根絕 [The establishment of Confucian learning and teaching and the origins of religious disputes], in *Tang Junyi quanji*, vol. 8, part 2, 59–64.

17. Tang Duanzheng 唐端正, ed., "Tang Junyi nianpu" 唐君毅年譜 [A year-by-year chronicle of the life of Tang Junyi], in *Tang Junyi quanji*, vol. 29, 111.

18. Tang Junyi, "Shijie liuda zongjiao liaojietang zhi jianli zhi ganxiang" 「世界六大宗教了解堂」之建立之感想 [Thoughts about the building of the Temple of Understanding for the world's six religions], in *Tang Junyi quanji*, vol. 8, part 2, 95–101.

19. Tang Junyi, "Wusi jinianri dui haiwai zhongguo qingnian zhi jige xiwang" 五四紀念日對海外中國青年之幾個希望 [A few hopes for overseas Chinese young people on the anniversary day of the May Fourth Movement], in *Tang Junyi quanji*, vol. 8, part 2, 336–337.

20. Tang Junyi, "Dongxi zhexue xueren huiyi yu shijie wenhua zhongzhi shuwai wenti" 東西哲學學人會議與世界文化中之「疏外」問題 [The East-West Philosophy Conference and the question of alienation in world cultures], in *Tang Junyi quanji*, vol. 8, part 2, 41.

21. Ibid.

22. Tang Junyi, "Huaguo piaoling ji linggen zizhi" 花果飄零及靈根自植 [Dispersion and relocation (of the Chinese) and the [need for] rejuvenating the roots for self-renewal], in *Tang Junyi quanji*, vol. 7, part 1, 41.

23. Tang Junyi, "Zhongguo xiandai shehui zhengzhi wenhua sixiang zhi fangxiang," 260.

24. Tang Junyi, "Dongxi zhexue xueren huiyi yu shijie wenhua zhong zhi shuwai wenti," 41.

25. Tang Junyi 唐君毅, Mou Zongsan 牟宗三, Xu Fuguan 徐復觀, and Zhang Junmai 張君勱, "Zhongguo wenhua yu shijie: Women dui zhongguo xueshu yanjiu ji zhongguo wenhua qiantu zhi gongtong renshi" 中國文化與世界——我們對中國學術研究及中國文化與世界文化前途之共同認識 [Chinese culture and the world: Our position toward the study of Chinese learning and the future of Chinese culture in world civilization], in *Tang Junyi quanji*, vol. 4, 14–15. For a discussion of the 1958 Manifesto, see Ming-huei Lee's chap. 5 herein.

26. Tang Junyi, "Zhongguo xiandai shehui zhengzhi wenhua sixiang zhi fangxiang," 245.

27. Tang Junyi, "Shijie renwen zhuyi yu zhongguo renwen zhuyi" 世界人文主義與中國人文主義 [World humanism and Chinese humanism], in *Tang Junyi quanji*, vol. 8, part 2, 57.

28. Tang Junyi, "Xiandai shijie wenhua jiaoliu zhi yiyi yu genju," 425–426.

29. Tang Junyi, Mou Zongsan, Xu Fuguan, and Zhang Junmai, "Zhongguo wenhua yu shijie," 18.

30. Tang Junyi, "Wenhua yishi yu daode lixing: zixu" 文化意識與道德理性: 自序 [Cultural consciousness and moral rationality: An introduction], in *Tang Junyi quanji*, vol. 20, 26–27.

31. Ibid.

32. Tang Junyi, "Wenhua yishi yu daode lixing: zixu," 26–27; see also Tang Junyi, "Xiandai shijie wenhua jiaoliu zhi yiyi yu genju," 427.

33. Tang Junyi, "Xiandai shijie wenhua jiaoliu zhi yiyi yu genju," 427.

Part Three

Social Responsibility and Social Action

11

Worshipping Ancestors in Modern China

Confucius and the Yellow Emperor as Icons of Chinese Identity

Marc Andre Matten

For centuries, ancestral veneration has been a central element of Chinese culture. By performing regular rituals—such as at the Tomb Sweeping Festival—living family members try to provide deceased family members with continuous happiness and well-being in their afterlife. Deeply influenced by the Confucian tradition, these rituals are intended to show respect to ancestors and reinforce family unity and lineage. Anthropologist James Watson has identified the use of particular death rituals as central to the construction of Han Chinese family identity. These standardized rituals consisted of public notifications; the bathing of the corpse; the offering of food, money, and goods to the deceased; and setting up a soul tablet. Though the details of these rituals differ from place to place, their structure is largely the same. More importantly, these rituals are practiced across social strata, especially after Neo-Confucian texts (such as Zhu Xi's *Family Ritual*) gained popularity since the sixteenth century among the poor and uneducated.[1]

The classical writings on burial and funeral customs were the *Book of Rites* (*Liji*) and the *Book of Etiquette and Ceremonial* (*Yili*). Both works based this thinking on the idea of filial piety (*xiao*), which Confucius (551–479 BCE) put forward. This idea was so central to Confucian orthopraxy that even the Manchu rulers did not challenge it after founding the Qing dynasty in 1644. Although not of Han descent and not sharing their cultural practices, they continued to show filial reverence to icons of Chinese civilization that were popular among the Han population, such as Huangdi (Yellow

Emperor) and Confucius. For the former, the intention of the Qing was more to win the support of the Ming literati than to prove their sinicization. For the latter, as part of the state ideology, rituals were performed at the Temple of Confucius in Qufu during the eighteenth and nineteenth centuries.[2]

In late nineteenth century, the rise of nationalism caused momentous changes to both icons. Rather than confining to locally or socially restricted circles, the act of veneration evolved into a cultural practice that focused on the nation as the primary identity. The most prominent advocates of this change—such as Liang Qichao 梁啟超 (1873–1929), Kang Youwei 康有爲 (1858–1927), Zhang Taiyan 章太炎 (1868–1936) and Sun Yat-sen 孫逸仙 (1866–1925)—called for the creation of a collective identity that was greater than the family, the clan, or the local community. They emphasized the need to create a larger ancestor that could bring all Chinese into the new nation, including those at the lower strata of society and living far away from the capital. This creation of national ancestor could only occur after modern media (such as journals and newspapers) and general school education had been introduced into China during the last decades of the nineteenth century. Due to the rise of nationalism, the goal of ancestor worship had to change. As a national symbol based on bloodline, the Yellow Emperor was deployed as a political symbol to challenge the Qing government. Similarly, as a national symbol based on political legitimacy, Confucius was used to rally support to critique the imperial system.

This chapter examines these two discourses on national identity by focusing on their potential to create a convincing national imagination in the process of political modernization. Particular attention will be given to the performance of ritual worships at the tomb sites in Shaanxi and Shandong. As Emile Durkheim has shown, rituals and ceremonies create a sense of belonging. We can observe this in small communities (families, associations) as well as in large ones (religious groups, nations). This becomes obvious if a ritual is conducted at a site of high significance, such as the ceremony of flying the flag each morning at Tiananmen Square, the Independence Day parades in the United States, the Bastille Day events in France, or the wreath-laying ceremonies in honor of war victims. In these ceremonies, a sense of belonging is created by means of old legends, especially the belief that one's heroic ancestor rises in immortal spirit and its presence is alive in the community. Through collective remembrance, individuals are knit together by a holy object members of the community share.[3]

During the late nineteenth and early twentieth centuries, Chinese political and cultural elites repeatedly conducted ceremonies in Confucius's hometown and at the tomb of the Yellow Emperor. To create a new nation, they transformed these sites into national places of memory. According to Pierre Nora, a place of memory (*lieux de mémoire*) constitutes a symbolic entity that relates the physical place to the collective memory. It is a place "where (cultural) memory crystallizes and secretes itself."[4] Nora's notion of *lieux de mémoire* includes geographical places, historical personalities, monuments, emblems, and symbols, thus not only ideas but also material realities can give rise to collective identity. He argues that the concept of *lieux de mémoire* defines history as "a history in multiple voices . . . less interested in causes than in effects; . . . less interested in 'what actually happened' than in its perpetual re-use and misuse, its influence on successive presents; less interested in traditions than in the way in which traditions are constituted and passed on."[5]

To add to Nora's point, I consider the continuity of worship crucial to the formation of collective identity. Contrary to the current view that sees the worship of Huangdi and Confucius as "an invented tradition," I argue that their symbolism remained the same despite drastic political transformations. In fact, evidence shows that their political function in both traditional and modern China can only be understood properly if we take into account the worship before the rise of nationalism in the late imperial period. In what follows, we compare the political use of Huangdi and Confucius in late imperial China with that in twentieth-century China. In the comparison, we see parallels and continuities in the ritual ceremonies as well as the bold attempts to transform the two historical figures into icons of national identity.

Yellow Emperor as National Ancestor

The Yellow Emperor was propagated as a symbol of Chinese national identity at the end of the Qing dynasty. Various historians have argued in the past decade that he—being understood as the ancestor of the Chinese nation—played a crucial role in the process of nation-building.[6] As a matter of fact, since the late 1890s, Huangdi was presented in a variety of journals and publications by both reformists and revolutionaries. For instance, in his 1901 *Introductory Essay to a History of China* (*Zhongguoshi xulun* 中國史敘論), Liang Qichao pointed out that the Han race had inherited the civilization the Yellow Emperor founded.[7] Ou Jujia 歐榘甲 (1858–1912), a disciple of Kang Youwei, said the same in his pamphlet *The New Guangdong* 新廣東.[8] Liu Shipei 劉師培 (1884–1919), a classical scholar and radical nationalist, wrote in his *Book of Expulsion* (*Rangshu* 攘書) that "the descendants of Huangdi and Yandi are solely the Han."[9] In current scholarship, these writings are considered part of anti-Manchu propaganda after the first Sino-Japanese War (1894–1895). Some scholars point out that these writings are racist;[10] others defend them as a brief aberration in the Chinese discourse of the nation before it turned to multiethnicity. The latter interpretation would mean that the norm would be a pluralistic social order in which different ethnic groups live harmoniously together. This view is not new because during the first half of the Qing, Emperor Qianlong considered all five ethnicities—the Manchus, Han, Hui, Mongols, and Tibetans—to be part of his empire.[11]

For those who see the writings as racist, they argue that the writings were part of the discourse of the Chinese nation. They point to the fact that having witnessed the Qing's failure to revive the country, many Chinese intellectuals believed that the political order of the nation-state should replace the traditional vision of *tianxia* (all-under-heaven). This fundamental shift led to a crisis in collective identity, and in the years after the Sino-Japanese War, this new identity was increasingly defined in distinct ethnonational terms such as "the descendants of the Yellow Emperor" (黃帝子孫). To explain this change, historians Shen Sung-chiao and Sun Longji argue that the Yellow Emperor was "discovered" as a symbol of Han Chinese. For this reason, the two historians consider Yellow Emperor as a modern construct—or in the words of Eric Hobsbawm, an "invented tradition"—of the late nineteenth and early twentieth centuries.

A similar argument has been put forward for Confucius who was seen at the time as an alternative symbol of Chineseness.[12] In this context, both symbols faced significant limitations in the Chinese discourse of the nation. One of the problems was the abrupt paradigm shift after the 1911 Revolution. After the revolution, the young republic went back to imperial imagination of the national body in order to prevent a substantial loss of Chinese territory. The new Chinese leaders realized that Tibet, Manchuria, and Xinjiang, as well as Mongolia, would have been lost if China only included the Han race. Surrounded by imperialist nations such as England, Russia, and Japan, the young republic needed to keep these territories, which it achieved by presenting the Yellow Emperor and Confucius as the collective ancestors of the Chinese nation, now called *Zhonghua minzu* 中華民族. The Chinese Communist Party (CCP) later resorted to the same strategy when it tried to win the support of ethnic minorities in their fight for liberation, and it was also for this reason that it strongly supported the veneration during the 1980s and 1990s when socialism lost its ideological appeal and was replaced by patriotism as the new civic virtue.

Yellow Emperor and Confucius as Rival National Icons

In Chinese tradition, lineage has been an important issue. Proving that one is related to a mythical or past heroic figure can raise one's social status. One way of proving one's lineage is compiling a genealogy. In compiling a genealogy, the writers always deemphasize mixed marriages, particularly the marriages between Han and non-Han people. The writers are keen to create a text that would produce maximum social impact, or in the words of Maurice Freedman, "a political statement."[13]

In the late nineteenth and early twentieth centuries, this strategy was employed in creating the cult of the Yellow Emperor.[14] As part of the rise of Han nationalism, the memory of the Yellow Emperor was expanded from families and clans to include the entire Chinese nation, as if all Han-Chinese were all biologically linked to this ancient figure.[15] Zhang Taiyan was one of the first writers who created this new memory of the Yellow Empire. In his political writings, Zhang often employed the language of descent to define the differences between the Han and the Manchu. His comprehensive knowledge of the classical writings allowed him to depict the Chinese people as a group of individuals who shared an unbroken lineage. As a scholar, Zhang was convinced that the dominance of the Manchus had resulted in the Han people losing memory of their own, great lineage (*dazong* 大宗). For Zhang, the new Chinese nation should resemble—in accord with the Confucian ethics—a family. After his flight to Japan in 1902 where Zhang met Sun Yat-sen and Liang Qichao, he began to include evolution theory and anthropology into his discussion of the Chinese nation. He attempted to clarify the relationship between race, clan, and political power, thus creating a new political order based on race and lineage. As we know, the essence of Zhang's vision was to exclude the Manchus. To some people, Zhang's vision is an obvious expression of racism, despite the fact that (in contrast to Europe) phenotypical characteristics such as skin color do not play a role in Zhang's definition of the Chinese race. The only measurable distinction was lineage.

In order to promote anti-Manchuism, the late Qing radical nationalists argued that the Yellow Emperor is an ancestor of the Han race. As such, Huangdi was used as a symbol to define racial boundaries, aiming at establishing a monoethnic nation. A prime example of this political use of Huangdi is the creation of a new calendar that would replace the year counting according to dynasties with the counting according to Huangdi (thus defining the year 1905 as 4616, the year of his accession to the throne).[16] For obvious reason, the Qing administration considered this change unacceptable and banned journals using this calendar. For those who were less radical, they preferred a calendar that took Confucius's birth as its beginning. The first issue of the reform-oriented *Journal of Self-Strengthening* (*Qiangxuebao*) Kang Youwei published in 1895 named Confucius as the father of Chinese civilization and preferred a calendar based on Confucius's life.[17] Radical nationalists (such as Liu Shipei) rejected the calculation according to Confucius, emphasizing that the goal was not to protect the teachings of the sage (*baojiao* 保教), but to protect the Chinese race (*baozhong* 保種). According to Liu, a calendar following the ethnic ancestor would show that—similar to the historical data in the *Records of the Grand Historian*—the Chinese history started with Huangdi rather than Confucius, and at the same time the current Qing emperor would be reminded that the country was not his private property.[18]

These examples show how the choice for either Huangdi or Confucius was highly political and related to the question of legitimate rule. For the radical nationalists, the exclusion of the Manchus was considered absolutely necessary. However, less radical scholars regarded ethnic ancestry an unreliable criterion for defining membership to the Chinese nation, as Kang Youwei showed in his opus magnum *Datongshu* 大同書.[19] In the same vein, Liang openly rejected ethnic revolution, arguing instead that state-nationalism should be the basis of political revolution. Liang's rejection of ethnic revolution was partly a result of Kang's influence. As Kang's student, Liang took seriously his teacher's warning in an open letter in 1902 that he should not join Sun Yat-sen's movement because the Manchus had the legitimacy to rule China. This was also the reason why in the early twentieth century Kang propagated Confucianism as state religion. His call for making Confucius a national icon, however, was only partially successful. Taking Christianity as a role model, Kang had argued for a national religion to awaken the population and make China a strong nation.[20] However, given the Qing admiration for the Confucian belief system, his efforts failed to transform the great sage into a national symbol for two reasons.

First, the anti-Manchu movement in the last decade of the Qing clearly described the Manchu's use of Confucian ideology as a conscious strategy for legitimacy, which Zou Rong 鄒容 (1885–1905) had argued in his radical tractate, *The Revolutionary Army* (革命軍). In defense, Liang Qichao argued that a strong nation had to have a constitutional government that respected the equality of all ethnicities. He warned that a racial intervention against the Manchus would mean a downfall of the government, leading to disintegration of China and to foreign intervention. And yet, Liang's argument did not turn the tide. Second, Confucius faced mounting difficulties to be accepted as a national icon, especially during the May Fourth Movement (1915–1923). For instance, in *A Madman's Diary* (*Kuangren riji* 狂人日記), Lu Xun 魯迅 (1881–1936) described Confucianism as a cannibalistic ideology that ate away the individual. Accordingly, the movement called for "smashing the Confucius's shop" and abandoning the "uncrowned king." In the ensuing decades, the CCP inherited this legacy and after 1949 launched many campaigns against superstition, material waste, and folk religion (such as the famous "Criticize Lin and Criticize Confucius Campaign" in 1974). Their fights against Confucius included destroying tombs to create more arable land and officially banning the traditional burial in a cemetery in the name of protecting the environment.[21]

Despite the radical critique of traditional customs after 1949, the worship of historical figures (either heroes or martyrs) did not stop totally. As long as these personages were considered meaningful and significant to the state or society, their worship was not only permissible but also state-sponsored. This was the case for well-known heroes (such as Lei Feng 雷锋, 1940–1962), model workers (such as Chen Yonggui 陳永貴, 1913–1986, and Wang Jinxi 王進喜, 1923–1970), martyrs (such as Liu Hulan 劉胡蘭, 1932–1947), and important historical figures of ancient and recent past (such as the national ancestor Huangdi,)[22] the National Father Sun Yat-sen 孫逸仙 (1866–1925),[23] and the Great Helmsman Mao Zedong 毛澤東 (1893–1976).[24] Contrary to the worship of private ancestors, the CCP provided sufficient opportunity, space, and financial support for enabling citizens and party and state representatives to express their filial piety and respect, most prominently tomb sites of revolutionary heroes at the Babaoshan Revolutionary Cemetery 八寶山革命公墓[25] or the tombs of deceased imperial rulers.

The tombs of Huangdi and Confucius were, and still are, no exception. The practice of presenting sacrificial offerings and reciting eulogies to the national ancestors did not stop during the Maoist period. More strikingly, since the late 1990s, CCP has started to show increased interest in these ceremonies to promote patriotism. In the last decade particularly, the worship of Confucius has been aimed at creating a sound and proper political consciousness among the population. In view of these developments, we have to ask what has led to this revival of interest in worshipping national ancestors. Is it a result of intense coverage by mass media, such as newspaper and television (during the 1990s some of the ceremonies were broadcasted nationwide)? Or is it a tacit recognition that the CCP needs Huangdi and Confucius to give legitimacy to its rule?

The Worship of the Yellow Emperor in Shaanxi

During the twentieth century, the tomb of Huangdi in Shaanxi Province was gradually turned into a national pilgrimage site. According to the chronicle of the tomb of Huangdi, *Huangling zhi* 黃陵志 (compiled by Li Jinxi in 1944), the origins of the temple at the tomb can be found in the Han dynasty. The tomb gained central political significance in the early Ming dynasty when Zhu Yuanzhang 朱元璋 commissioned a team in 1371 to determine the exact site of the tomb and to organize regular sacrificial ceremonies.[26] This tradition continued during the Qing when the first emperor Shunzhi 順治 (reign 1644–1662) visited the tomb in 1651. During the visit, Shunzhi legitimized his rule by offering sacrifices and presenting a eulogy (*jiwen* 祭文) stating that the Qing had taken over the mandate of heaven 天命 from the Ming and that Han and Manchus were part of the same family.[27] During the reign of Kangxi 康熙, nine similar ceremonies were performed, two during Yongzheng 雍正, eleven during Qianlong 乾隆, four during Jiaqing 嘉慶, and three during Daoguang 道光.[28] The enumeration of these dates indicates that the veneration of Huangdi continued nonstop from the seventeenth century to the nineteenth century. Until the end of the Qing, these ceremonies—partly also conducted in Beijing—were aimed at legitimizing the rule of the emperor, continuing ancestral worship, and above all, offering an opportunity to pray or ask for support in times of crisis.

As mentioned earlier, during the late Qing, the purpose of the worship of Huangdi was changed. At a gathering of the Shaanxi branch 同盟會陝西分會 of the *Tongmenghui* at the tomb on the ninth day of the ninth month in 1908, representatives of Sun Yat-sen prayed for the restoration of the nation 復興民族, essentially discrediting the Qing government as the legitimate ruler.[29] The significance of this ceremony is that it was, for the first time, directed against the imperial authority based on a clear distinction between the state (i.e., the Qing dynasty) and the nation (i.e., the Han race). When the state authority was restored after the Wuchang uprising in October 1911, the local revolutionary government decided to dedicate a sacrifice to the Yellow Emperor, thanking him for the military success. Representing the *Tongmenghui*, the later president of the republic, Li Yuanhong 黎元洪 (1864–1928), gave a eulogy in which he thanked the ancestor for helping to end the 240 years of Han oppression.[30]

Ironically, after the founding of the Chinese Republic on January 1, 1912, Huangdi was again put into the service of the state (and not of the nation). This became obvious in the ceremony Sun Yat-sen ordered in March 1912. Sun sent a delegation from Beijing to the tomb in Shaanxi to make a sacrifice. In contrast to Li Yuanhong's ceremony a few months ago, the Huangdi was remembered as the founder of the Chinese civilization, while his role as ancestor of the Han race was downplayed. Furthermore, Sun deliberately avoided any reference for the Han race; instead he adopted a new and ambiguous term, "*Zhonghua.*" Similarly, in *Huangdi gongde ji* 黃帝功德紀 (1935), historian Yu Youren 于右任 (1879–1964) praised the Yellow Emperor for his cultural achievements and emphasized that the Chinese nation included the Tibetans, Hui, Mongols, and Manchu. In the same year, representatives of the Kuomintang (KMT), including Zhang Ji 張繼 (1882–1947) and Shao Yuanchong 邵元沖, and the national government, including Deng Jiayan 鄧家彥 (?–?), went to the grave to ask the ancestor to support the expulsion of the Japanese imperialists and the restoration of Chinese sovereignty 光華復旦.[31]

After the Xi'an December 1936 Incident, which led to cooperation between the CCP and the KMT in the fight against Japanese aggression, worship ceremonies at the grave of Huangdi were jointly conducted in 1937 and 1938. In 1937 Zhang Ji 張繼 (KMT), Sun Weiru 孫蔚如 (?–?) (government official of Shaanxi), and Lin Zuhan 林祖涵 (?–?) (as envoy of Mao Zedong 毛澤東), and Zhu De 朱德 (1886–1976) participated in the ritual.[32] In 1938 a KMT general, Cheng Qian 程潛 (1882–1968), installed an inscription bearing the signs *renwen chuzu* 人文初祖. Between 1939 and 1943, reflecting the worsening relationship between the KMT and the CCP, the national government organized several worship ceremonies, but no CCP representative was allowed to attend. In 1939 an administrative body was established to restore the tomb, and in 1942 Chiang Kai-shek 蔣介石 (1887–1975), then president of the republic, dedicated a stone tablet inscribed with *Huangdiling* 黃帝陵.[33]

In the years after the founding of the People's Republic of China, worship ceremonies at the tomb of the Yellow Emperor continued. A few weeks after the liberation of the prefecture Huangling (where the tomb is situated) on March 10, 1948, the vice president of the front area Shaanxi-Gansu-Ningxia, Liu Jingfan 劉景範 (1910–1990), the deputy commander of the People's Liberation Army (PLA) in northwest China, Zhao Shoushan 趙壽山 (1893–1965), and the head of the political section of the PLA, Gan Siqi 甘泗淇 (1904–1964), gathered at the tomb. During the 1950s, official CCP representatives visited the tomb, giving speeches emphasizing the importance of the increase of production, the national defense, and the fight against U.S. imperialism. These speeches were not traditional eulogies (*jiwen*), as in the 1955 speech.[34] Rather, they were written in plain vernacular (*baihua*) declaring that the primary task of building socialism in China was to improve people's livelihood.[35] In 1961 the State Council (*Guowuyuan* 國務院) declared the tomb a national treasure. The veneration of Huangdi was stopped during the Cultural Revolution, but in 1976 the Chinese Communist Party showed interest again in the tomb again when the Bureau for

Cultural Affairs of Shaanxi provided money for the reconstruction of buildings destroyed earlier. In 1978 the Bureau for the Management of Cultural Relics (*Wenwu guanlisuo* 文物管理所) was established, and beginning in 1979 sacrificial ceremonies took place regularly. The number of participants was quickly rising, with 6,000 in 1986 and more than 10,000 in 1993.[36]

In 1994, at the heyday of the Patriotic Education Movement in mid-1990s, Li Ruihuan 李瑞環 (member of the Politburo and chairman of the Political Consultative Conference) offered flowers at the tomb at the *Qingmingjie*. Li's participation officially ended the communist taboo of worshipping ancestors, and afterward prominent politicians such as Zhu Rongji 朱鎔基, Wu Bangguo 吳邦國, and Li Tieying 李鉄映 did likewise.[37] The sharp rise in visitors compelled the CCP to provide money to enlarge the site. More than 80 million RMB was spent completely reconstructing the site, providing better travel connections, and turning it into a major tourist destination.[38] The Foundation for the Yellow Emperor's Tomb 黃帝陵基金會, founded by Li Ruihuan with the purpose of collecting funding in China and abroad, paid for some of the reconstruction.[39] These activities show clearly the importance of the tomb for the central government in Beijing.[40] In 1997 the site was finally declared to be one of the 100 Sites for Patriotic Education百個愛國主義教育示範基地.[41] In the end, the Yellow Emperor was propagated among the population by various medial means, including live coverage of the Qingming festivities, a homepage dedicated to the ancestor and his tomb, historical materials (see www.hdlinfo.com, formerly also with the possibility of making online sacrifices), television documentaries,[42] and sculptures of Emperors Yan and Huang completed as currently the fifth tallest statues in the world (106 meters).

This list of homages paid to Huangdi shows that the tomb is undoubtedly a place of memory that is constitutive for the creation of a national/collective identity. The creation of identity is not solely related to the physical presence of the tomb, but it has to be explained by the importance of Huangdi in the collective memory of the Chinese people. While much of the memory of Huangdi was constructed, the memory has been sustained and reinvigorated to create a homogeneous Chinese nation. However, this essentialism is precisely what makes—as one would assume—Huangdi a difficult icon of collective identity, even though the current interpretation shares elements of the Qing era. Facing counter voices against a too Han-centrist interpretation of Huangdi—such as in the case of the Miao ethnicity[43]—the party state soon turned to an icon that promised to be less problematic because of its nonethnic character, namely the great sage and teacher Confucius.

The Worship of Confucius in Qufu

In contrast to Huangdi, the veneration of Confucius is widely perceived as less artificial because it is not based on the assumed belief of a given ethnic descent, but on a number of ethical principles that are supposed to work beyond ethnic, religious, or cultural boundaries. The CCP's recent promotion of Confucian values is not restricted to the Chinese nation, but also includes a global vision that extends from the ethnic minorities within China to achieving harmony around the world.[44] Confucius is obviously an important, if not the most important, national icon of China if one looks at the ritual ceremonies conducted at *San Kong* 三孔 (the three historic sites related to Confucius)—his temple (*Kong miao* 孔廟) in the city of Qufu, his burial in the Confucius Forest (*Kong lin* 孔林), and the Kong Family Mansion (*Kong fu* 孔府). All three places are categorized as the first AAAA tourist scenic spot in China, and thereby a major attraction of Qufu's tourist industry. Since 1994 the three places are listed as a United Nations Educational, Scientific, and Cultural Organization (UNESCO) World Heritage Site, opened to visitors from all parts of the world.[45]

The Temple of Confucius—consisting of 460 rooms, with most of them dating from the fifteenth century—was a place where imperial sacrifices were made to Confucius. Official chronicles list the sacrifice offered by the first emperor of the Han dynasty, that is, Han Gaozu (206–195 BCE), as the first imperial sacrifice. When China was going through a period of disunity in the fifth century, a structured imperial cult was established that was no longer limited to his descendants and his followers.[46] The Tang dynasty then elevated Confucius to royal statues and developed even more detailed rituals. In the year 739 Confucius was posthumously bestowed with the title Exalted Duke of Propagating Culture (*wenxuan wang* 文宣公),[47] and this treatment of Confucius was continued in the ensuing dynasties until the first emperor of the Ming removed the posthumous titles for all gods and spirits with the exception of Confucius. Despite the high appreciation of Confucius in the first decades of the Ming, officials at the court later reexamined his status, when finally in 1530 his royal title was removed and Confucius was since that time given the name "Ultimate Sage, First Teacher Master Kong" (*zhisheng xianshi Kongzi* 至聖先師孔子").[48] During the Qing, the imperial court donated different inscriptions to the Confucius Temple in Beijing, starting with emperor Kangxi in 1684 who gave him the title Exemplary Teacher of the 10,000 Generations (*wanshi shibiao* 万世师表),[49] which is until today one of the most prominent categorizations of the sage of the past (thus also his reintegration into the school curricula since the 1990s).

Since the Ming dynasty, statues of Confucius were venerated in his temples. Fearing the influence of Daoism and Buddhism, Neo-Confucian thinkers discredited this habit and convinced the Jiajing 嘉靖 emperor (reign 1522–1566) to issue a decree that called for the removal of all images in Confucian temples, replacing the statues with spirit tablets (*shenwei* 神位). Local chronicles after 1530 reported that this change was problematic as the local population was used to worshipping sculptural representations of Confucius. Hence, a solution was found whereby the images of Confucius were no longer godlike, but rather showed him as a teacher. The most well-known image of Confucius is the one created by Wu Daozi 吳道子 (ca. 689–755) who modeled it after the portrait in the Confucius Temple in Qufu. Considered to be the most authentic picture of Confucius, the image has been reprinted many times for teaching materials in schools and academies.

The imperial decree to remove icons of Confucius did however exclude the temple of Confucius in his hometown, where not only his descendants but also the state made sacrificial offerings. In the end, the ritualists who had argued against the use of images in temples accepted the use of portraits in family worship.[50] Accordingly, the main sacrificial hall (*Dachengdian* 大成殿) housed sculptural images of Confucius, and in addition paintings of his disciples, former worthies and former scholars. This made the Qufu temple unique, even though the one in Beijing was, ideologically speaking, more important for the imperial court. Yet, when a 1724 fire destroyed the main hall in Qufu, Emperor Yongzheng sent a team of artisans from his palace to create replacement for the images of Confucius and his four correlates,[51] which were completed in 1730.

The unique position of the temple in Qufu ensured the continuity of the iconography despite the decree of 1530 which was in effect until the twentieth century. After 1949, due to ideology, Confucian ideas were suppressed, Confucian temples were destroyed, and Confucius as a teacher was expunged from public memory.[52] During the Cultural Revolution, Red Guards damaged the *Konglin* (孔林)—the forest houses the tomb of Confucius and his more than 100,000 descendants who have been buried there since the late Zhou Dynasty, with the most recent ones belonging to the seventy-sixth and seventy-eighth generation.[53] Led by Tan Houlan 譚厚蘭, Red Guards from Beijing came to Qufu and established together with students from the local Qufu Normal College a Revolutionary Rebel Liaison Station to Annihilate the Kong Family Business 徹底搗毀孔家店革命造反聯絡站 that held mass rallies and organized both the students and the masses to destroy the steles on the cemetery and to dig up the tomb of Confucius in late November 1966.[54] The destruction also entailed pulling down stone stelae and the statue of Confucius in the temple, with the latter even paraded through the streets in order to vilify the archenemy.

After the destruction frenzy, the Confucius Temple and the Kong Family Mansion were restored.[55] Accordingly, the Qufu branch of the People's Bank of China bought back the gold found in the tombs by the locals (spending 101,000 RMB), and the Qufu County Cultural Relics Management Committee used 300,000 RMB to buy back funerary objects that had disappeared among the masses in the late 1960s.[56] Likewise, the smashed icons were reconstructed in 1984, and Hong Kong and overseas Chinese donors erected large statues of Confucius at schools and temples. In 1999 the government-supported China Confucius Foundation (*Zhongguo Kongzi jijinhui* 中国孔子基金会) issued a limited edition of 1,000 gold statuettes to honor the 2,500th anniversary of his birth, claiming that this statue was the most authentic representation. As expected, the image was based on the Wu Daozi's rendition.[57] Interestingly enough, some of the newly designed statues depicted Confucius without his sword, thereby implying that modern teacher-philosophers no longer carry weapons.[58]

Figure 11.1. Worship of Confucius at his tomb in March 2012. (*Source*: Author's photo.)

Figure 11.2. Statues of Confucius in Qufu at (*top left*) Confucius Research Institute, (*top right*) Qufu Normal University, and (*bottom*) Lunyu Garden (*Source*: Author's photo.)

In 2011 the newly opened National Museum in Beijing included a 31-foot, 17-ton bronze statue by sculptor Wu Weishan 吳為山. The statue disappeared four months later (arguably moved to a less prominent location). After the decades-long condemnation of Confucius that had started with the May Fourth Movement and continued during the Great Proletarian Cultural Revolution, the CCP under the leadership of Hu Jintao tried to restore Confucianism as a means to fill the ideological vacuum after the introduction of market economy and capitalism. It was supposed to remedy the various negative consequences of market reforms by emphasizing ethical behavior, respect for the elderly, and social harmony.

The renaissance of Confucianism has not been confined to China, and it became a central tenet of the promotion of Chinese soft power abroad. A fascinating example of these efforts is the 1996 founding of the Confucius Research Institute (*Kongzi yanjiuyuan*) in the center of Qufu. Being a large-scale cultural project ratified by the State Council, its goal is to sponsor academic research, organize exhibitions, collect documents, and establish cultural exchanges with scholars around the world. It publishes monographs and two journals (*Kongzi wenhua* 孔子文化 and *Kongzi xuekan* 孔子學刊), sponsors international academic symposiums,[59] and is establishing a "modern comprehensive Confucius document center" to gather documents on Confucius and Confucianism from the ancient times until the present. It also houses a Confucius Culture Museum that is "fully displaying the characteristics of oriental culture."[60]

On its premises, the institute houses on 9.6 hectares several buildings, a hotel, a library, and an exhibition hall. Construction started in 1996 and the last buildings were completed in 2010, with total building costs amounting to 190 million RMB. Planned and designed by Wu Liangyong 吳良鏞,[61] a famous architect and former professor in urban planning, the institute is a public space open for tourists who want to know more about Confucius[62] and those who have a genuine interest in the great sage's teachings. The institute not only houses a small park that assembles inscriptions of the Four Books of Confucianism (*sishu* 四書), but also has two statues of Confucius, one of which resembles the standard version of the statue, and the other is more postmodern.

This unorthodox sculpture of Confucius notwithstanding, the popularity of both Confucius and Confucian values gained political momentum. In late November 2013, the current national leader Xi Jinping even visited the Confucius Research Institute and pointed out that Confucius can play a positive role in China's development not only for academics but also for business people.[63] The institute reports proudly on its homepage that the Secretary-General visited the exhibition hall and "interestingly read the

Figure 11.3. Confucius sculpture in the Park of the Four Books (Sishuyuan 四书苑). (*Source*: Author's photo.)

books and publications showing the research achievements of Confucius Research Institute one by one."⁶⁴ The institute's current director, Yang Chaoming 杨朝明, reported that because of the high praise from Xi, Confucianism should regain its worldwide significance. For this aim, its five contemporary values were most central and are described thusly:

> The first is the world significance. Confucius is a world-class philosopher enjoying equal popularity with Socrates and Plato, and his thought belongs to the most basic of human civilization, the fundamental symbol of Chinese culture going to the world is Confucianism's going to the world. Secondly, Confucianism is the link of the whole China and Chinese nation, and the deepest spiritual pursuit of Chinese nation. Confucius has put up such thought as constructing the family and the country, and taking the welfare of the public as one's own duty, and so on, which has constituted the common pursuit of Chinese people and inspired generations of Chinese people. Thirdly, Confucianism is the deepest cultural soil of localization of Marxism

in China and socialism with Chinese characteristics. Fourthly, it has great significance to the present social governance and construction of the Party conduct and of an honest and clean government. Confucius's thoughts such as ruling by virtue and rite, valuing education after becoming rich, cultivating oneself to keep reverent, view on the relationship between righteousness and interest, [and] the doctrine of the mean have great influence on government. Fifthly, Confucianism has the effect of improving self-cultivation, and training the thinking outlook of the youngsters.[65]

Given the political role attributed to Confucianism in transforming China, we should not be surprised that Qufu has developed in the recent decades into an important place for cultural tourism. In addition, the family mansion is one of the 100 Sites for Patriotic Education since its inception in 1997.[66] At the same time, the town of Qufu decided to develop the tourist infrastructure in the larger context of economic reconstruction. Before 2000 tourism was directed toward the three major sites—the Confucius Temple, the Cemetery, and the Kong Family Mansion—but since 2002 these three sites have been integrated into a greater framework of "three Confucian spots, four mountains, and two cities" (三孔, 四山, 两城) that is largely defined by cultural tourism.[67]

In many ways, tourism helps transform Confucius into a brand. Accordingly, the daily Confucius's Dream performance, the reenactment of opening the Ming dynasty city gate twice a week, and the performance of regular ritual worship ceremonies have become part of the tourist attraction, as well as the numerous festivals and academic conferences in Qufu.[68] These performances are widely reported on not only in the local media but also in the regional, provincial, and national media,[69] especially at the important holidays such as the Tomb Sweeping Day (April 5), Teachers' Day (September 10), and Confucius's birthday (September 28). By doing so, Confucius became an icon of Chinese culture and Chinese identity helping create a sound and proper national pride. For this reason the local government in Qufu is the major force of organizing and administrating the heritage, thereby showing a great deal of creativity in either inventing or reenacting performances.

Conclusion

The preceding analysis has shown that both the Yellow Emperor and Confucius have served as symbols of Chinese national identity in the twentieth century. Both social and political forces have used their tombs to create a sense of belonging sustained by worship rituals. These rituals—once limited to the imperial court or the educated elite—are now open to the public. In recent years, nationwide media coverage on these rituals (television, Internet, newspapers, and journals) enables the veneration of the Yellow Emperor and Confucius to reach every home in China.

However, the question remains how Huangdi (the national ancestor) or Confucius (the national teacher) is able to represent the entire Chinese nation. The heated debate between Kang Youwei and Zhang Taiyan in the last decade of the Qing dynasty shows that the understanding of Huangdi as an ethnic or even racial ancestor has the tendency to exclude subgroups. While the veneration of Confucius seems to avoid this ethnic pitfall, it does not mean that he is a better icon of identity. Currently, CCP leaders seem to favor Confucius over Huangdi for countering the ill effects of market economy. At the same time, they cannot do away the ethnic forefather. Similar to the introduction of the concept of *wuzu gonghe* in 1912 by which Sun Yat-sen justified the integration of Manchu, Mongols, and Tibetans,[70] the current worship of Huangdi downplays the racial-ethnic element and depicts him as a nonethnic ancestor. Interestingly leaders of both pre-1927 Republican China and contemporary China understand Huangdi as the ancestor of the heterogeneous and multiethnic community *Zhonghua minzu*, and as such, Huangdi is remembered for his cultural achievements, such as his astronomical discoveries, his invention of the calendar, his improvement on agricultural tools, and his contributions to Chinese medicine. A closer look at the official webpage dedicated to his tomb in Shaanxi Province shows a comprehensive list of these qualities. As such, like Confucius, Huangdi becomes a cultural icon or a brand whose meaning is difficult to define.

Nevertheless, when observing the use of the two icons in the media, one can discern that Huangdi seems to be more convincing because of the belief in blood lineage. On the other hand, Confucius is clearly an empty signifier, or a moneybag (as Arif Dirlik describes) created for consumption.[71] One can even say that Confucius has become a postmodern persona because he means anything that anybody wants him to be. This includes social harmony that has recently developed into a new political ideology, even though the Chinese are facing increasing social, economic, and political conflicts as a result of market economy.

Notes

1. James Watson, "The Structure of Chinese Funerary Rites: Elementary Forms, Ritual Sequence, and the Primacy of Performance," in *Death Ritual in Late*

Imperial and Modern China, edited by James Watson and Evelyn S. Rawski (Berkeley: University of California Press, 1988), 3–19.

2. An impressive list of rituals—including the eulogies and description of rituals—can be found in the local gazetteers of Qufu, see, e.g., *Shandong shengzhi—Kongzi gulizhi* 山东省志孔子故里志 [Chronicle of Shandong Province: The annals of the former residence of Confucius], edited by Shandong sheng difang shizhi bianzuan weiyuanhui 山东省地方史志编纂委员会 (Beijing: Zhonghua shuju, 1994).

3. Emile Durkheim, *The Elementary Forms of the Religious Life* (New York: Free Press, 1965), 424–427. For the political significance of rituals in early Republican China see Peter Zarrow, "Political Ritual in the Early Republic of China," in *Constructing Nationhood in Modern East Asia*, edited by Chow Kai-Wing, Kevin M. Doak, and Poshek Fu (Ann Arbor: University of Michigan Press, 2001), 149–188.

4. Pierre Nora, "Between Memory and History: Les Lieux de Mémoire," *Representations*, no. 26 (1989): 7–24, here 7.

5. Pierre Nora, *Realms of Memory: Rethinking the French Past* (New York: Columbia University Press, 1996), vol. 1: xxiv.

6. Sun Longji 孙隆基, "Qingji minzuzhuyi yu Huangdi chongbai zhi faming" 清季民族主义与黄帝崇拜之发明 [Late Qing nationalism and the invention of the Yellow Emperor worship], *Lishi yanjiu* 历史研究 [Historical studies], no. 3 (2000) 68–79; Shen Sung-chiao 沈松僑, "Wo yi wo xue jian Xuanyuan—Huangdi shenhua yu wan Qing de guozu jiangou" 我以我血薦軒轅—黃帝神話與晚清的國族建構 [I will give my blood to honor Xuanyuan: The myth of the Yellow Emperor and the nation-building in Late Qing], *Taiwan shehui yanjiu jikan* 臺灣社會研究季刊 [Quarterly for the studies of Taiwan society) 28 (1997): 1–77; Térence Billeter, *L'Empereur jaune—Une tradition politique chinoise* (Paris: Les Indes savantes, 2007); Marc Andre Matten, *Die Grenzen des Chinesischen—Nationale Identitätsstiftung im China des 20. Jahrhunderts* (Wiesbaden: Harrassowitz-Verlag, 2009).

7. *Liang Qichao quanji* 梁启超全集 [Collected Writings of Liang Qichao], vol. 10 (Beijing: Beijing chubanshe, 1999), 45.

8. Quoted from *Xinhai geming qian shinian shilun xuanji*, 306 (vol. 1a). The *New Guangdong* was published originally in 1902 in the *Datong ribao* 大同日報 in San Francisco, in the same year a reprint appeared in Yokohama. Ou argues in this text that more autonomy (*zili*) of the provinces is the only way to save China.

9. *Huangdihun*, 2 (originally published in the first issue of *Guomin riribao*).

10. Kauko Laitinen, *Chinese Nationalism in the Late Qing Dynasty—Zhang Binglin as an Anti-Manchu Propagandist* (London: Curzon Press, 1990); Wang Chunxia 王春霞, *Pai Man yu minzuzhuyi* "排满"与民族主义 [Anti-Manchus and nationalism] (Beijing: Shehui kexue wenxian chubanshe, 2005).

11. Wang Ke 王柯, *20 seiki Chūgoku no kokka kensetsu to minzoku* 20 世紀中国の国家建設と「民族」 [Twentieth-century China and the construction of the Chinese nation-state] (Tokyo: Tokyo daigaku shuppankai, 2006); Marc Andre Matten, ed., *Places of Memory in Modern China—History, Politics, Identity* (Leiden: Brill, 2012); Murata Yūjirō 村田雄二郎, *Sun Zhongshan yu xinhai geming shiqi de "wuzu gonghe" lun* 孙中山与辛亥革命时期的「五族共和」论 [Sun Yat-sen and the

theory of "Republic of the Five Races" during the 1911 Revolution], *Fuyin baokan ziliao—Zhongguo jindaishi,* 复印报刊资料: 中国近代史 [Reprints of newspapers and journals: Modern Chinese history], no. 1 (2005): 84–91.

12. See Kuo Ya-pei, "In One Body with the People: Worship of Confucius in the Xinzheng Reforms, 1902–1911," *Modern China* 35, no. 2 (2009): 123–154.

13. Maurice Freedman, *Chinese Lineage and Society: Fukien and Kwangtung* (London: Athlone, 1966), 31.

14. See Wang Mingke 王明珂, *Yingxiong zuxian yu dixiong minzu—genji lishi de wenben yu qingjing* 英雄祖先與弟兄民族—根基歷史的文本與情境 [Heroes, ancestors, brothers, and race: The text and context of basic history] (Taipei: Yunchen, 2006), 78–83; Patricia Ebrey, "Surnames and Han Chinese Identity," in *Negotiating Ethnicities in China and Taiwan,* edited by Melissa J. Brown (Berkeley, CA: Institute of East Asian Studies, 1996), 11–36.

15. See Anthony Smith, *Nationalism and Modernism* (London: Routledge, 1998).

16. See Takeuchi Hiroyuki 竹内弘行, "Shinmatsu no shikinen nitsuite" 清末の私紀年について, *Nagoya gakuin daigaku ronshū—jinbun-shizen kagaku hen* 31, no. 1 (July 1994): 77–96.

17. The year 1895 is defined as the 2,373rd year after the death of Confucius 孔子卒後二千三百七十三年. On Kang Youwei's proposal see the study by Murata Yūjirō 村田雄二郎, "Kō Yūi to Kōshi kinen" 康有為と孔子紀年, in *Xueren (di er qi)* 学人 (第二期), edited by Wang Shouchang 王守常, Wang Hui 汪晖, and Chen Pingyuan 陈平原 (Nanjing: Jiangsu wenyi chubanshe, 1992), 513–546.

18. *Huangdi jinianlun,* 276, in *Guomin riribao,* no. 1. In fact, Liu Shipei argues the Japanese calendar commenced with Jimmu Tennō, the legendary first ruler of Japan. The corresponding date, 660 BCE, is the traditional founding date of Japan, but (as Yabuuchi Kiyoshi has shown) it is a fictive date that was defined only in 1873 by the Meiji government (and in this sense, it is an invented tradition). See Yabuuchi Kiyoshi 薮内清, *Rekishi wa itsu hajimatta ka* 歴史はいつ始まったか (Tokyo: Chūō kōron sha, 1980).

19. See Laurence G. Thompson, *Ta t'ung shu: The One-World Philosophy of K'ang Yu-wei* (London: Allen and Unwin, 1958).

20. Kung-chuan Hsiao, *A Modern China and a New World: K'ang Yu-Wei, Reformer and Utopian, 1858–1927* (Seattle: University of Washington Press, 1975).

21. Change to cremation and reduction of rites conducted at the tomb site (funeral, burial, and mourning obligations) helped to weaken the conception that the individual's fate depended on patrilineal descent and property transmission, thus necessitating appropriate worship rituals. On the implementation of funeral reforms in post-1949 China, see Martin K. Whyte, "Death in the People's Republic of China," in *Death Ritual in Late Imperial and Modern China,* edited by Watson and Rawski, 289–316.

22. Not to forget Chiang Kai-shek, see here Matten, "The Chiang Kai-shek Memorial Hall in Taipei: A Contested Place of Memory," in *Places of Memory in Modern China,* edited by Matten, 51–90.

23. See Chen Yunqian 陈蕴茜, *Chongbai yu jiyi: Sun Zhongshan fuhao de Jiangou yu Chuanbo* 崇拜与记忆: 孙中山符号的建构与传播 [Worship and memory: The construction and propagation of the political symbol of Sun Zhongshan] (Nanjing: Nanjing daxue chubanshe, 2009); Li Gongzhong 李恭忠, *Zhongshanling: Yi ge xiandai zhengzhi fuhao de dansheng* 中山陵:—个现代政治符号的诞生 [The Sun Yat-sen mausoleum: The making of a political symbol in modern China] (Beijing: Shehui kexue wenxian chubanshe, 2009); Lai Delin, "Searching for a Modern Chinese Monument: The Design of the Sun Yat-sen Mausoleum in Nanjing," *Journal of the Society of Architectural Historians* 64, no. 1 (2005), 22–55.

24. See Rudolf Wagner, "The Implied Pilgrim: Reading the Chairman Mao Memorial Hall," in *Pilgrims and Sacred Sites in China*, edited by Susan Naquin and Chu Yuan-fang (Berkeley: University of California Press 1992), 378–423; Frederic Wakeman Jr., "Mao's Remains," in *Death Ritual in Late Imperial and Modern China*, edited by Watson and Rawski, 254–288; Daniel Leese, "A Place Where Great Men Rest? The Chairman Mao Memorial Hall," in *Places of Memory in Modern China*, edited by Matten, 91–129.

25. At the national cemetery of China, space is allotted according to the rank of the cadre buried there (with the largest sites being about 24 square feet), with most tombs being in cremation niches and allowed to remain for a designated period. Because space is limited despite efforts to enlarge the cemetery, the remains in the tomb niches have to be moved to another cemetery or removed by the family to their hometown after ten or more years. Leading cadres can have large tomb sites with big tombstones and flower decorations. Despite official rhetoric during the revolutionary period, this cemetery enjoyed special privileges that were outstripped only by Mao Zedong's Mausoleum on Tiananmen Square. In this case, all calls for frugality and simplicity were simply ignored, although Mao himself had warned against a personality cult.

26. The historical records mention ceremonies taking place in 1396, 1414, 1426, 1450, 1462, 1506, 1531, 1556, 1563, 1570, 1573, 1600, and 1621. For the renovations and rebuildings conducted during Ming and Qing dynasties, cf. *Huangling xianzhi*, 635–637. The chronicle lists renovations in the years 1667, 1680, 1691 (Kangxi), 1729 (Yongzheng), 1760, 1772, 1790 (Qianlong), 1807 (Jiaqing), and 1842 (Daoguang).

27. Shunzhi as well as Kangxi are known for their Confucian way of legitimizing rule. See Bo Ming 柏明 and Li Yingke 李颖科, *Huangdi yu Huangdi ling* 黄帝与黄帝陵 [Yellow Emperor and his tomb] (Xi'an: Xibei daxue chubanshe, 1990), 111, 131.

28. Descriptions of the various ceremonies from Han dynasty until 1989 can be found in Bo Ming and Li Yingke, *Huangdi yu Huangdi ling*, 107–166. A detailed analysis of the ceremony in 1688 is provided in Billeter, *L'Empereur jaune*. Records of the ceremonies at the Tomb of the Yellow Emperor were kept until 1851.

29. For the text of the eulogy cf. Bo Ming and Li Yingke, *Huangdi yu Huangdi ling*, 134. A discussion of the ceremonies is found in Zhao Qixiang, *Zhongguo renmin zhengzhi xieshang huiyi—Shaanxi sheng weiyuanhui* 中国人民政治协商

会议陕西省委员会: *Shaanxi xinhai geming huiyilu* 陕西辛亥革命回忆录 [Shaanxi memories of the 1911 Revolution] (Xi'an: Shaanxi renmin chubanshe, 1982).

30. See Hu Zushun 胡祖舜, *Wuchang kaiguo shilu* 武昌開國實錄 [Annals of the starting a nation in Wuchang] (Hankou: Jiaotonglu jianguo shuju, 1948), 61–62; for the translation see Henrietta Harrison, *Inventing the Nation—China* (London: Arnold, 2001), 133.

31. See *Huangling zhi*: *Huangling zhi* 黃陵志, 1944, in *Huangling zhi Yanling zhi* 黃陵志—炎陵志, edited by Li Jinxi 黎錦熙, which appeared in the series *Zhongguo cimu zhi congkan 16* 中國祠墓志叢刊16 (Yangzhou: Guanglin shushe, 2004), 74–75. After the event, a similar ceremony was conducted each year at *Qingmingjie*, the traditional Tomb Sweeping Day, see Bo Ming and Li Yingke, *Huangdi yu Huangdi ling*, 144.

32. On this occasion, Mao Zedong donated a stone tablet with the inscription, "A history of 5,000 years, a width of 30,000 miles" 上下五千年，縱橫三萬里 that was erected on April 5, 1937, 清明節, when the KMT and CCP collectively worshipped the Yellow Emperor, praying for support in their fight against Japanese aggression. See *Huangling xianzhi* 黃陵縣志 [Chronicle of Huangling County], which appeared in the series *Shaanxi difangzhi congshu* 陝西地方志叢書, edited by Huanglingxian difangzhi bianzuan weiyuanhui 黃陵縣地方志編纂委員會 (Xi'an: Xi'an ditu chubanshe, 1995), 632.

33. *Huangling zhi*, 9.

34. Billeter, *L'Empereur jaune*, 101–107. For the eulogies, see Yao Minjie 姚敏傑 and He Bingwu 何炳武, eds., *Huangdi jiwen ji* 黃帝祭文集 [A collection of memorial writings for the Yellow Emperor] (Xi'an: Sanqin chubanshe, 1996).

35. Thus, not surprisingly, the current tombstone with the inscription "Tomb of Huangdi" 黃帝陵—composed by the literate Guo Moruo 郭沫若 (1892–1978)—dates from May 1958.

36. *Huangling xianzhi*, 634; Billeter, *L'Empereur jaune*.

37. See the list in *Huangling nianjian* 黃陵年鑒 [Annals of the tomb of the Yellow Emperor], edited by Huanglingxian renmin zhengfu 黃陵县人民政府 and Huanglingxian xianzhiban 黃陵县县志办 (Xi'an: Xi'an chubanshe, 2002), 65–66. A detailed description of the contemporary ritual can be found in Xu Xiaoyan 徐晓燕, "Shenzhou Xuanyuan ziguchuan—gongji Xuanyuan Huangdi xindianli ceji" 神州轩辕自古传—共祭轩辕黄帝新典礼侧记, *Liang'an guanxi* 兩岸关系 [Relations across the Taiwan Strait] (2004): 12–16.

38. Li Ruihuan was also officially in charge of the reconstruction work (*Huangling nianjian*: 63). Impressive photos of the reconstructed site can be found in the article *Baiye Shaanxi Qiaoshan Huangdiling* 拜谒陕西桥山黄帝陵, in *Wenhua jiaoliu* 2 (2005).

39. The budget of the foundation and its activities are discussed in Billeter, *L'Empereur jaune*, 122–125.

40. See Li Ruihuan's speech on the occasion of the tenth anniversary of the foundation, held on October 26, 2002: *Zai Huangdiling jijinhui chengli shi zhounian ji zhengxiu Huangdiling gongzuo zuotanhui shang de jianghua* 在黄帝陵基金会成立

十周年暨整修黄帝陵工作座谈会上的讲话, in *Xue zhexue, yong zhexue* 学哲学, 用哲学 [Leaning philosophy and applying philosophy], edited by Li Ruihuan 李瑞环, (Beijing: Zhongguo renmin daxue chubanshe, 2005), 689–691.

41. See the list of 100 Sites for Patriotic Education 百个爱国主义教育示范基地名单 in *Renmin ribao* 人民日报 [People's daily], June 11, 1997, 4.

42. In March 2008, China Central Television (CCTV) broadcast a documentary in the serial production *Exploring* (*Tansuo—Faxian*) about the town of the Yellow Emperor (*Huangdicheng*, 黄帝城). This five-part documentary aimed to prove the historical existence of the Yellow Emperor by presenting the newest archaeological findings.

43. When Huangdi became an important symbolic resource in defining a shared identity in the late 1980s and early 1990s, the CCP faced a severe problem with Huangdi being mostly understood as the ancestor of the Han (and not the *Zhonghua minzu*). In the end, the battles and conflicts between Huangdi and his rival Chiyou were widely downplayed in textbooks, historical dramas, and the popular media, because highlighting them would have meant excluding the Miao from the nation. When two historical dramas, *The Emperors Yandi and Huangdi* (*Yan Huang erdi* 炎黄二帝) and *The Great Alliance of Fushan* (*Fushan dajiemeng* 釜山大結盟), were broadcasted in the late 1990s, the Miao—already organized in their Miao Culture Study Society (苗族文化学会, cf. also their homepage http://www.3miao.net)—protested against these dramas because they seemed to imply that the Miao were not part of China. See Yang Zhiqiang 楊志強, "Enkō shison" to "chūka minzoku": Kindai Chūgoku ni okeru kokumin tōgō o meguru futatsu no gensetsu 炎黃子孫」と「中華民族」：近代中国における国民統合をめぐる二つの言説," in *Keiō gijuku daigaku daigakuin shakaigaku kenkyūka kiyō—Shakaigaku shinrigaku kyōikugaku, ningen to shakai no tankyū*, no. 64 (2007): 121–137.

44. The recent publications by Yan Xuetong and Zhao Tingyang on this issue are too many to mention.

45. See http://whc.unesco.org/en/list/704, accessed Dec. 1, 2013.

46. Thomas Wilson reports that the *History of the Later Han* (*Hou Hanshu*) mentions only four other times that Han emperors (either personally or through representatives) have visited Queli, namely in the years 29, 72, 85, and 124 CE. See Wilson, "Sacrifice and the Imperial Cult of Confucius," *History of Religions* 41, no. 3 (2002): 259–261.

47. Since that year the most senior Kong in each generation had the title of duke. In 1055 he was then given the title of Duke of Perpetuating the Sage (*Yansheng gong* 衍聖公). See Wilson, "Sacrifice and the Imperial Cult of Confucius," 63, 67.

48. *Ming shi* 50, 1296–1299. On the details of the imperial cult of Confucius see Wilson, "Sacrifice and the Imperial Cult of Confucius," 269–271.

49. Emperors Yongzheng (1725), Qianlong (1737), Jiaqing (1799), Daoguang (1821), Xianfeng (1851), Tongzhi (1862), and Guangxu (1875) gave inscriptions. On the state cult of Confucius, see John Knight Shyrock, *The Origin and Development of the State Cult of Confucius* (New York: Paragon Book, 1966); Leon E. Stover, *Imperial China and the State Cult of Confucius* (Jefferson, NC: McFarland, 2005).

50. Jan Stuart and Evelyn Sakakida Rawski, *Worshiping the Ancestors: Chinese Commemorative Portraits* (Stanford, CA: Stanford University Press, 2001), 35–49.

51. These were his disciples: Yanzi 颜子, Zengzi 曾子, Sizi 思子, and Mengzi 孟子.

52. For more details on the destruction of the Three Kong sites in Qufu see Julia K. Murray, "'Idols' in the Temple: Icons and the Cult of Confucius," *Journal of Asian Studies* 68, no. 2 (2009): 371–411; Deborah A. Sommer, "Destroying Confucius: Iconoclasm in the Confucian Temple," in *On Sacred Grounds: Culture, Society, Politics, and the Formation of the Temple of Confucius*, edited by Thomas A. Wilson (Cambridge, MA: Harvard University Asia Center, 2002), 95–133; Wang Liang, "The Confucian Temple Tragedy of the Cultural Revolution," translated by Curtis Dean Smith, in *On Sacred Grounds: Culture*, edited by Thomas A. Wilson, 376–398.

53. Kong Decheng 孔德成 (1920–2008), Confucius's descendant of the seventy-seventh generation, died 2008 in Taiwan.

54. See the well-researched paper by Geremie Barmé and Sang Ye, "Commemorating Confucius in 1966–67—The Fate of the Confucius Temple, the Kong Mansion and Kong Cemetery 孔庙, 孔府, 孔林," in *China Heritage Quarterly*, no. 20 (2009), here taken from http://www.chinaheritagequarterly.org/scholarship.php?searchterm=020_confucius.inc&issue=020 (accessed Dec. 3, 2013).

55. The buildings of the Kong family mansion dated originally from 1877 after the previous ones had been destroyed by fire.

56. For this detail see Barmé and Sang, "Commemorating Confucius in 1966–67."

57. Yet, there were intense debates in China on this issue. See here Murray, "'Idols' in the Temple," 2009. For the Foundation see also their detailed homepage http://www.chinakongmiao.org (accessed Dec. 4, 2013).

58. See here the report Zhongguo xinwenwang 中國新聞網 (2006): Zhongxuanbu pizhun Kongzi jijinhui zhengji. Kongzi biaozhun xiang 中宣布批准孔子基金會征集孔子标准像, taken from http://news.sina.com.cn/c/2006-01-26/14408977148.shtml (accessed Dec. 3, 2013). See also Murray, "'Idols' in the Temple."

59. With Tu Wei-ming and Cheng Zhongying participating regularly, such as in the case of the annual World Confucian Conference (*Shijie ruxue dahui* 世界儒學大會). See Zhuang Jinlan 庄金兰 and Yang Chaoming 杨朝明 ed., *Kongzi yanjiuyuan* 孔子研究院 [Confucius Research Institute] (Beijing: Zhongguo wenhua chubanshe, 2011).

60. See here http://www.confucius.gov.cn/Item/1946.aspx, accessed Dec. 3, 2013. Importantly, actual contribution of the institute to research on Confucianism is still limited, and many of the publications are in line with the official interpretation of Confucius and his teachings.

61. Born in 1922 Wu Liangyong taught at Tsinghua University for more than fifty years. He developed the new library of Beijing and oversaw the enlargement of Tiananmen Square. He received many architectural prizes in and outside of China.

62. With ticket prices of 40 RMB per person, however, the number of visiting tourists is virtually nil, especially when considering that the actual Confucius Temple—a place with true historical authenticity—is close by.

63. For the latter group the Confucius Research Institute offers regular courses and trainings, integrating so-called Confucian values into business behavior. Not surprising, then, the term "Confucian businessmen" (*Rushang*) that came to enjoy a rising popularity among entrepreneurs in Shanghai and other parts of China during the 1990s is not seen as an oxymoron because from the view of the Confucian businessperson, righteousness and profits are equally important. I thank Julia Hauser for pointing me out to the *rushang*.

64. See http://www.confucius.gov.cn/Item/2379.aspx (accessed Dec. 3, 2013).

65. Song Zhenzhong 宋振中, *Yang Chaoming xiang Xi zhuxi huibaole ruxue de wuge dangdai jiazhi* 杨朝明向习主席汇报了儒学的五个当代价值, seen on http://www.confucius.gov.cn/Item/2372.aspx (accessed Dec. 3, 2013).

66. See the list of 100 Sites for Patriotic Education 百个爱国主义教育示范基地名单 in *Renmin ribao* 人民日報 [People's daily], June 11, 1997, 4.

67. See for instance the self-description by the government of Qufu, Peng Guang 彭广 (2009): Wo shi fahui pinpai youshi zuoda zuoqiang wenhua lüyou chanye 我市发挥品牌优势做大做强文化旅游产业, posted Sept. 7, 2009, http://www.qufu.gov.cn/past/display2.asp?id=3841 (accessed Dec. 4, 2013). On a classification of tourism resources in Qufu see Aiping Ma, Lina Si, and Hongfei Zhang, "The Evolution of Cultural Tourism: The Example of Qufu, the Birthplace of Confucius," in *Tourism in China: Destination, Cultures and Communities*, edited by Chris Ryan and Huimin Gu (New York: Routledge, 2009), 188.

68. For a list of new performances the tourism industry created in Qufu see the list in Ma, Si, and Zhang, "The Evolution of Cultural Tourism," 190ff.

69. This includes television, newspapers, journals, and of course the Internet where all important Qufu tourist spots have a homepage of their own (http://qufu.gov.cn, http://www.kmgzj.com).

70. Regarding debates surrounding the concept of *wuzu gonghe*, see Murata Yūjirō, *Sun Zhongshan yu xinhai geming shiqi de "wuzu gonghe,"* and Andō Kumiko 安藤久美子, "Son Bun no gozoku kyōwa hihan to Tai Kitō no renpō kyōwasei ron" 孫文の「五族共和」批判と戴季陶の連邦共和制論 [Sun Yat-sen's critique of Republic of the Five Races and Dai Jitao's discussion of Republic of United States], *Shisō* 思艸, no. 46 (2005): 13–41. This concept was however not an invention of Puyi or Sun Yat-sen, as often argued, but entailed a vision of China present already during the reign of Qianlong, during which China was already considered to be a unified state whose government "represents" or acts in the name of different nations/ethnic groups. Some scholars question whether Sun Yat-sen created the term *wuzu gonghe*. See Murata Yūjirō, *Sun Zhongshan yu xinhai geming shiqi de "wuzu gonghe."*

71. Arif Dirlik, "Confucius in the Borderlands: Global Capitalism and the Reinvention of Confucianism," 22 *Boundary 2*, no. 3 (1995): 229–273.

12

The Chinese Media's Campaign for Confucianism

Motivations, Implications, and Problems

Junhao Hong, Miao Liu, and Wen Huang

In recent years, Confucian studies have been revitalized in mainland China. This revitalization has manifested itself in many ways, from the government's effort to encourage literacy in classical Chinese and the establishment of Confucius Institutes (CIs) to the wide popularity of *The Analects of Confucius* among Chinese people. This chapter investigates the revitalization of Confucianism as a broad-based cultural phenomenon by examining media campaigns in China over the past decade, offers some conclusions regarding the spread and revival of Confucian culture in today's China, and points out some problems associated with the promotion of Confucianism.

Confucianism was criticized and banned in China immediately after the Chinese Communist Party (CCP) took power. Mao Zedong launched the first massive criticism of Confucianism in the early 1950s along with the massive criticism of the movie *The Story of Wu Xun*. During the Cultural Revolution (1966–1976), once again Confucianism became a target of political campaign. In the early 1970s Mao and his followers launched another massive campaign to criticize Confucianism along with the massive criticism of Mao's former "closest revolutionary partner" Lin Biao. After the Third Plenary Session of the Eleventh Central Committee in 1978, the CCP reestablished a pragmatic Marxist ideology and allowed the implementation of "thought liberation" movement in the field of ideology and culture. Since then, thanks to several external and internal forces, Confucianism gradually began to receive realistic and practical assessments in mainland China. After the bastion of anti-Confucianism for three decades, nevertheless, the first

Confucianism conference was held in 1978 in communist China.[1] Since then, the authorities have shown increasing interest in the Confucian culture, although mostly out of the political calculation. However, because of this change, the academics and the public are able to respect Confucius again. And along with the recent "national studies heat" (*guoxue re*) and "Confucius heat" (*Kongzi re*), Confucianism has once again become the source of intellectual vitality and the object of reinterpretation among academics, despite the fact that the contemporary Confucian revival was perceived as a betrayal of Maoism by some scholars.[2]

The Mass Media's Promotion of Confucius

The official ideology toward Confucius and Confucian culture has transformed from criticizing and banning it to accepting and promoting it. Confucianism is now perceived as a valuable asset to boost its soft power. For example, the 2008 Summer Olympics highlighted Confucian themes, quoting the *Analects* at the opening ceremony and in booklets given to visiting journalists.[3] The associations and organizations such as China Confucian Culture Promotion (CCPA) sponsor the CIs and promote Confucian culture across the world.

In today's globalized world, the communicative power of media—especially movies, television, and the Internet—is phenomenal, and this sort of power is used for different purposes by different users at different times. In China, many television programs and movies have used the elements of traditional Chinese culture for the CCP's political and ideological agendas. For instance, in 2006 Yu Dan, a well-known professor at Beijing Normal University, gave seven daily lectures on the *Analects* for a program on China Central Television (CCTV), the most powerful and influential state-run television network in China. This kind of lecture-format television program has existed for a long time, but was not initially successful. For example, in 1999 the Hunan Economic television station broadcast Yu Qiuyu's talk on "Chinese Culture into the Twenty-first Century." In 2001, Phoenix TV and CCTV, respectively, launched the "Century Forum" and "Lecture Room." Neither of these programs attracted great attention until after "Lecture Room" was broadcast on CCTV. In May 2004, Yan Chongnian, a famous historian, started to give lectures on the "Mysteries of the Qing Emperors" on CCTV, which garnered a viewership rate of 0.57 percent, ranking first among all CCTV programs. After that, "Lecture Room" changed its strategy to focus on history and cultural topics, and its rating rose considerably. In 2007 Yu Dan's "Thoughts on Zhuangzi" was broadcast during "Lecture Room," setting a new record of viewership and inspiring a nationwide boom in interest in classical Chinese thoughts. Concomitantly, Yu Dan's books, including *Thoughts on the Analects of Confucius*, *Thoughts on Zhuangzi*, and *Reflections on the Analects of Confucius*, sold 3 million copies in mainland China and became popular in overseas markets, although her books are controversial with the public because many readers criticize her for being a "spokeswomen of the government." As Tongdong Bai and Steven Angle note in their chapters herein, scholars of classical Chinese thoughts also criticize Yu Dan for depoliticizing and simplifying classical Chinese thoughts. Nonetheless, the popularity of her books suggests that many nonacademic, nonpolitical Chinese people find value in her interpretations of the sages' moral ideals.

Released in 2009, for the first time in the history of China, a positive movie about Confucius, *Confucius*, was made in mainland China, artistically presenting a positive image of Confucius and conveying his teaching and doctrines to audiences by dramatizing events and conflicts in his life. As a sixtieth anniversary tribute to the People's Republic of China, the movie *Confucius* was released during the National Day of 2009. It was shown at a time when China was rapidly being integrated into the global economy and when China was trying to cope with the challenges of the age of globalization, interdependence, and uncertainties.[4] Furthermore, the movie signaled the official recognition of the contribution of Confucianism to Chinese history. Even though many scholars have criticized the movie as a political propaganda, the debates surrounding it inspired many people to read the Confucian classics. Thus, it may have played a role in spreading Confucian learning.[5]

In 2010 a 102-episode cultural television series on Confucius, including the world's first video version of the *Analects*, was filmed in Qufu, Shandong, Confucius's hometown. This television series successfully recreated the setting in which Confucius gave lectures to his disciples, vividly demonstrating the original spirit of the *Analects* and giving the audience a better understanding of Confucius's teaching and philosophy. To ensure its historical authenticity, the producers of the *Analects* television series employed thirteen famous Confucian experts as special advisors. Many scenes were shot in Qufu to give a sense of what life may have looked like during Confucius's time. This television series is classified as a part of the official Chinese traditional culture educational materials for the National Youth Organization. It was also one of the audio-visual publishing planning projects of China's Eleventh Five-Year Plan carried out by the State Press and Publication Administration. Thus, the impact of the television series was felt throughout the country.

In 2011 the Wuhan Digital Media Engineering Technology Company produced an animated series of *The Story of Confucius*, which was broadcast on China Network Television (CNTV). *The Story of Confucius* was produced in flash format, making it suitable for web broadcasting on the Internet. Within three days after being posted on the Internet, users accessed it more than 15,000 times. This animated series rejects the stereotype of Confucius as a sage and presents him as an ordinary person struggling to cope with life's challenges. The series also presents Confucius's doctrine in a more easily accessible way, opening a new channel for disseminating Confucian culture. This new promotional effort of Confucian culture is likely to be more appealing to younger generations because most young Chinese people tend to use the Internet as their major communication platform.

Every year, the Chinese National Office for Teaching Chinese as a Foreign Language (or Hanban) organizes many activities to promote Chinese culture and language. Among them, *Hanyuqiao* (Chinese Language Bridge) is the most influential where young people around the world compete in their proficiency in Chinese. Held for twelve years by 2013, *Hanyuqiao* is Hanban's most significant international education and exchange program. It attracts students all over the world who study Chinese as their second language. It also encourages Chinese language learners to learn Chinese culture more broadly by training them to learn Chinese songs, dances, martial arts, and other aspects of Chinese culture. The official state-run Chinese newspapers, magazines, television and radio stations, and the Internet always give wide coverage of these activities.

These examples show that the Chinese government has made tremendous efforts in promoting Chinese language and Chinese traditional culture. With the increasing number of cultural products every year, the influence of Chinese culture most likely will continue to grow not only in China but also in other countries.

The Confucius Memorial Ceremony

As Marc Matten states in chapter 11 herein, the Confucius memorial ceremony has also become another way for the Chinese authorities to promote Confucianism. Using cultural festivals to celebrate Confucius is not new, but it has become less political and more appealing. For instance, in 2004, the Qufu municipal government hosted a memorial ceremony for Confucius. This was the first government ceremony for Confucius in mainland China after 1949, and it had a major impact both at home and abroad. In 2006 the Qufu Confucius Temple, the Taipei Confucius Temple, and the Tainan Confucius Temple jointly organized memorial ceremonies for Confucius. It was the first time in contemporary China where the worship of the sage was done simultaneously in mainland China and Taiwan. In 2008 the First

The Chinese Media's Campaign for Confucianism / 213

World Confucianism General Assembly was held in Qufu, the hometown of Confucius, providing an opportunity for scholars from various countries to exchange ideas and experiences. On January 11, 2011, a 30-foot tall statue of Confucius was erected on the north square of National Museum of China and joined other prominent symbols in Tiananmen Square. The location of this statue at such a significant site indicates that promoting traditional culture has become an important initiative of the Chinese government. To further prove this point, a list of activities that promote Confucius and Confucianism follows.

Confucius Institutes

The CIs are nonprofit organizations in name but they are actually sponsored by the Chinese government. While publicly their goal is to promote Chinese culture and language, the government's real purpose is to use the CIs to boost China's soft power globally. Based in Beijing, the CIs' headquarters administers CIs around the world with each CI forming a partnership between a Chinese university and a foreign university. In addition to CIs, the CI headquarters designates Confucius Classrooms in primary and secondary schools, supplying them with Chinese language teaching materials and other resources.

The first CI was founded in November 2004 in Seoul, Korea. Since then, the number has increased rapidly. By the end of 2013, 477 CIs and more than 500 Confucius Classrooms had been established in 105 countries and regions. Figure 12.1 shows the increasing number of CIs from 2004 to 2013. In the meantime, the number of people who study Chinese language

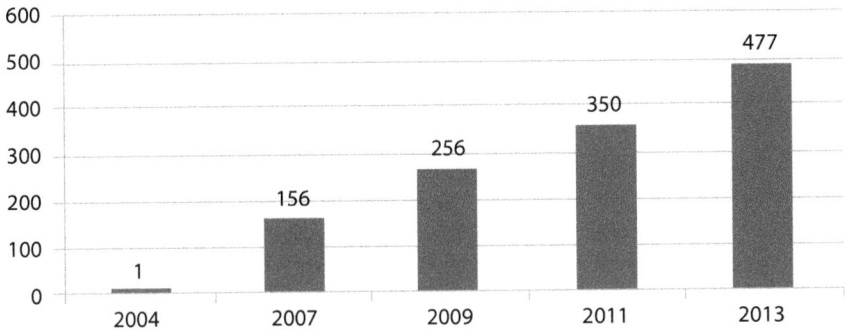

Figure 12.1. Growth of Confucius Institutes (2004–2013). (*Source:* Hanban, China, 2013).

worldwide has also increased by 39 percent. North America and South America alone, for example, have more than 65 CIs and 350 Confucius Classrooms. The Chinese government provides US$100,000 for each new CI as a start-up budget, with matching funds from the host institution.

Since 2008, a 24-hour television program about CIs is produced by Yellow River Television and serviced by the American SCOLA Education Network. The Yellow River television program has been available at more than 400 foreign universities, over 7,000 American secondary schools, and more than 50 urban cable television networks in the United States, and its audience has reached 13 million. Apparently the Chinese government intends to use these programs to promote global learning of Chinese language and to spread Chinese culture widely and quickly.

Importantly, the swift expansion of CIs across the world has not only become a controversial issue, but also a serious concern among faculty members at some U.S. and Canadian universities. For example, in April 2014, 100 professors at University of Chicago signed a petition requesting the university's top administrators to block the renewal of CI at the university. A similar activity occurred at a Canadian university earlier.

Advocating Confucianism on the Internet

Chinese authorities have extensively used the Internet, the most advanced and fastest method of communication, to spread Confucianism. In addition to establishing CIs across the world, the CI headquarters has also established a virtual CI at http://www.chinese.cn/. This website is presented in ten languages, including English, Japanese, Korean, French, and Spanish. It also provides numerous resources and information for people who are interested in learning Chinese culture and Chinese language. People who want to learn Chinese language can go to a virtual classroom on the website. Other websites include China Confucius website (http://www.chinakongzi.org/), which is specifically dedicated to Confucianism and is sponsored by the China Confucius Foundation.

Many Confucian culture organizations and institutions have established their own professional websites. According to incomplete statistics, the number of such sites is between twenty and thirty. The following are some active, high-profile websites: the Confucian Network (http://www.confuchina.com/), Contemporary Confucianism Network (http://www. cccrx.com /), the International Confucian (http://www.ica.org.cn/indexdemo.php), Confucianism and the Point Forum (http:www.yuandao.com/), Confucian China (http:// www.rujiazg.com/), the Guoxue network (www.guoxue.

com/), Confucius 2000 (http://www.confucius2000.com/), and the Confucius Research Institute (http://www.confucius.gov.cn/Category_10/Index.aspx).

The Confucianism websites have a strong communicative power and can increase the size of the audience for the transmission of Confucian cultural values. In order to promote Confucianism globally, many Confucius-related websites provide English versions, including the Chinese Confucius Research Institute (http://www.confucius.gov.cn/Category_80/Index.aspx) and, the Confucius Institute Online (http://english.chinese.cn/).

From the above, the Chinese government's efforts to promote Chinese traditional culture are clearly to serve its political needs. For example, the Education Ministry of China has added the studies of the Confucian classics to the secondary school syllabi. The government has also established an experimental school specialized in learning classical Chinese language. Some first rate universities, including Peking University and Tsinghua University, have also initiated Chinese studies classes that integrate Chinese studies into enterprise management. From cases such as the establishment of the Chinese Studies College at Renmin University of China, the government's establishment of the Confucius Institutes to promote Confucianism abroad, and its support to the movie Confucius from filming to release, the Chinese government is clearly committed to using the Confucian culture to achieve its political goal in the era of globalization.

The Motives behind the Chinese Government's Promotion of Confucianism

The Basis of National Unity and Cultural Identity

In imperial China, authorities had repeatedly used Confucianism as a ruling ideology. It also served as a foundation of the Chinese family system and the kinship society. As a result, Confucianism became part of the fabric of Chinese culture emphasizing the pursuit of harmony, especially the harmony between the inner and outer dimensions of human life, and between man and nature. Despite the anti-Confucian campaigns (such as during the May Fourth Movement in the 1920s and the political movements during Mao's era), Confucianism remains the pillar of the national spirit of China. It is indeed the bedrock of the Chinese nation, bringing different ethnic groups together under one cultural system.

Contemporary China, however, faces challenges and difficulties in terms of maintaining social stability. Every year, numerous incidents of ethnic unrest and social upheaval occur, especially in the western part of China where many are seeking political independence from China. For instance, many Tibetans maintain close contact with people in Nepal and India; members of the Dai minority in China have close contact with people in Laos, Burma, and Thailand; some non-Han people in Xinjiang (Hui, Uyghurs, and Kazakhs) and some Inner Mongolians have close contact with people who share their languages and culture in Central Asia, Turkey, Mongolia, and Russia. Similarly, Chinese Koreans have close contact with people in South Korea, let alone the case of Xinjiang, where more ethnic upheavals have occurred in recent years than in any other ethnic regions of China. Under these circumstances, the Chinese government sees Confucianism as a useful tool to maintain social stability in the ethnic regions, even though it did not work out well.

Maintaining Social Stability and Building a Harmonious Society

As we know, two core values of Confucianism are benevolence and proper conduct. "Benevolence" means carrying out benevolent governance with the principle of loving members of society and making it possible for them to enjoy life and happiness. Proper conduct refers to using moral education to establish social order so that members of the society will have a clear moral orientation and a firm moral commitment. Generally speaking, once a moral standard is established, the majority of the members of a society will be able to manage their lives and to live peacefully.

In recent years, China has been undergoing rapid social and economic development. Unbalanced socioeconomic development has resulted in a series of social problems. For instance, with high-speed economic development and improvement of living standards, many Chinese people lose their faith and directions. In general, national cohesion in many aspects has decreased significantly in the last few decades. At the same time, the ideology and culture have become more diverse, creating new challenges to China's social stability. In response, the government promotes Confucianism to stabilize society. As Daniel Bell points out, in an age of individualism, Confucianism is an effective force to promote social responsibility and social harmony.[6] For example, Confucianism encourages filial piety and instructs young people to take care of their parents. It shapes people's behavior and changes people's attitude, particularly in regard to conflict management and conflict resolution. As such, even though the moral code of Confucianism may not be entirely suitable to modern society and economy, from the perspective of the authorities it is a valuable tool for maintaining social stability.

The Need to Build Cultural Power and Enhance the Image of China

To a great extent, culture is a soft power that is as important as economic, political, and military power. However, as China's economic power continues to grow, the country still lacks cultural products that are influential worldwide. For instance, China imports large numbers of cultural products from developed countries such as the United States and Japan, but exports only a few literary works, movies, and works of arts to Western countries. In order to enhance China's cultural soft power, the government has made great efforts to promote Chinese culture across the world. One of the efforts, as mentioned earlier, is the worldwide establishment of CIs. Figure 12.2 presents the geographic distribution of CIs around the world, and as is shown, CIs are now operated in most areas of the globe.

Domestically, the Chinese government has also made tremendous effort to promote traditional Chinese culture among the younger generation. The government is concerned that young Chinese who grow up watching cartoons and television series from the United States and Japan will lack knowledge of traditional Chinese culture, becoming pro-Westernized instead. Even though the primary and secondary school textbooks include famous excerpts from the Chinese classics, Chinese youth's knowledge of

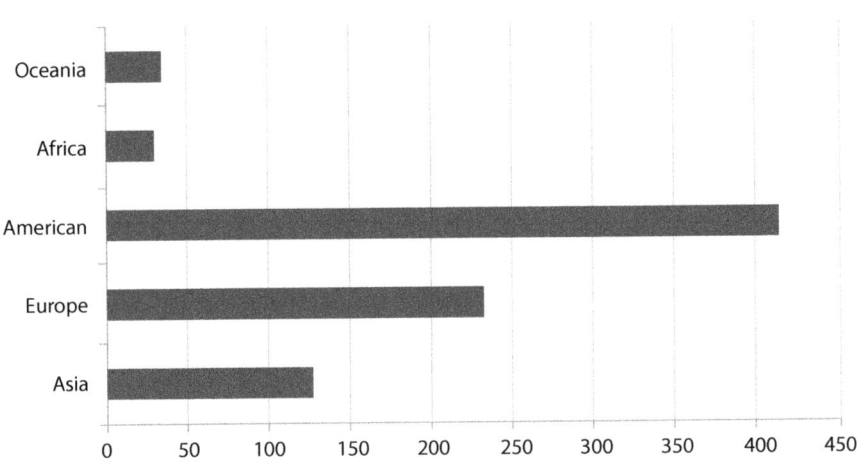

Figure 12.2. Geographic distribution of Confucius Institutes. (*Source:* Retrieved from http://data.163.com/12/0528/14/82JN7I0700014MTN.html).

traditional culture is still much weaker than that of young people in neighboring Japan and Korea.

To the Chinese government, promoting Confucian culture to the outside world is in part an attempt to resist the invasion of Western cultural values. For example, former Party Secretary General Hu Jintao's report to the 17th National Congress of Communist Party of China in 2007 clearly reflects this, stating: "At present, culture has increasingly become an important source of national cohesion and creativity and act[s] as an important force in the competition of comprehensive national strength. China should inherit its heritage and culture and follow the 'Going Out' mode for cultural innovation in the 12th Five-Year Plan in order to enhance international competitiveness and impact of Chinese culture, and in the meantime, to enhance the soft power of the State." In fact, China's influence has gone beyond East Asia. It has become a world power with significant impact on global affairs.

Dissemination of Chinese Values and Improving International Relations

In recent years, the Chinese government has been vigorously promoting the Confucian idea of "harmonious but different" (*he er butong*), which the Chinese government now widely uses to grapple with contentious issues domestically and to handle relations with foreign countries. To strengthen China's national cohesion, a scholar points out, "[d]omestically, the affirmation of harmony is meant to reflect the ruling party's concern for all classes."[7] Some Confucian concepts, such as "harmonious but different," has also become an important criterion for Chinese people to deal with interpersonal relations. As Daniel Bell suggests, Confucianism insists that the good life lies in social ties and that entails certain social responsibilities.[8]

In terms of foreign policy, the concept of "harmonious but different" is central to China's attempt to promote peaceful coexistence with other countries. It also informs China's handling of complex international relations. For instance, the Chinese government put forward the Five Principles of Peaceful Coexistence "to seek common ground while reserving differences." With increasing communication with countries around the world, Chinese leaders have used the concept of "harmonious but different" to manage global affairs. However, in international arena, China has not yet acquired a strong cultural position similar to its economic and political status. In response, the Chinese government decides to continue to promote Chinese culture in foreign countries, hoping to convince more countries to accept the Chinese view of the global order.

Problems and Weaknesses

Based on the above, the Chinese government is clearly promoting "state Confucianism," meaning that Chinese authorities use the recent Confucian revival as a tool to support its rule. As a result, even though the Chinese government has invested considerable resources in promoting Confucianism, after a while, the enthusiasm for Confucianism and the Confucian classics gradually lessens. In fact, Chinese people have been overwhelmed by excessive media campaigns. For example, despite its large budget, the film *Confucius* had box office sales of only 28 million RMB (which is less than US$5 million) in its first week of release in 2009. The sale was far less than that of the Hollywood blockbusters *Avatar* and *Pirates of the Caribbean 4*, each of which earned billions of RMB in the first week when first shown in China. Also, as interest in ancient classics spreads, problems become more apparent, such as wrong annotations, poor quality of the relevant publications, and various mistakes in the book contents. Many books about ancient China are simply imitations of earlier publications. Consequently, the chaos in the book market has had a negative impact on the promotion of Confucianism.

In short, although interest in Confucianism has increased across China, it is more a result of the support of government organizations. By contrast, nongovernment grass-root Confucian organizations are still weak. In fact, compared to government organizations, grass-root Confucian organizations have fewer resources and less influence. In order to increase the influence of Confucianism on ordinary Chinese people, the government must give grass-root Confucianism organizations equal access to resources and funding, which unfortunately is not promising because, as mentioned earlier, the government's purpose for promoting Confucianism is to maintain control rather than to share power based on Confucian teaching.

The Impact of the Promotion of Confucianism

For whatever motivations, the recent promotion of Confucianism has had and will continue to have a positive impact on the spread of Chinese culture to the world. A case in point is "Chinese fever" where foreigners are enthusiastic about learning Chinese language and culture. According to the records, the number of Chinese language learners is rapidly growing compared to other language learners in the world. For instance, by the end of 2013, more than 150 million people outside China were learning Chinese and that number is increasing every day.

In recent years, aside from government-supported media campaigns, the number of mass media products including books, movies, and television series that make use of the elements of Chinese traditional culture has been constantly increasing in recent years. According to China State Administration of Radio Film and Television data, in 2011, 469 television series received distribution licenses, of which, 219—46.7 percent—contain historical themes.

Nevertheless, the government's goal in promoting Confucianism is to strengthen its power and to maintain social order. In order to reduce social tension and stabilize society, Chinese leaders are keen on using Confucian culture as a tool to subdue discontentment against the CCP among Chinese citizens. Consequently, the utilitarian use of Confucianism has not produced results that the Chinese authorities hoped to achieve. According to a 2014 survey of 500 college students in the United States the authors of this chapter and their research team conducted, only one in three said they may have some kind of interest in learning about Chinese culture (see fig. 12.3). As for learning the Chinese language, the percentage is significantly lower: just 4 percent, but even this 4 percent represents people who "intended" to learn the language; the number of the people who would actually start learning Chinese language and would keep using it is even smaller. That explains why the number of students enrolled in Chinese class decreases after a period of time when students become disinterested after encountering difficulty in learning a complex language.

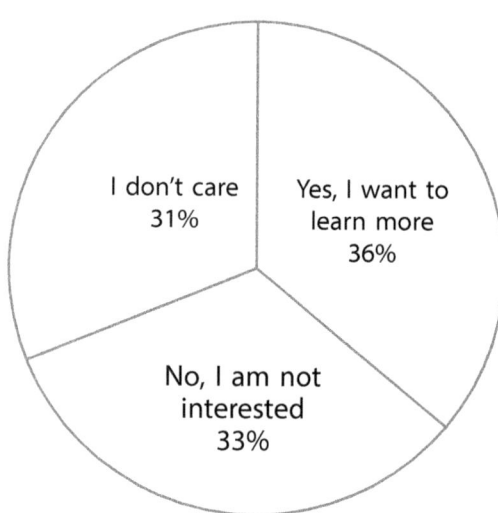

Figure 12.3. Are you interested in learning about Chinese culture?

The Chinese Media's Campaign for Confucianism / 221

Although most of the surveyed college students are not interested in learning about Chinese culture, nevertheless, they have a not-so-positive perception of Chinese culture (see fig. 12.4). When the college students were asked why they are not interested in learning about Chinese culture, one in four answered because they feel Chinese culture simply has nothing to do with their life (see fig. 12.5).

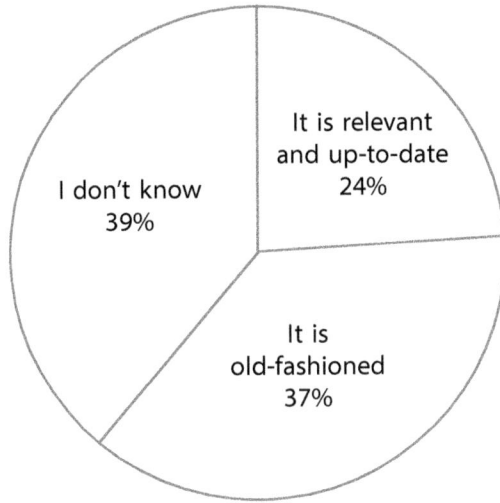

Figure 12.4. How do you feel about Chinese culture?

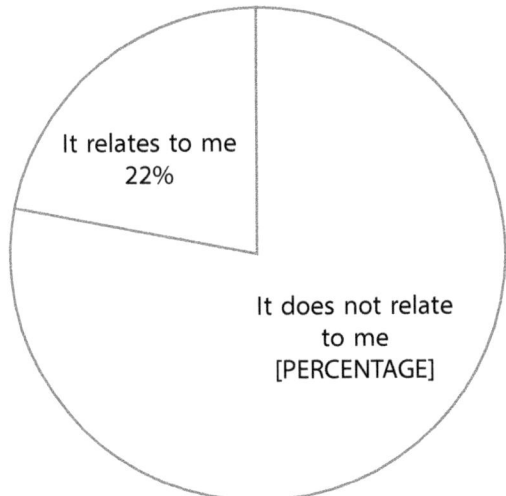

Figure 12.5. Why are you not interested in learning about Chinese culture?

According to the same survey, despite the efforts of the Chinese authorities to establish numerous CIs in the United States and other countries, attempting to disseminate Chinese culture across the world, most people in United States still obtain their knowledge of Chinese culture through the media and cultural products of their own country (see fig. 12.6). This means the efforts of the Chinese authorities in this regard is currently not effective.

Furthermore, Chinese authorities have been trying to use Confucianism to boost China's soft power, but the U.S. college students surveyed still think the number one element of China's soft power is its government, not its culture (see fig. 12.7). Therefore, for people outside China, China's soft power unfortunately still comes from the government's force and not from the influence of the Chinese culture.

Conclusion

Intermittently Confucianism has dominated China for more than 2,000 years, and its intellectual and cultural vitality has been repeatedly recog-

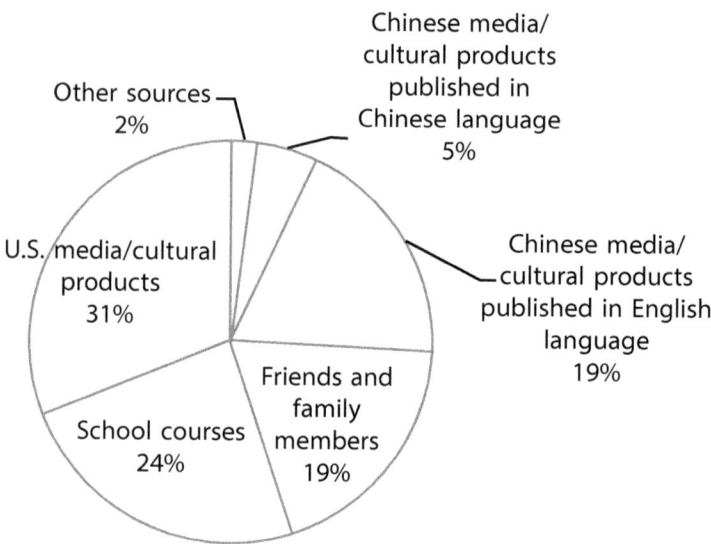

Figure 12.6. Where do you obtain your knowledge of Chinese culture?

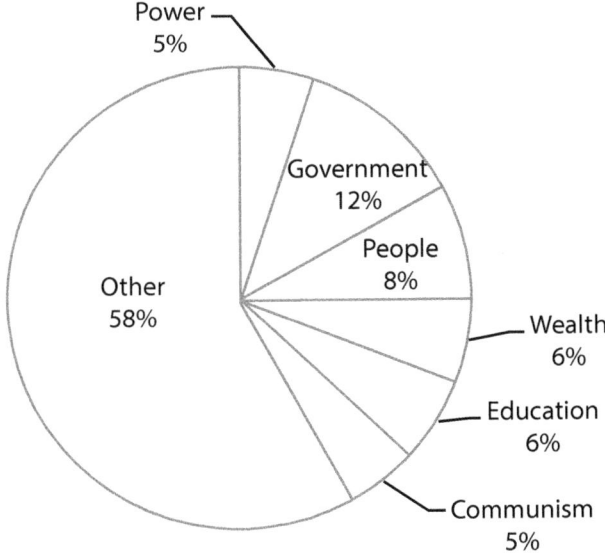

Figure 12.7. What is the most important element of China's soft power?

nized. Some even say that parts of the Confucian teaching are applicable to people's lives in contemporary society. Importantly, however, China still has a long way to go to restore the status of Confucianism. First and foremost, Confucianism must be recognized as an essential element of Chinese modern culture and be used to enhance the cohesion of Chinese people and society. Second, cultivating the spirit of Chinese nationality based on Confucianism is crucial. In order to establish the glory of Chinese culture at this new historical stage, China must create a new form of Confucianism that directly responds to the challenges of the contemporary world.

Notes

1. Arif Dirlik, "Confucius in the Borderlands: Global Capitalism and the Reinvention of Confucianism" 22 *Boundary 2*, no. 3 (1995): 229.
2. Ibid.
3. Daniel A. Bell, *China's New Confucianism: Politics and Everyday Life in a Changing Society* (Princeton, NJ: Princeton University Press, 2010).
4. Joseph Tse-Hei Lee, Ronald K. Frank, Renqiu Yu, and Bing Xu, "From Philosopher to Cultural Icon: Reflections on Hu Mei's 'Confucius,'" *Global Asia Journal* (2010). Retrieved from http://digitalcommons.pace.edu/global_asia_journal/11.

5. Ibid.
6. Ulara Nakagawa, "The Confucian Comeback," *The Diplomat* (Mar. 2, 2011). Retrieved from http://thediplomat.com/new-emissary/2011/03/02/the-confucian-comeback/.
7. Bell, *China's New Confucianism*, 9.
8. Nakagawa, "The Confucian Comeback."

Epilogue

Beyond New Confucianism

Expanding the Contemporary Rudao

JOHN H. BERTHRONG

First, and imperative to remember, Confucianism, while an immensely important aspect of Chinese culture, is not alone in defining Chinese culture. Confucianism does not equate to China, or vice versa. Numerous other traditions, including Daoism, Buddhism, and now Marxism, which are three major classical and modern forces in Chinese life, have equally defined the contours of Chinese philosophical and religious history. Underlying all three great elite traditions of Confucianism, Daoism, and Buddhism is the massive substrate of Chinese regional, local, and popular vernacular culture. For instance, the *Yijing* 易經 *Classic of Change* is a canonical source text for all Chinese traditions, large and small, elite and popular.[1] Even with this recognition of great cultural diversity, the Confucian Way has been highly instrumental in the self-definition of Chinese (and other East Asian countries) ethos for centuries. And now the Confucian Way appears to be making a remarkable comeback after one of its more difficult centuries of decline, denunciation, and self-criticism.[2] In order to place the articles in *Beyond New Confucianism* in a proper perspective, we need to begin with a short review of the history of Confucianism and its various transformations over the last two millennia. The contemporary discussions of New Confucianism, pro and con, arise from a long and complex history.

Second, the chapters in this volume reflect the amazing, diverse, and growing current revival of Confucian discourse in the last three decades.[3] But before we assay the current state of Confucian scholarly debates and trends, we need to reflect on the recent historical odyssey of the *rudao* 儒道. For the terms of this review of the question of getting "beyond New

Confucianism," we need only think back to the beginning of the twentieth century to gauge the depth of the problems the Confucian Way encountered over the last century and the beginning of the twenty-first century.[4]

Arguably no other great philosophical or religious tradition suffered as much from its encounter with Western Enlightenment modernity and the imperial West (including Japan in this list) in the last century as did the Confucian Way. At the end of the nineteenth century and the beginning of the twentieth century Confucianism still dominated many features of Chinese society. This was so much the case that many people would consider China really Confucian China. Families, especially the educated elite, often ordered themselves around ritual lives devised by great scholars such as Zhu Xi 朱熹 (1130–1200). Educating the elite, including merchants, took the teaching of the Confucian Way with utter seriousness. Furthermore, appointment to and membership in the ruling elite in the Song, Ming, and Qing dynasties depended on passing the highest levels of an imperial examination, which was based on Confucian texts and learning. To be successful in twentieth-century China demanded a pervasive understanding and probably a strong commitment to the Confucian Way.

All of this vast integration of the Chinese state, culture, and the Confucian Way was in complete turmoil by the end of the second decade of the twentieth century. The analogy of the fate of the Titanic comes to mind. When the Titanic (China in this case) smashed into the iceberg that sank the great ship, the captain and the senior members of the crew where Confucians, the very people charged to protect the mighty vessel. When a ship sinks, the blame immediately accrues to the captain and crew, and these were all Confucians in our metaphor for the fall of imperial China. By 1905 the imperial civil service examinations were abolished, thereby ending the long control of much of the Chinese state by Confucian educated statesmen and officials. The ladder to success in China, so long based on command of a Confucian intellectual sensibility and education, was yanked from the control of the Confucian tradition. Education was transformed on a Western model that now ended in graduate studies in universities and not in Confucian academies. Families abjured what they felt were outdated and useless Confucian ritual systems. As China suffered humiliating defeat after humiliating defeat at the hands of the Western imperial powers and the rising Japanese empire, Chinese intellectuals were forced to look for different captains for the ship of state, much less ordering family life and the education system. In the end the choice was a Chinese form of Marxism.

By the early 1920s many Chinese public intellectuals felt that the whole Confucian Way needed to be abandoned if China was to be saved from what was called a semicolonial state of affairs. Even during the late 1960s the great historian Joseph Levenson, who thought well of many aspects of Confucianism, came to the conclusion that Confucianism would no longer play a living role in the future of Chinese society.[5] Sadly Levenson believed that Confucianism would only continue to exist in the museum of Chinese history, a theme scholars still echo today. The *rudao* could become an object of study but never again an object of a life well lived. In the early part of the twentieth century numerous attacks were made on Confucianism for its manifest role contributing to the manifold catastrophes in the rapidly failing Chinese state and society. The sooner Confucius and Sons were purged from the Chinese system, the better.

One wonders if any other reaction would have been possible given Chinese history in the nineteenth and twentieth centuries. These were terrible times indeed. Many Chinese (and no doubt Manchus) could remember vividly when China was a supreme and dominant power East Asia. As recently as the mid-eighteenth century the Qing Dynasty's army saved the Russians in Central Asia from yet another inner Asian tribal confederacy that threatened to run the Russians out of their Siberian conquests. But these halcyon days were long gone. Ever since the 1840s China had been under constant attack from the Western imperial powers. And while China was never formally colonized, its various regions were parceled out to the Western powers as semicolonial spheres of influence. And if the Western incursion were not enough, the catastrophe of the Taiping Rebellion almost destroyed the Qing dynasty and devastated huge parts of southern and central China. Some scholars have argued that perhaps more people died in this gigantic rebellion than World War II. The immense Taiping Rebellion simply was another event leading to the death of the Confucian state.

Things did not get any better in the early twentieth century after the downfall of the Qing and the rise of republican China. China joined the Allied cause in World War I in the hope of regaining a measure of its international integrity, but this was not the case. What the Chinese discovered is that, although Germany had been defeated in Europe, the German sphere of influence (Shandong for instance), had secretly been transferred not to China but to the rising power of the militant Japanese empire, and the situation seemed to get progressively worse. Whatever merits the Confucian state may have had, it was now viewed as hopelessly fossilized and completely unable to provide any meaningful support to the reform and restoration of Chinese cultural and political power and dignity.

All Chinese officials, therefore, regardless of political or philosophical beliefs, had good reasons for rejecting the Confucian Way as a path forward for China in the twentieth century. But the case became even more complex as increasingly more young Chinese intellectuals returned from study in North America and Europe to take teaching positions in China's new Western-style universities. What happened was yet another example of multiculturalism in action. These young intellectuals used Western philosophies and categories of analysis they had learned in London, Cambridge, Paris, Berlin, and Boston. The study of Chinese philosophy was completely transformed by the new models of Western intellectual historiography. As On-cho Ng writes, the study of Confucianism, either by Western or Chinese scholars, has, of necessity, become an example of comparative global philosophy.[6] The material being studied might be Chinese classical texts for instance, but the methodology used to analyze these texts was now informed by Western philosophical categories, methodologies, and sensibilities. In some case this would mean that texts that had long fallen out of favor with Chinese intellectuals, such as the *Mozi*, returned to be studied because the classical Mohist tradition was uniquely interested in the kind of logic found in Western philosophy. Chinese scholars in search of texts infused with an interest in what Western intellectuals would recognize as logic and science found that the *Mozi* fit the bill much better than any "Confucian" text from the classical Warring States Period.

The work of Hu Shi and then Feng Youlan in the 1920s and 1930s are highly illustrative of the work of Western-trained historians of Chinese philosophy in the sense that they both created the first highly influential Western-style histories of Chinese philosophy. Along with logical texts such as the *Mozi* both Hu and Feng went in search of theories about the one and the many, universals and particulars, epistemology, logic, and a host of other Western cosmological, ontological, and metaphysical tropes in the classical and later Chinese traditions. This tradition continues today, although scholars have begun to question whether simply importing Western research paradigms is always an effective way to study Chinese intellectual history. The chapters in this volume represent a new trend in the study of Chinese philosophy, namely one that tries to balance the received Western methodologies with a stronger concern for articulating Chinese ways of thinking and acting. But before we return to the range of topics the chapters included in this collection address, we need to look even father back in the history of the Confucian Way for possible parallels to the current debates between and among New Confucians.

The Third Epoch of the Confucian Way

Although we can examine the historical development of the Confucian Way in many ways, one of the most productive is to explore what scholars have called the three epochs of the Confucian Way. The notion of the three epochs is now closely identified with Professor Tu Wei-ming, formerly of Harvard University and now Peking University, but the term and the ideas behind it was probably first used by Tu's famous teacher, Mou Zongsan (1909–1995). The division of the Confucian Way into three epochs focuses attention on three decisive transformations in Confucianism's long history.[7] The first epoch is that of the classical, foundational period. Traditionally this begins with Master Kong, although Kongzi would not have thought of himself as the founder of a tradition. Rather he felt that he transmitted and did not create. What he transmitted was the inherited sage lore of the Shang and Zhou dynasties. Kongzi focused attention specifically and in most detail on the Dao of King Wen, King Wu, and the Duke of Zhou.

Of course later scholars of the Confucian Way, including Mengzi, the second of the Warring States masters, counted Kongzi as a sage: a sage without a crown, perhaps, but a sage nonetheless. Kongzi himself never claimed the rank of a sage. This classical period ran from Kongzi to Xunzi at the end of the Warring States Period and forward to the synthesizing work of the Western Han scholar-official Dong Zongshu. While there were later great arguments about who constituted the genuine transmission of Kongzi's Dao, there is no argument but that this collection of teachings from Kongzi to Dong Zongshu created the rich philosophical lexicon that has endured to this day as the literary expression of the Confucian Way.

We must remember, however, that the classical epoch shares an important feature with the second and third epoch, namely external debates with other scholars representing other schools, such as Mozi, Laozi, and Zhuangzi just to mention three of the most famous disputers of the Dao. Each epoch of the Confucian Way is marked by these kinds of vital debates with non-Confucian scholars about shared topics such as the mind-heart, human nature, self-cultivation, ritual civility, *qi* as vital force, and the constitution of the cosmos. These great extramural debates were often accompanied by fierce struggles within the community of scholars who honored Kongzi as the first teacher, such as the famous quarrel Xunzi had with Mengzi's theory of the goodness of human nature. This pattern of internal and external dispute and transformation has marked and continues to mark the second and third epochs of the Confucian Way.

The second epoch is the long period after the fall of the Han in the third century CE until the nineteenth century. Along with the revival of Daoism, the most memorable aspect of the challenge that gave rise to the maturing of the second epoch in the Northern Song dynasty was the arrival and flourishing of Buddhism. Imagining the most distinctive schools of the second epoch of the Confucian Way without the stimulus of Chinese

Buddhism would be impossible. Of course, as scholars such as Hoyt Tillman and Peter Bol have reminded us,[8] there were plenty of internal Confucian disputes in the Northern Song and Southern Song. Even if New Confucian scholars reject the notion that they simply hijacked and then deployed various forms of Buddhist thought for their own purposes, they admit that what is called the Neo-Confucian revival of the Northern and Southern Song dynasty was done in order to provide a Confucian response to the intellectual and religious achievements of Buddhism. Of course, the robust Daoist schools and institutions of the Wei-Jin and Tang dynasties also challenged Confucianism just as their ancestors, Laozi, Zhuangzi, and Liezi did in the classical period.

Moreover, a fascinating parallel exists between the kinds of debates that occurred in the second epoch and that are now occurring again in the third epochs of the Confucian Way, and the general pattern I find is the kind that is beginning to engage the diverse intellectual agendas of the New Confucian movement. The structure of the debate has two aspects, and in naming them we, of course, oversimplify both emerging sides of the debates. The dispute is around (1) the role of the philosophical nature of the writings of the majority of first and second generations New Confucians such as Tang Junyi and Mou Zongsan[9] and (2) the now-perceived need for a much more politically and socially engaged and sensitive contribution to the revival and renewal of the Confucian Way by thinkers such as Jiang Qing and Fan Ruiping.

Anyone who has read about the debates among various Confucian scholars in the Northern Song has the distinct feeling that Confucians have walked and talked over this ground before. Both the second and third epochs of the Confucian Way were and are marked by (1) complex and sustained philosophical elaboration and reconstruction of the classical resources, as well as by (2) an intense desire to apply these insights to the political and social life of China.[10] For instance, we only have to think of the debates about the Northern Song New Reforms of Wang Anshi with other Northern Song philosophers. Moreover, the scope and detail of this Northern Song reform project was much more ambitious than anything that has been proposed from the politically minded New Confucians.[11]

Additionally, the political program seems to have predated the most sophisticated philosophical projects of the Northern Song and the Southern Song scholars. It was as if, often out of office, the people we now know as the Neo-Confucian philosophers, such as Zhou Dunyi, Shao Yong, Zhang Zai, Cheng Hao, and Cheng Yi, and later Zhu Xi, had the time and felt the need to offer critiques of the New Reforms. These critiques were not only aimed at the particulars of the reforms but also sought to provide a philosophical vision of the Confucian Way that would sustain Wang Anshi's critique.

But the point about the internal debates in the second and third epoch is striking here in two ways. The first is that this kind of debate between the philosophers and the political public intellectuals seems to be a strong feature of both the second and now emerging third epoch of the Confucian Way. Moreover, as the later Qing evidential research scholars noted with some asperity, the Neo-Confucian philosophical project was much too much interconnected with Buddhism for its own Confucian good. Many of the political thinkers among the New Confucians make the same case about their current philosophical colleagues, although Western philosophy has now replaced Buddhist discourse. While the political public intellectuals (who are as wonderfully philosophical as the "philosophers" per se) acknowledge the scholarly brilliance of the philosophers, they also argue that they are too concerned to philosophize via an intense intercultural exchange with Western philosophy or to propose modern Confucian cultural reforms. If the second epoch Neo-Confucian philosophers were accused of being Buddhists in a Confucian disguise, then third epoch New Confucian philosophers are seen as being too concerned with great Western thinkers such as Kant and Hegel. This leads to one of the main themes of the contemporary Confucian political thinkers, namely the need to devise a New Confucianism that is conceptually linked to Classical Confucian resources and is not always carried out in what is basically a Western mode of philosophical discourse.

Many, if not almost all, contemporary professional Chinese philosophers and public intellectuals are extremely well acquainted with Western philosophy. Since the early work of Hu Shi and Feng Youlan, historians of Chinese philosophy have tried to find ways to compare and match Chinese texts and modes of expression with analogous terms in the Western philosophical lexicon. However, most scholars have again noticed that while this can be a fascinating and rewarding enterprise, a successful mapping from one tradition to another does not always happen. Increasingly more Contemporary New Confucians philosophers have come to this conclusion as well. Therefore, along with a call for a more socially active Confucianism, there is a concurrent call for a form of presentation, both in Chinese and English, which will honor the Confucian side of the comparative equation. The chapters in this book are excellent examples of the shifting perspectives, goals, and even vocabulary of the New Confucian movement in its various forms.

Yet another question surfaces with New Confucianism in all its emerging and various forms that most scholars on both sides of the "philosophers" and "public social intellectuals" avoid, and this is the question of social praxis, or what the previous Confucians would have called *li* 禮, ritual propriety and civility.

Social Praxis: The Role of *Li* 禮

At the beginning of the twentieth century one of major casualties of the collapse of late imperial Confucianism was the hold of Confucian ritual 禮 on many aspects of Chinese life. Of course, the effects of Confucian ritual theory and praxis were most prominent at the elite level of society, but Confucian forms of social conduct permeated all levels of Chinese society.[12] All the New Confucians know this was the case and some of them are wondering, as is everyone interested in the fate of New Confucianism, what will be the outcome of some kind of ritual reform or revival of ritual as civility—if there is to be one.

But even in the wider Chinese Diaspora where some forms of Confucian rituals remained, they are greatly diminished in form and function from what Confucian ritual life was prior to the end of the nineteenth century. Confucians were masters of ritual theory and practice. In fact, many scholars now believe that Confucianism itself arose during the Zhou dynasty as a class of professional ritual masters. In the first two epochs of the Confucian Way ritual reform went hand in hand with the philosophical, social, and political achievements of scholars as diverse as Xunzi in the late Warring States and Zhu Xi in Southern Song China. Xunzi predicated the whole Confucian project on the role of ritual in helping to found and sustain a flourishing social system.

Zhu Xi thought about ritual *li* as much as Xunzi and would have thought any kind of promotion of the Confucian Way impossible without rituals to sustain and nourish its role in the daily lives of the Chinese people. In fact, Zhu Xi authored the most important ritual text of the last eight hundred years, namely the work that has come to be known as *Master Zhu's Family Rituals*.[13] Zhu's text was not only famous in China but also became the standard ritual text in Korea. Furthermore, many Korean scholars have noted and argued that Koreans followed Zhu's ritual text even more closely than did their Chinese cousins. One cannot overestimate how much Zhu relied on ritual to teach and educate people in the Confucian Way.[14] Zhu argued, and was successful in doing so, that Confucian ritual was not only the prerogative the imperial elite but also for anyone who sought to become a student of the Confucian Way. A much wider audience now practiced Zhu's family rituals than before the transition of Chinese society from the aristocratic world of the Tang to the literati social elite of the Song. Of course, this would have been possible only for the wealthy literati and merchant families to carry out all the rituals in Zhu's manual, but this was actually a great expansion of Confucian ritual into Chinese social life. Along with the domination of the education system and government officialdom, classical early modern Confucian ritual life fell apart at the end of the nineteenth century and is certainly not to be found in any part of cultural China in the twenty-first century.

So what to do about ritual in the New Confucian world? Although hardly a rigorous social science research project, my personal conversations with all types of New Confucians leads me to believe that each one is concerned about the future role of ritual in the New Confucian Way. Moreover, everyone is also aware that this is a difficult task. Some contemporary Confucians, as we have seen in some chapters in this book, such as Jiang Qing, have even tried to revive some traditional ritual forms and institutions.[15] Jiang was at one time a highly successful professor in one of China's modern Western-style universities. He resigned his university professorship in order to promote a more traditional form of Confucian revival and founded a traditional Confucian academy in order to teach the Confucian Way. Colleagues of Jiang, such as Fan Ruiping,[16] have also looked at what can be called a Confucianized (ritual) policy for medical service in China. This work, however, is inferior to the original work of the New Confucians, although this is not a criticism of the sincerity of the effort of New Confucians such as Jiang and Fan, when compared to Zhu's impact on Chinese ritual life in post-Song imperial China. Of course, it is simply much too early in the revival efforts of the New Confucians to claim that they too will find a new way to express *li* 禮.

I have also talked with colleagues about other forms of "Confucian" ritual revival in modern China. But here things become difficult to analyze. For instance, as we mentioned before, "Confucian" does not equal everything Chinese, especially in the world of ritual action. But equally all kinds of alternative rituals are associated with various forms of Buddhism and Daoism. Any visit to a sacred spot such as Mt. Tai (Taishan 泰山) in central Shandong Province will make this point. The main Daoist temple on Taishan is now festooned with thousands, even tens of thousands, of padlocks attached to all parts of the temple seeking good luck for all kinds of reasons. This is clearly not a revival of a traditional Daoist ritual; nor did the learned Daoist monk leading our party around the mountain, who also had a master's degree in religious studies from Shandong University, believe that it was anything like what had been done before in the temple. Modern padlocks are just that, although seeking the aid of the mountain spirits is certainly an extension of previous ritual.

If elite Confucianism, Daoism, and Buddhism can be likened to three great waves on the sea of Chinese life worlds, then as we slide down these waves we enter the broader water of regional and local ritual forms and then into the vast ocean of popular Chinese religious and ritual culture. Here designating that a particular ritual is Confucian—much less Daoist and Buddhist in any sense that a scholarly practitioner of the elite traditions would recognize as his or her own—is difficult.

Moreover since there never was or is a central controlling authority for defining Confucian ritual in the general society, tracking popular ritual revivals of what were traditionally considered Confucian rituals is even more confusing.[17] For contemporary Daoism and Buddhism, schools, temples, and monasteries exist wherein more and more educated monks and nuns are available to discuss the revival of their traditions. One possible outcome of the New Confucian revivals, chronicled in this book, might well be New Confucian institutions that, as elite educational and social organizations, could commend reformed and new forms of Confucian rituals. I have heard, for instance, of families again making use of Zhu's family rituals for marriages in modern settings.

Yet another dramatic change also appears to be emerging with the rituals of ancestor veneration *xiao* 孝. If there was ever a set of rituals that closely defined Confucian life, it was the range of practices generalized as the rituals surrounding ancestor veneration. One of the key features of this practice was the role of the son (the eldest male) in leading the rituals for the death of parents. This need for a male liturgist was so ingrained that if a family did not have a son to carry out the rituals, the family would often adopt a nephew or cousin from the same lineage in order to have a "son" to perform the death rituals. In the contemporary world, however, the eldest daughters are now playing this critical ritual role. And as some female colleagues have said to me, why not indeed? With the policy of one child per family this makes a lot of sense. Moreover Chinese women have emerged from the inner quarters of late imperial China to play active roles in all sectors of modern Chinese society. If this is the case, then why should a daughter not play the role of the eldest child in the loving veneration of the ancestors, one's own parents? The family register of names now includes women where previously only men were listed. Confucian rituals can change.

The Diversity of Change: "Getting Beyond New Confucianism"

By now we see that getting beyond New Confucianism can mean different things to different scholars and public intellectuals. For instance, let us remember the range of topics addressed in this book: traditional values and China's foreign policy; global capitalism in its Chinese form; Asian economic development; how Confucianism has followed Weber in terms of socialist modernization according to Chen Lai; Jiang Qing's political Confucianism as the conservative Confucian rejection of an overly "philosophical" New Confucianism; Confucianism and civil society; self-restriction in the social philosophy of Mou Zongsan and progressive Confucianism; recent approaches to Confucian morality; Tang Junyi's Confucian humanism; Mou Zongsan's reformed Confucian and philosophically reconstructed morality for the contemporary world; the place of historical memory and the modern media in China; the motives and implications of the Chinese media's promotion of Confucianism; and the possibility of democracy and New Confucianism. This is certainly a wide-ranging list of topics.

What strikes anyone interested in the developing history of New Confucianism (social, political, and philosophical in a broad sense) is how the movement has moved beyond its early origins in the reconstruction of classical and Neo-Confucian philosophy via its global comparative engagement with various strains of Western philosophy and the social sciences. Its discourse moves from Kant to Weber forward to modern political theories of democracy and the social and political sciences, including economics. Contemporary Confucians have even begun to address the question of ritual, which is such a vital part of the traditional Confucian way.[18] And yet another caveat is to be made here about the political (New) Confucian criticism of their more philosophically inclined colleagues. I doubt that even the political thinkers can escape the need to engage in philosophical reconstruction. The very nature of the Chinese philosophical lexicon demands it because of its continuity over time. For instance, Confucians from the days of Kongzi, Mengzi, and Xunzi to Zhu Xi and now the modern New Confucians continue to talk about *xing* 性, *xin* 心, *li* 理, *xiao* 孝 filial piety, and general forms of *li* 禮 ritual propriety or civility. Of course, just like their predecessors in the first and second epochs, contemporary Confucians of all political opinions infuse new layers of meaning to the inherited Confucian philosophical lexicography. A certain amount of cosmological and axiological speculation simply cannot be avoided by anyone working in Chinese philosophical traditions. Of course, there will still be intense debates and radically different social and intellectual programs will still be proposed as the twenty-first century progresses.

What is fascinating about these chapters, beyond the manifest excellence of all the individual contributions, is that they collectively provide a panorama of the development of contemporary Confucianism. They actually do so in two ways. The first, as the title says, is to go beyond a discussion of the intricacies of the various philosophical systems and discourse that has dominated what constituted the first phase of New Confucianism. However, we must remember that New Confucianism itself, like its Song predecessor in Zhu Xi's *daotong* (Transmission of the Way), is a postdated creation, especially since the 1980s and 1990s the New Confucian movement has tended to be identified with the group of scholars who wrote the famous January 1958 "A Manifesto for a Re-appraisal of Sinology and Reconstruction of Chinese Culture."[19] Because this was a group of philosophers, the New Confucianism they proposed became identified with "New Confucian" philosophy per se. For example, the great historian Qian Mu did not sign the Manifesto and hence many of Qian's students do not consider Qian a New Confucian, even though few modern Chinese scholars have done more to revivify the study of Confucianism than Qian. Again this modern pattern echoes or even mirrors Zhu Xi's pattern of selecting of certain philosophers to merit being the true restorers of the Confucian Way after its (strange) occlusion after the death of Mengzi. And just as in the Song Dynasty, many remarkable Song and now contemporary historians have looked somewhat askance at the hubris of their philosopher friends in trying to define the Confucian Way.

But if we step back from the iconic moment of the publication of the 1958 Manifesto, we see other features of the revival of Confucianism emerge in the twentieth century besides what is certainly a remarkable philosophical moment. One only has to think of the great Liang Shuming, once even considered the last Confucian.[20] Though a great scholar, Liang was equally famous for his attempts at rural reconstruction in Shandong in the 1930s. Liang's brilliant efforts at social reform were thwarted by the long war with Japan, the civil war that followed World War II, and finally the victory of the Chinese Communist Party (CCP) in 1949. However much individual communist leaders might have admired Liang, there was clearly no place for Confucian rural reconstruction in China after 1949; or at least until the dramatic transformation of China in the 1980s. But the point still stands that there was a social and even active political aspect to the modernizing Confucianism in the early and mid-twentieth century China. The various Nishan Forum conferences and summer seminars now actively promote these discussions of the social role of Confucianism. Contemporary Confucianism has many themes and topics, including proposed emerging institutional forms.

Mou Zongsan, probably the most famous philosopher of the second generation of the New Confucians, argued in many places that a revived and reformed New Confucianism (not a term he used) had to do many things, but three were critical for the potential success and influence of the Confucian Way in modern China, including a revised role for the equality of women along with a timely appropriation of ecumenical science and democracy. Of Mou's three revisionary projects, the role of science is the least contested, and in fact universally accepted and flourishing in modern China. Most agree that modern ecumenical science and Confucianism not only can coexist but also can provide positive and mutual support.

Of the remaining two items, the role of women was not included in the chapters, although clearly everyone would agree with Mou about the necessity for the full equality for women in modern China and within a revived Confucian Way. However, we now find a growing literature about a New Confucian vision for women. For instance, Li-Hsiang Lisa Rosenlee has written a very perceptive study of the relationship of Confucianism and women.[21] Her basic conclusion, after a careful review of the philosophical history of the Confucian Way, is that no essential or fundamental impediment exists for Confucianism to embrace a resolutely modern view of the role of women as completely equal and valued members of society. She ends her philosophical reflections with a short outline of what such a New Confucian feminist agenda will and should entail.

Because the main point where some contemporary Confucians distinguish themselves from other New Confucians concerns the theory and praxis of democracy, this was often a focal point for several of the chapters herein. Simply put, there is no consensus on the future relationship of Confucianism and Western-style democracy. While democracy is only one part of the larger positive reform agenda for many New Confucians, other public intellectuals equally contest it, in a purely Western form, on practical and theoretical grounds. The most influential critic of Western democracy being imported without modification in modern China is Jiang Qing, a person of great interest to number of the chapter authors of this book. The most pressing questions are: (1) whether Western-style democracy is suitable for China as a practical form of governance and social organization, and (2) whether it is compatible with a revived modern Confucianism.

Actually this is a continuation of a debate that began early in the rise of New Confucianism. The question of whether Confucianism is compatible with democracy has been raised often. In one sense it is an odd empirical question. For instance, South Korea, Japan, and now Taiwan have robust democratic governments and no one would deny that they have strong Confucian heritages. Koreans often argue that they were the most "Confucian" country in East Asia after the fall of the Ming dynasty. Of course, critics in all of these countries often argue that Confucianism does not always provide positive reinforcement for the new democratic institutions. They contend that one has to work around Confucianism in order to bring democracy to East Asian societies. Other scholars argue the opposite and believe, just as is the case for modern ecumenical science, there is nothing intrinsic to the main thrust of the Confucian Way that is ultimately inimical to democracy with Chinese characteristics. Modern China can love and provide a home for Beethoven and forms of democratic life equally well.

The debate about democracy and the role of merit in any political system are symptomatic of the debate about importing both Western philosophies and political, social and cultural forms of Western social life. Those who seek to get "beyond" New Confucianism both want to expand the conversation in all the ways listed above and want to find a distinctive Chinese lexicography to describe their reformed Confucian visions of a new society. The discussion of merit and the role of meritocracy is actually one of the more fascinating motifs that has emerged in most Confucian theorizing about politics representing a distinctively traditional and contemporary part of Confucian theory. Political Confucians point out that one of the debilitating effects, in many cases, of Western-style democracies is that they have few places for merit or the work of a meritocracy when compared to the often low intellectual standards of elected parliaments or congresses. The point being made here is that without listening to intellectual and scientific meritocracies, a democratic government will simply live in the moment without giving proper care to the impact of current policies for future generations.

The benefit of clear and carefully informed and merit-based public policies needs a way to be implemented and Western democracies find this hard to do effectively according to the politically minded contemporary Confucian thinkers. How do we balance meritocracy with democratic electoral politics? As a major example, the ecological crisis provides, according to this contemporary Confucian cohort, a perfect example of a situation that demands the merited input of many types of experts who embody various forms of scientific and social analytic excellence. These political New Confucians argue that the Confucian tradition has championed this kind of respect for merit and ought to do so in the future. This is surely a form of Confucian discourse emic to the tradition and one that needs to be considered in the emerging globalized world of the twenty-first century. Some Confucian meritocracy is sorely needed in a world beset with a massive ecological crisis.

Notes

    1. Although I have not encountered one, I suspect that somewhere a Marxist reading of the *Yijing* exists.

    2. Certainly the late nineteenth and twentieth centuries were difficult times for traditional Confucianism; one is tempted to say the most difficult but this would be a matter for much more sustained study and reflection on the long history of Confucianism.

    3. Of course, most scholars now locate the intellectual lineage of the Contemporary New Confucians with a group of public intellectuals in the early twentieth century. For instance, Xiong Shili (1885–1968), Liang Shuming (1893–1988), and Ma Yifu (1883–1967) are almost always perceived as critical figures, among others, in the emergence of what will become "New Confucianism."

    4. I have used the term *rudao* 儒道 or the Confucian Way as my way of discussing what is commonly called Confucianism. Of course we know that the term "Confucian" and "Confucianism" are Western neologisms and that there is no precise Chinese analog. Over the last century, however, the English usage has become familiar to Chinese scholars and has generally been accepted as a working translation of the rich Chinese tradition. I also like to use Confucian Way to point out, as do many of the chapters herein, that "Confucianism" is not just a philosophical tradition, but also a "way" of life that encompassed an immense range of Chinese cultural, social, artistic, economic, and political theories and practices. Whatever one makes of it, Confucianism was a way of life for many generations of Chinese people.

    5. See Joseph R. Levenson, *Confucian China and Its Modern Faith: A Trilogy*, 3 vols. (Berkeley: University of California Press, 1968).

    6. On-cho Ng, "The Ethics of Being and Non-Being: Confucian Contestations on Human Nature (*xing*) in Late Imperial China," in *Deconstruction and Ethical Thought in Asian Thought*, edited by Youru Wang (London: Routledge, 2012), 87–99.

    7. Hoyt Tillman also has a very fine short outline of the philosophical developments of these three major epochs. He reminds us that the interpretation of the nature of each epoch has been contested, such as the debate in Southern Song between Zhu Xi and Chen Liang (1143–1194). Zhu overwhelmed Chen, but Chen still had a fascinating take on the history of Confucian philosophy. See Hoyt Tillman, "Creativity and Evolving Confucian Traditions: Some Reflections on Earlier Centuries and Recent Developments," *Journal of Chinese Philosophy* 33, no. 2 (June 2006): 213–223.

    8. See Tillman, "Creativity and Evolving Confucian Traditions"; Peter K. Bol, *"This Culture of Ours": Intellectual Transition in T'ang and Sung China* (Stanford, CA: Stanford University Press, 1992); Peter K. Bol, *Neo-Confucianism in History* (Cambridge, MA: Harvard University Asia Center, 2008).

    9. This is sometimes call "Mind" Confucianism; in this case "mind" means philosophy as well as the various forms of ethical self-cultivation that were such

important aspects of the second, Neo-Confucian, epoch of the tradition. The second, of course, is the political aspect or agenda of Confucian public intellectuals.

10. Galia Patt-Shamir has a defense of the Neo-Confucian elaboration of classical Confucian thought. Following Mou Zongsan, she argues that however much Buddhist philosophers stimulated the Neo-Confucian masters and Daoist thought, the Confucians were still true to the classical Confucian vision of what she calls, to paraphrase, a "moral world informed by ethical terminology." See Galia Patt-Shamir, "Moral World, Ethical Terminology: The Moral Significance of Metaphysical Terms in Zhou Dunyi and Zhu Xi," *Journal of Chinese Philosophy* 31, no. 3 (Sept. 2004): 349–362.

11. Of course, Contemporary New Confucians in China need to be aware of just how far they can push a political program while under the watchful eye of the government. While intellectual history and systematic philosophy is one thing, political action is an entirely different reality in modern China it appears.

12. Richard Smith has some excellent chapters on the role of Confucian ritual in late imperial China and shows how much it suffused all levels of Chinese society. See Richard J. Smith, *Mapping China and Managing the World: Culture, Cartography and Cosmology in Late Imperial Times* (London: Routledge, 2013).

13. For a translation of Master Zhu's Family Rituals (*Zhuzi jiali*), see Chu Hsi's *Family Rituals: A Twelfth-Century Chinese Manual for the Performance of Cappings, Weddings, Funerals, and Ancestral Rites*, translated and edited by Patricia Buckley Ebrey (Princeton, NJ: Princeton University Press, 1991). Along with her exemplary translation of Chu's Family Rituals, Professor Ebrey published a companion volume on the role of ritual in Confucianism that helps explain why ritual was such a critical part of Zhu's *daoxue*. See Patricia Buckley Ebrey, *Confucianism and Family Rituals in Imperial China: A Social History of Writing about Rites* (Princeton, NJ: Princeton University Press, 1991).

14. Hoyt Tillman has an extended discussion of how Zhu's ritual prayers to Kongzi are connected to the concept of *daotong* 道統. As Tillman points out so well, Zhu's axiological cosmology was as much in service to the praxis of ritual action as it was to the formulation of a complex philosophical system. Ritual engagement with ghosts and spirits was as vital to Master Zhu as the contemplation of the *li-qi* 理氣 dyad. See Hoyt Tillman, "Zhu Xi's Prayers to the Spirit of Confucius and Claim to the Transmission of the Way," *Philosophy East and West* 54, no. 4 (Oct. 2004): 489–513.

15. See Jiang Qing, *A Confucian Constitutional Order: How China's Ancient Past Can Shape Its Political Future*, translated by Edmund Ryder and edited by Daniel A. Bell and Ruiping Fan (Princeton, NJ: Princeton University Press, 2013).

16. See Ruiping Fan, *Reconstructionist Confucianism: Rethinking Morality after the West*. (Dordrecht: Springer, 2010).

17. Of course, Richard Smith reminds us that the Qing dynasty published elaborate descriptions of ritual; beyond the most elite elements of officialdom, however, these did not have the kind of impact that Zhu's text would have had for Confucian families. See Smith, *Mapping China and Managing the World*.

18. Ing and Smith both have fascinating discussions of the role of ritual in Chinese history. Ing's is especially revealing because it looks at what Confucians believed happens when a ritual fails. New Confucians certainly are interested in how rituals fail in modern China in their almost complete absence, and even where there is ritual, as there clearly is, how it fails to meet the mark of authentic Confucian praxis. See Michael David Kaulana Ing, *The Dysfunction of Ritual in Early Confucianism* (Oxford, UK: Oxford University Press, 2012), and Smith, *Mapping China and Managing the World*.

19. Carsun Chang, *The Development of Neo-Confucian Thought*, 2 vols. (New York: Bookman Associates, 1957–1962), vol. 2, 455–483.

20. Guy S. Alitto, *The Last Confucian: Liang Shu-ming and the Chinese Dilemma of Modernity* (Berkeley: University of California Press, 1979).

21. Li-Hsiang Lisa Rosenlee, *Confucianism and Women* (Albany, NY: State University of New York Press, 2006).

Bibliography

Alitto, Guy S. *The Last Confucian: Liang Shu-ming and the Chinese Dilemma of Modernity.* Berkeley: University of California Press, 1979.

Andō Kumiko 安藤久美子. *Son Bun no gozoku kyōwa hihan to Tai Kitō no renpō kyōwasei ron* 孫文の「五族共和」批判と戴季陶の連邦共和制論 [Sun Yat-sen's critique of Republic of the Five Races and Dai Jitao's discussion of Republic of United States]. *Shisō* 思艸, no. 46 (2005): 13–41.

Angle, Stephen C. "The *Analects* and Moral Theory." In *The Dao Companion to the Analects*, edited by Amy Olberding, 225–257. Dordrecht: Springer, 2014.

———. *Contemporary Confucian Political Philosophy: Toward Progressive Confucianism.* Cambridge, UK: Polity Press, 2012.

———. *Sagehood: The Contemporary Significance of Neo-Confucian Philosophy.* New York: Oxford University Press, 2009.

Bai, Tongdong. *China: The Political Philosophy of the Middle Kingdom.* London: Zed Books, 2012.

———. "A Confucian Version of Hybrid Regime: How Does It Work, and Why Is It Superior? In *The East Asian Challenge to Democracy—Meritocracy in Comparative Perspective*, edited by Daniel A. Bell and Chenyang Li, 55–87. Cambridge, UK: Cambridge University Press, 2013.

———. "How to Rule without Taking Unnatural Actions (无为而治): A Comparative Study of the Political Philosophy of the *Laozi.*" *Philosophy East and West* 59, no. 4 (Oct. 2009): 481–502.

———. "A Mencian Version of Limited Democracy." *Res Publica* 14, no. 1 (2008): 19–34.

———. "Nietzsche, Mencius, and the Nature of Compassion as a Modern Virtue," manuscript.

———. "Preliminary Remarks: Han Fei Zi—First Modern Political Philosopher?" *Journal of Chinese Philosophy* 38, no. 1 (Mar. 2011): 4–13.

———. "The Price of Serving Meat—On Confucius's and Mencius's Views of Human and Animal Rights." *Asian Philosophy* 19, no. 1 (Mar. 2009): 85–99.

———. "Renguan gaoyu zhuguan: Mengzi de Zhengyi zhanzheng guan 仁权高于主权: 孟 的正义战争观 [Humanity (*Ren*) Overrides Sovereignty—On Mencius's View of a Just War]. *Journal of Social Sciences* 社会科学 1 (2013): 131–139.

———. Review of *Contemporary Confucian Political Philosophy* by Stephen C. Angle. *Notre Dame Philosophical Review* (Jan. 1, 2013). http://ndpr.nd.edu/news/36870 contemporary-confucian-political-philosophy/; accessed on Jan. 23, 2014.

———. "Xiandai guojia rentong yu guoji guanxi: Rujia de lilun jiqi dui minzu guojia yu ziyou zhuyi fanshi zhi youyue xing" 现代国家认同与国际关系: 儒家的理论及其对民 国家与自由主义范式之优越性 [National identity of modern states and modern international relations—A Confucian theory and its superiority to the nation-state and liberal models]. *Intellectual Forum* 知识分子论丛 11 (2013): 103–119.

Barmé, Geremie, and Ye Sang. "Commemorating Confucius in 1966–67—The Fate of the Confucius Temple, the Kong Mansion and Kong Cemetery" 孔庙、孔府、孔林. *China Heritage Quarterly*, no. 20 (2009), here taken from http://www.chinaheritagequarterly.org/scholarship.php?searchterm=020_confucius.inc&issue=020 (accessed Dec. 3, 2013).

Bauman, Zygmunt. *Modernity and the Holocaust*. Ithaca, NY: Cornell University Press, 2000 (1989).

Béja, Jean Philippe. "The Rise of National-Confucianism?" *China Perspectives* 2 (Nov.–Dec. 1995): 6–11.

Bell, Daniel A. *Beyond Liberal Democracy: Political Thinking for an East Asian Context*. Princeton, NJ: Princeton University Press, 2006.

———. *China's New Confucianism: Politics and Everyday Life in a Changing Society*, new ed. Princeton, NJ: Princeton University Press, 2010.

Bell, Daniel A., and Avner de-Shalit. *The Spirit of Cities: Why the Identity of a City Matters in a Global Age*, new ed. Princeton, NJ: Princeton University Press, 2013.

Bell, Daniel A., and Yingchuan Mo. "Harmony in the World 2013: The Ideal and the Reality." *Social Indicators Research* 118, no. 2 (Sept. 2014): 797–818.

Berger, Peter L., and Hsin-huang Michael Hsiao, eds. *In Search of an East Asian Development Model*. New Brunswick, NJ: Transaction Books, 1988.

Billeter, Térence. *L'Empereur jaune—Une tradition politique chinoise*. Paris: Les Indes savantes, 2007.

Billioud, Sébastien. "Carrying the Confucian Torch to the Masses: The Challenge of Structuring the Confucian Revival in the People's Republic of China." *Oriens Extremus* 49 (2010): 201–224.

———. *Thinking through Confucian Modernity: A Study of Mou Zongsan's Moral Metaphysics*. Leiden: Brill, 2011.

Billioud, Sébastien, and Joël Thoroval. "Confucianism, 'Cultural Tradition,' and Official Discourse in China at the Start of the Century." *Chinese Perspectives*, no. 3 (2007): 50–65.

———. "Jianhua: The Confucian Revival as an Educative Project." *Chinese Perspectives*, no. 7 (2007): 4–20.

———. *Le Sage et le people: Le renouveau confucéen en China*. Paris: CNRS Éditions, 2014.

Bo Ming 柏明 and Li Yingke 李穎科. *Huangdi yu Huangdi ling* 黃帝与黃帝陵 [Yellow Emperor and his tomb]. Xi'an: Xibei daxue chubanshe, 1990.
Bol, Peter K. *Neo-Confucianism in History*. Cambridge, MA: Harvard University Asia Center, 2008.
———. *"This Culture of Ours": Intellectual Transition in T'ang and Sung China*. Stanford, CA: Stanford University Press, 1992.
Bresciani, Umberto. *Reinventing Confucianism: The New Confucian Movement*. Taipei: Ricci Institute for Chinese Studies, 2001.
Brook, Timothy. "Profit and Righteousness in Chinese Economic Culture." In *Culture and Economy: The Shaping of Capitalism in Eastern Asia*, edited by Timothy Brook and Hy V. Luong, 27–44. Ann Arbor: University of Michigan Press, 1997.
Brown, Elizabeth A. R. "The Tyranny of a Construct: Feudalism and Historians of Medieval Europe." *American Historical Review* 79, no. 4 (1974): 1063–1088.
Bunnin, Nicholas. "God's Knowledge and Ours: Kant and Mou Zongsan on Intellectual Intuition." *Journal of Chinese Philosophy* 35, no. 4 (2008): 613–624.
Callahan, William A. "Chinese Visions of World Order: Post-Hegemonic or a New Hegemony?" *International Studies Review* 10 (2008): 749–761.
Carlson, Allen. "Moving beyond Sovereignty? A Brief Consideration of Recent Changes in China's Approach to International Order and the Emergence of the *Tianxia* Concept." *Journal of Contemporary China* 20, no. 68 (2011): 89–102.
———. "Reimagining the Frontier: Patterns of Sinicization and the Emergence of New Thinking about China's Territorial Periphery." Paper presented at the Civilizations and Sinicization Workshop, Beijing University, Beijing, Mar. 25–26, 2011.
Chakrabarty, Dipesh. "Towards a Discourse on Nationalism." *Economic and Political Weekly* 22, no. 28 (July 11, 1987): 1137–1138.
Chan, Joseph. "Democracy and Meritocracy: Toward a Confucian Perspective." *Journal of Chinese Philosophy* 34, no. 2 (June 2007): 179–193.
———. "Territorial Boundaries and Confucianism." In *Boundaries, Ownership, and Autonomy*, edited by David Miller and Sohail H. Hashmi, 89–111. Princeton, NJ: Princeton University Press, 2001.
Chan, N. Serina. *The Thought of Mou Zongsan*. Leiden: Brill, 2011.
Chang, Carsun (Zhang Junmai). "A Manifesto for a Re-appraisal of Sinology and Reconstruction of Chinese Culture." In *The Development of Neo-Confucian Thought*, edited by Carsun Chang, 455–483. New York: Bookman Associates, 1962.
Chang, Hao. "New Confucianism and the Intellectual Crisis of Contemporary China." In *The Limits of Change: Essays on Conservative Alternatives in Republican China*, edited by Charlotte Furth, 276–302. Cambridge, MA: Harvard University Press, 1976.
Chen Guanzhong 陳冠中. "Zhongguo tianchaozhuyi yu xianggang" 中國天朝主義與香港 [China's tributary system and Hong Kong]. *Xianggang: Dushi*

xiangxiang yu wenhua jiyi guoji xueshu yantaohui 香港: 都市想像與文化記憶國際學術研討會 [Hong Kong: Imagining the city and cultural memory international Academic Symposium], Dec. 17, 2011.

Chen Lai 陈来. *Chuantong yu xiandai: Renwen zhuyi de shijie* 传统与现代: 人文主义的视 [Tradition and modernity: The scope of humanism]. Beijing: Beijing daxue chubanshe, 2006.

———. "Duoyuan wenhua jiegouzhong de ruxue ji qi dingwei" 多元文化结构中的儒学及其定位 [Ruxue and its place in multicultural structures]. *Zhongguo luntan* 中国论坛 [China forum] 27, no. 1 (1988): 21–23.

———. "Ershi shiji wenhua yundong de jijin zhuyi" 二十世纪文化运动的激进主义 [Radicalism in twentieth-century cultural movements]. In *Zhishi fenzi lichang: Jijin yu baoshou zhijian de dongdang* 知识分子立场: 激进与保守之间的动荡 [Intellectual positions: The turbulence between radicalism and conservatism], edited by Li Shitao 李世涛, 293–308. Changchun: Shidai wenyi chubanshe, 1999.

———. "Ershi shiji Zhongguo wenhua zhong de ruxue kunjing" 二十世纪中国文化中的儒学困境 [The predicament of Confucianism in twentieth-century Chinese culture]. *Zhejiang shehui kexue* 浙江社会科学 [Zhejiang Social Sciences] 3 (May 1988): 26–32.

———. "Guoxue re' yu chuantong wenhua yanjiu de wenti" 国学热'与传统文化研究的问题 [The "national studies craze" and the problem of research on traditional culture]. *Kongzi Yanjiu* 孔子研究 [Confucius research] no. 2 (1995): 4–6.

———. "Huajie 'chuantong' yu 'xiandai' de jinzhang: 'Wusi' wenhua sichao de fansi" 化解 '传统' 与 '现代' 的紧张: '五四' 文化思潮的反思 [Dissolving the tension between tradition and modernity: Reflections on the cultural trend of "May Fourth"]. In Chen Lai, *Chen Lai zixuanji* 陈来自选集 [Self-selected works of Chen Lai], 373–398. Guangdong: Guangdong shifan daxue chubanshe, 1997.

———. "Jiushi niandai bulü weijian de 'guoxue yanjiu' 九十年代步履维艰的 '国学研究' [National studies research of the 1990s: Walking with difficulty]. *Dongfang* 东方 [Orient] 2 (1995): 24–28.

———. "Shisu rujia lunli yu houfa xiandaihua 世俗儒家伦理与后发现代化" [Vulgar Confucianism and the modernization of late developing countries]. *Ershiyi shiji* 二十一世纪 [Twenty-first century] 22 (Apr. 1994): 112–120.

———. "Zhenxia qiyuan 贞下起元" [A propitious new start]. *Ershiyi shiji* 二十一世纪 [Twenty-first century] 10 (Apr. 1992): 10–11.

Chen Yunqian 陈蕴茜. *Chongbai yu jiyi: Sun Zhongshan fuhao de Jiangou yu Chuanbo* 崇拜 与记忆: 孙中山符号的建构与传播 [Worship and memory: The construction and propagation of the political symbol of Sun Zhongshan]. Nanjing: Nanjing daxue chubanshe, 2009.

Chen Zehuan. "Individuals, Nation States, and the World: A Study of Liang Qichao's Views on Human Rights." Paper presented at CASS, Beijing, 2010.

Chen Zhaoying 陳昭瑛. "Xu Fuguan yu ziyou zhuyi de duihua" 徐復觀與自由主義的對話 [The dialogue between Xu Fuguang and the liberals]. *Sixiang* [Thought] 20 (Nov. 2012): 175.

Cheng Chung-yi鄭宗義. "Tang Junyi lun renwen xueshu" 唐君毅論人文學術 [Tang Junyi on the Humanities]. In *Xianggang Zhongwen Daxue de dangdai ruzhe. Qian Mu, Tang Junyi, Mou Zongsan, Xu Fuguan* 香港中文大學的當代儒者。錢穆, 唐君毅牟宗三, 徐復觀 [Contemporary Confucians of the Chinese University of Hong Kong. Qian Mu, Tang Junyi, Mou Zongsan, Xu Fuguan], edited by Cheng Chung-yi, 345–366. Hong Kong: Chinese University Press, 2006.

Chow, Kai-wing. *The Rise of Confucian Ritualism in Late Imperial China: Ethics, Classics and Lineage Discourse*. Stanford, CA: Stanford University Press, 1994.

Chow, Tse-tsung. The May Fourth Movement: Intellectual Revolution in Modern China. Cambridge, MA: Harvard University Press, 1960.

Ciaudo, Joseph. "Questioning Sinodicy: An Inquiry into Zhang Junmai's Cultural Discourse (1919–1937)." PhD diss., College de France, 2016.

Clower, Jason. *The Unlikely Buddhologist: Tiantai Buddhism in Mou Zongsan's New Confucianism*. Leiden: Brill, 2010.

Davis, Gloria, ed. *Voicing Concerns: Contemporary Chinese Critical Inquiry*. Lanham, MD: Rowman and Littlefield, 2001.

de Bary, William Theodore. *The Message of the Mind in Neo-Confucianism*. New York: Columbia University Press, 1989.

———. "The New Confucianism in Beijing." *American Scholar* (Spring 1995): 175–189.

DeBlasi, Anthony. "Selling Confucius: The Negotiated Return of Tradition in Post-Socialist China." In *The Sage Returns: Confucian Revival in Contemporary China*, edited by Kenneth J. Hammond and Jeffrey L. Richey, 67–92. Albany, NY: State University of New York Press, 2015.

Dikotter, Frank. *The Discourse of Race in Modern China*. Hong Kong: Hurst, 1992.

Dirlik, Arif. "Confucius in the Borderlands: Global Capitalism and the Reinvention of Confucianism." *Boundary 2* 22, no. 3 (Fall 1995): 229–273.

Doyle, Michael. "Kant, Liberal Legacies and Foreign Affairs, Part I." *Philosophy and Public Affairs* 12, no. 3 (Summer 1983): 205–235.

———. "Kant, Liberal Legacies and Foreign Affairs, Part II." *Philosophy and Public Affairs* 12, no. 4 (Autumn 1983): 323–353.

Durkheim, Emile. *The Elementary Forms of the Religious Life*. New York: Free Press, 1965.

Ebrey, Patricia Buckley, trans. and ed. *Chu Hsi's Family Rituals: A Twelfth-Century Chinese Manual for the Performance of Cappings, Weddings, Funerals, and Ancestral Rites*. Princeton, NJ: Princeton University Press, 1991.

———. *Confucianism and Family Rituals in Imperial China: A Social History of Writing about Rites*. Princeton, NJ: Princeton University Press, 1991.

———. "Surnames and Han Chinese Identity." In *Negotiating Ethnicities in China and Taiwan*, edited by Melissa J. Brown, 11–36. Berkeley, CA: Institute of East Asian Studies, 1996.

Elstein, David. "Mou Zongsan's New Confucian Democracy." *Contemporary Political Theory* 11 (Aug. 2011): 192–210.

Esherick, Joseph W., Paul G. Pickowicz, and Andrew G. Walder, eds. *The Chinese Cultural Revolution as History*. Stanford, CA: Stanford University Press, 2006.

Fan, Ruiping. *Reconstructionist Confucianism: Rethinking Morality after the West*. Dordrecht: Springer, 2010.

Fan Wenlan 范文澜. *Zhongguo jindai shi* 中国近代史 [History of modern China]. Beijing: Renmin chubanshe, 1955.

Fang Chaohui 方朝晖. *Xuetong de mishi yu zaizao: Rujia yu dangdai Zhongguo xuetong yanjiu* 学统的迷失于再造：儒家与当代中国学统研究 [The loss and reconstruction of intellectual paradigms: Studies of Confucianism and contemporary intellectual paradigms]. Xi'an: Shaanxi shifan daxue, 2010.

Fang Keli 方克立. "Guanyu xiandai xin rujia yanjiu de jige wenti" 关于现代新儒家研究的几个问题 [On some issues in New Confucianism research]. In *Xiandai xin ruxue yanjiu lunji* 现代新儒学研究论集 [Collected essays on New Confucianism studies], edited by Fang Keli 方克立 and Li Jinquan 李锦全, vol. 1, 1–13. Beijing: Zhongguo shehui kexue chubanshe, 1989.

———. "Lüelun jiushi niandai de wenhua baoshou zhuyi sichao" 略论九十年代的文化保主义思潮 [A brief discussion of the cultural conservative trend of the 1990s]. In *Zou shenme lu: Yu Zhongguo jinxiandai lishi shang de ruogan zhongda shifei wenti* 走什么路：与中国近现代历史上的若干重大是非问题 [Which way to go: Some major disputes on modern Chinese history], edited by Sha Jiansun 沙健孙 and Gong Shuduo 龚书铎, 145–161. Jinan: Shandong renmin chubanshe, 1997.

———. *Xiandai xinrujia yu Zhongguo xiandai hua* 现代新儒家与中国现代化 [Modern New Confucianism and China's modernization]. Tianjin: Tianjin renmin chubanshe, 1997.

Fang Keli 方克立, and Li Jinquan 李錦全, eds. *Xiandai xinrujia xuean* 现代新儒家學案 [Intellectual biographies of modern New Confucians]. Beijing: Zhongguo shehui kexue chubanshe, 1995.

Fang Keli 方克立, and Zheng Jiadong 鄭家棟, eds. *Xiandai xinrujia renwu yu zhuzuo* 现代新儒家人物與著作 [The modern New Confucians and their writings]. Tianjin: Nankai daxue chubanshe, 1995.

Feuchtwang, Stephan. *Popular Religion in China*. Surrey, UK: Curzon Press, 2001.

Freedman, Maurice. *Chinese Lineage and Society: Fukien and Kwangtung*. London: Athlone, 1966.

Fröhlich, Thomas. "'Confucian Democracy' and Its Confucian Critics: Mou Zongsan and Tang Junyi on the Limits of Confucianism." *Oriens Extremus* 49 (2010): 167–200.

———. "Confucian Philosophy Reconsidered: Recovering Tang Junyi's Modern Confucianism as Civil Theology" (forthcoming).

———. "The Exilic Prism of Modernity: New Perspectives on the Post-War Philosophy of Tang Junyi." *Oriens Extremus* 52 (2013): 37–82.

———. "Regulating, Governing, and Pacifying the Modern World: Optimism Regarding the Civilizational Progress in Chinese Interpretations of the *Great Learning* in the Twentieth Century" (forthcoming).

———. "Tang Junyi, Max Weber und die Mächte des Dämonischen. Zum Politikverständnis eines modernen Konfuzianers." *Asiatische Studien / Etudes Asiatiques* 57, no. 4 (2003): 813–848.

Gan Chunsong 干春松. *Rujia gailun* 儒学概论 [An introduction to Confucian studies]. Beijing: Zhongguo renmin daxue chubanshe, 2009.

———. "Wangzhi wuwai yu yixia zhi fang: Gongyang san shi shuo yu yixia guannian de chongtu yu xietiao" 王者无外 与 夷夏之防: 公羊三世说与夷夏观念的冲突与协 调 [The kingly way without outsiders and protection against barbarians: The conflict and compromise between the Gongyang shishuo and the concept of barbarians]. Paper presented at People's University of China, Beijing, Oct. 24, 2010.

Gan Yang 甘陽. "Ruxue yu xiandai—jian lun ruxue yu dangdai Zhongguo" 儒學與現代—論儒學與當代中國 [Confucian learning and the modern age: A study of Confucian learning and contemporary China]. In *Ruxue fazhan de hongguan toushi. Xinjiapo 1988 nian ruxue qunyinghui ji shi* 儒學發展的宏觀透視。新加坡 1988 儒 學群英會紀實 [A Macro study of the development of Confucian learning: A chronicle of the 1998 Singapore conference], edited by Tu Wei-ming 杜維明, 595–623. Taibei: Zhengzhong shuju, 1997.

Gan Yang 甘陽, ed. *Bashi niandai wenhua yishi* 八十年代文化意识 [The cultural consciousness of the 1980s]. Shanghai: Shijie chuban jituan, 2006.

Ge Zhaozhao 葛兆兆. "Songdai [Zhongguo]—Yishi de tuxian—Guanyu jin shi minzuzhuyi sixiang de yi ge yuanyuan" 宋代《中国》意识的凸显—关于近世民族主义思想的一个远源 [The prominence of "China" consciousness in the Song Dynasty: A distant source of nationalist thought in modern times], *Wen shi zhe* 文史哲 [Journal of literature, history and philosophy], no. 1 (2004): 5–12.

Gill, Bates, and Yanzhong Huang. "Sources and Limits of China's Soft Power." *Survival* (Summer 2006): 17–36.

Glanville, Luke. "Retaining the Mandate of Heaven: Sovereign Accountability in Ancient China." *Millennium* 39, no. 2 (2010): 323–343.

Gregor, A. James. *Marxism, Fascism, and Totalitarianism: Chapters in the Intellectual History of Radicalism*. Stanford, CA: Stanford University Press, 2009.

Guo, Yingjie. *Cultural Nationalism in Contemporary China: The Search for National Identity under Reform*. London: Routledge Curzon, 2004.

Guomin riri bao 國民日日報 [Citizens' daily]. Edited by Zhang Shizhao 章士釗, Zhang Ji 張繼, and Su Manshu 蘇曼殊, 4 issues, Shanghai, 1913.

Hammond, Kenneth J. "The Return of the Repressed: The New Left and "Left" Confucianism in Contemporary China." In *The Sage Returns: Confucian Revival in Contemporary China*, edited by Kenneth J. Hammond and

Jeffrey L. Richey, 93–111. Albany, NY: State University of New York Press, 2015.

Hammond, Kenneth J., and Jeffrey L. Richey. "The Death and Resurrection of Confucianism." In *The Sage Returns: Confucian Revival in Contemporary China*, edited by Kenneth J. Hammond and Jeffrey L. Richey, 1–9. Albany, NY: State University of New York Press, 2015.

Hegel, G[eorg] W[ilhelm] F[riedrich]. *The Philosophy of History*. With prefaces by Charles Hegel and the translator, J. Sibree. Kitchener, ONT: Batoche Books, 2001.

———. *Philosophy of Right*. Translated by S. W. Dyde. Kitchener, ONT: Batoche Books, 2001.

Harrison, Henrietta. *Inventing the Nation—China*. London: Arnold, 2001.

Hobsbawm, Eric, and Terence Ranger, eds. *The Invention of Tradition*. Cambridge, UK: Cambridge University Press, 1983.

Hon, Tze-ki. "National Essence, National Learning, and Culture: Historical Writings *Guocui xuebao*, *Xueheng*, and *Guoxue jikan*." *Historiography East and West* 1, no. 2 (2003): 242–295.

———. *Revolution as Restoration:* Guocui xuebao *and China's Path to Modernity, 1905–1911*. Leiden: Brill, 2013.

Hsiao, Kung-chuan. *A Modern China and a New World: K'ang Yu-Wei, Reformer and Utopian, 1858–1927*. Seattle: University of Washington Press, 1975.

Hu Zushun 胡祖舜. *Wuchang kaiguo shilu* 武昌開國實錄 [Annals of the starting of a nation in Wuchang]. Hankou: Jiaotonglu jianguo shuju, 1948.

Huang Zhaoqiang 黃兆強. *Xueshu yu jingshi—Tang Junyi de lishi zhexue ji qi zhongji guanhuai* 學術與經世—唐君毅的歷史哲學及其終極關懷 [Learning and statecraft: The philosophy of history and the ultimate concerns of Tang Junyi]. Taipei: Xuesheng shuju, 2010.

Huangdihun 黃帝魂 [The spirit of the Yellow Emperor]. Edited by Huang Zao 黃藻. N.p.: N.p., 1903.

Huangling nianjian 黃陵年鉴 [Annals of the tomb of the Yellow Emperor]. Edited by Huanglingxian renmin zhengfu 黃陵县人民政府 and Huanglingxian xianzhiban 黃 县县志办. Xi'an: Xi'an chubanshe, 2002.

Huangling xianzhi 黃陵縣志 [Chronicle of Huangling County]. Edited by Huanglingxian difangzhi bianzuan weiyuanhui 黃陵縣地方志編纂委員會, and appeared in the series *Shaanxi difangzhi congshu* 陝西地方志叢書. Xi'an: Xi'an ditu chubanshe, 1995.

Huangling zhi 黃陵志 [Chronicle of the tomb of the Yellow Emperor], originally published in 1944. In *Huangling zhi Yanling zhi* 黃陵志—炎陵志, edited by Li Jinxi 黎錦熙, and appeared in the series *Zhongguo cimu zhi congkan 16* 中國祠墓志叢刊 16. Yangzhou: Guanglin shushe, 2004.

Hung, Chang-tai. "The Cult of the Red Martyr: Politics of Commemoration in China." *Journal of Contemporary History* 43, no. 2 (2008): 279–304.

———. *Mao's New World: Political Culture in the Early People's Republic*. Ithaca, NY: Cornell University Press, 2011.

Hutchinson, John. *The Dynamics of Cultural Nationalism: The Gaelic Revival and the Creation of the Irish Nation State*. London: Allen and Unwin, 1987.

Ing, Michael David Kaulana. *The Dysfunction of Ritual in Early Confucianism*. Oxford, UK: Oxford University Press, 2012.

Jensen, Lionel M. "Culture Industry, Power, and the Spectacle of China's 'Confucius Institutes.'" In *China in and beyond the Headlines*, edited by Timothy B. Weston and Lionel M. Jensen, 271–299. Lanham, MD: Rowman & Littlefield, 2012.

Jiang, Qing 蒋庆. *A Confucian Constitutional Order: How China's Past Can Shape Its Political Future*, translated by Edmund Ryden, edited by Daniel A. Bell and Fan Ruiping. Princeton, NJ: Princeton University Press, 2013.

———. *Shenming xinyang yu wangdao zhengzhi: Rujia wenhua de xiandai jiazhi* 生命信仰与王道政治:儒家文化的现代价值 [A faith in life and the Kingly Way of politics: The modern value of Confucian culture]. Taipei: Yang Zheng Tang, 2004.

———. *Zailun zhengzhi rujia* 再论政治儒学 [Political Confucianism revisited]. Shanghai: East China Normal University Press, 2011.

———. *Zhengzhi rujia: Daidai ruxue de zhuanxiang tezhe ji fazhen* 政治儒学: 代儒学的转向、特质与发展 [Political Confucianism: The changing direction, particularities, and development of Contemporary Confucianism]. Beijing: Sanlian shudian, 2003.

Jiang Shigong 强世功. *Zhongguo Xianggang: Wenhua yu zhengzhi de shiye* 中國香港: 文化 政治的視野 [China's Hong Kong: The establishment of culture and institutions]. Hong Kong: Oxford University Press, 2008.

Jing Haifeng 景海峰. *Xinruxue yu ershishiji Zhongguo sixiang* 新儒学与二十世纪中国思想 [Contemporary New Confucianism and twentieth-century Chinese thought]. Zhengzhou: Zhongzhou guji chubanshe, 2005.

———. "Zongjiaohua de xinrujia: Lüelun Tang Junyi chongjian zhongguo renwen jingshen de quxiang" 宗教化的新儒家: 略論唐君毅重建中國人文精神的取向 [Making New Confucianism a religion: A study of Tang Junyi's plan for rebuilding the Chinese humanistic spirit]. In *Xiandai xinrujia yanjiu lunwenji* 現代新儒學研究論集 [Collected essays on Contemporary New Confucianism], edited by Fang Keli 方克立 and Li Jinquan 李錦全, vol. 2, 226–243. Beijing: Zhongguo shehui kexue chubanshe, 1991.

Johnston, Alasdair Ian. *Cultural Realism: Strategic Culture and Grand Strategy in Chinese History*. Princeton, NJ: Princeton University Press, 1995.

Joseph, William, Christine P. W. Wong, and David Zweig, eds. *New Perspectives on the Cultural Revolution*. Cambridge, MA: Council on East Asian Studies, 1991.

Kahn, Herman. *World Economic Development*. Boulder, CO: Westview, 1979.

Kang Youwei 康有为. *Kang Youwei zhenglun ji* 康有为政论集 [A collection of Kang Youwei's essays on politics], 2 vols. Beijing: Zhonghua shuju, 1981.

Karl, Rebecca. "Foreword." In *The End of the Revolution: China and the Limits of Modernity*, edited by Wang Hui, vii–x. London: Verso, 2009.

King, Ambrose Y. C. "Confucianism, Modernity, and Asian Democracy." In *Justice and Democracy: Cross-Cultural Perspectives*, edited by Ron Bontekoe and Marietta Stepaniants, 174–177. Honolulu: University of Hawaii Press, 1997.

Knöbl, Wolfgang. *Spielräume der Modernisierung. Das Ende der Eindeutigkeit*. Weilerswist: Velbrück Wissenschaft, 2001.

Kongmiao liyue kao 孔廟禮樂考, edited by Qu Jiusi 瞿九思, series Zhongguo cimu zhi congkan 25 中國祠墓志叢刊 25. Yangzhou: Guangling shushe, 2004 (1609).

Koselleck, Reinhart. *Futures Past: On the Semantics of Historical Time*. Translated and with an Introduction by Keith Tribe. New York: Columbia University Press, 2004 (1985).

Kuo, Ya-pei. "In One Body with the People: Worship of Confucius in the Xinzheng Reforms, 1902–1911." *Modern China* 35, no. 2 (2009): 123–154.

Lai, Delin. "Searching for a Modern Chinese Monument: The Design of the Sun Yat-sen Mausoleum in Nanjing." *Journal of the Society of Architectural Historians* 64, no. 1 (2005): 22–55.

Laitinen, Kauko. *Chinese Nationalism in the late Qing Dynasty: Zhang Binglin as an Anti-Mandchu Propagandist*. London: Curzon Press, 1990.

Lau, D. C., trans. *Confucius: The Analects* [paperback bilingual edition]. Hong Kong: Chinese University Press, 2002.

——. *Mencius*, rev. and bilingual ed. Hong Kong: Chinese University Press, 2003.

Ledderose, Lothar. "Die Gedächtnishalle für Mao Zedong: Ein Beispiel für Gedächtnisarchitektur" [The Memorial Hall for Mao Zedong: An example of memorial architecture]. In *Kultur und Gedächtnis* [Culture and memory], edited by Jan Assmann and Tonio Hölscher, 321–345. Frankfurt: Suhrkamp Verlag, 1988.

Lee, Joseph Tse Hei, Ronald K. Frank, Renqiu Yu, and Bing Xu. "From Philosopher to Cultural Icon: Reflections on Hu Mei's 'Confucius.'" *Global Asia Journal*, paper 11 (2010). Retrieved from http://digitalcommons.pace.edu/global_asia_journal/11.

Lee, Ming-huei 李明輝. "Culture et démocratie: Réflexions à partir de la polémique entre libéraux taiwanais et Néo-Confucéens Contemporains." *Extrême-Orient, Extrême-Occident* 31 (2009): 33–62.

——. *Dangdai ruxue zhi ziwo zhuanhua* 當代儒學之自我轉化 [The self-transformation of Contemporary Confucianism]. Taipei: Zhongyang yanjiuyuan Zhongguo wenzhe yanjiusuo, 1994.

——. *Der Konfuzianismus im modernen China*. Leipzig: Leipziger Universitätsverlag, 2001.

——. *Konfuzianischer Humanismus: Transkulturelle Kontexte*. Bielefeld: Transcript, 2013.

——. *Ruxue yu xiandai yishi* 儒學與現代意識 [Confucianism and modern consciousness]. Taipei: Wenjin chubanshe, 1991.

——. "Wang Yangming's Philosophy and Modern Theories of Democracy: A Reconstructive Interpretation." *Dao: A Journal of Comparative Philosophy* 7 no. 3 (2008): 283–294.

Lee, Ming-huei 李明輝, ed. *Rujia sixiang zai xiandai Dongya: Zonglun pian* 儒家思想在現代東亞: 總論 篇 [Confucianism in modern East Asia: A general perspective]. Taipei: Zhongyang yanjiuyuan Zhongguo wenzhe yanjiusuo, 1998.

Leese, Daniel. "A Place Where Great Men Rest? The Chairman Mao Memorial Hall." In *Places of Memory in Modern China: History, Politics, Identity*, edited by Marc Andre Matten, 91–129. Leiden: Brill, 2012.

Levenson, Joseph R. *Confucian China and Its Modern Fate: A Trilogy*. 3 vols. Berkeley: University of California Press, 1968.

Li Chenyang. "The Confucian Ideal of Harmony." *Philosophy East and West* 56, no. 4 (Oct. 2006): 583–603.

———. "Where Does Confucian Virtuous Leadership Stand?" *Philosophy East and West* 59, no. 4 (2009): 531–536.

Li, Fang 李方. "*Shilun Tangchao de 'Zhongguo' yu 'Tianxia'* 试论唐朝的 '中国' 与 '天下' [A study of "China" and "*Tianxia*" in Tang dynasty]. *Zhongguo bianjiang shidi yanjiu* 中国边疆史地研究 [Research on the history and geography of China's borderlands] 17, no. 2 (June 2007): 10–20.

Li, Feng. *Bureaucracy and the State in Early China*. Cambridge, UK: Cambridge University Press, 2008.

———. *Landscape and Power in Early China*. Cambridge, UK: Cambridge University Press, 2005.

Li Gongzhong 李恭忠. *Zhongshanling: Yi ge xiandai zhengzhi fuhao de dansheng* 中山陵: 一个现代政治符号的诞生 [The Sun Yat-sen Mausoleum: The making of a political symbol in modern China]. Beijing: Shehui kexue wenxian chubanshe, 2009.

Li Ruihuan 李瑞环. *Xue zhexue, yong zhexue* 学哲学, 用哲学 [Leaning philosophy and applying philosophy]. Beijing: Zhongguo renmin daxue chubanshe, 2005.

Li Yangfan 李扬帆. "*Tianxia*" guannian 《天下》观念" [On the concept of "*Tianxia*"] *Guoji zhengzhi yanjiu* 国际政治研究 [Research in international politics] 1 (2002).

Li Zehou 李泽厚. *Zhongguo jindai sixiang shi* 中国近代思想史 [History of modern Chinese thought]. Beijing: Renmin chubanshe, 1979.

———. *Zhongguo xiandai sixiang shilun* 中国现代思想史论 [Studies of contemporary Chinese thought]. Beijing: Dongfang chubanshe, 1987.

———. *Zou wo ziji de lu* 走我自己的路 [Going my own way]. Beijing: Sanlian, 1986.

Li Zehou 李泽厚 and Liu Zaifu. *Guobie geming: Huiwang ershi shiji Zhongguo* 告别革命: 回望二 十世紀中國 [Farewell to revolution: Looking back on twentieth-century China]. Hong Kong: Tiandi tushu youxian gongsi, 1995.

Liang Qichao 梁啟超. *Liang Qichao quanji* 梁启超全集 [The collected work of Liang Qichao]. Beijing: Beijing chubanshe, 1999.

Liang Tao 梁涛 and Gu Jianing 顾家宁, eds. *Guoxue wenti zhengming ji (1990–2010)* 国学 问题争鸣集 (1990–2010) [A collection of polemical writings on national learning, 1990–2010]. Guilin: Guangxi shifan daxue chubanshe, 1990.

Lin, An-wu 林安悟. "Cong waiwang dao neisheng: Hou xin ruxue de xin sikao" 從「外王」到「內聖」: 後新儒學的新思考 [From the outer king to the inner sage: The new thought of post–New Confucianism]. *Ehu* [Legein monthly] 鵝湖 30, no. 2 (Aug. 2004): 16–25.

———. "Cong 'yixin kongshen' dao—'shenxin yiru': Yi Wang Fuzhi zhexue wei hexin jianji yu Cheng-Zhu, Lu-Wang de taolun" 從「以心控身」到「身心一如」: 以王夫之哲學為核心兼及於程朱、陸王的討論 [From "controlling the body by the mind" to "the combination of body and mind": A study of Wang Fuzhi's philosophy and the debate between the Cheng-Zhu and Lu-Wang schools], *Guowen xuebao* 國文學報 30 (June 2001): 77–96.

———. *Dao de cuozhi: Zhongguo zhengzhi chuantong de genben kunjie* 道的錯置: 中國政治傳統的根本困結 [Misplaced Dao: The essential problem of Chinese political thought]. Taipei: Taiwan xuesheng shuju, 2003.

———. "Hou xinruxue de shehui zhexue: Qiyue, zeren yu 'yiti zhiren'—maixiang yi shehui zhengyilun wei hexin de ruxue sikao" 後新儒學的社會哲學: 契約、責任與「一體之仁」—邁向以社會正義論為核心的儒學思考 [The social philosophy of post–New Confucianism: Contracts, duties and the one body of humanity—Confucian thought on social justice], *Si yu yan* 思與言 [Thought and Utterance] 39, no. 4 (2001): 57–82.

———. *Mou Zongsan qianhou: Dangdai xin rujia zhexue sixiang shilun* 牟宗三前後: 當代新儒家哲學思想史論 [Before and after Mou Zongsan: A historical account of the philosophical thoughts of Contemporary New Confucians]. Taipei: Taiwan xuesheng shuju, 2011.

———. *Rujia lunli yu shehui zhengyi* 儒家倫理與社會正義 [Confucian ethics and social justice]. Beijing: Zhongguo yanshi chubanshi, 2005.

———. *Rujia yu Zhongguo chuantong shehui zhi zhexue xingcha* 儒學與中國傳統社會之學省察 [A philosophical critique of Confucianism and Chinese traditional society]. Taipei: Youshi wenhua shiye, 1996.

———. *Rujia zhuanxiang: Cong xin ruxue dao hou xinruxue de guodu* 儒學轉向: 從「新儒學」到「後新儒學」的過渡 [A change of direction in Confucianism: The transition from New Confucianism to post–New Confucianism]. Taipei: Taiwan xuesheng shuju, 2006.

———. *Ruxue geminglun: hou xin rujia zhexue de wenti xiangdu* 儒學革命論: 後新儒家哲學的問題向度 [Revolution in Confucianism: On the philosophy of post–New Confucianism]. Taipei: Taiwan xuesheng shuju, 1998.

———. *Wang Chuanshan renxingshi zhexue zhi yanjiu* 王船山人性史哲學之研究 [A study of Wang Chuanshan's philosophy on humanistic history]. Taipei: Dongda tushu gongsi, 1987.

———. "Xin rujia, hou xinrujia, xiandai, yu houxiandai: Zuijin shinianlai de xingcha yu sikao zhi yiban" 「新儒學」、「後新儒學」、「現代」與「後現代」——最近十年來的省察與思考之一斑 ["New Confucianism," "Post–New Confucianism," "modernity," and "postmodernity": My views and thoughts in the last ten years], *Ehu* [Legein monthly] 鵝湖 30, no. 12 (June 2005): 8–21.

———. "Yingjie hou Mou Zongsan shidai de lailin: Mou Zongsan quanji chuban ganji" 迎接「後牟宗三時代」的來臨——《牟宗三先生全集》出版感紀 [Welcome the arrival of the post–Mou Zongsan era: Thoughts on *The Complete Works of Mou Zongsan*], *Ehu* [Legein monthly] 鵝湖 28, no. 9 (May 2003): 1.

Lin Yusheng 林毓生. "Miandui weilaide zhongji guanhuai: Tang Junyi quefa piping jingshen" 面對未來的終極關懷：唐君毅缺乏批評精神 [The ultimate concern in facing the Future: Tang Junyi's lack of critical spirit], *Zhongguo luntan* 中國論壇 15, no. 1 (Aug. 1982): 21–24.

Lin, Yü-sheng. *The Crisis of Chinese Consciousness: Radical Antitraditionalism in the May Fourth Era*. Madison: University of Wisconsin Press, 1979.

———. "The Suicide of Liang Chi: An Ambiguous Case of Moral Conservatism." In *The Limits of Change: Essays on Conservative Alternatives in Republican China*, edited by Charlotte Furth, 151–168. Cambridge, MA: Harvard University Press, 1976.

Ling, Trevor O. "The Weberian Thesis and Interpretive Positions on Modernisation." In *The Triadic Chord*, edited by Tu Wei-ming (q.v.), 57–85. Singapore: Institute of East Asian Philosophies, 1991.

Liu Honghe. *Confucianism in the Eyes of a Confucian Liberal. Hsu Fu-kuan's Critical Examination of the Confucian Political Tradition*. New York: Lang, 2001.

Liu Junping 刘军平. "'Tianxia' yuzhouguan de yanbian yu qi zhexue yiyun" 天下'宇宙观的 演变及其哲学意蕴 [The development and philosophical meaning of the cosmological concept of *"Tianxia"*], *Wen shi zhe* 文史哲 [Journal of literature, history, and philosophy], no. 6 (2004): serial no. 285, 101–107.

Liu, Kang. "Is There an Alternative to (Capitalist) Globalization? The Debate about Modernity in China." *Boundary 2* 23, no. 3 (Fall 1996): 193–218.

Liu Shuxian [刘述先]. *Lun Rujia zhexue de sanda shidai* 论儒家哲学的三个大时代 [On the Three Epochs of Confucian philosophy]. Guiyang: Guizhou People's Press, 2009.

———. *Rujia sixiang kaituo di changshi* 儒家思想开拓的尝试 [Attempts to explore Confucian thoughts], edited by Jiadong Zheng 郑家栋. Beijing: Chinese Social Sciences Press, 2001.

———. *Understanding Confucian Philosophy: Classical and Sung-Ming*. Westport, CT: Praeger, 1998.

Liu Xiaoyan. *Frontier Passages—Ethno politics and the Rise of Chinese Communism, 1921–1945*. Stanford, CA: Stanford University Press, 2004.

Louie, Kam. "Confucius the Chameleon: Dubious Envoy for "Brand China." *Boundary 2* 38, no, 1 (2011): 77–100.

Luo Zhitian. *Tianxia yu shijie: Qingming zhiren guanyu renlei shehui renzhi de zhuanbian* 天下到世界: 清末士人关于人类社会认知的转变 "From *"tianxia"* [all-under-heaven] to "the World": Changes in the Late Qing Intellectuals' Conceptions of Human Society," *Zhongguo shehui kexue* 中国社会科学 [Social sciences in China] 29, no. 2 (May 2008): 93–105.

Lynn, Richard John. *The Classic of Changes: A New Translation of the* I Ching, as interpreted by Wang Bi. New York: Columbia University Press, 1994.
Ma, Aiping, Lina Si, and Hongfei Zhang. "The Evolution of Cultural Tourism: The Example of Qufu, the Birthplace of Confucius." In *Tourism in China: Destination, Cultures and Communities*, edited by Chris Ryan and Huimin Gu, 182–196. New York: Routledge, 2009.
MacIntyre, Alasdair. *After Virtue*. Notre Dame, IN: University of Notre Dame Press, 2007.
Makeham, John. *Lost Soul: "Confucianism" in Contemporary Chinese Academic Discourse*. Cambridge, MA: Harvard University Press, 2008.
——, ed. *New Confucianism: A Critical Examination*. New York: Palgrave Macmillan, 2003.
——. "The New Daotong." In *New Confucianism: A Critical Examination*, edited by John Makeham, 55–78. New York: Palgrave Macmillan, 2003.
——. "The Retrospective Creation of New Confucianism." In *New Confucianism: A Critical Examination*, edited by John Makeham, 25–53. New York: Palgrave Macmillan, 2003.
Marquard, Odo. *Schwierigkeiten mit der Geschichtsphilosophie*. 4th ed. Frankfurt am Main: Suhrkamp, 1997.
Matten, Marc Andre. "The Chiang Kai-shek Memorial Hall in Taipei: A Contested Place of Memory." In *Places of Memory in Modern China: History, Politics, Identity*, edited by Marc Andre Matten, 51–90. Leiden: Brill, 2012.
——. *Die Grenzen des Chinesischen—Nationale Identitätsstiftung im China des 20 Jahrhunderts*. Wiesbaden: Harrassowitz, 2009.
Matten, Marc Andre, ed. *Places of Memory in Modern China: History, Politics, Identity*. Leiden: Brill, 2012.
Metzger, Thomas A. *A Cloud across the Pacific: Essays on the Clash between Chinese and Western Political Theories Today*. Hong Kong: Chinese University of Hong Kong Press, 2005.
——. *Escape from Predicament: Neo-Confucianism and China's Evolving Political Culture*. New York: Columbia University Press, 1977.
Mou Zhongjian 牟钟鉴. "She *tianxia* yi jia haishi ruorouqiangshi" 是天下一家还是弱肉强食 [Is it *tianxia* or the strong prey on the weak?]. *Benkan tegao* 本刊特稿 [Special issue of Benkan], no. 1 (2007): 10–14.
Mou Zongsan 牟宗三. *Daode de lixiang zhuyi* 道德的理想主義 [Moral idealism]. Taipei: Xuesheng shuju, 2000.
——. *Wang Yangming zhi liangzhi jia* 王陽明致良知教 [Wang Yangming's teaching of extending good knowing]. Taipei: Zhongguo wenhus shuju, 1954.
——. "Xianxiang yu wu zisheng" 現象與物自身 [Phenomenon and thing-in-itself]. In *Mou Zongsan quanji* 牟宗三全集 [The complete works of Mou Zongsan], vol. 21. Taipei: Lianjing chubanshe, 2003.
——. *Xianxiang yu wu zishen* 現象與物自身 [Phenomena and things-in-themselves]. Taipei: Xuesheng shuju, 1975.
——. *Xinti yu xingti* 心體與性體 [The metaphysical principle of the mind and the metaphysical principle of nature]. Taipei: Zhengzhong shuju, 2002.

———. *Zhengdao yu zhidao* 政道與治道 [Authority and governance]. Taipei: Xuesheng shuju, 1991.

———. "Zhide zhijue yu zhongguo zhexue" 智的直覺與中國哲學 [Intellectual intuition and Chinese philosophy]. In *Mou Zongsan quanji* 牟宗三全集 [The complete works of Mou Zongsan], vol. 20. Taipei: Lianjing chubanshe, 2003.

———. "Zhongguo zhexue de tezhi" 中國哲學的特質 [Characteristics of Chinese philosophy]. In *Mou Zongsan quanji* 牟宗三全集 [The complete works of Mou Zongsan], vol. 28. Taipei: Liangjing chubanshe, 2003.

———. *Zhongguo zhexue shijiu jiang* 中國哲學十九講 [Nineteen lectures on Chinese philosophy]. Taipei: Xuesheng shuju, 1983.

Mou, Zongsan 牟宗三, Junmai Zhang, Fuguan Xu, and Junyi Tang. *Wei zhongguo wenhua jinggao shijie renshi xuanyan* 为中国文化敬告世界人士宣言 [A manifesto to the world's people's on behalf of Chinese culture]. In *Dangdai xin rujia* 当代新儒家 [Contemporary New Confucians], edited by Zusheng Feng 封祖盛, 1–52. Beijing: Sanlian Shudian, 1989.

Murata Yūjirō 村田雄二郎. "Kō Yūi to Kōshi kinen" 康有為と孔子紀年. In *Xueren [di er qi]* 学人 [第二期], edited by Wang Shouchang 王守常, Wang Hui 汪晖, and Chen Pingyuan 陈平原, 513–546. Nanjing: Jiangsu wenyi chubanshe, 1992.

———. "Sun Zhongshan yu xinhai geming shiqi de 'wuzu gonghe' lun" 孙中山与辛亥革命时期的「五族共和」论 [Sun Yat-sen and the theory of "Republic of the Five Races" during the 1911 Revolution.] In 复印报刊资料: 中国近代史 *Fuyin baokan ziliao—Zhongguo jindaishi* [Reprints of newspapers and journals: Modern Chinese history], no. 1 (2005): 84–91.

Murray, Julia K. "'Idols' in the Temple: Icons and the Cult of Confucius." *Journal of Asian Studies* 68, no. 2 (2009): 371–411.

Nakagawa, Ulara. "The Confucian Comeback." *The Diplomat* (Mar. 2, 2011). Retrieved from http://thediplomat.com/new-emissary/2011/03/02/the-confucian-comeback/.

Neville, Robert Cummings. *Boston Confucianism: Portable Tradition in the Late-Modern World*. Albany, NY: State University of New York Press, 2000.

Ng, On-cho. "The Ethics of Being and Non-Being: Confucian Contestations on Human Nature [*xing*] in Late Imperial China." In *Deconstruction and Ethical Thought in Asian Thought*, edited by Youru Wang, 87–99. London: Routledge, 2012.

Nora, Pierre. "Between Memory and History: Les Lieux de Mémoire." *Representations*, no. 26 (1989): 7–24.

———. *Realms of Memory: Rethinking the French Past*. New York: Columbia University Press, 1996.

Ottmann, Henning. *Geschichte des politischen Denkens. Das 20. Jahrhundert. Der Totalitarismus und seine Überwindung*, vol. 4/1. Stuttgart: Metzler, 2010.

Patt-Shamir, Galia. "Moral World, Ethical Terminology: The Moral Significance of Metaphysical Terms in Zhou Dunyi and Zhu Xi." *Journal of Chinese Philosophy* 31, no. 3 (Sept. 2004): 349–362.

Perry, Elizabeth J., and Liu Xin. *Proletarian Power: Shanghai in the Cultural Revolution*. Boulder, CO: Westview, 1997.

Pines, Yuri. "Changing Views of *Tianxia* in Pre-Imperial Discourse." *Oriens Extremus* 43 (2002).

Qi Liang 启良. *Xin rujia pipan* 新儒學批判 [The critique of New Confucianism]. Shanghai: Sanlian shuju, 1995.

———. "Zou chu zhengzhi ruxue" 走出政治儒学 [Moving beyond political Confucianism]. In *21 shiji Zhongguo zhexue zouxiang—Di 12 jie guoji Zhongguo zhexue da hui. Lunwen ji zhi yi*. 21 世纪中国哲学走向—第 12 届国际中国哲学大会. 论文集之一 [Trends in Chinese philosophy of the twenty-first century—The twelfth international plenary session on Chinese philosophy. Collected writings, part 1], edited by Fang Keli 方克立案, 424–442. Beijing: Shangwu yinshuguan, 2003.

Queli zhi 闕里志 [Chronicle of Queli]. In *Zhongguo cimu zhi congkan* 中國祠墓志叢刊 [Collection of Chinese temple and tomb sources], edited by Chen Gao 陳鎬, vol. 21–23. Yangzhou: Guanglin shushe, 2004 (1505).

Rabinbach, Anson. "Moments of Totalitarianism" (review article). *History and Theory* 45 (Feb. 2006): 72–100.

Rawls, John. *The Law of Peoples with "The Idea of Public Reason Revisited."* Cambridge, MA: Harvard University Press, 1999.

Reischauer, Edwin O. "The Sinic World in Perspective." *Foreign Affairs* (Jan. 1974): 41–48.

Reynolds, Susan. *Fiefs and Vassals*. Oxford, UK: Clarendon Press, 1994.

Richey, Jeffrey L. "Chat Room Confucianism: Online Discourse and Popular Morality in China." In *The Sage Returns: Confucian Revival in Contemporary China*, edited by Kenneth J. Hammond and Jeffrey L. Richey, 113–125. Albany, NY: State University of New York Press, 2015.

Roetz, Heiner. "The 'Dignity within Oneself': Chinese Tradition and Human Rights." In *Chinese Thought in a Global Context*, edited by Karl-Heinz Pohl, 236–262. Leiden: Brill, 1999.

Roth, Guenther. "Introduction." In Max Weber, *Economy and Society: An Outline of Interpretive Sociology*, edited by Günther Roth and Claus Wittich, xxxiii–. Berkeley: University of California Press, 1978.

Rozman, Gilbert. *The East Asian Region: Confucian Heritage and Its Modern Adaptations*. Princeton, NJ: Princeton University Press, 1991.

Schluchter, Wolfgang. "Einleitung: Max Webers Konfuzianismusstudie: Versuch einer Einordnung," In *Max Webers Studie über Konfuzianismus und Taoismus: Interpretation und Kritik*, edited by Wolfgang Schluchter, 11–54. Frankfurt am Main: Suhrkamp Verlag, 1983.

Schwarcz, Vera. *The Chinese Enlightenment: Intellectuals and the Legacy of the May Fourth Movement of 1919*. Berkeley: University of California Press, 1986.

Shaanxi xinhai geming huiyilu 陕西辛亥革命回忆录 [Shaanxi memories of the 1911 Revolution]. Xian: Shaanxi renmin chubanshe, 1982.

Shandong shengzhi: Kongzi gulizhi 山东省志: 孔子故里志 [Chronicle of Shandong Province: The annals of the former residence of Confucius], edited by Shandong sheng difang shizhi bianzuan weiyuanhui 山东省地方史志编纂委员会. Beijing: Zhonghua shuju, 1994.

Shen Sung-chiao 沈松僑. "Wo yi wo xue jian Xuanyuan—Huangdi shenhua yu wan Qing de guozu jiangou" 我以我血薦軒轅—黃帝神話與晚清的國族建構 [I will give my blood to honor Xuanyuan: The myth of the Yellow Emperor and the nation-building in Late Qing]. *Taiwan shehui yanjiu jikan* 臺灣社會研究季刊 [The quarterly for the studies of Taiwan society] 28 (1997): 1–77.

Shyrock, John Knight. *The Origin and Development of the State Cult of Confucius*. New York: Paragon Book, 1966.

Smith, Anthony. *Nationalism and Modernism*. New York: Routledge, 1998.

Smith, Richard J. *Mapping China and Managing the World: Culture, Cartography and Cosmology in Late Imperial Times*. London: Routledge, 2013.

Sommer, Deborah A. "Destroying Confucius: Iconoclasm in the Confucian Temple." In *On Sacred Grounds: Culture, Society, Politics, and the Formation of the Temple of Confucius*, edited by Thomas A. Wilson, 95–133. Cambridge, MA: Harvard University Asia Center, 2002.

Song, Xianlin. "Reconstructing the Confucian Ideal in 1980s China: The 'Culture Craze' and New Confucianism." In *New Confucianism: A Critical Examination*, edited by John Makeham, 81–104. New York: Palgrave MacMillan, 2003.

Stuart, Jan, and Evelyn Sakakida Rawski. *Worshiping the Ancestors: Chinese Commemorative Portraits*. Stanford, CA: Stanford University Press, 2001.

Stover, Leon E. *Imperial China and the State Cult of Confucius*. Jefferson, NC: McFarland, 2005.

Sun, Anna. *Confucianism as a World Religion: Contested Histories and Contemporary Realities*. Princeton, NJ: Princeton University Press, 2013.

Sun Longji 孫隆基. "Qingji minzuzhuyi yu Huangdi chongbai zhi faming" 清季民族主义与 黃帝崇拜之发明 [Late Qing nationalism and the invention of the Yellow Emperor worship]. *Lishi yanjiu* 历史研究 [Historical studies], no. 3 (2000): 68–79.

Tai, Hung-chao, ed. *Confucianism and Economic Development: An Oriental Alternative?* Washington, DC: Washington Institute Press, 1989.

Takeuchi Hiroyuki 竹内弘行. "Shinmatsu no shikinen nitsuite" 清末の私紀年について. *Nagoya gakuin daigaku ronshū—jinbun—shizen kagaku hen* 31, no. 1 (July 1994): 77–96.

Tang Junyi 唐君毅. *Renwen jingshen zhi chongjian* 人文精神之重建 [The reconstruction of the humanistic spirit]. Hong Kong: Xinya shuyuan, 1974.

———. *Tang Junyi quanji* 唐君毅全集 [The collected works of Tang Junyi] vols. 23, 24. Taipei: Xuesheng shuju, 1989.

———. *Zhongguo wenhua zhi jingshen jiazhi* 中國文化之精神價值 [The spiritual values of Chinese philosophy]. Taipei: Zhengzhong shuju, 1997.

Tang, Yijie. "Some Reflections on New Confucianism in Mainland Chinese Culture of the 1990s." Translated by Gloria Davies. In *Voicing Concerns: Contemporary Chinese Critical Inquiry*, edited by Gloria Davies, 123–134. Lanham, MD: Rowman & Littlefield, 2001.

Tang Zhonggang 汤忠钢. *Dexing yu zhengzhi: Mou Zongsan xin rujia zhengzhi zhexue yanjiu* 德性与政治: 牟宗三新儒家政治哲学研究 [Virtue and politics: Research on Mou Zongsan's New Confucian political philosophy]. Beijing: Zhongguo Yanshi chubanshe, 2008.

Thompson, Laurence G. *Ta t'ung shu: The one-world philosophy of K'ang Yu-wei*. London: Allen and Unwin, 1958.

Tillman, Hoyt. "Creativity and Evolving Confucian Traditions: Some Reflections on Earlier Centuries and Recent Developments." *Journal of Chinese Philosophy* 33, no. 2 (June 2006): 213–223.

———. "Zhu Xi's Prayers to the Spirit of Confucius and Claim to the Transmission of the Way." *Philosophy East and West* 54, no. 4 (Oct. 2004): 489–513.

Travel, Taylor. "Regime Insecurity and International Cooperation: Explaining China's Compromises in Territorial Disputes." *International Security* 2, no. 30 (Fall 2005): 46–83.

Tu, Wei-ming. *Confucian Ethics Today: The Singapore Challenge*. Singapore: Curriculum Development Institute of Singapore, 1984.

——— [杜维明]. "Cong shijie sichao de jige cemian kan ruxue yanjiu de xin dongxiang" 从 世界思潮的几个侧面看儒学研究的新动向 [Looking at new development in New Confucianism from the perspective of several currents of world thought]. In *Rujia chuantong de xiandai zhuanhua*, edited by Yue Hua and Guan Dong, 303–329. Beijing: Zhongguo guangbo dianshi chubanshe, 1992.

———. "Hsiung Shih-li's Quest for Authentic Existence." In *The Limits of Change: Essays on Conservative Alternatives in Republican China*, edited by Charlotte Furth, 242–275. Cambridge, MA: Harvard University Press, 1976.

——— (杜维明). "Huajie qimeng xintai" 化解启蒙心态 [Beyond the Enlightenment syndrome]. *Ershiyi shiji* 二十一世纪 [Twenty-first century] 2 (Dec. 1990): 12–13.

———. "Introduction." In *Confucian Traditions in East Asian Modernity: Moral Education and Economic Culture in Japan and the Four Mini-Dragons*, edited by Wei-ming Tu, 1–10. Cambridge, MA: Harvard University Press, 1996.

———. "Introduction: Cultural Perspectives." *Daedalus* 122, no. 2 (Spring 1993): vii–xxiv.

———. "Multiple Modernities—Implications of the Rise of 'Confucian' East Asia." In *Chinese Ethics in a Global Context: Moral Bases of Contemporary Societies*, edited by Karl-Heinz Pohl and Anselm W. Müller, 55–77. Leiden: Brill, 2002.

———. *Neo-Confucian Thought in Action: Wang Yang-ming's Youth (1472–1509)*. Berkeley: University of California Press, 1976.

———. "The Rise of Industrial East Asia: The Role of Confucian Values." *Copenhagen Journal of Asian Studies* 4 (1989): 81–97.

——— (杜维明), *Ruxue disanqi fazhan de qianjing wenti: Dalu jiangxue, wennan, he taolun* 儒学第三期发展的前景问题: 大陆讲学, 问难 和讨论 [Prospective issues of the Third Epoch of Confucianism: Mainland lectures, questions, and discussions]. Taipei: Lianjing chubanshi gongsi, 1989.

———. [杜维明]. "Ruxue disanqi fazhan de qianjing wenti" 儒學第三期發展的前景問題 [The prospect for the development of the Third Epoch of Confucianism]. In *Rujia chuantong de xiandai zhuanhua: Du Weiming xinruxue lunzhu jiyao* 儒家传统的现代转化: 杜维明新儒学论著辑要 [The modern transformation of Confucian tradition: A collection of writings on New Confucianism by Tu Wei-ming], edited by Yue Hua 岳华 and Guan Dong 关东, 234–277. Beijing: Zhongguo guangbo dianshi chubanshe, 1992.

——— [杜维明]. "Rujia lunli yu dongya qiye jingshen" 儒家伦理与东亚企业精神 [The Confucian ethic and the East Asian entrepreneurial spirit]. In *Rujia chuantong de xiandai zhuanhua*, edited by Yue Hua and Guan Dong, 329–360. Beijing: Zhongguo guangbo dianshi chubanshe, 1992.

———. *The Triadic Chord: Confucian Ethics, Industrial East Asia and Max Weber Proceedings of the 1987 Singapore Conference on Confucian Ethics and the Modernisation of Industrial East Asia*. Singapore: Institute of East Asian Philosophies, 1991.

Tu, Wei-ming, Milan Hejtmanek, and Alan Wachman, eds. *The Confucian World Observed: A Contemporary Discussion of Confucian Humanism in East Asia*. Honolulu, HI: East-West Center, 1992.

Vollrath, Ernst. *Grundlegung einer philosophischen Theorie des Politischen*. Würzburg: Königshausen and Neumann, 1987.

Wagner, Rudolf. "The Implied Pilgrim: Reading the Chairman Mao Memorial Hall." In *Pilgrims and Sacred Sites in China*, edited by Susan Naquin and Chu Yuan-fang, 378–423. Berkeley: University of California Press, 1992.

Wakeman, Frederic, Jr. "Mao's Remains." In *Death Ritual in Late Imperial and Modern China*, edited by James L. Watson and Evelin S. Rawski, 254–288. Berkeley: University of California Press, 1988.

Wang, Aihe. *Cosmology and Political Culture in Early China*. Cambridge, UK: Cambridge University Press, 2000.

Wang Bangxiong 王邦雄. "Cong Zhongguo xiandaihua guocheng zhong kan dangdai xin rujia de jingshen" 丛中国现代化过程中看当代新儒家的精神 [The spirit of New Confucianism from the perspective of China's modernization]. In *Ping xinrujia* 评新儒家 [Assessing New Confucianism], edited by Luo Yijun 罗义俊, 74–97. Shanghai: Shanghai renmin chubanshe, 1989.

Wang Chunxia 王春霞. *Pai Man yu minzuzhuyi* "排满"与民族主义 [Anti-Manchus and Nationalism]. Beijing: Shehui kexue wenxian chubanshe, 2005.

Wang Dasan 王达三. "Rujia *tianxia* guannian yu shijie chengxu zhongjian 儒家天下观念与 世界秩序重建 [The Confucian concept of *Tianxia* and the reconstruction of global order]. http://vpapers.cn/rujia/137.

Wang, Hui. "Contemporary Chinese Thought and the Question of Modernity."

In *China's New Order: Society, Politics, and Economy in Transition*, edited by Theodore Huters, 139–187. Cambridge, MA: Harvard University Press, 2003.

———. *The End of the Revolution: China and the Limits of Modernity*. London: Verso, 2009.

Wang, Jing. *High Culture Fever: Politics, Aesthetics, and Ideology in Deng's China*. Berkeley: University of California Press, 1996.

Wang Ke 王柯. *20 seiki Chūgoku no kokka kensetsu to minzoku* 20世紀中国の国家建設と「民族」 [Twentieth-century China and the construction of the Chinese nation-state]. Tokyo: Tokyo daigaku shuppankai, 2006.

Wang, Liang. "The Confucian Temple Tragedy of the Cultural Revolution." Translated by Curtis Dean Smith. In *On Sacred Grounds: Culture, Society, Politics, and the Formation of the Temple of Confucius*, edited by Thomas A. Wilson, 376–398. Cambridge, MA: Harvard University Asia Center, 2002.

Wang, Liping. "Creating a National Symbol: The Sun Yatsen Memorial in Nanjing." *Republican China* 21, no. 2 (1996): 23–63.

Wang Mingke 王明珂. "Lun panfu: Jindai Yan Huangdi zisun guozu jiangou de gudai jichu" 論攀附: 近代炎黃子孫國族建構的古代基礎 [On making connections: The ancient roots of the contemporary construction of nation-states based on the genealogy of Yan and Huang emperors]. In *Zhongyang yanjiuyuan lishi yuyan yanjiusuo jikan* 中央研究院歷史語言研究所季刊 [The quarterly of the Institute of History and Language of Academia Sinica] 73, no. 3 (2002): 583–624.

———. *Yingxiong zuxian yu dixiong minzu—genji lishi de wenben yu qingjing* 英雄祖先與弟兄民族——根基歷史的文本與情境 [Heroes, ancestors, brothers, and race: The text and context of basic history]. Taipei: Yunchen, 2006.

Wang Yangming 王陽明. *Zhuanxi lu xiangzhu jiping* 傳習錄詳註集評 [Record of practice with detailed annotations and collected commentary]. Taipei: Xuesheng shuju, 1983.

———. *Wang Yangming chuanji* 王阳明全集 [The complete works of Wang Yangming], Shanghai: Shanghai Guji chubanshe, 2009.

Watson, James, and Evelyn S. Rawski, eds. *Death Ritual in Late Imperial and Modern China*. Berkeley: University of California Press, 1988.

Weber, Max. *Economy and Society: An Outline of Interpretive Sociology*. Edited by Günther Roth and Claus Wittich. Berkeley: University of California Press, 1978.

———. *The Protestant Ethic and the Spirit of Capitalism*. Translated by Talcott Parsons. New York: Scribner's Sons, 1958.

———. *The Religion of China: Confucianism and Taoism*. Translated by Hans Gerth. New York: Free Press and Collier-Macmillan, 1968.

Wei Zhengtong 韋政通. *Rujia yu xiandaihua* 儒家與現代化 [Confucianism and modernization]. Taipei: Shuiniu Chubanshe, 1989.

———. "Xiandai rujia de cuozhe yu fuxing: Zhongxin sixiang de pipan" 現代儒家的挫折與復興——中心思想的批判 [The challenge and the revival of contemporary Confucianism: A critique of its central concept]. In *Dangdai xinrujia* 當代新儒家 [Contemporary New Confucianism], edited by Feng Zusheng 封祖盛, 120–136. Beijing: Sanlian shudian, 1989.

Whyte, Martin K. "Death in the People's Republic of China." In *Death Ritual in Late Imperial and Modern China*, edited by James Watson and Evelyn S. Rawski, 289–316. Berkeley: University of California Press, 1988.

Wilson, Thomas A. "Sacrifice and the Imperial Cult of Confucius." *History of Religions* 41, no. 3 (2002): 251–287.

Xu Jilin 许纪霖 and Luo Gang 罗岗. *Qimeng de ziwo wajie: 1990 niandai yilai Zhongguo sixiang wenhua jie zhongda lunzheng yanjiu* 启蒙的自我瓦解: 1990年代以来中国思想文化界重大论争研究 [The self-dissolution of Enlightenment: Studies of the major intellectual and cultural debates since the 1990s]. Jilin: Jilin chuban jituan, 1997.

Xu Xiaoyan 徐晓燕. *Shenzhou Xuanyuan ziguchuan—gongji Xuanyuan Huangdi xindianli ceji* 神州轩辕自古传—共祭轩辕黄帝新典礼侧记 [The unbroken transmission of Xuanyuan in China: A record of the memorials for Xuanyuan Yellow Emperor]. *Liang'an guanxi* 兩岸关系 [Relations across the Taiwan Strait] (2004): 12–16.

Yabuuchi Kiyoshi 薮内清. *Rekishi wa itsu hajimatta ka* 歴史はいつ始まったか. Tokyo: Chūō kōron sha, 1980.

Yan Xuetong. "How Assertive Should a Power Be?" *New York Times*, Mar. 31, 2011.

———. *Ancient Chinese Thought, Modern Chinese Power*. Edited by Daniel A. Bell and Sun Zhe, and translated by Edmund Ryden. Princeton, NJ: Princeton University Press, 2011.

Yang, Ch'ing-k'un. Introduction to *The Religion of China: Confucianism and Taoism* by Max Weber, xiii–xliii. Translated by Hans Gerth. New York: Free Press and Collier-Macmillan, 1968.

Yang Zhiqiang 楊志強. "'Eno shison' to 'chūka minzoku': Kindai Chūgoku ni okeru kokumin tōgō o meguru futatsu no gensetsu" 炎黄子孫」と「中華民族」: 近代中国における国民統合をめぐる二つの言説. In *Keiō gijuku daigaku daigakuin shakaigaku kenkyūka kiyō—Shakaigaku shinrigaku kyōikugaku, ningen to shakai no tankyū*, no. 64 (2007): 121–137.

Yao Minjie 姚敏傑 and He Bingwu 何炳武, eds. *Huangdi jiwen ji* 黃帝祭文集 [A collection of memorial writings for the Yellow Emperor]. Xi'an: Sanqin chubanshe, 1996.

Yao, Xinzhong. *An Introduction to Confucianism*. New York: Cambridge University Press, 2000.

Yin Haiguang 殷海光. "Genzhe wusi de jiaobu qianjin" 跟著五四的腳步前進 [Going forward by following the footsteps of the May Fourth Movement]. In *Yin Haiguang quanji* 殷海光全集 [Collected works of Yin Haiguang], edited by Lin Zhenghong 林正弘, vol. 11, 577. Taipei: Guiguan tushu gongsi, 1990.

Yu, Dan. *Confucius from the Heart: Ancient Wisdom for Today's World*. New York: Atria Book, 2006.

Yu Ying-Shih 余英時. "Xiandai rujia de huigu yu zhanwang" 現代儒學的回顧与展望" [Review of and prospects for contemporary Confucianism]. In *Xiandai rujia de huigu yu zhanwang* 现代儒学的回顾与展望 [Review of and prospects for contemporary Confucianism], 132–186. Beijing: Sanlian Shudian, 2004.

Yu Youren 于右任. *Huangdi gongde ji* 黄帝公德纪 [Records of the Public Virtue of the Yellow Emperor]. Xi'an: Shaanxi renmin chubanshe, 1987 (1935).

Zarrow, Peter. "Political Ritual in the Early Republic of China." In *Constructing Nationhood in Modern East Asia*, edited by Chow Kai-Wing, Kevin M. Doak, and Poshek Fu, 149–188. Ann Arbor: University of Michigan Press, 2001.

Zhang, Feng. "Regionalization in the *Tianxia*: Continuity and Change in China's Foreign Policy." Paper presented at the China-West Intellectual Summit, Paris, Feb. 23–24, 2009.

———. "The *Tianxia* System: World Order in a Chinese Utopia." *Chinese Heritage Quarterly*, no. 21 (Mar. 2010), http://www.chinaheritagequarterly.org/tienhsia.php?searchterm=021_utopia.inc&issu=021.

———. "Rethinking the 'Tribute System': Broadening the Conception Horizon of Historical East Asian Politics." *Chinese Journal of International Politics* 2 (2009): 597–626.

Zhang Hao 张灏. *Youan yishi yu minzhu chuantong* 幽暗意识与民主传统 [Consciousness of darkness and the democratic tradition]. Beijing: Xinxing chubanshe, 2006.

Zhang, Junmai [Carsun Chang]. "A Manifesto for a Re–appraisal of Sinology and Reconstruction of Chinese Culture." In *The Development of Neo–Confucian Thought*, vol. 2, edited by Junmai Zhang, 455–483. New York: Bookman Associates, 1962.

Zhang Junmai 張君勱, Tang Junyi 唐君毅, Xu Fuguan 徐复觀, and Mou Zongsan 牟宗三. *Zhongguo wenhua yu shijie* 中國文化與世界 [A Declaration to the world for Chinese culture]. Hong Kong: N.p., 1958. [First published as "Wei Zhongguo wenhua jinggao shijie renshi xuanyan—women dui Zhongguo xueshu yanjiu ji Zhongguo wenhua yu shijie wenhua qiantu zhi gongtong renshi" 為中國文化敬告世界人士宣言—我們對中國學術研究及中國文化與世界文化前途之共同認識. *Minzhu Pinglun* 民主評論 [Democratic Critique] 9, no. 1 (1958): 2–21.

Zhang, Xudong. "The Making of the Post–Tiananmen Intellectual Field: A Critical Overview." In *Whither China? Intellectual Politics in Contemporary China*, edited by Xudong Zhang, 1–75. Durham, NC: Duke University Press, 2001.

Zhao, Tingyang. "All–Under–Heaven and Methodological Relationism: An Old Story and New World Peace." In *Contemporary Chinese Political Thought: Debates and Perspectives*, edited by Fred Dallmayr and Zhao Tingyang, 46–66. Lexington: University of Kentucky Press, 2012.

———. "Rethinking Empire from a Chinese Concept 'All-under-Heaven' (*tianxia*)." *Social Identities* 12, no. 1 (2006): 29–41.

Zheng Jiadong 郑家栋. *Mou Zongsan* 牟宗三. Taipei: Dongda Tushu gongsi, 2000.

Zhou Ailing 周愛靈. "Huaguo piaoling: Lengzhan shiqi zhimindi de xinya shuyuan" 花果飄零：冷戰時期殖民地的新亞書院 [The dispersion of flowers and fruits: The New Asia College under colonial rule during the

Cold War]. Translated by Luo Meixian 羅美嫻. Hong Kong: Shangwu yinshuguan, 2010.

Zhuang Guotu 庄国土. "Luelun chaogong zhidu de xuhuan: yi gudai zhongguo yu dongya de chaogong guanxi yi li" 略论朝贡制度的虚幻: 以古代中国与东南亚的朝贡关系 例 [An account of the fiction of the tributary system: An example of the relationships in tributary system in ancient China and East Asia]. *Nanyang wenti yanjiu* 南洋问题研究 [Research on problems in Nanyang] 3 (2005): 1–8.

Zhuang Jinlan 庄金兰 and Yang Chaoming 杨朝明, ed. *Kongzi yanjiuyuan* 孔子研究院 [Confucius Research Institute]. Beijing: Zhongguo wenhua chubanshe, 2011.

Zurndorfer, Harriet T. "Confusing Confucianism with Capitalism: Culture as Impediment and/or Stimulus to Chinese Economic Development." Paper presented at the Third Global Economic History Network Meeting, Konstanz, Germany, June 3–5, 2004.

Notes on Contributors

STEPHEN C. ANGLE received his B.A. from Yale University in East Asian Studies and his Ph.D. in Philosophy from the University of Michigan. Since 1994 he has taught at Wesleyan University, where he is now Mansfield Freeman Professor of East Asian Studies and Professor of Philosophy. His most recent books are *Contemporary Confucian Political Philosophy: Toward Progressive Confucianism* (2012) and, with Michael Slote, *Virtue Ethics and Confucianism* (2014).

TONGDONG BAI is Professor of Philosophy and the director of an English-based M.A. program in Chinese philosophy at Fudan University in China. His book *A New Mission of an Old State: The Comparative and Contemporary Relevance of Classical Confucian Political Philosophy* (in Chinese) was published in 2009, and his book *China: The Political Philosophy of the Middle Kingdom* was published in 2012. He is now working on an English translation and a drastically revised version of his 2009 book, which will explore Confucianism-inspired alternatives to liberal democracy in both domestic and global governance.

DANIEL A. BELL is Dean of the Faculty of Politics and Public Administration at Shandong University. He is the author of *The China Model*, *The Spirit of Cities*, *China's New Confucianism*, and *East Meets West* and he edits the Princeton China series. He writes frequently for leading media outlets in China and the West and his works have been translated into twenty-three languages.

JOHN H. BERTHRONG was educated at the University of Kansas and the University of Chicago in Chinese and East Asian religious and intellectual history. His special focus is on the rise of Neo-Confucianism and contemporary Confucian revivals and scholarship.

HOK YIN CHAN is Assistant Head of the Department of History and Chinese at City University of Hong Kong. His research focuses on the cultural history of late imperial and Republican China, particularly the nationalistic thought of Zhang Taiyan, the ethnohistory of Gu Jiegang, and the impact of Neo-Confucianism as a modernization theory. His 2014 book, *May Fourth in Hong Kong: Colonialism, Nationalism, and Localism* (in Chinese), won the 2015 Hong Kong Book Prize.

ELS VAN DONGEN is Assistant Professor of History at Nanyang Technological University, Singapore. She was trained in Chinese studies, with a specialization in the intellectual history of modern and contemporary China. She has published on official and intellectual discourses that revolve around the broader themes of modernization, historiography, nation-building, and migration in contemporary China.

THOMAS FRÖHLICH is Professor of Chinese Studies at Friedrich-Alexander University Erlangen-Nuremberg. He is a specialist of modern Chinese political thought and intellectual history. His publications include books and articles on the political philosophy of modern Confucianism, Chinese political thought of the Republican period, anti-colonialism in twentieth-century Taiwan, and Chinese intellectuals in exile after 1949.

TZE-KI HON is Professor of History at City University of Hong Kong. He is the author of four books: *The Yijing and Chinese Politics* (2005), *Revolution as Restoration* (2013), *Teaching the I Ching* (with Geffrey Redmond; 2014), and *The Allure of the Nation* (2015). He has coedited four edited volumes: *The Politics of Historical Production in Late Qing and Republican China* (2007), *Beyond the May Fourth Paradigm* (2008), *The Decade of the Great War* (2014), and *Confucianism for the Contemporary World* (2017). Currently, he is a member of the editorial board of *Sungkyun Journal of East Asian Studies* (Seoul, South Korea) and the Principal Investigator of the "Chinese views of the global order" research project funded by the SUNY Arts and Humanities Network of Excellence.

JUNHAO HONG is Professor of Communication at University at Buffalo, SUNY. His research focuses on global communication issues, relationships between media and society in Asian societies, and how media formations differ in different societies. He is the author of *The Internationalization of Television in China* (1998), *Internet Popular Culture and Jewish Values* (with L. Sherlick; 2008), and *Media Laws across the World: A Comparative Study of Their Evolution and Challenges* (with T. Su; 2016). He coedited *Series on*

Western Research in the Humanities and Social Sciences: Mass Communication (2007) and edited *New Trends in Communication Studies* (2014). Currently, he is an editorial board member of *Telematics and Informatics*, *Modern China Studies*, *Communication and Society*, *American Review of Chinese Studies*, *Journal of Chinese Communication*, among others.

WEN HUANG is Associate Professor at the Department of Science and Technology of Communication and Policy, University of Science and Technology of China.

MING-HUEI LEE, Ph.D., University of Bonn, is Research Fellow at the Institute of Chinese Literature and Philosophy at Academia Sinica, Taipei. He has written on Kant's philosophy, traditional Confucianism, and modern Confucianism.

AN-WU LIN is Director of the Institute for the Studies of Religions and Humanities, Tzu Chi University, Taiwan. He has published books and articles about New Confucianism.

MIAO LIU is a doctoral student at the Department of Communication, University of Utah.

MARC ANDRE MATTEN, Ph.D., is Associate Professor of Contemporary Chinese History at Friedrich-Alexander University Erlangen-Nuremberg, Germany. He has published extensively on the issues of Chinese nationalism and national identity, including *The Borders of Being Chinese: On the Creation of National Identity in Twentieth-Century China* (German; 2009) and *Places of Memory in Modern China: History, Politics, and Identity* (2011/2013).

KE SHENG is Assistant Professor of Philosophy at Capital Normal University, China.

KRISTIN STAPLETON is Professor of History at the University at Buffalo, State University of New York. She serves as the editor of the journal *Twentieth-Century China* and on the editorial board of *Education about Asia*, and she is executive secretary of the New York Conference on Asian Studies. Her research interests include Chinese and comparative urban administration, the history of Chinese family life, and humor in history. She is the author of *Civilizing Chengdu: Chinese Urban Reform, 1895–1937* (2000) and *Fact in Fiction: 1920s China and Ba Jin's* Family (2016). Her current research concerns Sino-Soviet cooperation in designing and managing "socialist cities."

Index

Analects. *See* Great Learning
Arendt, Hannah, 156–158
Asian capitalism, xiv–xvii, 8–14, 19–37

Boston Confucians, xxiv. *See* Tu Wei-ming

Carlson, Allen, 51–52
Chen Lai, xviii, 19–37, 235
Chen Yinke, 7
Cheng Chung-ying, 4, 11–12
Chinese University of Hong Kong, 170–171
civic Confucianism, xx, 9, 12–15
Confucian capitalism, 4, 28–33
Confucianism: as a moral critique of instrumental rationality, 22–35; as a lost soul, xxiv, xxixn42; as a theory of international relations, 45–59; as a theory of modernization, xviii, 22–35; as a political theory, 69–76, 81–89; three epochs of, xiv–xv, 108–110, 228–232; the triad chord of, xv; Weberization of, xv–xviii, 19–37, 135–139
Confucius: the animated series of, 211–212; as a commodity, xxiii, 183–199; as a cultural icon, xxiii, 183–199; and three historic sites in Shantong, 193–195; the movie about, 211; and the social practice of *li* (rituals), 232–234

contemporary New Confucianism. *See* New Confucianism
cultural craze, xiii, 7
Cultural Revolution, xi, xxiii, 3, 209

Declaration, The 1958. *See* Manifesto for a Re-appraisal of Sinology and Reconstruction of Chinese Culture
Dictionary on Confucius, 5, 12–15
Dirlik, Arif, xii–xv, 3–4, 9, 33–34
Du Weiming. *See* Tu Wei-ming

East Asian development model, xiv–xv, 12–14, 28–33

Fan Wenlan, 16n11
Fang Dongmei, 4, 11
Fang Keli, xvii, 4–15
farewell to revolution, 5–7, 15n8
Feng Youlan, 4, 11
Four Mini Dragons, xi, 4, 9
Fukuyama, Francis, 65

Great Learning (*Analects*), 49–50, 53, 67, 97–98

Habermas, Jürgen, 28, 107–108
He Lin, 4, 11
Heidegger, Martin, 126
Holocaust, xxii, 153–155
Hong Kong, xiii, 167–177
Hu Shi, 26

Japan, xi, 4, 9
Jiang Qing, xix, 14, 57, 66, 91, 100
Jing Haifeng, xiii, xxviin17

Kang Youwei, 7, 48, 57, 184, 188, 200

Lee Kuan Yew, 131
Li Yangfan, 45, 56
Li Zehou, xxvin15, 6
Liang Qichao, 26, 46–47, 184
Liang Shuming, 4, 11, 28
Lin Yü-sheng, 26, 118–119
Liu Shipei, 7, 185–186
Liu Shu-hsien, 4, 11–12
Liu Zaifu, 6
Lu-Wang School of Song-Ming Confucianism, xi, xviii, 10, 23
Lu Xiangshan, xviii–xi, 23
Luo Yijun, xiv, 14

Ma Yifu, 4, 11
MacIntyre, Alasdair, xx, 117–126
Mainland Confucians, xii–xiii
Makeham, John, xii–xiii, 5, 11, 57
Manifesto for a Re-appraisal of Sinology and Reconstruction of Chinese Culture (1958), xiii, xxii, 83–84, 236
Mao Zedong, 189, 209
May Fourth Movement, xi, xxiii, 3, 11, 21, 25–27, 66, 118–119
Mencius, 124
Mou Zongsan, xii–xvii, xx–xxii, 4, 10–11, 23, 67, 83–86, 91–102, 110–111, 117–127, 168, 235–237

National Essence group, 3–4
national learning craze, xiii, 7
New Asia College, xxi
New Confucian research project, xiv–xvii, 3–15
New Confucianism: as a critique of colonialism and capitalism, 167–177; as a critique of totalitarianism, 131–158; as a modernization theory, xvii–xix, 8–12, 19–37, 135–139, 173–179; as a moral foundation of democratic institutions, 81–89, 91–102, 107–113, 117–127; as one of the three intellectual currents of modern China, 5–8; relation to East Asian development model, xiv–xvii, 8–12, 19–37, 173–177; relation to foreign policy, 45–59; relation to mass media, xxiii–xxiv, 209–223; relation to nationalism, xxiii, 215–223; relation to the openness of the 1980s and 1990s, xii–xiii; a retrospective creation, 5, 15n9; as a theory of capitalism, 8–14, 19–37; as the third epoch of Confucianism, 108–110, 228–232
New Confucians, three generations, 8–12
Nora, Pierre, 185

openness of the 1980s and 1990s, xii–xiv, xxvin15

political Confucianism, 69–74
Post–New Confucianism, xx, 107–108
progressive Confucianism, 101–102

Qian Mu, 4, 236

reform and opening up, 6
retrospective creation of New Confucianism, 5, 15n9
revolutionary historiography, 5–6

San Kong. See three historic sites related to Confucius
Sartre, 125–126
socialism with Chinese characteristics, 4
Song Xianlin, xiii, 7
Song-Ming Neo-Confucianism, xi, xviii, 10, 23

Spring and Autumn Period, xix, 74
Story of Confucius, The (animated series), 211–212
Sun Yat-sen, 189

Tang Junyi, xiii, xvi, xxi–xxii, 4, 10–11, 23, 83–84, 119, 131–158, 167–177, 235
Tang Yongtong, 7
Third Way, xiv
three epochs of Confucianism, xiv–xv
three generations of New Confucians, 8–12
three historic sites related to Confucius (*San Kong*), 193–195
three intellectual currents of modern China, 7–8
Tianxia, xviii, 45–57
totalitarianism, 143–158
Tu Wei-ming, xiv–xvii, 4, 11–12, 20–24, 27–33, 36, 57

Wang Fuzhi, 110–111

Wang Jing, xii
Wang Yangming, xi, xviii, 10, 23, 100, 123
Warring States Period, xix, 47, 74
Weber, Max, xv, xvii, xviii, xxii, 19–33, 135

Xiong Shili, xii, xviii, 4, 11, 119
Xu Fuguan, xiii, xvi, 4, 10–11, 23, 83–84, 119, 168

Yan Chongnian, 210
Yan Xuetong, 50–56
Yellow Emperor, xxiii, 183–199
Yu Dan, xvi, 67, 210–211
Yu Ying-shih, 4, 11–12, 26

Zhang Junmai, xiii, 4, 11, 23, 26, 83–84
Zhang Taiyan, 4, 184, 200
Zhao Tingyang, 48–50, 54
Zhu Xi, 23, 48, 183, 226, 232–233, 236
Zou Rong, 188

www.ingramcontent.com/pod-product-compliance
Ingram Content Group UK Ltd.
Pitfield, Milton Keynes, MK11 3LW, UK
UKHW021844140426
5217IPUK00022B/1577